Once Upon a Time...

Storytelling to Teach Character and Prevent Bullying

**Lessons from
99 Multicultural
Folk Tales
for Grades K–8**

Elisa Davy Pearmain

CHARACTER DEVELOPMENT GROUP

Once Upon a Time: Storytelling to Teach Character and Prevent Bullying

Publisher: Character Development Group, Inc.
P.O. Box 35136, Greensboro, NC 27425-5136
336-668-9373, Fax: 336-668-9375
E-mail: Info@CharacterEducation.com, www.CharacterEducation.com

Text editing by Ginny Turner, layout by Sara Sanders, SHS Design
ISBN: 1-892056-44-5 $32.95
Printed in the United States of America

Story permissions

"Once Upon a Time" a poem by Bill Martin Jr. is reprinted here from *Bill Martin Jr's Treasure Chest of Poetry* by Bill Martin Jr., with John Archambault and Peggy Brogan (Allen, Tex.: DML Teaching Resources, 1986.)

"I'm Tipingee, She's Tipingee, We're Tipingee, Too," reprinted from *The Magic Orange Tree* (New York: Alfred A. Knopf, 1978) with permission from the author, Diane Wolkstein.

"How Bat Came to Be." Used with permission from *Keepers of the Night* by Michael J. Caduto and Joseph Bruchac. © 1999. Fulcrum Publishing, Inc., Golden, Colo. All rights reserved.

"The Brave Little Parrot," is reprinted here with permission from the author Rafe Martin from *The Hungry Tigress: Buddhist Myths, Legends, and Jataka Tales* (New York: G.P. Putnam and Sons, 1998).

"The Leopard's Revenge" is reprinted with the permission of Simon & Schuster Adult Publishing Group from *The Book of Virtues* by William J. Bennett. Copyright © 1993 William J. Bennett.

"Talk," is reprinted with the permission of Henry Holt & Co. from *The Cow-Tail Switch and Other West African Stories* by Harold Courlander. Copyright © 1947.

"Old Joe and the Carpenter" from *Thirty-Three Multicultural Tales to Tell* retold by Pleasant DeSpain. Copyright © 1993 Pleasant DeSpain. Reprinted on behalf of the publisher August House, by Marian Reiner.

"Sweet and Sour Berries" by Storyteller Linda Fang is reprinted here from *More Ready-to-Tell Tales from around the World*, ed. David Holt and Bill Mooney (Little Rock: August House Publishers, 2000) with permission from the author.

"Owl," reprinted from *The Magic Orange Tree* (New York: Alfred A. Knopf, 1978) with permission from the author, Diane Wolkstein.

"The Tail of the Linani Beast" is adapted here with permission from Margaret Read MacDonald. See her full work in *More Ready-to-Tell Tales from Around the World*, eds. David Holt and Bill Mooney (Little Rock: August House Publishers, 2000).

Acknowledgments

This book is dedicated to those who made made it possible:

Eddie, Joy, Bob, Claire, Vicki, and Bill, who love me no matter how much time I spend writing, and who have taught me much about character.

The librarians at the Lincoln Public Library in Lincoln, Massachusetts.

Doug Lipman, who first taught me how to do folk tale research.

Margaret Read MacDonald, whose research for the Storytellers Sourcebook made my research so much easier.

All of the teachers in the Lesley University Creative Arts in Learning Program, who brought the stories and exercises to their classrooms, and who shared with me their wisdom and experience.

All of the storytellers, folklorists, and authors who have labored to find, tell, and preserve the stories included in this book.

Contents

Introduction

FOR THE LAST TWENTY YEARS, I HAVE worked as a storyteller, traveling from schools to libraries and religious settings, sharing folk tales from around the world with students of all ages. There are few things as satisfying to me as the aliveness in the faces of young people who are experiencing a story through storytelling. Their bodies are relaxed, their hearts are open, and their minds are actively working, imagining, predicting, and weighing the justice of the events and outcomes in each story. I have seen the power of story to win over the most reluctant participator time and again.

I have also spent the last fifteen years traveling the country as an adjunct faculty member in the Lesley University graduate program, helping teachers to integrate storytelling into their classroom social cultures and curricula. It is so exciting for me to have witnessed every teacher's discovery that, after a try or two, he or she can tell a story and now has a new, invaluable tool that holds students' attention like nothing before.

In 1998, I published my first book, *Doorways to the Soul: 52 Wisdom Tales from Around the World* (Cleveland: Pilgrim Press, 1998). This book project was born out of a desire to collect short, wise folk tales from around the world to nourish me and other adults on our life journeys. The teachers whom I worked with through the Lesley program expressed to me a wish that there were a similar book with stories appropriate for younger children. As I worked in the schools, and also watched my daughter go through the elementary and middle school systems, it became clearer to me that as teachers are feeling more and more pressure to prepare their students for testing, there is less and less time to help our children to learn what it means to be a wise, caring, and courageous person of character—an education that endures far beyond most book learning. I also noticed that more and more schools were waking up to the problem of bullying and struggling for solutions that worked. While I don't for a minute believe that teachers are solely responsible for developing character in our young people, I do know that children spend a huge amount of time in school and on school work, and education is the arena that I have known best.

And so *Once Upon a Time: Storytelling to Teach Character and Prevent Bullying* was born. Students, families, religious educators, librarians, storytellers, and teachers alike can enjoy these tales and their follow-up activities. My hope is that the adults who read the book will be empowered to share the tales and to be examples of the qualities of character that they espouse. My hope is that students who hear the tales will have the chance to contemplate them deeply, and will find in them examples of how they can meet life as courageous, caring, and wise beings.

I think it is only right to begin the discussion of character education with a story. This story, like many that have inspired me, is from the Buddhist tradition:

Once Upon a Time...

Once upon a time in China, there lived a monk who sat all day and into the night upon a tree branch to meditate. Because he sat in a tree with birds perching upon his shoulders and arms, they called him Bird's Nest. At first the people would laugh at him, but soon they realized that he was a wise man, and they began to seek him out for advice.

One year the wealthy and powerful governor of the capital city heard about Bird's Nest's wisdom, and decided that he would travel to seek his counsel. He set off early one day with his retinue of servants and soldiers to protect and serve him. When he reached Bird's Nest's tree, the sun was high in the sky.

Looking up into the tree the Governor called, "Bird's Nest! I am the governor of this land. I have traveled all morning to seek your wisdom so that I might be a better ruler. I am powerful, I have wealth, but I am not very popular. How can I also gain the respect of those who serve me?"

For a while it was quiet up in the tree where Bird's Nest sat. At last he spoke. "The most important piece of advice that I can give to you, Governor, is to always do good. Don't do bad things. Always do good."

"Any four-year-old knows that, Bird's Nest!" laughed the Governor. "Don't tell me I traveled all this way to hear that bit of street advice."

Bird's Nest only smiled, and said, "A four-year-old may know it, Governor, but the eighty-year-old still finds it very difficult to practice. That is the best advice I can give you."

This tale is a fitting way to introduce the book. It reminds us that knowing something intellectually, and living that knowing on a consistent basis, are two different things. In the book I hope to share engaging stories that remind us of how to act for the highest good, as well as follow-up activities to help us to plant that knowing deeply in our everyday lives. Both are necessary parts of learning.

Knowing what is best and choosing to do what is best for all are not easy in a culture that gives us a barrage of mixed signals about what should be most important to us: Is it self, family, wealth, career, compassion, community service, religion, the perfect body? We cannot take for granted that anyone, young or old, will develop into wise beings by themselves. It requires lots of positive role modeling and conscious attention to understanding the positive traits of a person of character. Stories help us to explore the qualities of goodness by presenting them in an enjoyable context.

Here is a list of character traits, which I have fit into twelve categories for the purpose of this book.

Persons of character are:

- Respectful of themselves and others
- Responsible for their actions
- Courageous and willing to sacrifice for the greater good
- Thoughtful and wise in making choices

- Slow to anger
- Open-minded, inclusive, and nonjudgmental
- Optimistic
- Honest and fair
- Empathetic and compassionate
- Kind and loving
- Generous and helpful

- Loyal
- Forgiving
- Cooperative
- Creative in conflict resolution
- Persevering, patient, and diligent
- Tolerant and appreciative of difference in others

Persons of character also:

- cultivate good habits that allow them to act for the highest good.
- cultivate self-awareness of their emotions and thoughts so that they do not react from emotion

and ego, but rather choose to act consciously.
- have self-mastery and integrity. They act for the highest good.

- walk the talk, and their actions are in keeping with their value system.

What would you add to this list?

In this book I have put the above traits into twelve categories. I also include a chapter addressing bullying.

- **Cooperation:** Includes nonviolent conflict-resolution stories.
- **Courage:** Includes making difficult choices and sacrifice for the highest good.
- **Diversity Awareness:** Includes multicultural appreciation, inclusion, and tolerance for difference of all kinds.
- **Empathy:** Includes compassion, kindness, love, and caring.
- **Friendship:** Includes loyalty, forgiveness, and many other qualities.
- **Generosity:** Includes helpfulness, sharing, and balance.
- **Honesty:** Includes fairness and justice.
- **Leadership:** Includes good citizenship and democracy.
- **Perseverance:** Includes diligence and patience.
- **Respect:** Includes self-respect, respect for others, and respect for the earth.
- **Responsibility:** Includes responsibility for our actions (or lack of action) and the actions of those around us.
- **Self-mastery:** Includes integrity, emotional intelligence, self-control, and wisdom.

- **Bullying prevention:** While this is not a character trait, I have included many stories that help young and old to think about the traits and actions associated with bullying, and the steps that need to be taken to prevent it. You will find these stories listed in this chapter, and then integrated within the twelve sections. The follow-up suggestions with these stories address bullying behaviors and prevention directly.

"These (folk) tales help us sink our teeth into the dance between character and fate, for they show us that life is a collaboration between who we are, what comes to us, and what we do with both."

Erica Helm Meade, *The Moon in the Well*

My goal in collecting the stories and shaping the ideas and exercises in this book are to promote awareness of the positive traits of character in young people and in those who teach and care for them. When awareness of these traits is fostered, the overall result will be increased self-awareness, respect for self and others, and a safer, more supportive school environment. This awareness will be accomplished through experiencing these traits in story form, making personal connections to the stories, and applying that wisdom to daily life.

How can folk tales help promote character education and safe classrooms?

Storytelling may be the oldest educational and therapeutic tool on earth. People have been telling stories to impart values and information, and to make sense of life as long as we have had language. People of all ages love story. Stories are effective teaching tools because they engage our imaginations, our hearts, and our minds simultaneously. There is something in a storytelling experience for every type of learner.

The basic structure of story makes sense to human beings, because we live story daily, and use it to make sense of our lives. Stories all contain the same basic elements of life: a character we can relate to emotionally, a place we can picture with our imaginations, a problem that needs solving, and an array of possible solutions that arouse our curiosity and sense of justice. Story wisdom stays with us as we walk with the characters vicariously, and can later be applied to our own lives. Studies have shown that "even students with low motivation and weak academic skills are more likely to listen, read and write and work hard in the context of storytelling."[1]

Folk tales from around the world were created long ago to address the challenges of being human. Most of those challenges are still with us. The folk tale gives us simple scenarios and solutions that anyone from any culture of the world can relate to. Finding the commonalities of our humanity in stories from other cultures builds an essential quality of character, that of tolerance and appreciation. We have far more in common on this human journey than we have differences. Every culture has folk tales, stories without a known author, that have been handed down orally. Every child in your class can find stories from his or her culture of origin. That helps to strengthen a sense of belonging and pride and to raise self-esteem.

Storytelling was the primary way that character education was taught in the past, both in the home and in the formal schoolhouse—and even before there were school houses. I met a man who had been a teacher in Cambodia before having to flee as a refugee. He told me that in his homeland he primarily taught through the folk tales of his culture. I have heard the Abenaki Storyteller Joseph Bruchac describe how Native American cultures found storytelling to be a more effective means of responding to a child's naughtiness than physical punishment. I believe this was true for most cultures of the world.

Stories help to cement the values of a people. They were often cautionary: If you do this, that happens; if you do that, these are the consequences. Here is how I believe it worked: The storyteller would tell a story to a group of people. That story, its problem, characters, solution, and wisdom became commonly held knowledge. A common language sprang up by which the people could identify problems and solutions by simply mentioning the story, or its characters when a similar situation arose.

Sharing stories in the home, classroom or, even better, school-wide can have a similar effect. Catch phrases develop from stories that can serve to defuse situations. Stories offer a common language for looking at the challenges we all face. They offer unspoken opportunities for solutions that are acceptable to everyone. When children read stories, rather than hearing them told as a group, they do not always share that sense of common knowledge. A teacher in one of my college courses once reported telling a folk tale to one of the two middle school teams at her school. The story was about the hurtful effects of gossiping (see "Feathers" under Respect). The students who had heard the story demanded that the other team hear the story too, so that they would also be more reluctant to engage in gossiping behavior in the future. Story wisdom becomes shared responsibility, a way to hold people accountable.

Another benefit of storytelling in character education is that of retention. Studies have shown that when students are told a story rather than read it, they retain more information from the story and are better able to retell it to someone else.[2] They show greater comprehension of vocabulary words within the context of story as well. Telling stories, and then having the students retell them in some expressive form further cements the learning and assures retention.[3] Long ago, before written language was used, listeners were required to hear stories told over and over again to assure that they could be retained and passed on. One Native American storyteller from the Northwest told me that he had been instructed to commit over one thousand stories to memory as a young man. While few would argue that we should burn all our books and go back to relying solely on oral means of passing on wisdom, something has been lost in relying on books, and not committing things such as history and folk tale wisdom to memory.

What is the difference between storytelling and theater in the classroom?

Both storytelling and theater come out of the tradition of drama. The first difference is that, generally speaking, storytelling is a solo activity, while most theater is performed by a group. As a solo activity the teller becomes each of the characters. In a class play it is typical for a few students to get leading roles, while everyone else gets a line or two. In storytelling, each child is challenged with the responsibility for the whole story. Each child claims ownership of the story, as he or she shapes it to his or her imagination. Each child is allowed to rise to the occasion instead of letting the bolder students take center stage. In storytelling there is no scenery. The teller helps the listeners to make the scenery in their imagination through language and movement. Props and costuming are used minimally, if at all. Typically told stories are learned by heart, rather than memorized as in a play script, leaving the teller open to some improvisation to fit the needs of the audience and their own inspirations. Storytelling is easier to put together in a classroom in that you do not need whole-class rehearsals, and students can practice at home and in pairs. Storytelling does take more time to perform in that each child must be heard individually. Typically, however, students' stories are no more than a few minutes long.

Character education promotes self-awareness rather than brainwashes value systems.

Character education in this book is not about instilling religious beliefs, values, or political persuasions. Because of their power to evoke emotional responses, stories are often used as tools for brainwashing and manipulation, such as in advertising or politics. This is not my goal, nor that of most teachers. I use stories and story activities as tools to promote self-awareness, so that young people can make informed choices in their lives and grow up to be healthy, responsible citizens in the world. In order to become responsible and discerning citizens, we must carefully scrutinize all of the stories we are exposed to for their truths and the responses they elicit in us.

Shouldn't character education be limited to home and religious settings?

Character education is already a part of nearly every aspect of the curriculum, in its content and delivery. We are called to assess the actions of characters from history, and in literature and contemporary society. We are required to teach about other cultures in a manner that builds respect. Our own classrooms are increasingly culturally diverse and, as we are learning, are made up of learners with diverse learning styles. This diversity demands respect, tolerance, and appreciation of difference on the part of the teacher and the students to build a climate of safety in which learning can happen. As students get older, they are required to take more and more responsibility for their schoolwork and to learn to work harder. In the arts and in sports, students are required to apply diligence and perseverance to succeed at achieving goals and learning a craft.

The school experience is largely a social one for our students. Qualities of friendship and inclusion must be taught. Bullying must be dealt with and discouraged aggressively, as it is a problem in every school. Honesty is called into question as students work cooperatively on projects, and when copying and cheating happen. Children need constant encouragement to have the courage to do what is right, and not what is easiest. As students get older, they should be encouraged to take on leadership roles and to question the qualities of a good leader, so that they can begin to participate actively in our democratic society.

Character education is happening in between classes as well—on the school bus, in the halls, and at recess. We have an obligation to think proactively about the daily dilemmas that children face. Much of character education is about adult modeling. Bullying, teasing, and taking the easy way out are learned behaviors.

Simply put, if we focus only on the three R's, we may have young people who are brain smart, but who do not know how to navigate this complex world—a world based largely on social interaction, making tough choices, and the cultivation of good habits.

Is character education through story and story-telling just another subject foisted upon already overworked teachers and an over full curriculum?

Teachers are overworked and the curriculum is over full, largely due to the pressures of mandated testing and the lack of resources schools are given. But character education through story and storytelling dovetails with state standards and enhances curriculum. When classroom and schools explore character issues, they are simultaneously creating an environment that is more conducive to learning. Classrooms in which character education is addressed become emotionally and physically safer, which allows for greater risk taking, an essential component of learning. Stress is reduced, freeing teachers and students to focus on learning. Literacy, creative writing skills, and oral skills increase through the act of listening to, responding to, creating, shaping and telling stories.[4] Self-esteem is boosted as students build self-awareness skills, which also enhances a student's ability to access their learning strengths. Stories are also a natural springboard into any subject area. When children hear a story, their curiosity and sense of wonder are heightened, and they are more willing to explore the subject following the story. While research has not yet confirmed this, teachers are likely to see test scores go up as a result of time spent on character education through story.

Why teachers make great storytellers

- Teachers naturally know or have learned how to modulate their voices effectively to hold their students' attention.

- Teachers know how to reach the whole group at once.

- Teachers know what their students need, and can adapt the story in the moment to best meet the needs of each student. When telling a story, teachers can fully observe their audience experiencing the story and can adapt the telling to the listeners' needs.

- Teachers are models for students. A visiting artist will often be held on a pedestal, his or her art seeming esoteric and something that few can aspire to. But when a teacher who is well known to the students tells a story, it becomes accessible, especially when the teacher walks the students through the process they used to learn, develop, and tell the story.

- Teachers have always used stories to reach their students. Without often realizing it, teachers tell stories to their students every day. They tell stories about themselves to connect with their students, and they tell stories to explain things in a way that will engage each child.

- Storytelling is a place where your own personality and creativity shine through. It is an opportunity for students to get to know you better. It is a very intimate experience in which the listeners see and experience you. Particularly if you can put the book down, you can fully experience the responses of your audience and hold their complete attention. You will bring your own strengths to the telling; you do not need to try to be like anyone else.

Storytelling is a priceless skill for every teacher.

Stories have always been an effective alternative to lecturing young people on proper behavior. Ears and minds stay open when a story is being told, but seem to close when the drone of a lecture begins. Every culture has stories that help us think about the consequences of certain behavioral choices. These were used long before the printed page.

Storytelling promotes listening skills. Teachers that try storytelling in their classrooms are inevitably amazed at the level of attention they receive. Storytelling calls for the audiences to look, as well as to listen. Storytelling strengthens the students' ability to make mental pictures. This is an essential skill for focusing on a discussion or lecture, and also for concentrating on written material in reading, for writing effectively, and for problem solving. When teachers take the time to learn a story for telling, they have incorporated it more deeply into their hearts and imaginations and will naturally portray it more fully and emotionally than when reading it. The result is that the listeners will be more likely to be drawn into the story and to be excited by it afterwards.

Storytelling reaches learners of each type of dominant intelligence.
Whether linguistic, kinesthetic, logical, visual, spacial, intra- or interpersonal, storytelling uses all of these intelligences to engage the listener.

Teachers are models for effective public speaking. Look at the curriculum standards for any state in the country. You will see the value that is placed on oral skill development, of listening skills, speaking, audience awareness and interpretation of story, and yet, the amount of time spent training our students to be effective and confident speakers and lovers of language is minimal. Why? Is it a lost art? The visual media dominate our culture today. We do not have effective ways of assessing oral skills, so as we become more test focused, we spend less time on oral skill development, and yet, in real life we will need to use the skill of communicating through speech 90% of the time. When teachers model effective use of language and communication through storytelling, they are inviting their students to do the same. By taking risks, they make the risk taking less dangerous and more fun. They let students experience body language, the beauty of the spoken word, the expressiveness of the face, and the power of words to conjure images and feelings. They excite students to mimic them. Teachers should capitalize on this desire to mimic, which is natural in children. It will allow the children to try on storytelling with their bodies, voices, and hearts.

Teachers can gain new confidence as effective speakers in front of adults, parents, and peers.

Storytelling is noncompetitive. There are no pictures, so there is no craning to see them. Students can relax and focus on creating the pictures in their imaginations.

Students who learn storytelling skills will become more effective oral communicators. Studies have shown that most adults are almost as afraid of speaking in public as they are of being killed in a car crash. Many of us learned to hate public speaking in school. We'd stand up in front of the class to give a report, or even to answer a question, and we'd risk humiliation from our peers. We were boring—we knew it and they knew it. No one paid attention, and it felt awful. It is usually incredibly boring when students get up and read to one another. But when students are taught to be effective storytellers, or even effective readers, they can hold the attention of their peers. They see people paying attention and responding.

Students find the joy in using their individual strengths to convey a story that is fun for them. They learn that talking can be fun and effective. And oral reports are so much more fun to listen to for the fellow students and teacher!

Why should students become storytellers?

Students utilize and strengthen every intelligence in the process of developing a story for telling:

- **Logical/Mathematical**—Students learn to predict, sequence, etc.
- **Verbal/Linguistic**—Students learn to appreciate the sound and power of words to conjure images.
- **Spatial/visual**—Students learn to communicate visual images through language and use of space.
- **Intrapersonal**—Students learn about themselves as they connect to themes and images and ideas in the stories. Drawing from their imaginations, memories, and emotions, they each interpret a story uniquely.
- **Interpersonal**—Students learn how to communicate with and to others, including how to interpret and shape a story for an audience.
- **Musical**—Stories have shapes like musical pieces. A good story has a rhythm to it—sound pacing, changes in intonation, pauses, use of breath. Many stories utilize sound and song.
- **Kinesthetic**—Storytelling allows students to use their whole bodies, and through them to conjure images and emotions. Stories often involved the audience in participation, using their bodies and voices to enhance the telling.

Storytelling is a great assessment tool. Students need not be good readers or writers to be good storytellers. Other skills and talents can be appreciated through a focus on oral communication. A child considered "slow" by other students can suddenly shine as a physical comedian or by the ability to use his or her voice effectively. Storytelling is the great equalizer!

Storytelling builds self-confidence. As children learn to shape stories for telling, they put their own personal touch in the shaping and telling. They create a work of art that is theirs. This experience builds confidence and satisfaction. The more students practice expressive speaking in public, the easier and less threatening it becomes, if they receive positive feedback. Learning the basics of eye contact, voice modulation and projection, character development and expression, and effective use of movement and gesture greatly enhance the performance, and can easily be taught through this fun craft. As I mentioned above, learners with challenges can often shine in the realm of oral communication.

Storytelling is therapeutic. Children come to school with a whole range of emotional challenges that get in the way of learning. Storytelling is relaxing, it reduces stress, and is noncompetitive. Stories provide avenues for making sense of life. They offer examples of the kind of emotional challenges children face without being about them. Hearing stories helps students to feel less alone, as they hear about other creatures encountering similar dilemmas and overcoming adversity. Stories give them hope that there are solutions to their problems, and that they can grow up to be good and strong people. Stories provide heroes to emulate. Stories can also be a bridge by which a student finds the words and the courage to speak out about a secret they have held. Stories nurture children's imaginative capacity and train them to use their imaginations to solve problems creatively. I cannot emphasize enough the importance of nurturing children's imaginations with story images. Sadly our children are receiving less and less opportunity to simply listen and enter the imaginative world of story, as their lives are increasingly saturated with visual stimuli or computers, TV, and video games. Story images provide healthy material with which children can work out their own inner dilemmas through fantasy play and daydreaming.

Those of us who were lucky to grow up hearing stories know the power of story intuitively. Precious little research has been done on the healing effects of story, but in his book *Healing Fiction*, James Hillman quotes a study in which it was determined that patients who had heard stories as children got better faster than those who did not.[5] You will know when a story has reached a child where he or she is, when that child asks for the same one over and over again.

---

1. U.S. Department of Education, *What Works: Research About Teaching and Learning*, 1986.

2. "The Effects of Storytelling Experience on Vocabulary Skills of Second Grade Students," a research paper by Gail Froyen (unpublished M.A. Thesis, U. of Iowa 1987).

3. G. Brown, *Tales As Tools*, National Storytelling Association.

4. Robin Mello, PhD. "Creating Literate Worlds: The Effect of Storytelling on Children's Writing." The Hood Children's Literacy Project, http://www.lesley.edu/academic_centers/hood/currents/v3n1/mello.html.

5. James Hillman, *Healing Fiction* (Barrytown, N.Y.: Station Hill Press, 1983).

Once Upon a Time

by Bill Martin Jr.

Once upon a
Once upon a
Once upon a time,
Tell it again, Storyteller,
Tell it again,

The Storyteller came to town
To share his gifts sublime,
Tell it again, Storyteller,
Tell it again,

Doors flew open to him,
Kings begged him not depart,
And children tucked his stories
In the pockets of their heart,

Oh
Once upon a
Once upon a
Once upon a time,
Tell it again, Storyteller,
Tell it again.

"Once Upon a Time," a poem by Bill Martin Jr. is reprinted here from *Bill Martin Jr's Treasure Chest of Poetry*, by Bill Martin Jr., with John Archambault and Peggy Brogan (Allen, Tex.: DML Teaching Resources, 1986.)

Pre-Story and Follow-Up Activities

ANY TEACHER OR PARENT KNOWS that a good story is more likely to fix itself in a child's imagination than a lecture. But even good stories can go in one ear and out the other with little or no reflection, depending on the method of delivery, the ability of the listener to attend, the environment, and the time taken to process and connect the learning afterwards. So, how to deliver the stories more effectively? The first goal is to engage the heart and the imagination and make an impression that holds the story firmly in the mind with lots of associations, so that its wisdom can be available to the listener later. A second goal is to follow the stories with activities that will allow the students to explore the story ideas and their feelings and to make connections to the story in their own lives and the world around them. In offering character education, we are not seeking to give information to students so that they can parrot it back to us, pass a test, and then soon forget. We want students to put these ideas into practice, and to become more self-aware in the process.

Following each story I have a section titled "Tips for the Telling." In it you will find suggestions for pre-story, by which I mean setting the mood and the scene for the story before beginning. Often a story needs no introduction, but sometimes you will want to preface the story with some specific vocabulary words, an introduction to the geographical place the story comes from, or an activity that helps the students to be mentally and physically prepared to get the most from the story. This is an area that every teacher and teller will approach differently. Use your creativity!

Pre-story suggestions

1. Choose a time of day that is conducive to good attention (not right before lunch or right after a long period of sitting still).
2. Make sure that your location for telling is quiet and comfortable, so that all students can concentrate fully. Put yourself in a comfortable position relative to the students. If they are much smaller than you, you may be more comfortable down on the floor with them, but if your story or style demands full body movement, don't be afraid to stand.

Set up basics for effective storytelling

3. Put a "Do Not Disturb, Storytelling in Session!" sign on the door.

4. Discuss some basic rules for storytelling with the class. Your students are probably used to a format in which they can raise their hand at any point to ask a question or request to go to the bathroom. This too depends on the story and your style. Most tellers prefer to tell the story without the interruption to its flow by questions or comments. Review the rules of respectful listening: look at the teller, don't talk or move your bodies unless asked to do so, no side comments. If you wish (especially when a student is the teller) you can have applause afterwards.

5. Take the time to relax your body and make sure that everyone else is relaxed too.

6. Take a moment to picture in your mind the crowning moment near the end of the story when the conflict is resolved and there is an emotion of satisfaction. This will connect you emotionally to what you love about the story.

7. Establish eye contact with your audience and take a moment of silence to create expectancy.

8. Take a nice deep breath as you launch into the story, and take time to pause and breathe at every transition point.

Please go to the section called "How to Tell a Story" following this chapter for detailed steps on how to learn and tell a story.

Pre-story rituals for fostering excitement and attention

Have you ever noticed that the phrase "Once upon a time" has a magical quality about it? When those words are spoken, most listeners automatically quiet and relax. It is an invitation, and a familiar one, that is safe and invites them into another time and place. Often this is enough once children have heard a few stories told or read, but you can add to this invitation by having a specific ritual that you repeat each time. Rituals feel comforting for children as they are predictable and, with repetition, are easy to join in. The idea is to focus the students' attention, build their curiosity, calm their energy, and get their bodies into the right position so that you can begin with a rapt audience. Here are some suggestions for story-starting rituals:

• Ring a bell, or play a special instrument, or invite one student to do so.

• Move your "story chair" into position and sit down.

• Light a candle.

• Invite the students into the story space and dim the lights.

• Make a "story bag." Before each story, open the bag and bring out an object that will be featured in the story and place it in front of the class or in the middle of the story circle.

• Sing a song that speaks of entering the story magic. I once had a student who had her children sing a song about going to the land the story was from on a magic carpet. At the end of the story they would fly back again.

- Recite a poem together, such as Bill Martin's "Once Upon a Time" at the start of this section.
- Have a simple phrase to begin each story, such as "Once there was, and once there was not..."
- Create a "storyteller persona." Leave the room momentarily and come back with a costume (funny glasses, a hat or shawl) as the "storyteller."
- Create a silent movement poem with hands and sign language to signal that story time has begun.
- Do a warm-up stretch.
- Take the students on a short imagination journey with their eyes closed to prepare them to use their imaginations.
- It's important to end your storytelling time in ritual fashion as well. When the story, or the story and discussion time, is completed, do something that reverses what you did to begin the storytelling mood.

Tips for effectively telling each story

In the Tips for the Telling section after each story, you will find suggestions for telling the story as effectively as possible. I urge teachers to "tell" the story, rather than reading it. Telling means putting down the book and telling it in your own words, with expression. It is not about pat memorization. (See the Basic Storytelling Skills section.) When a story is told rather than read, the impact is greater for both teller and listener. For one, you have maintained eye contact with your listeners throughout, making the story more immediate. However, should you choose to read, these suggestions will help to make the experience more rewarding. They include:

- Creative ways to introduce the story
- Different media to deliver the story, including story boards and puppets
- Possible points of view to present the story from different effects
- Props to enhance the telling
- Movements to enhance the story
- Music or song to enhance the story
- Places to stop the story for discussion, or for students to make their own endings
- Opportunities for audience participation in the story
- Dramatic enactments involving the listeners as actors within the telling

---

Audience participation in storytelling

Storytelling is participatory by nature. The storyteller depends upon the responses of the audience, and the audience makes the images that the storyteller describes in their imagination. Some stories lend themselves best to listening, while others can be enhanced by inviting the audience to join actively in the telling. There are as many ways to involve an audience in a story as there are stories to tell. With young audiences, pre-K to grade 3, I suggest having lots of participation. Older students also enjoy it if they are comfortable and it is age appropriate.

The basic rule for audience participation is to find places in the story where there is repetition. This can be in the form of words or phrases, movements that are easy to mimic, sound effects, or where whole sections of the story repeat. You can also add songs, if it seems that they will enhance the story. It is best to stick with short songs that are easy to learn and can repeat through the tale. If you use repetitive movement, chances are good that your audience will naturally want to do it too.

Teaching elements of the audience participation before the story starts is usually a good idea. It builds anticipation, excitement, and a sense of responsibility. You will notice how well the students listen for their part. It can also work to introduce the participation within the story, depending on how complex the instructions are and if they interrupt the flow of the story. One example of teaching participation in advance would be to teach the students how to make the sounds of a rainstorm ahead of time, so that everyone does it the same way. If you have several parts in a story, you can divide the group and give each group a sound or movement. Practice makes perfect!

There are participatory stories in every chapter of this book.

> *"Tell me and I will listen.*
> *Involve me and I remember."*
>
> **Kronberg and McKissack,**
> *Piece of the Wind* (1997)

Follow-up activities

The structure of the follow-up activities used in this book was inspired in part by the writing of Kevin Ryan and Karen E. Bohlin in their excellent book, *Building Character in Schools* (San Francisco: Jossey-Bass Publishers, 1999). They talk about practical wisdom as involving the "head, heart and hand." One way to interpret this is that in order for persons of any age to develop positive character traits, they must understand them intellectually, they must make a personal, heartfelt connection to them, and they must practice them in daily life. I also used a similar format in my first book, *Doorways to the Soul: 52 Wisdom Tales from Around the World* (Pilgrim Press, 1998) in which readers are encouraged to make a deeper connection to the wisdom in the stories through a variety of exercises.

The Follow-Up Activities that follow each story in this book divide into four sections:

1. Tips for Increasing Story Retention

Studies have shown that when students have the chance to retell a story soon after hearing it, their retention and comprehension increase. When students are encouraged to mimic the expressive storytelling style of the storyteller, they also internalize a number of effective oral communication skills. These exercises will help students to cement the sequence of events, feelings, and images in their minds. They will also help to clarify students' questions and assess their level of understanding. The exercises include those that can be done as a group, with a partner or at home, and using various media, creative writing, and drama.

2. Making a Personal Connection

When students can see how a subject connects to their own lives, and when they are allowed to express and explore their feelings about something, they become more willing to invest themselves in it. These exercises help students to connect the ideas and feelings in the story to what is going on in their own lives, the classroom, home, community, and world. Storytelling followed through in this way can build emotional intelligence. This is the place to encourage the class to generate a list of questions that the story brought up for them, or that they would like to ask the characters. It is a place to help them to remember times in which they have grappled with the theme, or had similar successes and challenges. Making personal connections help them to reflect on personal choices past, present, and future.

3. Creative Exploration of the Story Ideas

When students have learned a story well enough to tell it to others, they have internalized a personal understanding of its meaning. When they can adapt the story and/or create original stories related to the ideas in a story, they have gained an even deeper understanding of their implications. Various exercises are presented throughout the book for students to retell, reshape, and/or create original stories based on the dilemmas and outcomes of the story.

4. Turning the Story Ideas into Action

When stories and their catch-phrases become part of a classroom or school-wide culture, they can be effective tools for talking about and resolving conflicts. The stories become symbolic means for starting dialogue and finding creative solutions to problems. Stories can also be springboards into collective and individual projects. Through multi-modal arts and class projects, students explore and deepen their experience of how positive character traits affect their daily lives—at home, at school, in their community, and the world.

Now, for a more detailed look at the four areas of follow-up. These suggestions can be applied generally to any of the stories in this book, but following each story, I offer very specific ones that work especially well with that story. I suggest that you read this section first so that you are familiar with the general model and purpose of follow-up activities. Then you can adapt them to suit your classroom.

These activities are various ways students can retell the stories, which helps firm them up in their memory.

Tips for increasing story retention

YOUNGER STUDENTS
• **Round-robin retelling:** In this whole-group activity, the students sit in a circle, and going around the circle in turn, each student adds a small part to retell the story. I suggest not allowing the students to "pass," as this gives them an easy out. Instead ask them to simply add a very small section, or to ask for help from a neighbor.

- **Whole-group dramatization:** Your youngest students will want to act the story out with their whole bodies, and they will remember it best if they do. You will want to have a fairly large carpeted area clear of objects. Set up behavioral ground rules, like "This sign means freeze." Then retell the story, inviting everyone to imagine that they are the characters in the story with their whole bodies, stopping to step into each character, to feel each feeling, and to try on each voice.

- **Volunteer retelling:** Individual students can volunteer to come up in front of the class and retell the story or some part of it for the class.

- **Telling the stories at home:** Assign the students to tell their favorite story to a parent. You may want to ask parents to sign a form stating that they have heard the story and have given some positive feedback to their child for their telling technique. You may have them make a pictorial outline to help with their retell if you wish. (See below.)

- **Sequential drawings:** Have students draw their favorite scene from the story. Take the pictures and let the students line them up on the floor in order of sequence. Then ask them to draw missing scenes to complete the story. Make them into a book.

- **Make a comic strip of the story:** From one simple picture, to a sheet divided into three scenes, to one with eight different scenes, your students can make a visual sequential outline of the story to help them to remember it. Have the students write a word or draw a picture to represent each scene in the story. My experience is that most students have excellent memories and the sheet can slow them down when they try to retell, but some benefit from using it or referring to it briefly first.

- **Pantomime retellings:** Assign small groups of students to pantomime different scenes from the story, and have the other students guess what was going on.

- **Scrambled retelling:** Teachers can retell the story while intentionally mixing up the sequence and let the students correct them.

- **Flannel board retelling:** Have a piece of cut flannel to represent each character. Model retelling the story using the flannel pieces, and then let the students try it in small groups on their own.

- **Retelling with puppets:** Make puppets, or have the students make puppets to represent each character. Model the use of puppets to retell the story, and let the students retell the stories to one another and to you.

OLDER STUDENTS

- **Round-robin retelling:** Older students can retell in round-robin style in small groups or with the whole class.

- **Partner retelling:** Students in pairs can retell the story to one another.

- **News reporter retelling:** With students in small groups, assign one in each group to pretend to be news reporters. Assign the others to be characters from the story. The reporters will interview the story characters to tell the television viewers what happened. Give them an example of what you want, such as: "Here we are at the site of an amazing scene. Just hours ago, the Big Bad Wolf was terrorizing this neighborhood, but it looks like he will not be back. Mr. and Mrs. Pig, can you tell me what happened?" A small prop such as a thick marker can serve as a microphone, giving more authenticity to the scene.

- **Town gossip:** This is similar to the news reporter, but this time pairs or small groups get together and retell the story as if it happened to someone in their town.

- **Dramatization:** Put the students into small groups and have them act the story out together and then for the class. This works best if one student takes the part of narrator and one the part of director to help place them in the scene and keep the action moving.

- **Comic strip outlines:** Older students can make more complex comic strips of the story than those mentioned above. Take a good-sized piece of paper (10" x 18" is ideal) and have them fold it until they have three to eight boxes (depending on age appropriateness). In each box have them draw a scene from the story from beginning to end, with captions for minimal dialogue. Once the comic strip is complete, the students can cut out each square and staple them together to make a small flip book for easy retelling.

Making a personal connection

These are activities that prompt students to think about how the ideas in the story, such as how to solve a complex problem, can be applied to their own lives. Once a young child identifies with the Little Engine That Could, he or she will be more willing to persist at many tasks.

Questions and discussion: Help your students to generate and respond to questions that will elicit thoughtful discussion and writing. Brainstorm a list of questions about the story or for the characters. These questions may be about scientific or cultural aspects of the story, or they may be moral questions. All questions will deepen their connections as they come from the students own style of learning. Questions you may want to ask:

- What lessons did they take from the story?
- Was there an image, phrase or message that stood out for them?
- Who was their favorite character, and why?
- Who was their least favorite character and why?
- What would they like to say to, or ask of the characters?

You can use a "story dissection" exercise, in which you retell the story and have the students yell, "Stop" every time they have a question, or want to make a point about a place in the story.

Connecting to the characters. There are several ways to explore the characters.

- Ask the students to identify with a character from the story and ask: How did that character feel? Make a list of feelings on the board.

- Play "hot seat," in which a student sits in a special seat at the front of the class and pretends to become a character from one of the stories. The other students ask questions of the "character." It helps if the teacher first models being in the hot seat, and models asking questions, such as, "Big, Bad Wolf, why are you making the pigs' life miserable?" This exercise can help the students to empathize with the characters and to try on many different emotions, which builds emotional intelligence.

- Encourage your students to explore their feelings and reactions to the story verbally and in journal writing.

- Pre-writers can make cards or letters for their favorite character, showing their favorite part and then explaining it to the class. Writers can add words to the card expressing what they felt about the story, or if something like that ever happened to them.

- Introduce a puppet character from the story who can speak directly to the students and invite honest story sharing and discussion.

Personal story sharing: Help the students to tell personal stories of their own experiences with the themes presented in the stories. When have they acted with generosity or felt greedy? When have they grappled with honesty or felt judged? I suggest that you tell a personal story that relates to the story theme, which can help to make a bridge to the students' own experiences. They will likely want to share these with the class, and one story will prompt another. I find that it is helpful to acknowledge that most of us have experiences in which we have been both kind and unkind, bullying and bullied, generous and greedy. Our point is to build awareness, not to increase shame. These stories remind students that they have rich resources for story material for their written assignments. Many state tests for English require that students write personal stories. This can be a good way to foster them.

With younger students you may find that students' stories do not have good form, and may go on and on, or seem to mimic one another. I suggest that you have a time limit for each story and a rule that people get one turn only. Also you can use an object like a "talking stick," a large sea shell, or other item that signifies who is allowed to talk so that others will be better listeners.

- Interviewing family: Have students tell the stories to family members and ask them to share stories of times when they have grappled with these issues. These family can then be shared in class. They can also interview school staff and collect their stories.

- Stories from biographical literature can also enhance the connection to personal story memories.

- Play "Truth or Lies," in which you share a story along a theme and the students guess whether it really happened or not. You try to make it sound real, with rich detail and emotion, but it can be made up. Then allow the students to tell this kind of story to their classmates and have them guess whether it is true or not. I find that younger students (grade 3 and under) mostly tell true stories to one another. This exercise helps them to think about what makes a story effective to tell and it generates lots of story ideas.

It is important to be aware of how we listen and respond to our students' stories, and especially those who come from cultures different than our own. See "What is Sharing Time For?" by Courtney B. Cazden in *The Need for Story: Cultural Diversity in the Classroom and Community*, eds. A. Dyson and C. Genishi (Urbana, Ill.: National Council of Teachers of English, 1994). This is a thoughtful chapter on how our biases affect how we listen to, censor, and interpret children's stories.

> **A note about inappropriate story content:** If you find that a student is beginning to tell a story that may be too personal, tell that student gently that this is a very special and important story, but that you want to hear it alone first. Then make the time to do this, or ask the school counselor to do so. Hearing graphic stories of abuse or family violence can be traumatizing for other children. It can also add to a child's trauma if other classmates (or the teacher) do not respond to the difficult stories they are sharing respectfully.

Creative exploration of the story ideas

This element is comprised of creative story making and storytelling activities. The premise is to help the students expand on the themes and apply them in new ways.

Students retelling the stories: Help your students to retell the stories you have shared with them formally in a storytelling presentation for reading buddies or other classes, as individual storytelling, or as a group dramatization. In the process, they are identifying with characters and processing the ideas. Storytelling and story making are great tools for assessing what the students have learned. Both individual telling and group dramas require effort on your part. Letting the students each retell allows everyone to be the star and to internalize the whole story. Students must prepare individually and require coaching. Dramatization usually involves a few students in major parts and many in minor parts. It requires greater coordination and cooperation among students.

Creative adaptation: Creating original stories based on this story's dilemma and outcomes helps students to further explore and gain some mastery over the topic. Students can approach this is a number of age-appropriate ways. Reshape the story as a group, with a partner, or individually by:

• Creating a new ending or introducing several alternate endings.

• Adding or changing characters. Change the people to animals or vice versa.

• Changing the setting. Make the story happen in the forest, or your school.

• Modernizing the story. Help the students to envision what would happen if the story were happening today.

• Changing the perspective from which the story is told. Encourage the students to tell the story as if they were one of the main characters. Changing the perspective from which a story is told is a powerful way to gain empathy and compassion and understanding. There are always two sides to a story, and being open to hearing other people's opinions is a difficult skill, but a definite quality of a person of character. Have students pick their favorite character from their stories. Then sitting with a partner or small group, have them introduce themselves in character. "Hello, my name is Turtle, do you see these cracks on my shell? Let me tell you how I got them!" Once they have gotten the feel for speaking in the first person, and where to start the story, let them tell each other the story in the first person. Then following the story, their classmates can ask the character questions which can help to enrich the story with detail. It is best if you model this process first.

• Creating original stories that contain the same dilemmas and themes but with entirely different circumstances.

Pourquoi stories. A number of the stories in this collection are stories that explain how something came to be. You might know them as "How and Why Tales." When children hear a pourquoi story, they are inspired to create one of their own. They will often ask, "Is that true?" Here is a good place to discuss with them the role of story making and storytelling in the lives of our ancestors, who were trying to make sense of the world around them without the aid of the scientific tools and information we have today. Making up stories to explain things is fun and a wonderful way to exercise the imagination. These tales are also excellent springboards into creative writing. The most reluctant writers can come up with stories using the formal structure of a pourquoi tale. (*Pourquoi* means "why" in French.)

Suggestions: Brainstorm a list of questions that your students are interested in relating to nature, such as: How did the zebra get its stripes? Why do dogs chase cats? What makes the wind? Then make up answers together as a group.

Example: Once upon a time there were no stars in the sky. Where does the story take place? Who was there? What was it like in that place and for these characters with no stars in the sky? (It was dark, or it was ugly in the sky.) What did they do to get light or beauty in the sky? What do stars remind you of? (Diamonds, tiny fireflies, teardrops) What happened to get those things into the sky? What was it like after the stars got in the sky?

After you have made up several as a group, let each student, pair, or small group make up one. Have them share them with other groups for feedback, and then with the class.

For the youngest children these tales can be as simple as: *Once there weren't any _____. Something happened _____, and then there were _____.* They fill in the blanks! Gradually you pull out the characters and details as they learn the ingredients of story!

Tell first—write later! I suggest that you do not have students write their ideas down before telling them. Most children speak better than they write and are bogged down by the mechanics of writing. Let them make outlines, pictures, and/or comic books of their ideas before sharing them orally. By conferencing and oral sharing, they have the chance to get all of their ideas out and shaped into story form. The writing will be richer for it. It will also be easier for them to share the final story orally if they have not committed a final version to writing. They will be less tied to the exact wording and more open to the freedom of expressive telling. After they have shared their stories orally, they can write the final version down with all of its details and dialogue. You can even tape-record the stories for them!

Dramatic discovery. Let the students pretend to be a jury to try the characters in the story and to decide on just punishments or rewards for behavior or to find new more suitable endings.

Researching stories. Older students can go online or to the library to find examples in history or current events that are similar to the events in the folk tales. They can then share these stories with one another.

Researching and sharing cultural variants of the tale. With the help of a reference librarian at your local library, you can often find cultural variants of a folk tale. Hearing the same basic tale told from several different cultural perspectives allows students to see commonalities between cultures, as well as learning about cultural differences. You may also find different endings or slants on the story that allow the students new meaning. These variants are a good springboard into their own creative adaptations. I suggest that you bring these versions into the classroom and let students read them and share the similarities and differences with one another. I have included examples of cultural variants after many of the stories. Storyteller, Librarian and Folklorist Margaret Read MacDonald's *Storyteller's Sourcebook* is an excellent reference book for finding cultural variants of a tale by motif (major or minor themes in a story).

Turning the story ideas into action

This element applies the story wisdom that the students have internalized to situations in the classroom, school, community and beyond.

Make a rubric with your class for the character trait you are focusing on. How will a student know what behaviors constitute an advanced ability to use this trait in daily life? What constitutes being proficient but not advanced? What are the basic skills that don't meet proficiency, but are beyond "just beginning"? What does it look like if we rarely or ever use this trait? Students can then have a positive guide to help them to develop these traits, rather than focusing on feeling ashamed that they don't, or worse, rebelling!

The Community of Caring Newsletter (www.communityofcaring.org, Winter 2003), describes how the Cresson Elementary School in Cripple Creek, Colorado, developed a behavioral rubric to positive effect.

Brainstorming: The best way to internalize positive traits is to practice them in everyday situations. Brainstorm with your students how you might put the ideas in the stories into practice in the classroom and in school.

Have the students share their stories at home and reflect with family members on how these themes are present in their home, and what they could do about it together.

Journaling for self-reflection: To help older students see how often they have opportunities to develop and use positive character traits daily, have them keep a journal to note and reflect on how and when these themes are encountered. These reflections often become stories.

Storytelling or drama: Share the stories throughout the school to create community.

- Have small groups of students go to different classrooms and share the stories, and then invite follow-up discussions.

- Have all-school or all-grade assemblies in which students act out the stories as plays for their peers. Have the students stay in character afterwards and ask the audience questions.

- Have students gather stories from other teachers, staff, and/or students who have at one time grappled with the themes in the stories. These tales can be shared in class, generating great discussions and reflections.

- Have a school-wide contest in which students write and tell stories related to a character education trait. The top three to five can perform or read them at an all-school assembly, or for smaller groups and parents.

Multimedia expressions: Create art in a variety of media to help spread the message of the story.

- Have the students make posters representing each story with a caption for school hallways or classroom walls, to remind everyone of the importance of behaviors. An example could be a picture of Beetle flying over Rat's head, with a caption by Parrot: "Don't judge people, get to know them!" (See "How Beetle Got Her Colors" on page 271, a great story for teaching respect and bullying prevention.)

- Have the students make 3D posters or artworks that can be manipulated to allow them to identify when a theme needs to be talked about (e.g., a bundle of sticks that rely on one another to stay standing). If someone feels that the class is not acting cooperatively, he or she can pull a stick out of the bundle. By having this common vocabulary of stories and their catch phrases, students and families will have an easy way to identify and discuss problems.

Classroom, school, community, and service-learning projects

You can follow up your discussions of character traits presented in the stories with projects that take the concepts into a larger community.

A **classroom project** is a project that involves only the classroom and not the larger school community. Examples are identifying social issues in the classroom and brainstorming ways to work on them; creating multimedia representations of story ideas to serve as reminders of the story ideas; starting a class recycling project; or raising money to buy something fun for the class. All of these projects help to develop skills of cooperation, leadership, responsibility, empathy, and friendship.

A school community project extends to the larger school population, in which students undertake to help in some aspect of the school community. An example might be related to bullying. Students could develop and administer a survey to find out where most bullying and teasing happens in school. Then, using the information, they could share it with teachers and students to find ways to stop it. One outcome of this could be that bus drivers and monitors are given a short training session on how to help stop bullying and teasing on the school bus. Learning would take place that would integrate many areas of the curriculum while developing awareness, empathy, and leadership skills. Another example could be turning a story into a play and sharing it with other classes and then leading a discussion about the issues in the story. There would be many opportunities for learning across many curriculum areas, particularly oral skills, confidence, and leadership skills.

According to the National and Community Service Trust Act of 1993, a service-learning project:

- Is a method whereby students learn and develop through active participation in thoughtfully organized service that is conducted in and meets the needs of communities.
- Is coordinated with an elementary school, secondary school, institution of higher education, or community service program and the community.
- Helps foster civic responsibility.
- Is integrated into and enhances the academic curriculum of the students, or the education components of the community service program in which the participants are enrolled.
- Provides structured time for students or participants to reflect on the service experience.

Examples of service learning projects could include:

- Older students helping in a preschool program and learning about working with small children. Many traits are learned including kindness, patience, and responsibility.
- Working directly in the town's wetland areas to determine levels of pollution and animal species, doing cleanup and town-wide education. Many traits are learned, including respect for the land and responsibility.
- Designing and implementing a school-wide recycling program, learning about the many issues related to recycling and putting on an educational event to educate members of the town community. Many traits are learned, including diligence and responsibility.
- Raising money to benefit a town soup kitchen or shelter, and learning about homelessness. Many traits are learned, including empathy and generosity.
- Providing companionship for elders in a council on aging or nursing home program while learning from the senior citizens. Many traits are learned, including appreciation for difference, generosity, and respect.

As you can imagine, the value of projects are greater the more they integrate into students' lives, communities, and curriculum. The more opportunities that students have to experience the connections between what they do and what happens in the larger world, the more they will see themselves as having a responsible place in the world. Students learn teamwork, critical thinking, research, and social skills while helping them to develop personally and academically. Ideally service-learning projects should be a part of the overall school strategy and should continue in all grades.

For examples of school communities that use service-learning projects see:

- www.ServiceLearn.com, www.MyWiseOwl.com, and www.learnandserve.org
- Sheldon Berman, Superintendent of Schools in Hudson, Massachusetts, has integrated service-learning projects into grades K-12. "Service as Systematic Reform" in *The School Administrator*, Aug. 2000.
- *How Can I Help*, by Ram Dass and Paul Gorman (New York: Alfred A. Knopf, 1985). This book written for adults has stories and examples of reflections on service to inspire teachers and parents.

How to Tell a Story

LEARNING TO TELL A STORY is intimidating at first to most of us. The idea of having to tell a story in front of peers causes initial anxiety in most of the teachers who take my classes toward a Master's of Education at Lesley University in Cambridge, Mass. Polls shows that, apart from death, what most of us fear most is public speaking. We imagine that as we face our audience, we will stumble or mumble, turn red or turn pale, and go completely blank. We will be laughed out of the room. Happily, by following some simple steps, teachers discover that they can tell stories very effectively. They have learned—as you can too—that they make often great, and certainly "good enough" storytellers to delight their students, and even their peers. Some of my teacher-students even chose to tell a story when their principal was observing them. You can too!

Step by step for teachers

Telling a story is not the same as giving a lecture in which a series of ideas must be laid out. A story has a structure that is very familiar to us as human beings. I speak of narrative: *There once was a character, in a place, who faces a problem. He or she uses various internal and external resources to solve the problem, and there is some kind of change or transformation as a result.* This is the story of our lives. We are all characters with problems and resources (or a lack of them), who are searching for solutions, and we are being changed all the time. This is what we care about and this is what is worth telling stories about. This is why we remember stories when the names and specifics are forgotten. They plug naturally into our mental hard drives. In the pages that follow, I will spell out the steps that have helped thousands of my students of all ages to learn to tell a story without memorizing.

The vast majority of storytellers down through history have spun their tales out without memorizing them word for word. A priceless beauty comes through the tale retold in one's own words, and with one's own imagination, heart, and body language. Because a storyteller is not using an exact script, he or she is able to adapt the story to the needs and responses of the audience, and the stirrings of his or her imagination during the telling. Storytelling is different from play-acting; you can change the words without messing up anybody else's lines! The key to learning a story is to learn the basic story sequence and then to play with it to find the way the story wants to be told in your own heart, body, and mind.

Why should you bother to learn a story for telling when you can read it?

Just ask an audience of children which they prefer. Just look at the level of attention you get when you put the book away and tell with your whole self. There is a startling difference. Storytelling is different than reading aloud. When you're telling a story, you have nothing between you and the audience. You are able to make full eye contact, to use your hands and your whole body if you choose. You can gauge your audience's interest and comprehension and you can ad lib within the story to bring greater meaning—enhancing a description here or stretching out some dialogue there—or to add your own insights or local references as you go. Because listeners are using their imaginations, there is no competition among the listeners to "see" the pictures. Because your full attention is on your audience, their whole attention will be on you, and thus on the story. In order to tell a story without the book you must internalize it to some extent. This means that you will give it back with more emotion and depth. It will become your story. The audience will be even more interested in the story because they will be interested in you, and will connect to your humanity through it.

A Few Basic Tips for Effective Storytelling

- Choose stories that you love, figure out why you love them, and make the aspects that you love stand out in your telling.

- Imagine the story unfolding before you with all of your senses, and your audience will imagine it vividly too.

- Feel what the characters are feeling and empathize with those characters, and your audience will empathize as well.

- Believe that the story is true in the moment and your audience will be invited to believe, entering a world of enchantment.

- Relax and have fun, and your audience will relax and have fun.

You can trip, drop something, get a frog in your voice, forget your place—it won't matter. They will be with you.

- When you tell a tale well, you will experience having the audience in the palm of your hand. It is a lovely responsibility. Use it well.

Learning a story without memorizing

The following simple steps give you a tale that you can tell every year for the rest of your life. Read my suggested order through and try it with a simple short tale with minimal dialogue. Then use these steps in the order that is right for you.

1. **Read the story** over several times, both silently and aloud.

2. **Write a brief outline** of the story in bullet form, only writing down the main points.

   - This happened,
   - then this,
   - then this.

If you are a visual learner, you can make a storyboard with boxes to represent each scene and draw stick-figure actors and settings instead of writing the words.

3. **Tell the story in its simplest form** to someone (or something, if no one is available) without trying to embellish or dramatize it at all. I call this the bare-bones or one-minute version. You are not timing yourself or trying to hurry, you just want to keep it simple. Put your outline away so that you are not tempted to look at it. If you forget sections, go back and look at the outline, but only then. Once you have told this short version successfully, you will see that you know the basic sequence of the story events. The rest is icing on the cake.

4. **Visualize your story setting** with your eyes closed. Imagine that you are a bird flying over the place where the story starts, surveying the geography of the land. Fly lower and lower, focusing on more and more detail, such as houses, colors, and movement below, until you land in the place where the story starts. Now walk through the story using all of your senses. Listen for sounds, imagine smells and tastes, see colors, and feel the ax, the dipper, the little mouse, or the magic peach pit. Is it warm or cold in the story, breezy or still? See the characters: How do they hold themselves? Listen to their voices: Do they reflect the character's nature? I do this before falling asleep at night or during the day when I need a little meditative break.

5. **Tell the story again, adding in the imagery.** I suggest that you begin to tell it to your students at this point. Let them know that you are trying to learn a new skill and that you'd like their support and feedback. Let them see the story evolve, from a one-minute outline to a dramatic experience. What great modeling for their creative oral expression and writing skills! Your willingness to share an unfinished piece will help them to take risks too.

6. Get to know your characters. **Change the perspective** from which you tell the story. Tell it as if you were one of the main characters. This works best if you introduce yourself to your listener as the character: "Hello, my name is _____. I am _____, and here is my story of how I came to be in such a place [or role, or whatever results at the end of the tale]." Tell the story as if you are remembering and reflecting on the events. This change of perspective allows you to gain a much stronger emotional connection to the characters, their feelings, and point of view. It also can help you to imagine them and how they would dress, talk, and present themselves. I like to try a story from the perspective of all of the main characters. It is important to *love all of your characters*, then they become three dimensional and the listener can care about them too. After this you can go back to telling from the narrator's view if you wish, but however you do it, you will have more insight, connection to, and respect for your characters.

7. **I write my stories down** in the process of shaping them. This may or may not work for you. The intention is not to memorize lines, but to

see how the story and dialogue flow on the page. This is one of the ways that I play with the story. Often when I actually stand up and tell it, it changes again. I never try to memorize what I have written unless I am telling Edgar Allen Poe or some such gifted author. Then the memorized wording comes only after I have fixed the story well in my mind.

8. **Add movement and gesture.** Tell the story standing up if you have not yet done this. See how much more energy to bring to it standing. Notice what gestures and movements you add. If this really isn't right for you, sit down again!

   - *Tell it without words* to further increase the use of movement. If there are objects in the story, try to show them with gesture and facial expression.
   - Try telling the story *with a favorite piece of music on.*
   - Tell your story *while walking* to increase your energy and to help you to get new ideas.

You may decide that you do not want to emphasize physicalizing characters, and that is fine, but you still need to know them. What is most important to get across is their intentions or their nature. This can be done just as effectively with very subtle gestures, body language, and a description such as "He was as tall as an oak tree," or "By the time she reached 80, she was as bent over as a question mark."

9. **Add audience participation.** (See more ideas about how to stimulate audience participation in the Pre-Story section.) Does this story have lots of repetition of words, actions, and/or sounds? Can you add sound effects? Your students can help you to find places to add participation to your story. Watch where they join you. You can also add a simple song to weave its way through a tale for young children. They will anticipate its coming and stay awake. Use a well-known tune and add your own words. Use this formula:

   AABA (Thanks to Storyteller Bill Harley for teaching me this.)
   A: She tiptoed down the hall
   A: She tiptoed down the hall
   B: Creak went the floor boards
   A: As she tiptoed down the hall.
   (Sung to *The Farmer in the Dell*)

10. **Focus on the language.** Tell the story while sitting on your hands. This can be just as hard for some of us as telling with no words. Does your use of expressive and image-rich language increase? Well-chosen language creates images and feelings in the listeners' imaginations and invites them to love words.

11. **Focus on the elements of diction.** As you tell the story without any use of movement or gesture, be aware of the quality of your speech—pitch,

rate, tone, and volume—and how it changes based on what is happening in the story. You must pause longer than feels natural at all transition points to give the audience a chance to catch up and move with you. When a teller speaks too quickly, the listeners have trouble keeping up with making mental images. Often they will give up and put their attention elsewhere.

12. **Think about the beginning.** Does it grab the listeners and quickly draw them in? Too much detail can bog down the mind. Not enough can leave the mind wandering.

   • Introduce the setting with simple, clear, and vivid imagery.

   • Introduce us to the main character in a way that makes us care about him or her and the problem quickly.

   • Introduce the problem pretty quickly too, so that we are beginning to wonder about and to predict how things are going to turn out early on in the story.

13. **Think about the ending.** Does it stop in the right place? What images are the listeners left with? Is the emotional focus strong in the end? Extra information at the end of the tale can dissipate that strong emotional feeling. Endings are often the last thing to coalesce in the story-shaping process, and they often change the more you tell the story. Resist the temptation to say, "The moral of the story is...." Your students will take something from the story. If they don't understand it, they need to be able to say so. If you tell them, "This is what this story means," you could be negating what they took from it. Trust that you get your message across in the body of the story.

> **Preserving your work:** Once you've learned a story, you want to remember how you told it so that you can tell it for years to come. Either write down the basic flow of the story with favorite phrases, or better, tape record yourself telling it. You can also write it out in your own words as a way of recording the version you have created. Keep a list of stories you have learned so that they will be available for you when needed.

Don't have time to do all of these steps? Then simply make the outline and tell the story to yourself in the car or the shower, or while you're out walking. Picture it as you lie in bed at night (a great way to overcome insomnia). And most importantly, tell it to your students. It will grow in your imagination, like a seed in the earth, even if you just live with it. You will be pleasantly surprised at what you create!

My teacher-students frequently ask if they can use props, music, and/or costumes in storytelling. In my mind there is no one right way to tell a story. You must be the final judge, and creativity should be your guide. Here is what I tell my students:

Props, music, costumes?

Props: When telling a story, try to show an object rather than actually bringing it in as a prop when possible. For instance, if the woman in the story wore a hat with a tall peacock feather, use your hands to put on the imaginary hat and to run your fingers up the length of the feather each time she puts it on. Listeners will soon be visualizing it and feeling the feathers on their imaginary hats. A simple gesture can conjure up almost anything, if you do with care. One need not be a professional mime to show an audience that you have a box with a delicate lid. With very young children, the use of props can be very helpful in holding their attention, but you do not want the children to become dependent on them. Our culture is so visually oriented that children are getting less and less practice at creating images in their minds. Storytelling without books or props is the best tool for strengthening the imagination, and thus the ability to attend.

Music: If you are a musician and can accompany a story with an instrument, you can enhance the telling considerably and can find many ways to involve the audience in singing and sound-making too. You can also tell a story and then give simple percussive instruments to the class. They can retell it with you, adding sound effects. You can also play quiet background music to set a tone or give a sense of the culture from which a story comes. I find this can be distracting unless the music is played very softly.

Costumes: What you wear can add to or detract from the believability of the tale. I usually dress simply so as to be able to slip in and out of all different characters. Most audiences can let go of the teller and focus on the tale, so what you wear should not matter that much. If I am telling a story in character then I will of course try to dress as they would have dressed. I also dress for comfort in movement when storytelling. This makes a great deal of difference.

Step by step for students

To help students of any age become better storytellers, and thereby better communicators, start by reflecting on what students know. Ask them what makes a story well told. What stories do they like best; which ones do they ask for? Once you have made storytelling a regular part of your class day, you will want to encourage your students to become storytellers. This greatly enhances their confidence and oral communications skills. So how do you begin?

Model effective storytelling yourself and, if possible, invite professional storytellers to your school or show videotapes and play audio tapes of storytellers. After the students have experienced live storytelling, help them to reflect on what made the storytelling effective. You can do this simply by having the students tell you what made the story fun to watch, or...

Demonstrate good and bad storytelling. Tell a story to your class as well as you can, and then tell a brief portion of it as badly as you can, using a monotone voice, no movement or expression, and staring over their heads at the wall while you tell. After you do the "bad" telling, ask the students to tell you what made the first one better and generate a list. They will tell you things like:

- eye contact
- use of movement
- changing the voice for different characters
- vocal variety—pacing, tone, pauses
- character development
- perspective changes
- vivid descriptions
- rich use of language
- relationship to the audience

Write the list with positive traits rather than negative. Reflect on each of the traits they have noticed. Examples: What does it feel like when someone won't look at you when they are talking? (Most students will say they feel left out.) What happens when someone talks too fast? (Most students will say that they stop listening.) The fact is that our minds are trying to make pictures or a sense of what we are hearing, but if the speaker talks too fast, we give up and stop listening.

Keep a copy of the list in your room and bring it out to reflect upon as the students are practicing their stories. It can be a guide to help them give each other praise and constructive criticism. It can be used to build a rubric (e.g., Maintains eye contact: all the time, most of the time, sometimes, rarely). You can use it to find positive things to say about each child's early efforts at storytelling. The students can use it to reflect on their own progress.

Helping pre-readers and early readers to learn a story

Pre-readers and early readers can create original stories or can retell stories that you have told or read to them. After hearing the story, these steps will help them internalize the story and develop some facility in telling it to others:

- Retell the story together using flannel boards, puppets, or drama.
- Draw a picture of what happens in the story.
- Make a three-part outline of the story. (Fold a piece of paper into thirds. Ask the children to draw pictures in the each section of beginning, middle and end.)
- Tell the story to a reading buddy, parent, or classroom helper.
- Have the students use a puppet or stuffed animal to be their favorite character. Let them animate that character, telling the story from that character's perspective of what happened.
- Make dioramas. (See below under Visual Representations.)

Helping young readers to learn a story without memorization

This is quite similar to the way you learned the story. Try the exercises you did, or modify them as I have described below:

- Have the students **read their story** through several times, or if it is an original tale, have them write it out in draft form.
- Have the students **make a comic strip outline**. Give them a large piece of paper, have them fold it into four to twelve sections (whatever you think is developmentally appropriate for their level of sequencing). Then have them map out in pencil what will be in each section, so that the story is retold in order through pictures. Tell them to draw stick figures so that they do not feel pressured to create an elaborate piece of art. Keep the

focus on the sequencing. They can color in the comic if there is time, once the sequence is right. Once they have the comic outline, they can share it with a partner, using it as a retelling tool. They can also cut up each square and **make a book** to take home.

- Have your students **take the story home and retell it** (using the outline or not) to family members.

- Have them do **one-minute retellings** to a partner. Have them switch partners several times, adding a minute to the length of the telling each time.

Shaping the tales for telling

Group visualization helps younger students become better storytellers by teaching them to focus on sensory details of a story. Lead them on an imagination journey in which you invite them to close or cast down their eyes and imagine that they are in their story. Draw them in by telling them to imagine that they are going to make a movie of the story in their minds. Invite them to get into their own private plane and to fly up over the place where the story starts. Tell them to film what they see, noting the geography of the land, then zooming down to see if there are roads, houses, rivers, etc. until they land their plane in the place where the story starts. Then have them get out of the plane and to walk through the story, filming it as it unfolds, remembering to listen to and record sounds and to capture smells, colors, sights, tastes, and feelings. At the end of the story, have them fly back to the classroom and to share what they saw with a partner.

Younger students may want to draw a more detailed picture after this exercise.

Older students can do a short writing assignment to write down the detail of what they saw.

An alternative to the group visualization is to have the students sit knee to knee with a partner, and both close their eyes. Have one partner at a time take the other through the beginning of the story using a lot of description so that the other can picture the setting and characters. The other can ask questions, such as what kind of a house did they live in? What color was the girl's hair?

Visual representations: Younger students, students with learning disabilities, and students with difficulty concentrating without props can have successes making a diorama of their story with a shoe box, some markers, clay, and small props. Show them how to use the clay to fashion the characters, and then to animate them as they retell the story standing over the box.

Older students can write and/or talk to a friend about what they most like about the story and be sure that they convey that clearly in the telling. They will need to tell it to others to know if their intended focus comes across.

The quickest way to be sure that your students can hold one another's attention is to help them to use physical expression in their story. Before having your students add movement and gesture to their stories, have them play **pantomime games**, such as charades, so that they can practice using movement to convey action and emotion. These games are fun and will help them to feel more comfortable being expressive in front of others.

A simple version of charades is to either have actions written on slips of paper and to pass one to each child, or to whisper an action into each child's ear. Tell them that they must convey that action without words to the class. Examples of actions are:

- making a peanut butter and jelly sandwich
- buying a soda from a soda machine
- blowing bubbles and popping them
- going fishing
- stepping on chewing gum

Students also enjoy portraying group scenes through pantomime, such as a day at the beach, making a snow person, a birthday party, or riding on the school bus.

Another fun exercise is to have the students stand in a circle and pass an invisible object from one to the next. Each child must change what the object is that they are passing, and must show what it is through movement. You might, for instance, pantomime that you are putting up and holding an umbrella. Then pantomime changing that object into something else, maybe turning it upside and having it become a cane, or shrinking it up until it is a lollipop. When they understand the concept, pass the object to a student next to you and ask him or her silently to make it into something else. When the students guess what the invisible object is, the pantomiming student passes it on.

After your students have played some pantomime games, have them retell their stories with the intention of showing the actions, emotions, and objects through movement and pantomime. Let them work in small groups to give one another suggestions. If students are working from a written story, they can also circle all of the places where there is an opportunity for movement.

Adding movement and gesture

Hint: Stand in a circle. If the students are using actions written on strips, have them give the strips back to you before their turn so you can help them if no one is getting what they are doing. Keep the performers confined to an area where they don't have their backs to anyone. Don't let the students talk or guess until the child has taken a small bow.

Changing the perspective

Your students will enjoy pretending to be the characters and telling the story from different perspectives. Model this with several examples, such as the Big Bad Wolf : "Hey, ya'll, I'm one big, bad wolf. At least I was until I got my tail all boiled away. It's a sad story..." Then invite a brave student to try it in front of the class. Then let the students work in pairs or small groups to retell their story from the perspective of one of the characters.

Another approach to connecting to the characters is to do the following exercise:

Have the students again close their eyes and visualize the character they are working with. Have them share the description with a partner. Have them write some similes and metaphors to describe the character: she was so proud her nose pointed straight up like steeple; he was as tall and strong as an oak tree; she was so strong she could pick up a school bus like it was a sandwich; he was so absent-minded he wore mismatched socks.

Before asking students to step into their characters physically, have them try this simple dramatic exercise to loosen up and to see how posture affects how we feel and what image we put forth. Using a large open space, have your students walk in a circle trying on different postures. Suggest movements like these:

- Stick out your chest and walk—How does it feel? Who walks like this?
- Hunch your shoulders—Who does that make you think of?

- Tiptoe quietly, then step on a creaky board.
- Be light on your feet.
- Drag your feet.
- Walk like a one-year-old who is just learning.

- Walk like a swaggering teen.
- Walk as if every joint was in pain.
- Walk as if you are carefree, sad, suspicious, angry, scared...

Now, invite your students to stand up and walk around, imagining that they are a story character, trying on that body for size—how would the Monkey King walk? Or the Tortoise, or the Loathly Lady? Ask them to note the character's posture and, when they begin to feel they can move like the character, let them speak from that body and explore how they would use their voice. Our speech is dependent on how we hold our bodies and how we modulate the air through our chest, throat, and face. You must find the body of a character before you can find the character's voice.

Trying on their character: To avoid class mayhem, invite several students at a time to come to the front of the class pretending to be a character in their story. Let them meet each other and tell each other a little bit about what they are doing while staying in character. For example, Big Bad Wolf could say, "I'm just on my way to my neighbor's to borrow a cup of sugar." Little Red Riding Hood could say, "I'm going to my grandmother's with this basket of goodies because she is sick." If you like, you can choose someone to be a director to suggest how each student could add more expression to their voice or body.

Practicing and peer coaching

Have the students practice as many times as possible, in class and at home, continually trying to add elements of expression to their telling. Each time they should receive positive and helpful critique. I suggest giving them each a rubric so that they can think about what they do well, and what they want to continue to work on.

Coaching: Invite brave students to tell their story for the whole class and you model giving positive, constructive feedback for your students. Don't assume that your students know how to give constructive feedback. You may want to make a rule that they have to say at least three things that they liked before they can give suggestions. Comments must always be in the form of suggestions such as, "It would be even better if..."

Projecting their projection and enunciation: What a shame to have a child work hard on a story, only to tell it in a tiny voice that no one can hear, or to mumble it through. Each child has a different speaking ability, and not all can speak loudly and clearly, but each child can make clear progress and gain self-confidence. What they need is for you to help them to be aware of their speaking habits and to give them tools for change. The first step is assessment.

Find a large space where the students can stand in two lines facing each other at least forty feet apart. If you can go outside, use the gym or an auditorium/cafetorium with a stage. Believe it or not, most of effective projection comes from *enthusiasm*. Ask your students to imagine that they are standing on opposite sides of a big playing field. Tell them that the person across from them in line is someone that they kind of know, but is not a good friend. Ask them how they would say "hi" to that person. They will make a somewhat enthusiastic, but not-too-loud sound. Now ask them to imagine that the person across the field is their very best friend. How would they say "hi." They should belt out the sound. Remind them that they did this with enthusiasm. If they can tell their story with the same enthusiasm, they will be heard.

Another approach if you have a stage in your school is to have half of the children up on the stage with the others at the back of the room. Have those on stage call out, "Once upon a time" and have them imagine that their nearly deaf grandmother has come to watch and is sitting in the back row. You can also have them imagine that they are telling a story to a king and queen as court jester to get more enthusiasm and grandeur.

Next have them *practice breathing* into their bellies and letting the breath out slowly. Have them practice saying "Once upon a time" clearly and loudly as they exhale the breath to the person in the line across from them. The partners will say if it was loud enough and the speakers may be asked to do it again. As the teacher, you stand with the group that is sending the words. Notice their body posture and make sure they are standing up straight, with their chins up, and with hands at their sides. Make sure they are projecting using belly breath rather than pushing the air out from their throats.

Next have them *practice exaggerated enunciation* as they call out, "Once upon a time in a far away land." The listening partners will say if they can hear each word clearly. Do any words drop off at the end of the sentence? This is a great assessment method. Finally have them say, "Once upon a time in a far away land," using clear enunciation, enthusiasm and projection. Have the partners say what they did well and what they want more of. When they prepare to tell their tales for the whole class, remind them of granny in the back row! Praise each child for his or her progress.

Final student story-sharing events

Class performances: Remember that your students' attention span is limited and that after about three to four stories they will need a break so they can give full attention to the next group of tellers. Even a five-minute stretch break will do. Do not try to do all of your students' stories at once, particularly on a parent night. It is too long. Better to divide the students into groups of five or six at the most.

Going to other classes: At least some of your students will want more opportunities to tell their tales. You can send them to other classes or to reading buddies or for school assemblies. If they go to younger grades, make sure the teacher of the class they go to prepares her students to be good listeners.

What do you do after the storytelling event?

Both students and adults need positive feedback after they have given a performance. I suggest that you give positive written feedback to each performer so that he or she has something to take away. This could be in the form of a printed award, or simply a short letter telling them what you liked. You can also have each student write something positive to each classmate. I would check them if you don't trust them to be nice. You can also give them feedback on areas to grow in. Particularly if they are older. A rubric may again be helpful here. Some states are now adopting standards by which to assess oral skills. Search the web to find these, or make up your own.

Process the experience through talking and journaling

Take some time to process the experience of learning a story and performing it for others. Students can do this as a group. I also suggest that they write in a journal how the experience felt and what they learned about themselves, as individuals and as storytellers. I always ask the students to name a strength that they saw in themselves during the storytelling, or one that others mentioned, as well as some areas that they would like to develop.

See How to Tell Stories in the Resource section on page 368 for books with more ideas about how to tell stories for and with children.

Starting a Character Education Program in Your School

ADDING A CHARACTER EDUCATION or social competency program to your school community will be most effective if teachers and parents are involved from its inception. I suggest having an introductory meeting with parents and teachers to brainstorm a list of character traits and social competencies that people would most like to see highlighted and strengthened in the school. Let the list be as long as people wish initially. Then decide which traits are similar, grouping them together, until you have a manageable number. Next have participants prioritize the traits to determine which ones they feel are most important to focus on. This may differ by grade level, so you may wish to break people into groups for this section. You could ask groups to come up with their "top three traits" for a school character trait motto.

Once you have a smaller number of trait headings identified, you can ask parents to brainstorm all of the ways that these traits can be taught without adding new time into the curriculum. Examples could be after-school or library projects, family-oriented projects, and town-wide focuses.

Next, meet with teachers to organize your character education program so that it best dovetails with the curriculum and school schedule. Once the traits have been identified, have members of the school community, which includes administrators and teachers, take a hard look at how the overall philosophy, values, and atmosphere of the school supports or detracts from a safe, respectful community in which positive character can naturally thrive. This includes things like teacher satisfaction, visibility of student work in the classrooms and halls, and a focus on learning rather than testing.

Here are strategies that various schools have taken:

- Choose one character trait cluster to be the permanent motto of your school. It might be a three-pronged approach such as: "Respect, Responsibility and Caring," "Sharing, Caring and Working Hard," or "Empathy, Ethics, and Service." Gear your activities to these three traits, make an effort to look at how these traits express themselves in your existing curriculum, and tell stories that build awareness about them throughout the year.

- Begin the year with an intensive focus on the traits. For the first few months, choose a story to tell each week that identifies and raises awareness about each of your chosen traits. You may choose to have teachers read or tell the stories to their classrooms, or have them shared in an assembly. Alternatively, you can assign different stories to individual classes to present to the whole school. This upfront approach builds a rich social/emotional vocabulary for the whole community to work with throughout the year and reinforces your school values tenfold.

- Choose three traits over the year and focus on them in trimesters.

- Choose a "trait of the month" on which all classes and grades focus, and have activities in each classroom and a culminating assembly in which classes share their work, as well as artwork in the halls.

- Choose traits for the year by grade as seems most developmentally appropriate, and have grades share with one another.

- Let individual teachers decide on their focus, and have their classes share with others at the end of the time of focus.

- Evaluate your approach at the end of the year and decide how to improve on it for future years.

For a fuller description of this process, and how to make it work at your school, check the list of books available from **Character Development Group** (www.charactereducation.com). Also see the Resources section at the back of the book for more extensive reading and organizations that can provide examples of how other schools have organized character education programs.

Cooperation

FEW THINGS EXIST IN OUR WORLD that were not made by a cooperative effort. This point can be well illustrated by looking at any natural process. Take the growing of a plant for instance, in which the elements of sun, rain, and good soil are all necessary. Few man-made products are created solely by one person either. Even the solitary profession of a fine arts painter involves many other people: teachers, patrons, gallery owners, those who make and sell the painter's tools, models, and even the subjects that are painted. When looked at in this way, our lives are a web of cooperation with others that we may not even see. Taking the time to acknowledge the function of cooperation helps us to appreciate the role that others play in our lives. Contrary to the old saying, it usually takes many cooks to make a truly great broth. The trick is to respect one another for our best contributions.

Learning is a cooperative effort. We learn best when we learn together because we benefit from so many points of view, and from other people's questions and insights. Howard Gardner's multiple intelligence theory (*Frames of Mind: The Theory of Multiple Intelligences*, New York: Basic Books, 1983) has taught us that we have a great diversity of approaches to learning within any classroom or family, and all make a valuable contribution to the learning process.

Democracy is a cooperative effort, relying on each citizen to be guided by the principles of respect and responsibility, and to obey the laws that allow everyone to safely and freely pursue happiness. Building an environment that is safe for the risk taking that learning involves requires cooperation. All parties must agree to behave respectfully and responsibly, and to follow rules that assure the safety of all. Stories that discuss cooperation help us to remember the advantages of creating a healthy community in which every student plays an equal part and deserves equal respect.

Some of the themes that rise up through a study of cooperation are safety, inclusion, risk taking, respecting differences, valuing each person's contribution, creative nonviolent conflict resolution, dividing the work, compromise, patience, communication skills, decision-making skills, strength in unity, and protecting one another.

For all of the reasons above, cooperation is a great start-of-the-year kickoff theme for creating a safe, productive, and close-knit classroom climate.

What themes do your students come up with when thinking of cooperation? Have your students brainstorm a list of the natural processes that require cooperation. Have your students brainstorm human-made products or professions and the role that cooperation plays to make them work. Can they think of any natural elements, products, or professions that do not rely on cooperation? Have them research scientific or geographical discoveries that have been credited to one person to learn about the other people without whom which it might not have happened. An example is Admiral Perry, who was literally carried to the North Pole by Matthew Henson, an African-American man who accompanied him on all of his excursions. Henson befriended the Inuit, who served as guides, and literally blazed the trail for Admiral Perry, who could no longer walk and was pulled on a sled. It was Henson who planted the flag at the North Pole. In part because of his ethnicity, he received no recognition at the time.

Talk about multiple intelligence theory in your classroom and help each student to identify his or her strengths, and how this adds up to a whole and balanced learning environment. Explore this with exercises in which everyone contributes their best efforts to one project.

Homework: Have your students observe and write about activities at home that demand cooperation to work their best.

The Bundle of Sticks

Once upon a time, an old man lived on a beautiful farm in the country. From his window, the old man could see pasture lands, fields of grain, barns filled with animals, orchards, and forests beyond. The farm was special to him because it has been his father's and grandfather's before him. He had raised his family there. Now his wife was dead, and he too was in the last days of his life. The old man should have been content after such a fortunate life, but he was not. He lay on his bed worrying about his children. They could not seem to get along. He heard them quarreling day and night, each one envious and angry with the other. Though he tried talking to them about forgiving and forgetting, they seemed to grow increasingly bitter by the day. He felt sure that they would not be able to keep the family farm after he had died, because they could not seem to work together.

Then one night as his strength waned, he had an idea. He called his six grown children to his bedside. "I have one last favor to ask of you my children, " he said. "I would like each one of you to go to the forest and find two sticks. Bring them here tomorrow and I will explain."

The children did as he asked and came to his room the next day with two sticks each. "Thank you, children," he said. "Now put one down, and see if you can break the other one in half." The children easily broke their sticks in half.

"Now, please gather the remaining sticks into a bundle." The children bundled the remaining sticks. "Please pass this bundle of sticks among you and tell me—is it as easy to break the bundle?" The six children passed the bundle between them but none of them could break the bundle of sticks.

"You, my children, are like these sticks," the old man said. "If you work together, value what you share in common, and care for each other, nothing in life can break you. But if you quarrel and see yourselves as separate from one another, you will be easily broken by the trials of life. Find strength and joy in one another's company, and you will live well."

The children took their father's lesson to heart, forgiving one another and focusing on what they could accomplish together. The old man died peacefully, and the farm remained in the family for many years.

Aesop

Grades K-8

THEMES: Cooperation, tolerance, creative conflict resolution, sacrificing for the greater good, loyalty, appreciating similarities and differences, forgiveness

As support for the story, I always tell the children a little bit about Aesop. While there are conflicting stories of who Aesop was, and precious little reliable historical data remains, numerous stories say that he spent part of his life, roughly around 620-560 BCE, as a slave for the Roman rulers. He may have lived on the Greek island of Samos. Stories also go on to say that he was able to avoid the most difficult forms of physical labor, owing to his gift of telling stories, which he did for his Roman masters. Aesop is thought to have created and gathered hundreds of fables in his lifetime, but to have written none down. One story tells that Socrates spent his last days in jail writing out Aesop's tales.

I tell the students that I believe that Aesop, being as wise as he was, probably was not just thinking about children in a family when he told this story. I imagine that he was thinking of students in classrooms, people in a neighborhoods or towns, differing tribes or countries sharing a piece of land, and all of us sharing this earth and her resources.

Tips for the telling

This is a story that lends itself to a lot of student participation. You can either tell the story once without the participation, and then have the students act it out, or as I prefer to do, add the participation into the first telling. The latter approach grabs their attention more effectively.

Buy or save enough Popsicle or craft sticks for each student in your room to have two. (Uncooked spaghetti will work for the littlest hands.) Have a rubber band on hand too. When you get to the part in the story in which the old man's children gather sticks in the forest, you can hand out two sticks to each student, or have them find them around the classroom. Have the children do what the grown children in the story do, breaking the first stick, and bundling the second. They will love trying to break the bundle, and this activity will engage all ages and make for a great discussion. I set ground rules that they can only try to break the bundle with their hands, as using feet, furniture etc., can be dangerous, and can result in a broken bundle if worked at long enough. The way I word the question is: "Is it as easy to break the bundle?" The answer is always "No."

You may also wish to have a number of dimes on hand to show them the picture of the bundled grain, with the motto E Pluribus Unum, or "Out of Many, One" engraved in them.

Follow-up activities

Follow the guidelines in the Introduction on follow-up activities, and then try out these specific activities as age appropriate.

Tips for story retention

• For younger students, have each child make a picture or comic strip version of the story, and take the paper home to aid them in retelling the story to family members. If you can, send Popsicle sticks home with the students as well, or have them gather sticks from the woods.

- For older students, let them retell with a partner or the whole class to cement the sequence of events. They too can go home and share the story with family.

- **Questions, discussion and story sharing:** Teachers can tell a story about a time when they did something better because of doing it with others. Sit in a circle, and let each child take a turn telling about a time when they did something better as a group.
- **Have the students go home and ask their parents** about a time when they accomplished something with a group of people. Make a list of all the things that would be better done cooperatively.

- **Creative adaptations:** Have the students act out the story out in small groups, changing an element of the story, such as who the people are who can't get along, or what they use as a substitute for sticks (e.g., set in an Italian village using pasta in a bunch). Students can then write down their new versions or tell them to the group individually.
- **Have the students make endings for the story.** What happened after the father died? What are some examples of how the children learned to work together?
- **Encourage the students to share their stories** with the class, with other classrooms, or for a whole-school assembly.

- **Make a class contract for cooperative projects:** Let your students reflect on things that are hard for them to do with a group. This can be a place for students to explore the challenges and benefits of working together. From this you can make a contract to ease cooperative atmosphere and to allow for different styles. Some children, for instance, need quiet, while others need to talk aloud and walk around.
- **Visual representations of the story:** Have the class make a 3D poster of the bundle of sticks, with actual sticks, perhaps using a cup to hold the bundle, and put it on the wall. When individuals or groups are having a hard time with cooperation, they can untie the string around the bundle as a symbolic gesture. If they think cooperation went especially well, they can acknowledge the bundle. It can help students have a way to talk about what they are feeling and observing.
- **Enlist the music teacher** to help the students to make up a school song with a refrain about "sticking together."
- **Service-learning projects:** Have the class brainstorm a project that they could all do together in the classroom to help make it a better place, or in the school or community that would involve them all using their best talents. Examples of these are class feasts, cleanup projects, collecting for a good cause, entertaining at a senior center or nursing home, talent day where everyone teaches their classmates to do something new. It is best for the students to think up their own project. They may need to come up with a decision-making strategy too.

Once Upon a Time...

The Turnip

Russia

Grades Pre-K–2

THEMES: Cooperation, small beings making a big contribution, respect, perseverance

Once upon a time in Russia, and old man and an old woman lived on a farm with their granddaughter, their horse, their cow, their goat, chickens, their dog, and their cat. They worked hard, but it was a happy life. One day the old woman decided that it was time to plant her turnips. She went into her garden with her granddaughter and together they planted turnip seeds in a straight long row. After the seeds were planted and had begun to grow, the grandmother showed her granddaughter how to weed and water the plants. Every day she tended them and sang to them. The granddaughter noticed that one plant was growing especially large, so she watered it the most and sang to it the longest. This turnip grew and grew and grew, until she could see that it was enormous under the ground, as big around as the hugest pumpkin ever grown.

One day the grandmother and grandfather decided that it was time to pick this turnip. The old man grabbed hold of the stem,

And he pulled and he pulled, and he huffed and he puffed,

But that stubborn turnip would not come up.

[This repeating refrain can be chanted or sung with audience participation.]

"I think I need some help, old woman," he called. So the old woman put her arms around the old man. The old man held on to the turnip stem,

And they pulled and they pulled, and they huffed and they puffed.

But that stubborn turnip would not come up.

"I think we need your help, granddaughter," the old woman said. So the little girl put her arms around the grandmother, who put her arms around grandfather, who grabbed hold of the turnip.

And they pulled, and they pulled, and they huffed and they puffed.

But that stubborn turnip would not come up.

"I think we need to ask the horse," the little girl cried. "Horse!" The horse came and put his hooves around the little girl, who put her arms around the grandmother, who put her arms around grandfather, who grabbed hold of the turnip.

And they pulled and they pulled, and they huffed and they puffed.

But that stubborn turnip would not come up.

"I think we need to ask the cow," said the horse. "Cow!" So the cow came and put her hooves around the horse, who put his hooves around the little girl, who put her arms around the grandmother, who put her arms around grandfather, who grabbed hold of the turnip.

And they pulled and they pulled, and they huffed and they puffed.

But that stubborn turnip would not come up.

"I think we need to ask the dog," said the cow. "Dog!" So the dog came

46

and put his paws around the cow, who put her hooves around the horse, who put his hooves around the little girl, who put her arms around the grandmother, who put her arms around grandfather, who grabbed hold of the turnip.

And they pulled and they pulled, and they huffed and they puffed.

But that stubborn turnip would not come up.

"I think we need to call the cat," said the dog. "Cat!" So the cat came and put his paws around the dog, who put his paws around the cow, who put her hooves around the horse, who put his hooves around the little girl, who put her arms around the grandmother, who put her arms around grandfather, who grabbed hold of the turnip.

And they pulled and they pulled, and they huffed and they puffed.

But that stubborn turnip would not come up.

"I think we need to ask the chicken," said the cat. "Chicken!" So the chicken put her skinny legs around the cat, who put his paws around the dog, who put his paws around the cow, who put her hooves around the horse, who put his hooves around the little girl, who put her arms around the grandmother, who put her arms around grandfather, who grabbed hold of the turnip.

And they pulled and they pulled, and they huffed and they puffed.

But that stubborn turnip would not come up.

They looked around. There was no one left to ask, and that stubborn turnip was still in the ground. But just then, they heard a tiny squeak. "Can I help?" A little field mouse had been watching from under a leaf. "You!" cackled the hen. "You!" mewed the cat. "You!" barked the dog. "You!" said everyone else all at once. "You are too little! How could you help?"

"I'd like to try," the mouse pleaded. The animals and humans looked at each other and decided to give it one last try with the help of the mouse, even though they thought it was silly. So the mouse put her tiny paws around the chicken, and the chicken put her skinny legs around the cat, who put his paws around the dog, who put his paws around the cow, who put her hooves around the horse, who put his hooves around the little girl, who put her arms around the grandmother, who put her arms around grandfather, who grabbed hold of the turnip.

And they pulled and they pulled, and they huffed and they puffed.

And they pulled and they pulled, and they huffed and they puffed.

And guess what? That stubborn turnip finally came up!

That turnip was so big; there was enough for everyone, even the mouse, who lived on turnip soup all that winter!

SOURCES

"The Turnip," in *My First Big Story Book*, by Richard Bamberger, translated by Emanuela Wallenta (London: Oliver & Boyd, 1965).

The Turnip, retold by Harriet Ziefort (New York: Viking, 1996).

The Enormous Turnip, retold by Alexei Tolstoy (San Diego: Harcourt, 2002).

Tips for the telling

This is a wonderful story to act out with your students. When the students have heard the story once through, you can give them parts and they can help you retell. Students can stand in a line, and either hold on gently to one another's waists (gently is the operative word,) or if you are afraid that they will pull each other over, they can pull on an imaginary or real rope instead of each other. You can ask the students for other animals that could join the line if you want parts for more children at one time.

Follow-up activities

Tips for story retention

- **Sequencing through drawing:** Have the students each draw a picture of one of the characters that helped in the story. Then sequence them together in the proper order. You can also make pocket story sheets in which the students draw a picture of each scene, and then take it home and tell the story to family members.

- **Round-robin retelling** would also work well as there is lots of participation to keep the group interested as each student added a character or action to the story.

Making a personal connection

- **Questions, discussion and story sharing:** Your students may relate to this story personally, as they are often the smallest beings around. Everyone looks much bigger, stronger and smarter, and they may feel that their input is not needed or wanted. A story like this reminds them that even very small people can have an important part to play and that we should never laugh at or underestimate what a small person can do. It is also a story about not giving up and about working together.

- **Encourage your students to talk** about times when they did or did not feel that they could make a difference. Perhaps they were laughed at for being so small, or told that they were too young to do something. Also, talk about situations in which the students felt like giving up but persevered and had a success. Your stories here will help them remember their own.

Creative exploration

- **Creative adaptation:** Let your students come up with new animals to join in. Set the story in a different place, with different types of animals, or in a family with a littlest brother or sister.

- **Research:** Ask the students to go to the library and ask the librarian for story books in which something or someone small succeeds in helping. Have your students share these stories with one another.

Turning the story ideas into action

- **Brainstorm** with the students ways in which they can work together to make the classroom or school a better place. Choose a class project that will be done much more quickly if done together, and that everyone can help with equally.

Stone Soup

France

Grades Pre-K-3

THEMES: Working together, greed, cleverness, fear of strangers

Long ago in the French countryside, three soldiers were marching towards home. The war had been long and hard, and they were tired and hungry. They had not eaten in two whole days. Suddenly, in the distance they heard the sounds of a village. "Ah, perhaps we will be able to get some food, and a bed to sleep in!" they said with weary smiles.

This was a village that did not like strangers, and the villagers did not like to share, even with each other. They kept their food well hidden in their houses and kept a lookout for strangers. When the lookout saw the soldiers approaching, he ran and alerted all of the villagers. "Three soldiers are coming! They look hungry and tired. Hide your food. They will eat us out of house and home!"

So the villagers quickly set about hiding their food even more carefully. Then they put on their saddest, leanest faces and waited for the knock on the door.

The three hungry soldiers entered the village and knocked upon the first door they came to. "Could we please have a bite to eat and a place to rest for the night? We are so hungry and tired."

"Oh, sirs, I am so sorry," said the couple behind their half-opened door. "We have had a very bad year, and have very little to eat ourselves. We could not possibly spare anything. And as for the bed, all of our beds are full!"

So, the soldiers went on to another house where they received the same message. "We have to feed my old parents, who are sick. We barely have enough food to keep skin on our bones. We cannot share with you." On and on they went to every home, and at each home, they met with the same reply.

"Well," they said to one another, "What are we to do? We cannot keep walking without any food in our bellies." They sat upon the town green looking very sad, and the villagers watched them from their homes. Suddenly one of the soldiers sat up straight. "I have it!" he announced. "Do you remember my granny's recipe for stone soup? I think we will have to make some." He winked at his companions and picked up the biggest, roundest, smoothest stone he could find. "We'll need a couple more of these." His companions each gathered a stone. "Now, if only we had a big pot to cook our stone soup, we could share it with these hungry people," the soldier said in a loud voice. "As I am remembering, it is very, very tasty."

One of the villagers who had been listening, called from her house, "I think I might know where a big pot is." She came running out with a large stew pot.

"Ah, yes," said the soldier. "This will allow us to make stone soup for the whole village, but we will need a good deal of water, and wood to cook this soup."

"I might be able to spare some water," said a woman as she sent three large children scurrying with buckets to the well. "And I might have some extra wood," said a man from another house as he sent his children out with armfuls of wood. Soon a fire was burning and the water in the pot was starting to steam.

"Now, didn't you say that a little salt and pepper really draws out the flavor from the stones?" one of the other soldiers wondered loudly. "I might have a little extra salt and pepper," declared a woman. "Now that will be good," said the soldier, sprinkling the pot with salt and pepper. "But my granny always told me that it was even better with a few carrots."

"I might have a few extra carrots," said an old man, who went hobbling off.

"And cabbage," dreamed the soldier aloud. "Granny said that cabbage would give it more bulk."

"I might be able to spare a cabbage for such a great soup," said the preacher's wife. Soon they had brought and chopped these ingredients and the soup was simmering nicely.

"Oh that is starting to smell so good," said the soldier. "If only we had a bit of meat and a few potatoes, this soup would be fit for a rich person's table. The villagers looked at one another. "I might be able to find a bit of meat," said a farmer. "And I might know where a few potatoes are," said another. The meat and potatoes were brought, chopped, and added to the pot.

The soldiers stirred and the villagers stepped in close to catch the delicious smells. "You know the King himself liked our stone soup, didn't he?" the soldier asked his friends. "Oh yes, he did," one replied, "but that time, as I recall, we threw in a bit of barley and a touch of milk, as we were in such rich company."

"Well if it's good enough for a King," said the Mayor, "it's good enough for us. I do know where a bit of barley and milk are stored." He ran off to his home. Soon those ingredients were stirred into the soup and wonderful smells filled the square.

"I think it's ready," the soldiers said. " We just need tables and bowls, and we'll have quite feast."

The villagers began to scurry about gathering tables, chairs, bowls, and spoons. Soon everyone was seated. The villagers sat and the bowls were served. It really did smell delicious. They felt like kings. "If we are to eat like kings," one woman said to the villagers, "we should add bread and cider to our table!"

Yes!" they all cried and several people ran to their houses and retrieved some bread and cider from under their beds.

Now the feast began in earnest. There was quiet and then laughter and many calls for seconds and thirds. Then the villagers began to dance and sing together, and the soldiers joined in. At the end of the evening, the Mayor stood up and silence fell. "We need to thank you for teaching us how to make stone soup. You have shown us a wonderful new recipe and the joy of sharing our food together. For such a gift, you should sleep in our finest beds tonight." Suddenly everyone was shouting, "Stay with us! Our feather pillows are the softest!"

The next day the soldiers were given a fine goodbye breakfast, and they set off down the road toward home. Their bellies were full, their feet were rested, and they knew that they would never go hungry again!

SOURCES—PICTURE BOOKS

Stone Soup, retold by Marcia Brown (New York: Charles Scribner and Sons, 1947).

Stone Soup, retold by Jon Warren Stewig, (New York: Holiday House, 1991). (Female heroine)

Fox Tail Soup, adapted by Tony Bonning (New York: Simon and Schuster, 1991). (Animals as main characters)

Tips for the telling

This story can be told very simply, or elaborated to make it last as long as your students are interested in adding ingredients. I would consider bringing a prop of a large smooth stone, or maybe a pot into which the children can add their imaginary foods. It will hold everyone's focus and be the center of attention. There are many versions of this story in picture book form. In some versions, the characters are all animals. In one version, a lone girl teaches the villagers to work together. You can decide who your children would like the main characters to be, either in your first telling or when you retell it together. In a barnyard setting, each animal character could offer something that it likes to eat, or that it produces, such as eggs or milk.

Follow-up activities

Tips for story retention

- **Round-robin retelling:** Let each student add in a small part of the story.

- **Visual sequencing and reenacting:** The teacher or students make cards with pictures or words for each food item that was needed in the soup. Let each student pick one card from the hat. Retell the story as if you were the first soldier. When you call out, "If only we had some_____," the student can run up as if bringing that item and add it to the imaginary pot.

Making a personal connection

- **Questions and discussion:** This story is about hunger, sharing, and the joy of doing something together. It also brings up issues of fear of poverty and fear of strangers. There is a lot of room for good discussion here, and lots of personal story sharing. You can also use this story to initiate a discussion about stranger awareness and safety.

- **Story sharing:** Have you ever been really hungry? Did you ever forget your lunch and have to beg friends to share some of theirs? Who has ever had a hard time sharing with a friend? Who has worried if there would be enough to eat? Who has felt wary of a new kid in school or the neighborhood, only to discover that they could be a friend? You can share your stories with these experiences.

Creative exploration

- **Creative story making:** Help the class to make up a story that happens in school. Here is a starter idea: One student forgets her lunch and has to ask everyone for food. Everyone refuses at first except the teacher, who gives her some crackers. She gets an idea and asks if anyone wants to help her make "Super delicious cracker sandwiches," and "Cracker Dessert Surprise." Students start volunteering little bits of food, like cheese and bologna, brownie crumbs, bits of cookie, and carrot sticks, and soon she has a great lunch and dessert, which everyone wants to try. Share this story with another classroom. Have the students make an illustrated book version of their new story.

- **Make stone soup in the classroom!** Decide as a group what to bring from home, or make a bunch of foods available and bring them. See how it helps if everyone brings something. You can even add up the cost of each item and see how expensive it would be if one person bought everything, and how cheap when everyone brings a small amount.

- **Class creative project:** Explore the fun of making something together, like a piñata, or a castle out of sugar cubes. Have everyone agree to bring some of the needed ingredients. Help the students to explore what works well in their collective process and what bugs need to be worked out.

- **Service-learning projects:** This is a good story to introduce a discussion on hunger. In 2001 in North America there were 23 million people who sought emergency food.[1] including the number of people who are "food insecure" or at risk for hunger and the number grew to 36 million.[2] This may be hard for your students to imagine. Twenty-three million people are equivalent to the combined populations of people in the ten largest U.S. cities.[3] Maybe some of the students in your school participate in the breakfast program. You would not want to call attention to this, as poverty can be a huge source of shame for children. Rather focus on other people in a different town and let everyone get in on the joy of giving. Is there a local food pantry to which they could donate food? Could you donate to a group like Feed the Children and have the class adopt a child? For a small amount of money each month ($8.00 or less) you can feed one or several children. They send photos and information. Give your children a few options of ways they can help together and let them discuss them with parents. Maybe they can have a bake sale to raise money or do chores at home.

Contact numbers

America's Second Harvest—The nation's largest hunger-relief organization. www.secondharvest.org. You can find your local food bank contact information through this site.

Feed the Children—Helps feed millions of children in North America and around the world. www.feedthechildren.org. Through this group your class can sponsor a child and help to feed them. You will receive photos and thank-you letters.

---

1. America's Second Harvest Hunger in America 2001 Report—www.secondharvest.org
2. U.S.D.A.'s Economic research Service, Household Food Security in the United States, 2001.
3. America's Second Harvest, ibid.

The Flock of Quail

India (Jataka)

Grades 2-8

THEMES: Working together, leadership, self-mastery

Once upon a time, a flock of quail lived at the edge of the forest, pecking seeds and bugs from the ground. The quail had a leader who would sing a simple song that would gather them all together. Together they would sing and peck seeds in a close group, happy in each other's company.

One day a hunter entered this part of the forest. He listened and watched, and he learned the quail's song. The hunter whistled the quail song, which caused the birds to gather. As they pecked and sang, the hunter threw his net over the birds. They panicked and fought one another to get free of the net, but the more they fought, the more hopelessly caught they became. With one swift move, the hunter gathered up the net and slung it over his shoulder, taking many of the quail to their death.

The next week the hunter came again. Again he sang, again the birds gathered, and again he threw his net over them. Again too the birds began to fight and peck at one another in their panic to break free. Many of the birds were taken. This happened week after week, until the flock was quite diminished.

Finally, the leader of the quail called the birds together. "We must do something differently when the hunter comes with his net," he said. "Soon we will be all gone. The next time he throws his net over us, do not panic and fight. Hold your heads up high. Stick your heads through the holes in the net. I will tell you what to do."

That is what happened. The hunter called the birds and threw his net. But this time the birds stayed calm. They held their heads up high through the holes in the net.

"Quickly now, my friends," called the leader, "spread your wings and fly away—high into the forest! Fly to the bramble bushes!"

That is what the birds did. They spread their wings and flew up away from the hunter, over the trees to the bramble bush, where they easily got free of the net. When the hunter finally found his net, it was impossible to untangle from the briars.

Repeatedly the birds used this new strategy, until finally the hunter had run out of nets and moved to a different part of the forest.

SOURCES

Jataka Tales: Fables from the Buddha, edited by Nancy Deroin (New York: Dell Publishing, 1977).

The Jataka Tales of India, retold by Ellen C. Babbitt (New York: Appleton-Century-Crofts, 1912, 1940).

Buddhist Parables, translated from Pali by Eugene Watson Burlingame (Delhi: Motilat Banarsidass Publishers, 1991)

In the older forms of this story, there is a second part in which the birds begin to quarrel again, their plan ceases to work, and they are caught. I prefer this version however, which makes the same point in a more hopeful manner.

This is a story that works for many ages. With younger audiences you can be sure that they will want to act it out, whether in their seats, pretending to be the quail, or as a group moving around the room as you tell it. Find a cooing sound that you can easily repeat, and that the class sings with you.

- **Group retelling:** Try acting it out as a group to music. A good way to cement a sequence of events with younger students is for them to act out the story physically. Let the students come up with stylized movements for pecking, flying, fighting, etc. In the story, the birds must use self-control to work together. Practicing this physically can help students to understand its value.

- **Older students** can enjoy acting it out too, but will want to do it in their own way.

- **Questions and discussion:** The birds in this story are too busy fighting for survival to work together. It is only when they work together that they save themselves. What makes it hard for your students to work together with others? This story involves one of the birds taking a leadership role. Discuss what makes it easier or harder to follow the leadership of another student. Make a list of rules that would make it easier.

- **Related discussion:** With middle school students you could use this story to initiate a discussion about pedophiles and how they often trick children into coming with them by pretending to be like someone else, such as a police officer or a person looking for his puppy.

- **Creative adaptation:** Have the students modernize this story. (One suggestion would be to make it about an evil alien who pretended to be a substitute teacher who was taking them to her space ship and how when they learned to work together to outwit her. This idea would be too scary for the younger students, but could be very fun for older students.) Share this story with other classes and talk about ways in which we do or don't work together. Let the students make up stories about someone who tries to do something without any help from anyone.

- **Trying on the roles:** Let different children pretend to be the leader of the birds, and let them experiment with different styles of leadership as the story is acted out. Discuss what leadership styles the class find effective.

- **Group cooperative projects with changing leadership roles:** Brainstorm a list of activities that would work better if done as a group. Choose an activity and make a plan to carry it out as a group. Let different students try being in the role of leader.

Heads or Tails

Source unknown

Grades 3-5

THEMES: Cooperation, wise thinking

Once upon a time, a herd of wild horses roamed the plains of the midwest. Their numbers were strong, but over time, more and more wolves were forced into their area, as settlers moved west, and they had been attacking their numbers. The horses decided to stick together to minimize the number of strays that could be picked off. They knew that they were strong and that they could fight the wolves if they had to. But they were not used to fighting, and it frightened them.

One evening just as the sun was setting, there came a cry from a horse that a pack of wolves was heading their way.

"Quickly, circle together. Protect yourselves!" the elder horses cried. The horses made a circle with their heads facing out to see the wolves coming. But as the wolves began to attack, the horses panicked, kicking out their

hooves. Who do you think they hit except each other? This was better than nothing, though some of the horses were hurt by other horses, and several horses were still killed by the wolves.

When the fighting was over and the wolves had been chased off, the horses gathered. "We must do something differently," said one. "Putting our behinds together only made us kick one another. Let us try to put our heads together next time. Perhaps we will kick the wolves."

The next time the wolves were sighted, the horses put their heads together in a circle. They found that not only did they not kick one another, but also they could talk about what to do as the wolves were approaching. They could see the situation from all angles and easily report to one another what to do. There were no casualties, and the wolves left without a meal.

"From now on we will put our heads, instead of our tails together," they said, and laughed.

This is a wonderful story to tell at the beginning of the year. The catch phrase "Let's put our heads together" can be referred to all year and will have more meaning than before. This story can be told in a straightforward manner. The group can also act it out. I suggest telling the story standing in a circle with your students. I would let some of them pretend to be wolves coming from outside and use the word "freeze" to allow the horse characters to decide what the best formation would be. You can also make this story into a game in which the horses have to decide which strategy works best in keeping the wolves from attacking them.

Tips for the telling

- **Acting it out as a group:** This is an easy story to remember, especially when it is acted out. Try the suggestions above in Tips for the Telling.

Follow-up activities
Tip for retention

- **Questions, discussion and story sharing:** Help the class to brainstorm times when they worked best by putting their heads together, or when they put their tails together and things didn't go so well. It helps if you can come up with a few examples from your experience. Have the students share their stories. Have them tell this story at home. Have them make a list of activities at home that go better when the family decides together how to do them, and bring those back to share. Older students can interview grandparents about events in history when people did or did not put their heads together, and the results.

Making a personal connection

- **Creative adaptation:** Divide the class into small groups to make up creative versions of this story set in a modern setting, with people instead of animals.

- **Cooperative story making:** Since you are trying to promote cooperation I would instruct them to make up a story cooperatively, perhaps brainstorming together. At the end of the process have them reflect on the process, and what made cooperative story making work more easily, and what were the challenges. Have them act these stories out for one another.

Creative exploration

- **Artistic representations:** Have the students make posters showing the horses kicking in or out with a quotation to remind themselves to work together.

- **Brainstorm** a list of situations in the school in which they could apply this principle. Examples might be in teamwork at a given sport, or in sticking up for someone who is being bullied by literally putting their bodies between the bully and the victim.

- **Creative problem solving:** Have your students literally put their heads together to come up with solutions to the problems they have identified, or problems that you give them.

Turning the story ideas into action

The Six Chinese Brothers

China

Grades K-5

THEMES: Cooperation, valuing individual strengths, loyalty, self-esteem

Once upon a time in China, there lived six brothers. They all looked exactly alike, but each had a special gift all of his own. One of the brothers could see for miles and miles. They called him See Well. Another could hear sounds that were hundreds of miles away. They called him Hear Well. A third was as strong as iron, and could not be bent or broken. They called him Strong as Iron. A fourth could stand in the middle of a fire and would not be burned. He was called Cannot Be Burned. A fifth could grow his legs so tall he could walk a mile in a minute. He was called Grow Tall. The sixth could swallow anything. They called him Swallower.

One day, when the brothers were eating their noontime meal together, Hear Well heard a distant sound of distress. "Someone is in trouble," he said. See Well stood up and looked as far as he could see. He saw that the Emperor was in trouble. He was riding past a mountainside when an avalanche had fallen on his party. A huge boulder was perched on his carriage and any second would crush him. The Emperor was trapped. "Don't worry," cried Strong as Iron. "I will go and save him." He ran to where the Emperor's party lay in shambles against the mountainside and easily lifted the great boulder, freeing the Emperor and his family.

"You have saved my life!" cried the Emperor with glee. "You must come and live with me at the palace and be my personal guard." Strong as Iron thanked the Emperor, but told him that he preferred to stay in the country with his family. The Emperor begged and pleaded, but when Strong as Iron would not give in, he grew angry. "This one who is surely the strongest man alive refuses to serve me. I say he is a danger to me if he is not my guard. Have him arrested. He will be executed at dawn."

Strong as Iron was arrested and put in prison. He was to be beheaded in the morning. In the morning, the Emperor's executioner tried to behead Strong as Iron, but no matter what they did, they could not even make a dent in his skin. Finally the Emperor, more afraid than ever, declared, "We shall throw him in the mile-deep pit with the sheer walls from which there is no escape!" Strong as Iron began to cry, for though he was very strong, he could not climb sheer walls of a mile-deep pit.

Hear Well heard his brother crying. See Well looked far away and saw that his brother was to be thrown into the pit in the morning. "Don't worry," cried Grow Tall. "I shall go and take his place." Grow Tall went and stole into the prison and took Strong as Iron's place. The next day he was thrown into the deep pit. No sooner did his feet hit the bottom then his legs started to grow. Up and up they went, until he was looking out over the rim of the pit, smiling. He easily pulled himself up and walked out of the pit.

58

"He will be burned at dawn!" screamed the Emperor, growing more terrified by the minute. Grow Tall was led away to the jail cell. Grow Tall began to cry, for he could not withstand the heat of flames. Again, Hear Well heard his cries, and See Well saw what was happening. "Don't worry," said Cannot Be Burned. "I will go and take his place." And so, he did.

Now the burning went much as the other attempts to rid the Emperor of the brothers. Cannot Be Burned stood bravely in the flames and laughed as they tickled his skin. The Emperor was growing desperate. "This scoundrel must be drowned. We will take him out into the middle of the sea and we will drown him in water that is many miles deep. Nothing can save him from that."

Cannot Be Burned now began to cry, and far away his brother heard him. "Don't worry," said Swallower. " I will go and take his place." That is what he did. Now the Emperor and his guards took Swallower onto a boat and the boat sailed way out into the sea where the water was many miles deep. Then Swallower was thrown overboard. Down, down he plunged. But, when he hit the ocean floor, he opened his mouth and began to drink the ocean down. Gulp by enormous gulp, the water in the ocean went down and down until the Emperor's ship was sitting on the ocean floor right next to Swallower. The Emperor and his guards did not recognize him, for he was many times bigger than the largest whale. Swallower began to cry because he could not walk away from the Emperor's ship. His brothers heard and saw him and Strong as Iron came and carried him up to the edge of the sea. Then Swallower let all of that water back out of his stomach. This created such and enormous wave that the Emperor and his ship were swept away to the other side of the world and never seen again. The six Chinese brothers lived happily and at peace after that, and so did all of the other people in China.

SOURCES

Six Chinese Brothers, An Ancient Tale, retold by Cheng Hou-tien, with scissor-cut illustrations by the author (New York: Holt, Reinhart and Winston, 1979).

The Seven Chinese Brothers, retold by Margaret Mahy (New York: Scholastic, Inc., 1990).

Seven Magic Brothers, retold by Kuang-Tsai Hao, translated by Rick Charette (Taipei, Taiwan: Yuan-Liou Publishing Co., Ltd., 1994). Told in English and Chinese.

Tips for the telling

Tell the story through without participation, or by stopping within the story to ask the students who they think would be called upon to help at each stage. You can have fun acting out the qualities of each character. You can also invite one student up to the front to act out each of the six characters, or divide the group into six parts and let them each come up with a sound and a movement for each character that will be repeated throughout the story.

Follow-up activities

Tips for story retention

- **Whole-group retelling:** Try a round-robin retelling in which the students sit in a circle and each one adds in a short section of the story action.
- **Small-group dramatizing:** Let them retell it in small groups of seven with six brothers (or sisters) and one narrator.
- **Visual sequencing:** Younger students could make pictures or puppets of each character and hold them up when it was their turn to be in the story.

Making a personal connection

- **Identifying with characters:** We all have special strengths, interests, and talents. Let the students write about their own strengths and give themselves a name as if they were one of the brothers or sisters. Then have them share with the class how they might help. Give some fun examples, such as: Hilary who loves soccer more than anything is Far Kicker; Max who draws tanks all over everything is called Tank Drawer.
- **Discussion:** Invite the students to brainstorm times when they helped to solve a problem by using their own special skills or interests. They can also go home and ask their parents about their special skills, talents, and interests, and times when those helped them or others to solve a problem.

Creative exploration

- **Creative story adaptation:** This is a story that lends itself to adaptation. What a great opportunity for acknowledging the many varied strengths, interests, and talents of your student body. You might try dividing your students into small groups and have them each brainstorm the skills, special interests, likes and strengths of one another and make up a fun story in which each skill is used to save themselves from some sort of tragedy. Have them act these out for one another and/or make books.
- **Research:** Many cultures tell stories in which a challenge is overcome with the help of a number of people's skills used together in turn. Have groups of students research or explore cultural variants of the tale and tell it to classmates. Have grades 4+ go to the library, or have different versions of these tales available for reading in the 3+ classroom. Have the students read and retell them for the class. This is a great way to demonstrate cultural similarities through literature. For other cultural variants see:

  —*Anansci the Spider* from Ghana, retold in picture book form by Gerald McDermott (New York: Holt, Rinehart and Winston, 1972).

—"Anansci," in *Moon Tales* by Rina Singh, in which Anansci's sons save his life using each of their unique strengths. This story also explains how the moon came to be in the sky.

—"Anansci's Rescue from the River," in *A Treasury of African Folklore* by Harold Courlander (New York: Marlowe & Company, 1996).

—The "Cow-Tail Switch" in *The Cow-Tail Switch and Other West African Stories*, edited by Harold Courlander (New York: Henry Holt & Co., 1947), in which it requires all of a man's sons to bring him back to life, but most valued is the one son who never forgot him in the first place.

—"Long Broad and Sharpsight," (Slavonic) found in *Bringing Out Their Best* by Norma Livo (Libraries Unlimited, 2003).

—"Seven Clever Brothers" (Jewish) found in magical *Tales from Many Lands*, retold by Margaret Mayo (New York: Dutton, 1993).

Turning the story ideas into action

- There is great benefit in acknowledging and celebrating how we each bring a unique contribution to the school community. **Do a survey** of the school community and see how many adults are needed to make the school run, and the unique strengths and talents they bring. You can take this opportunity to **highlight different teachers and staff** all year long in a school magazine or assembly. You can do the same thing with **all of the students in the classroom**, featuring a student every other week. Remember this story throughout the year as problems come up that require unique strengths to best solve them and draw these out for the students until they are doing the same themselves.

The Sun and the Wind

Aesop

Grades K-8

THEMES: Creative conflict resolution, kindness vs. force, strength vs. power, and cooperative action, awareness of assertive vs. aggressive styles of behavior, bullying

One day the Sun and the Wind began an argument over who was stronger. Seeing a man walking on the road down on earth, the Wind had an idea. "Let us have a contest," he suggested. "The one who can most easily get that man's cloak off will clearly be stronger."

"Fine," said the Sun. "You go first."

So the sun went behind a cloud and the wind began to blow down upon the man. It blew harder and harder until the man was bent nearly double. But the harder the wind blew, the more tightly the man pulled his cloak around himself. The wind could not get it off.

And then the Sun came out and the Wind hid. The sun shone down upon the man and he straightened up. It shone a bit more brightly and the man sighed and loosened his grip upon his cloak. It shone more brightly still and the man loosened the clasp. The sun continued to radiate warmth down upon the man until he laughed. "I don't need this anymore," he said. Removing the cloak, he flung it over one shoulder, and went upon his way.

"There," laughed the Sun. "I guess it all depends on how you measure strength. What you wind could not do through force, I did easily with gentleness."

See page 44 for information on Aesop.

This is a fun story to tell using movement, as it has three simple characters that do a limited number of movements. I have seen it done effectively with mime, meaning no words at all! You may wish to tell it through once, and then invite the audience to be the person with the coat, and see how they react to the two forces. You can also try it from the perspective of the different characters.

This is more about creative conflict resolution than cooperation. This story provides a powerful metaphor for what kinds of environments or atmospheres are more conducive to openness and learning, and which cause people to withdraw into self-protection. This story is perhaps most useful for the teacher to contemplate his or her teaching style, and how to accomplish goals of discipline through gentle, but effective, means. Perhaps you can reflect on this with the students in terms of asking them, "We need to do such and such, do you want me to be a sun or a wind here?"

Tips for the telling

- **Small-group retelling:** Have groups of four act the story out together. Have a narrator, sun, wind, and person. Have them try this with words, or using only movement and no words. Have the students try retelling the story from each point of view. Have groups share with one another.

- **Questions and discussion:** What questions and observations do the students have about this story? Learning to approach problem solving with courtesy, creativity, and without violence are important aspects of cooperation. Young people frequently encounter frustrating situations in which they may want to change someone's behavior. The sun demonstrates in this story that it is easier to influence someone through positive, or cooperative, action than by negative action.

- **Relating to the characters:** Play "hot seat." Let someone sit in the hot seat pretending to be one of the characters in the story. Have the rest of the class ask them questions about how they felt, such as how the person wearing the cloak felt when the wind beat on him vs. when the sun shone on him.

- **Sharing personal stories:** Help the students to tell stories about their own experiences of being treated with kindness or force. Did someone ever want you to do something for them or give them something and they went about asking for it by force? How did that feel? How did it feel when someone asked you for something using warmth or kindness? Did you ever try to get something from someone using kindness or force? Which worked better? Sibling stories are often good for this.

- **Creative story adaptation:** Help your students to generate modern examples of this story, change the setting, the characters, and the object of clothing. Retell it to other groups of students, and let the students lead a discussion of the stories afterwards.

Follow-up activities
Tip for retention

Making a personal connection

Creative exploration

Turning the story ideas into action

- **Practicing courtesy and kindness in conflict resolution:** As situations of conflict come up in your classroom, reflect back on this story and ask the students to comment on how they could solve the problem by acting with courtesy and kindness, rather than force or unkindness. Older students may wish to reflect on this in journal form, or to fictionalize a true event in their lives with a new ending.

- **Practicing assertive instead of aggressive behaviors:** This can be a place to discuss passive, assertive, and aggressive styles of behavior. There are many good books out now on assertiveness training for children. Once you have taught students how to treat others respectfully and to ask for what they want assertively, rather than aggressively (or passive aggressively), you can start asking them to notice when they are doing which behavior.

- **Artistic representations:** Let the students make posters demonstrating assertive vs. aggressive behaviors.

- **Generate a dialogue about world affairs** and discuss how certain conflicts in current events remind them more of the sun or the wind's behavior.

I'm Tipingee, She's Tipingee, We're Tipingee, Too

There was once a girl named Tipingee who lived with her stepmother. Her father was dead. The stepmother was selfish, and even though she lived in the girl's house, she did not like to share what she earned with the girl.

One morning, the stepmother was cooking sweets to sell in the market. The fire under her pot went out. Tipingee was in school and the stepmother had to go herself into the forest to find more firewood. She walked for a long time, but she did not find any wood. She continued walking. Then she came to a place where there was firewood everywhere. She gathered it into a bundle. However, it was too heavy to lift up onto her head. Still, she did not want anyone else to have any of the firewood. Standing in the middle of the forest she cried out: "My friends, there is so much wood here and at home I have no wood. Where can I find a person who will help me carry the firewood?"

Suddenly an old man appeared. "I will help you to carry the firewood. But then what will you give me?"

"I have very little," the woman said. "But I will find something to give you when we get to my house."

The old man carried the firewood for the stepmother, and when they got to the house he said, "I have carried the firewood for you. Now, what will you give me?"

"I will give you a servant girl. I will give you my stepdaughter, Tipingee."

Now Tipingee was in the house and when she heard her name, she ran to the door and listened.

"Tomorrow I will send my stepdaughter to the well at noon for water. She will be wearing a red dress. Call her by name—Tipingee—and she will come to you. Then you can take her."

"Very well," said the man and he went away.

Tipingee ran to her friends. She ran to the houses of all the girls in her class and asked then to wear red dresses the next day.

At noon, the next day the old man went to the well. He saw one little girl dressed in red. He saw a second little girl dressed in red. He saw a third girl in red.

"Which one of you is Tipingee?" he asked.

The first little girl said, "I'm Tipingee."

The second little girl said, "She's Tipingee."

The third little girl said, "We're Tipingee too."

"Which of you is Tipingee?" asked the old man.

Haiti

Grades 4-8

THEMES: Friendship, sacrifice, courage, empathy, cooperation, unity in action

Then the little girls began to clap and jump up and down and chant:

> I'm Tipingee
> She's Tipingee
> We're Tipingee, too.
>
> I'm Tipingee
> She's Tipingee
> We're Tipingee, too.

Rah! The old man went to the old woman and said, "You tricked me! All the girls were dressed in red and each one said she was Tipingee."

"That is impossible," said the stepmother. "Tomorrow she will wear a black dress. Then you will find her. The one wearing a black dress will be Tipingee. Call her and take her."

But Tipingee heard what her stepmother said and ran and begged all her friends to wear black dresses the next day.

When the old man went to the well the next day, he saw one little girl dressed in black. He saw a second little girl dressed in black. He saw a third girl in black.

"Which of you is Tipingee?" he asked.

The first little girl said, "I'm Tipingee."

The second little girl said, "She's Tipingee."

The third little girl said, "We're Tipingee too."

"Which of you is Tipingee?" asked the old man.

Then the little girls began to clap and jump up and down and chant:

> I'm Tipingee
> She's Tipingee
> We're Tipingee, too.
>
> I'm Tipingee
> She's Tipingee
> We're Tipingee, too.

"Which one of you is Tipingee?" asked the man.

And the girls joined hands and skipped about and sang:

> I'm Tipingee
> She's Tipingee
> We're Tipingee, too.
>
> I'm Tipingee
> She's Tipingee
> We're Tipingee, too.

The man was getting angry. He went to the stepmother and said, "You promised to pay me and you are only giving me problems. You tell me Tipingee, and everyone here is Tipingee, Tipingee, Tipingee. If this happens a third time, I will come and take you for my servant."

"My dear sir," said the stepmother, "tomorrow she will be in red, completely in red. Call her and take her."

And again Tipingee ran told her friend to dress in red.

At noon the next day the old man went to the well. He saw one little girl dressed in red. He saw a second little girl dressed in red. He saw a third girl in red.

"Which one of you is Tipingee?" he asked.

"I'm Tipingee," said the first little girl.

"She's Tipingee," said the second little girl.

"We're Tipingee too," said the third little girl.

"WHICH ONE OF YOU IS TIPINGEE?" the old man shouted.

But the girls just clapped and jumped up and down and sang:

I'm Tipingee
She's Tipingee
We're Tipingee, too.

I'm Tipingee
She's Tipingee
We're Tipingee, too.

The old man knew he would never find Tipingee. He went to the stepmother and took her away. When Tipingee returned home, she was gone. So she lived in her own house with all her father's belongings, and she was happy.

Reprinted from *The Magic Orange Tree* (New York: Alfred A. Knopf, 1978) with permission from the author, Diane Wolkstein.

SOURCES

This story was collected by Diane Wolkstein in Haiti and is included in her collection of Haitian folk tales called *The Magic Orange Tree* (New York: Alfred A. Knopf, 1978).

Tips for the telling

This is a wonderful story for audience participation. It has a built-in song, and there is dancing on the part of the children. I have often had the whole class act it out after the first telling. Personally, I have trouble with mean stepmother stories, as I know that many of the children in the classes I work with have stepmothers, and are or have gone through difficult divorces in their families. My way of avoiding this is to call the stepmother an "auntie." Far fewer people have to live with an aunt than a stepmother. You decide what you are comfortable with.

Follow-up activities

Tip for retention

- **Group retelling:** Divide the students into small groups of about seven and retell the story with a narrator and actors, or do one large class retelling with many students taking the part of a larger body of friends who all dress in red or black and sing the song. You may also choose a small group of students to be the directors.

Making a personal connection

- **Questions and discussion:** Allowing the students to ask questions and to talk about what this story means to them will bring this story from a not very real scenario (luckily) to their everyday lives. I would introduce the word, "solidarity" here, as the children in the story were acting in solidarity with Tipingee.

- **Story sharing:** Have students share examples of times when they have stuck by or acted in solidarity with friends or family members to protect or help them, or when friends or family have done the same for them. Have them share about times when they wish they had stuck by someone, or someone had stuck by them. It helps if you the teacher can share examples from your experience.

Creative exploration

- **Adapting the story:** Guide your students to come up with their own versions of this tale, whether they be modernized, set in a different place, animal characters, or students in a school thwarting a bully. Their main goal is to have people in the story act in solidarity with the main character to overcome a problem.

- **Looking to history:** There are always examples of community events in which people have come together to help or show support for someone in need, whether in the town or across the globe. Have the students find and share these examples. Through history, one can find dramatic examples, such as during the Holocaust when the Jews were marked and others chose to mark themselves so that the oppressed would not be singled out. While visiting in Nigeria, West Africa, I observed that certain ethnic groups intentionally scarred their faces in solidarity with those who had been marked as slaves long ago. In my own community, I have witnessed people who have shaved their heads in solidarity with friends who were undergoing chemotherapy, which had caused hair loss. Sitting in at lunch counters where people of color had been denied service was an act of solidarity. Even something as simple as the yellow ribbons on people's cars is an act of solidarity with soldiers overseas.

Turning the story ideas into action

- **Brainstorm** examples of problems in the school, community, and world that need solidarity and cooperative action to solve, and choose a project that they could undertake together for positive change.

- **Role-play different scenarios** in which friends and bystanders stand up with someone who is being bullied.

Once Upon a Time...

The Difference Between Heaven and Hell

Japan

Grades 3-8

Themes: Generosity, cooperation, sharing

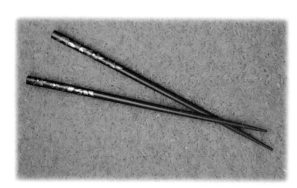

Long ago in Japan, an old woman wished to see for herself the difference between heaven and hell before she died. The monks in her local temple agreed to grant her request. They put a blindfold around the old woman's eyes.

"First you shall see hell," the monk said, after carrying her what felt like a great distance. When the blindfold was removed, the old woman saw that she was standing at the entrance to a great hall. The hall was filled with round tables, each piled high with the most delicious foods. Despite the smell and bounty of the food, the old woman noticed that the people in hell were gaunt and their pale faces were convulsed with desperation. She soon saw why this was so. The people in hell had arms that would not bend. They were forced to sit at arm's reach from the food. They had been given long chopsticks, but their arms could not bend to bring the food back to their mouths. As she watched a hungry, angry sound filled the air.

"Enough!" cried the old woman. "Let me see heaven."

Again the blindfold was put around the old woman and she was carried a great distance. When the blindfold was removed, the monk said, "Now you shall see heaven." The old woman blinked and rubbed her eyes. This scene looked just like the previous one. There were people seated just out of reach of tables piled high with food, but again they could not bend their arms, and they had those same chopsticks! Then she noticed a difference. The people in heaven were plump and rosy cheeked, and as she watched, the happy sound of laughter filled the air. Then the woman was laughing too, for now she understood. The people in heaven were using those long chopsticks to feed each other.

This story works well when told as a riddle that the audience has to solve. Try stopping the story at the part when the old woman notices that people in paradise are plump and happy, and ask, "Why?"

You might want to think about the language that you use. As a Japanese story, the concept of heaven and hell are different from those held by some in the United States. Some students may be upset by the use of the word "hell." Some versions of this story use the word "paradise" instead of "heaven."

- **Group dramatizing:** Have the students sit in one big circle. Have them pretend to be trying to reach food with arms that do not bend. Then have the students figure out how to feed one another.

- **Artistic representations:** Have the students draw pictures of the two scenarios of heaven and hell.

- **Questions and discussion:** This is a story about how we can solve our problems by helping one another to make things possible that we could not do alone. Asking for help can be difficult. Reaching out to help those that we may not know that well can be difficult.

- **Connecting to the characters:** Have the students put themselves in the shoes of the people in heaven or hell, by acting this one out, imagining that they have just arrived and are finding themselves sitting with unbendable arms in front of plates of delicious foods. Talk about what challenges they would feel in this situation.

- **Story sharing:** Let the drama lead into sharing of stories of times when you or your students had to ask for help from others and or had to decide whether or not to offer help to those they might not know or like that well.

- **Creative adaptation:** Make up modern-day versions of this story in which people find themselves in some challenging situation and how one group tries to solve it working individually and the other collectively.

- **Dramatic retelling:** Put this story on as a class play that you can take around to different classrooms. Invite the audience to feast (on muffins or something easy to pick up with chopsticks) afterwards by feeding each other, making sure that they work it out so that everyone is fed in an organized way.

- **Discuss** how this story relates to world affairs. The people in hell were paralyzed by their handicap, while the people in heaven used their creativity to work out a way to use their handicaps to the advantage of all. What situations in current events remind your students of the heaven scenario, and what of hell? Discuss alternatives that they can imagine.

- **See resources** on groups that help ameliorate hunger and statistics on hunger in North America, at the end of the story called "Stone Soup."

Follow-up activities
Tips for story retention

Making a personal connection

Creative exploration

Turning the story ideas into action

Favorite picture books

Brer Tiger and the Terrible Wind, told by William Faulkner (New York: Morrow Junior Books, 1995). This is an African-American folktale about a greedy tiger that hoards the only source of water and food in the jungle during a terrible drought. Brer Rabbit helps all of the animals to work together to trick the tiger into thinking that a terrible storm is coming. The Tiger begs to be tied up so that he will not blow away, and the other animals are able to share the food and water. There are many opportunities for participation in this story.

Swimmy, by Leo Leoni (New York: Scholastic, 1989). In this charming story, a giant fish is hunting a group of small fish. One little fish feels different from his school because of his color. He finds a way to help the whole school when he teaches them to swim in the shape of a big fish, and he becomes the eye of the fish, chasing the predator fish away.

See suggestions for Cooperative Games books on page 370 in the Resource section. In these books you will find many examples of noncompetitive games in which children work together to solve problems.

Courage

PROBABLY THE NUMBER-ONE KEY TO LEARNING SUCCESS is a safe environment in which risk taking can occur. No learning occurs without making mistakes. That is how most discoveries are made. Thomas Edison could not have invented the light bulb if he was afraid to keep trying. Only after countless failed attempts did he succeed. Students need to feel free to ask questions, to say that they do not understand, to risk presenting an unusual view on a subject. Studying courage gives us an opportunity to give one another credit for risk taking. It is a chance to talk honestly about fears and when risks are too big to take. It is a good chance to talk about taking an unpopular stance—at home, at school, and in the world.

Courage studies evoke discussions of what defines courage, heroes, and heroic acts. It calls us to explore who our heroes are, and why. We can start by acknowledging the everyday heroes in our family and community. We need to give ourselves credit for the many ways in which we are heroic, and to imagine how to move towards courage in other areas of our lives.

There are so many ways to be courageous. It is good to ask the students what they think is an example of a courageous act, and to start with everyday courage. Examples of this could be getting on the bus alone, asking a new friend to play, telling someone that your feelings are hurt, standing up for someone when others are teasing them, daring to like something that others think is different, or trying something new like zucchini or rollerblading. It takes courage to live with integrity. It takes courage to take a stand against bullying. It takes courage to be yourself. It takes courage to be a teacher!

Acknowledging our own courageous acts is important psychologically. Everyone faces times of great fear and challenge. Remembering when we were able to meet challenges and overcome fears helps us to navigate the inevitable rough spots along our life journeys. Stories of how others have found courage provide a vicarious experience of hope and promise that we can draw from as well.

You may want to start by discussing and defining courage and heroism with your students. Older students will benefit from keeping a journal of all the courageous and risk-taking acts they notice in themselves and others. Some schools have a system of recognizing and rewarding courageous acts. Students and teachers can nominate one another by filling out a form and placing it in a central box, which are then shared at assemblies or over the loudspeaker.

The Brave Little Parrot

India

Grades K-4

THEMES: Persistence, courage, love, compassion, sacrifice, being a good example

Once, long ago, the Buddha was born as a little parrot. One day, a storm broke upon his forest home. Lightning flashed, thunder crashed, and a dead tree, struck by lightning, burst into flames. Sparks leapt on the wind and soon the forest was ablaze. Terrified animals ran wildly in every direction, seeking safety from the flames and smoke.

"Fire, fire!" cried the little parrot. "Run! Run to the river!" Flapping his wings, he flung himself out into the fury of the storm, and, rising higher, flew towards the safety of the river. But as he flew, he could see that many animals were trapped, surrounded by the flames below, with no chance of escape.

Suddenly, a desperate idea, a way to save them, came to him. He darted to the river, dipped himself in the water, and flew back over the now raging fire.

The heat rising up from the burning forest was like the heat of an oven. The thick smoke made breathing almost unbearable. A wall of flames shot up—now on one side, and now on the other. Crackling flames leapt and danced before him. Twisting and turning through the mad maze of fire, the little parrot flew bravely on. At last, over the center of the forest, he shook his wings and released the few drop of water that still clung to his feathers. The tiny drops tumbled like jewels down into the heart of the blaze and vanished with a hsssssssss.

The little parrot once more flew back through the flames and smoke to the river, dipped himself in the cool water, and flew back again over the burning forest. Back and forth he flew, time and time again, from the river to the forest, from the burning forest to the river. His feathers were charred. His feet were scorched. His lungs ached. His eyes, stung by smoke, burned red as coals. His mind spun as dizzily as the spinning sparks. But still the little parrot flew on.

At this time, some of the devas, gods of a happy realm, were floating high overhead in their cloud palaces of ivory and gold. They happened to look down and they saw the little parrot flying through the flames. They pointed at him with perfect hands. Between mouthfuls of honeyed foods they exclaimed, "Look at that foolish bird! He's trying to put out a raging forest fire with a few sprinkles of water! How ridiculous! How absurd!" And they laughed.

But one of the gods did not laugh. Strangely moved, he changed himself into a golden eagle and few down down towards the little parrot's fiery path.

The little parrot was just nearing the flames again when the great eagle, with eyes like molten gold, appeared at his side. "Go back, little bird!" said the eagle in a solemn and majestic voice. "Your task is hopeless!" A few drops of water can't put out a forest fire! Cease now and save yourself— before it is too late."

But the little parrot only continued to fly on through the smoke and flames. He could hear the great eagle flying above him as the heat grew fiercer, calling out, "Stop, foolish little parrot! Save yourself! Save yourself!"

"I don't need a great, shining eagle," coughed the little parrot, "to give me advice like that. My own mother, the dear bird, might have told me such things long ago. Advice! (cough, cough) I don't need advice. I just (cough) need someone to help."

And the god who was that great eagle, seeing the little parrot flying through the flames, thought suddenly of his own privileged kind. He could see them floating high up above. Yes, there they were, the carefree gods, still laughing and talking while many animals cried out in pain and fear from among the flames below. Seeing that, he grew ashamed, and a single desire was kindled in his heart. God though he was, he just wanted to be like that brave little parrot and to help.

"I will help!" he exclaimed, and flushed with these new feelings, he began to weep. Stream after stream of sparkling tears poured from his eyes. Wave upon wave they washed down like cooling rain upon the fire, upon the forest, upon the animals, and upon the little parrot himself.

Where those tears fell, the flames died down and the smoke began to clear. The little parrot, washed and bright, rocketed about the sky, laughing for joy. "Now that's more like it!" he exclaimed.

The eagle's tears dripped from the burned branches and soaked into the scorched earth. Where those tears glistened, new life pushed quickly forth— shoots, stems, and leaves. Buds unfurled and blossoms opened. Green grass pushed up from among still-glowing cinders.

Where the teardrops sparkled on the parrot's wings, new feathers now grew. Red feathers, green feathers, and yellow feathers too. Such bright colors! Such a handsome bird!

All the animals looked at one another in amazement. Washed by those tears, they were whole and well. Not one had been harmed. Up above, in the clear blue sky, they could see their friend, the little parrot, looping and soaring in delight. When hope was gone, somehow he had saved them. "Hurray!" they cried. "Hurray for the brave little parrot and for this sudden, miraculous rain!"

"The Brave Little Parrot," is reprinted here with permission from the author Rafe Martin, from *The Hungry Tigress: Buddhist Myths, Legends, and Jataka Tales* (New York: G.P. Putnam and Sons, 1998).

SOURCES

The Hungry Tigress: Buddhist Myths, Legends, and Jataka Tales, edited by Rafe Martin (Somerville, Mass.: Yellow Moon Press, 1999). Check out his website for more books and programs: www.rafemartin.com

Picture book version: *The Brave Little Parrot*, retold by Rafe Martin, illustrated by Susan Gaber (New York: G.P. Putnam and Sons, 1998).

Tips for the telling

This is a Jataka tale, meaning that it is one of hundreds of tales translated from Buddhist sources. The Jataka are stories of the former lives of the Buddha who took many forms, both animal and human. The Buddha used these stories as a teaching device, as have many other spiritual teachers. The first line of this story may be too confusing to your students, and if you do not intend to teach them about Jataka and Buddhism, I would suggest simply saying that, "Once there was a little parrot."

This is a pourquoi story, meaning one that explains how something came to be. This is how the parrot got its beautiful colors. You might start by showing a picture of the bird. I would suggest beginning by creating a real feel for the jungle. You can list all of the animals that might live in the jungles of India. You can have your students close their eyes before you begin the story to use their imaginations to hear, smell, and see the richness of jungle life. This story tells of gods sitting in the sky eating and drinking. In the Hindu tradition, it is believed that there were many gods that could look down on earth and that could assume different forms. You might tell the students about this before starting the story so that it does not confuse them in the middle.

Follow-up activities

Tip for story retention

- **Imagination journey.** Have students close their eyes and take a moment to revisit the story as a movie in their imaginations. You can guide them by moving through each section of the story and asking them to picture it, or if they are older, you can ask them to see the whole scene as if they were one of the gods or an eagle or flying in an airplane above. Then have the class each share their favorite image and ask if there were any sections that they had trouble picturing or remembering.

Making a personal connection

- **Questions, discussion and story sharing:** What did the story make you wonder about? What would you like to say to the little parrot? Why didn't the other animals think they could help? Why didn't the gods want to help at first? What changed the one god's mind? The little parrot was passionate about saving his friends and the forest. What do you feel passionate about? Are there things that you would risk your life for? Have you ever started something and had other people first laugh at you? Did you ever start something and have other people help you after a while? Teachers can help by telling their stories to get things going.

Creative exploration

- **Dramatization:** This is a great one to act out as a class. There can be plenty of small parts and few larger ones. Students can even be trees or dancers with flames and smoke running through the forest. Take it to other classes and then generate discussions about courage.

- **Creative adaptation:** Give your students the chance to explore the theme of this story by creating their own version, which might explain how some other animals helped and got their characteristics too. In the Pre-Story section under Creative Adaptation, there are ideas for making up your own pourquoi stories, explaining how things came to be.

- **Research:** Older students can research people throughout history who single-handedly undertook projects to make change and succeeded in getting others to join with them.

- **Brainstorm** with your students to help them to identify what they care a lot about. Let children stand up and talk about a project or action that they would undertake even if no one else would join them. What kinds of projects could they start as a group that other students in the school would be inspired to join? See if they can agree on one project with the hope of encouraging others to join them.

How the Bat Came to Be

Native American
(Anishinabe—
Eastern Woodland)

Grades K-5

THEMES: Sacrifice,
courage, gratitude,
perseverance, reward

Long ago, as the Sun began to rise one morning, it came too close to the earth and became tangled in the top branches of a tall tree. The harder Sun tried to escape, the more he became caught. So the dawn did not come.

At first, the birds and animals did not notice. Some woke, then went back to sleep, thinking that they had been mistaken and it was not yet time for morning. Animals that love the night, like the panther and the owl, were happy that it remained dark and continued to hunt. But after a while, so much time had passed that all the birds and animals knew something was wrong. They gathered together in the dark to hold a council.

"Sun has become lost," the eagle said.

"We must search for him," said the bear.

So all of the birds and animals began to look for Sun. They looked in caves and in the deep forest and on the mountains and in the swampy lands. But Sun was not there. None of the birds or animals were able to find Sun.

Then one of the animals, a small brown squirrel, had an idea. "Perhaps Sun is caught in a tall tree," he said.

Then the small brown squirrel began to go from tree to tree, going further and further toward the east. At last, in the top of a very tall tree, he saw a glow of light. He climbed up and saw that it was Sun. Sun's light was pale and he looked weak.

"Help me, Little Brother," Sun said.

The small brown squirrel came close and began to chew at the branches in which Sun was caught. The closer he came to Sun, the hotter it became. The more branches he chewed free, the brighter Sun's light grew.

"I must stop now," said the small brown squirrel. "My fur is burning. It is all turning black."

"Help me!" said Sun. "Don't stop now."

The small brown squirrel continued to work, but the heat of the sun was very great now and it was even brighter.

My tail is burning away," said the small squirrel. "I can do no more."

"Help me," said the Sun. "Soon I will be free."

So the small squirrel continued to chew. But the light of the sun was very bright now.

"I am growing blind," said the small squirrel. "I must stop."

"Just a little more," said the Sun. "I am almost free."

Finally, the squirrel chewed free the last of the branches. As soon as he did so, Sun broke free and rose up into the sky. Dawn spread across the land and it was day again. All over the world the birds and animals were happy.

But the small squirrel was not happy. He was blinded by the brightness of the sun. His long tail had been burned away and what fur he had left was all black. His skin had stretched from the heat and he clung to the top branches of that tree which had held the sun, unable to move.

Up in the sky, Sun looked down and saw the small squirrel. He had suffered so much to save him. Sun felt great pity and he spoke.

"Little Brother," Sun said, "you have helped me. Now I will give you something. Is there anything that you have always wanted?"

"I have always wanted to fly," said the small squirrel. "But I am blind now and my tail has been burned away."

Sun smiled. "Little brother," he said, "from now on you will be an even better flyer than the birds. Because you came so close to me, my light will always be too bright for you, but you will see in the dark and you will hear everything around you as you fly. From this time on, you will sleep when I rise into the sky and when I say goodbye to the world each evening, you will wake."

Then the small animal, which had been a squirrel, dropped from the branch, spread his leathery wings, and began to fly. He no longer missed his tail and his brown fur, and he knew that when the night came again it would be his time. He could not look at the Sun, but he held the joy of the Sun in his heart.

And so it was, long ago, that Sun showed his thanks to the small brown squirrel who was a squirrel no longer, but the first of the bats.

Tips for the telling

This story involves a transformation of the main character, so attention to detail is important to convey the change effectively, without giving away what the squirrel is changing into.

Follow-up activities

Tips for story retention

- **Retell with puppets:** Create a tree prop and sun and squirrel/bat puppets, or let the students make them with Popsicle sticks. Get them into groups of three. One holds the tree and does the narration while the other two take on the parts of sun and squirrel-turned-bat. You can also add puppets for the other animals in the beginning of the story.

- **Drawing the sequence:** Have students draw pictures of the squirrel as it makes the transformation to bat. You can have them divide the paper into six parts: healthy squirrel; fur burned black; tail gone; skin to leather; eyes blinded; bat. Using this device, they can tell the story to reading buddies or at home.

Making a personal connection

- **Questions, discussion and story sharing:** This story brings home the point that when we have the courage to take a risk and to make sacrifices for the greater good, we are transformed. Help your students to tell stories about experiences that have changed them.

- **Discussion point:** Sacrifice is often a large part of courage, when become willing to give of ourselves for the sake of others. Saving the sun was something that life on earth depended upon. It is important that when we make sacrifices, we feel that it is for a worthy cause and that we do not feel taken for granted. This can be a good story to use to teach assertiveness skills. When do we say no, and when do we give of ourselves for the good of others? I think that everyone has a story of a time that they did something for someone else and felt good afterwards, and a time when they felt taken advantage of and angry. It is important to help students to learn to distinguish the two.

Creative exploration

- **Creative adaptation:** Have your students tell the story with another animal as the hero or heroine. It might be a horse that has to stretch its neck so long to reach the sun that it becomes the first giraffe. In the Pre-Story section under Creative Adaptation, there are ideas for making up your own pourquoi stories, explaining how things came to be. Have them tell the story to other classes and to parents.

- **Let students make up stories** with themselves as the hero/heroine, in which they save the earth in some way and are changed by it. Maybe their hair turns red, they get an interesting scar, or their hands turn to paws. Encourage creativity!

Turning the story ideas into action

- You can help your students to experience making a sacrifice for some greater good. **Brainstorm** with them some ways that they could experience sacrificing for a good cause. Could they practice giving up one week's allowance to donate to a worthy cause, such as spending a Saturday afternoon cleaning up trash in the town, or holding a bake sale rather than watching TV? After they carry out these sacrifices, it is important to process how it felt and what they learned.

Androcles and the Lion

Aesop

Grades 2-6

THEMES: Courage, sacrifice, friendship, loyalty, compassion

Long ago, when the Romans kept slaves, a man named Androcles suffered under the hand of a cruel and violent master. Although Androcles was strong and worked hard, he was barely given enough food to eat and was beaten nearly every day. Androcles had often heard tales of how slaves who tried to run away were caught and punished or died of thirst or were killed by beasts in the forest. But one day he decided that such a fate would be better than to go on living this way. One night he slipped from the master's land and into the woods that skirted the desert. He walked and walked, looking for a bit of food or a place to sleep, when suddenly he heard a strange sound—a moaning, groaning, and crying coming from a cave. He peered into the cave and jumped with fear. For there was a full-grown lion just inside the entrance.

The lion did not see him right away, as he was frantically licking and gnawing at his paw. Androcles saw that a large thorn was buried deep in the lion's paw, and that the paw was swollen and bleeding. He felt a surge of pity for the animal. Stepping forward carefully and quietly, he spoke so as not to startle the lion. "I won't hurt you, my friend. If you let me, I think I can pull out the thorn." The lion growled, but did not move to strike.

Androcles bent down and knelt before the lion. He picked up the large paw in both hands and laid it upon his leg, feeling the claws against his skin. Quickly he pulled out the thorn and wrapped his paw in a bandage made from the cloth of his own shirt.

The lion licked Androcles' hand in thanks, and from that time on, they were friends. They slept together in the cave, and the lion shared his meat with Androcles. They lived together in peace. However, one day the lion did not return from hunting. Androcles searched for him and discovered many human footprints in the sand near the watering hole. He realized that his friend had been captured by hunters. Not long after that, Androcles, now wandering the countryside, was also caught and brought to the city for punishment for running away from his master.

The punishment for his crime in those days was to be thrown to the lions that the Emperor kept in his palace. Many people from the city would crowd into the arena to watch the spectacle. On the day Androcles was to be killed, even the Emperor had come to watch. The soldiers dragged Androcles into the center of the arena and left him there. Then they lifted the door to a pen where a hungry lion stood waiting. Androcles sat down and closed his eyes. The end would come soon. The crowd was shouting, egging the lion on, and Androcles tried to shut out the sound by remembering his happy times with the lion in the forest. But suddenly the crowd gasped and grew silent. He opened his eyes and his heart jumped. For there, sitting but a few feet from him, was *his* lion! Androcles cried out with joy and embraced his friend.

The Emperor stood up and called to Androcles. "Who are you, that you can tame the fiercest of beasts?"

Androcles stood and bowed before the Emperor. "Your Highness, I once helped this lion when he was injured, and he became the most faithful friend I have known in this hard life."

The Emperor invited Androcles to tell him his whole story. When he was done, the Emperor was quiet a while. "You have shown great courage and kindness. I will reward you and the lion with your freedom. Return to the forest and live out your days in peace." That is just what they did.

I suggest introducing your students to Aesop if they are not already familiar with him. See my introduction on page 44. Aesop was also said to have been a slave.

This is a listening tale, without many opportunities for participation. If you can picture the story, and take time to build up the feelings of Androcles, you will hold your listeners' attention and open their hearts.

Your students may have a hard time understanding how people could be so cruel as to make sport of watching a person be eaten by lions. You can choose to downplay this part and focus on the Emperor watching. The subject is rich if you are studying history.

Tips for the telling

- **Retell using different creative media:** This story can be retold with simple puppets, or by making a diorama of clay and letting the children move the main characters around.

Follow-up activities
Tip for retention

- **Questions, discussion and story sharing:** This is a beautiful story about compassion, trust, friendship, and loyalty. It often takes courage to reach out to someone new. Reminding ourselves of previous courageous acts helps us to step up to the plate when we are frightened and raises our self-esteem. Help your students to think and talk about times when they did something scary because they knew it was the right thing to do. Help them to remember a time when they helped someone that they didn't know that well, and how that person may have helped them in some way at a later time. It helps to brainstorm a list of types of activities that require courage, such as raising your hand when you have a question, saying no to someone when it would be easier to say yes, standing up to a bully, doing something alone. For homework, the students can interview a family member about times when they did something scary that took courage.

Making a personal connection

- **Dramatization:** Have the students act this one out as a group. Small groups can do it by asking the audience to play the bystanders in the stadium. Share this story with other groups of students.

- **Creative writing/telling:** Make a book of everyone's personal stories of courage and/or share the stories orally with another class or parents.

Creative exploration

- **Help the students think about someone new** that they could reach out to in the class or school. Brainstorm ways of reaching out and then try them and reflect on them afterwards.

- **Brainstorm** ways to go about overcoming fears. Brainstorm a list of scary actions that have to do with school and everyday living. Help students to set goals to try new things every day. Then give them credit for what they have done, and help them to give one another credit.

Turning the story ideas into action

The Burning of the Rice Fields

Japan

Grades 3-8

THEMES: Courage, sacrifice, generosity, compassion, wise action

Every few hundred years in Japan, a tidal wave, or tsunami, will wreak havoc on a village, leaving huge destruction and loss of life in its wake. This is a story that may have actually happened over two hundred years ago.

Long ago in Japan, there stood a village at the foot of a great mountain and at the edge of the sea. The people farmed the gentle slopes of the mountain and fished for their food. In and out of the terraced rice fields that rose from the sea wove a red clay road. At the top of the road was one house, high above the village. In that house lived a man named Hamaguchi Gohei. The people called him Ojiisan, which means grandfather, or one who is wise. Ojiisan lived with his grandson Tada. One day the two of them looked out from their balcony. They saw the wheat that was ready for harvest in the fields. They saw the villagers below preparing for the harvest celebration. They saw thick dark clouds hanging over the village. They noticed that the air was especially still. "It looks like earthquake weather," Ojiisan said to his grandson. Sure enough, before long, there came a rumbling, grumbling from way out under the sea. It shook the house, and then was still.

Looking down on the village, they saw that the people had gone down to the water's edge. The water was running out to the horizon, leaving behind fish and rocks and sand. The people did not know what to make of it, but Ojiisan knew. He remembered a story that his grandfather had told him, and he knew what the sea was going to do.

He had to think quickly. "Tada, bring me a lit torch from the kitchen fire." Tada ran to the house and returned with a flaming torch. Ojiisan took it and ran down to his fields of grain. He began to run between the stalks, licking each one with the flames. Tada ran behind him yelling, "Ojiisan, why are you burning our foods?" But Ojiisan did not answer. He thought only of the lives of the villagers and continued to weave in and out of his field. Finally, a thick black cloud of smoke rose over the field.

The Buddhist monks in the temple below saw it and rang the temple bell. The people turned from the sea and saw the smoke. "Ojiisan's fields are on fire! We must help him put them out!" they cried. They all began to grab their pails and to fill them at the well. They ran up the hill, the old and small coming behind slowly or on donkey back.

Ojiisan stood by his balcony and watched the fields burn. He also watched the sea, which was still running away to the horizon. He watched the people come and urged them to come faster. Soon the first people arrived and tried to throw their water on the fields.

84

"Let them burn! Everyone must come," warned Ojiisan.

When the last of the villagers arrived, Tada ran to them and cried, "Ojiisan's gone mad! He burned our fields on purpose."

"Yes," said another, "he has gone mad! Next he'll burn ours."

They went to grab him, but he pointed toward the sea. "Look!" he cried. All eyes turned and saw a shadow like a coastline on the horizon where no coastline was. Now it was coming toward them, faster than galloping horses, higher than a giant wall. "It's a tsunami!" they screamed and ran up the mountain as high as they could.

The giant wave rolled in and crashed on the village, sending a sheet of foaming water hundreds of feet up the mountain. It pulled back and crashed several more times, until slowly the water began to calm and to pull away again. Finally, the people were able to come out of their hiding places. They looked down upon their ruined village. There was nothing left but wood and stone scattered about. Then they took stock of who was there, and the cry went up. "Everyone is here! Everyone is here!"

One after another the villagers, over four hundred in number, knelt down before Ojiisan and thanked him for saving their lives.

SOURCES

This story was collected and recorded by Lafcadio Hearn in *Gleanings in Buddha Fields: Stories of Hand and Soul in the Far East* (Boston: Houghton Mifflin, 1897).

The Burning Rice Fields, retold by Sara Cone Bryant (New York: Holt, Rinehart and Winston, 1963).

Picture Book: *The Wave*, retold by Margaret Hodges (Boston: Houghton Mifflin, 1964).

Tips for the telling

I have been telling this story in performances since 1983. It has taken on new meaning since the Indonesian tsunami of 2004. It made me sad to think that so many people have lost the folk tales and nature lore to know the warning signs. Apparently in Japan, where the tsunamis are more common, everyone knows these stories and this information. I read on the Internet also about a North American fourth grader vacationing with her family in Thailand when the tsunami hit. She had been studying tsunamis in school and warned her parents when she observed the sea moving away from the shore. They were able to get to safety before the wave came in. This story could be a wonderful bridge to link folklore to weather studies.

Before you tell the story, you should decide whether you would like to include the introduction, or if you want the tidal wave to be a total surprise. Take time to build up the description of the place, so it is clear that the villagers must climb up the hill to reach the burning fields. I like to use sound effects to evoke the sea, both when it is calm and stormy. Note how the tension builds in the story as the old man realizes that it is a tsunami that is coming toward his village. Try to capture this in the volume and pitch of your voice and your rate of speech. This story lends itself to visual, auditory, and kinesthetic telling. I use my whole body to portray the wave, but you may choose to use images to show its strength, sound, and fury.

Follow-up activities
Tip for retention

- **News reporter retelling** works for this dramatic event story. Get students into groups of four with a reporter, the grandfather, grandson and one villager, and let them retell the events in the tale as if it has just happened.

Making a personal connection

- **Questions, discussion and story sharing:** Your students may want to tell stories that they have heard about the 2004 tsunami. What character traits did the main character utilize in this story? This is a story about sacrifice, quick thinking, and caring. Every day we make small sacrifices for others, whether they are time, money, energy, material things, or food. Help your students to think about times when they have made sacrifices for the sake of others. It will help if you begin by sharing stories in which you grappled with sacrifice. You can also focus on how a town or group of people recover together after a disaster.

Creative exploration

- **Story research:** Students are fascinated with natural disaster and storm stories. Let your students go online or to the library to find storm or natural disaster-related stories in which real people helped others. Share these with other classes or in a class book.

- **Story creation:** Set a story with the same basic theme in your town. What kind of natural disaster might take place? What quick thinking solution would your hero/heroine use, and what would be the sacrifice and the reward?

- **Brainstorm local issues:** What local needs require help or sacrifice? Make a list of people or animals that might be in need of help. Make a list of the type of sacrifices that students could make.
- **Interview town or school officials** and learn about people who have already sacrificed. They could tell their stories and give them a recognition award.

Turning the story ideas into action

Descent into the Maelstrom
(abridged)

Edgar Allen Poe

Grades 7-8

Themes: Courage, sacrifice, risk taking, fear

The fishing between the islands offshore of one particular spot on the Norwegian coastline was especially good, but of all the fishermen in the area, only two brothers ever dared to fish there. For twice each day, between the islands and the shore, a horrendous whirlpool some half-mile in diameter would form and suck down every object or living thing that came within several miles of it. People called it "The Great Maelstrom."

One day these two brothers, sure of perfect weather, set sail to the islands, enjoyed a marvelous catch, and then headed home well before the pool was to form. Suddenly, however, the winds changed, stranding them. Before they could row back to the islands, a hurricane wind was upon them, tossing them wildly about and snapping their mainsail's mast.

The younger brother clung to a ring bolt at the front of the boat, and the elder brother grabbed an empty barrel that was lashed to the back. They rode this way for some time. Suddenly, as they crested a wave, they saw that their tiny boat was heading straight toward the forming pool. In his terror, the elder brother at the back lunged forward and forced the ring bolt from his brother's hand. The younger brother did not contest the other's fear, but went to the back and held on to the water cask.

Finally, the inevitable moment came and the tiny boat careened into the whirlpool. The younger brother closed his eyes, said a prayer, and waited for certain death. After a moment, however, when death hadn't come, he opened his eyes to find that the boat had not fallen into the abyss, but was hanging on the edge of the pool, riding around and around, going slowly down.

Looking up at the sides of the pool and knowing now that death was unavoidable, his fear all but left him. He began to notice with fascination that there were many other objects in the pool—trees, boats, and furniture. He began to take interest in the differing speeds with which the objects fell and finally plunged into the swirl. As he watched, a stunning realization was forming in his mind: The lighter, cylindrical objects fell more slowly, while the heavier objects dropped more quickly into the abyss.

This realization set his heart to pounding and his mind to racing. He knew that their only hope of surviving was to lash themselves to the empty water cask and throw themselves out of the boat. He motioned to his brother, and using hand signals, explained his plan. But his brother dropped his head and gripped the ring ever harder, choosing the familiarity of his boat over the uncertainty of the waters. At last, resigning him to his fate, the younger brother cut free the water cask, lashed himself to it, and jumped into the cold black wall of the pool.

It was just as he had hoped. His barrel sank but little more, while the small boat went steadily down and finally hurtled his poor brother to his death. Soon the pool began to change. The whirl began to slow and the bottom to rise up. It was not long before he found himself again on the surface of the water with the shores of his home in sight.

Early the next morning some fishermen from his own village found him floating on his barrel. But the fishermen knew him not. For when he had left that morning, his hair had been as black as a raven's. When they hauled him in, it was as white as snow.

SOURCE

The Complete Stories and Poems of Edgar Allan Poe (Garden City, N.J.: Doubleday & Co., Inc. 1996). This story is in the public domain. I suggest you read the full version. I have shortened it considerably here to fit in this collection. While it is not a folk tale that I know of (we don't know how Poe came to this tale, which is not typical for him), it is a personal favorite.

Tips for the telling

Being a longer story and a literary one, I suggest that you take the time to learn some of the language by heart, as it is beautiful. I do this best by writing down the story several times over. It is a story that demands a quiet space and a thoughtful moment afterwards. The more the teller can be in the moment with the story, the more the audience will go with you. The descriptions of the way the sea changes are important. Take your time so that you and the listener can be inside that maelstrom together. The metaphors are very powerful. You may also choose to read Poe's entire longer story.

Follow-up activities

Tips for story retention

- **News reporter retelling:** Divide them into groups of three with one as reporter, one as the brother who survives, and one as fisherman who hauls him in.

- **Retelling in pairs:** Partners sit facing one another with eyes closed. One begins, telling a portion of the story using vivid imagery. The other picks up after a while and they go back and forth until the story is told.

Making a personal connection

- **Questions and discussion:** Why did the brother up front not join his brother in jumping out of the boat? What character traits did the brother use that allowed him to survive? Why do you think the surviving brother's hair turns white? How do you imagine this experience changes his life?

- **Telling personal stories:** Have you ever been in a situation in which you thought you might be seriously injured or killed? What type of quick thinking did you or someone else do to get you out of it? The brother who survived had to be willing to let go of what was safe for him in order to survive. Have you ever had an experience in which you had to risk losing something that was familiar or important to you in order to gain something else? One way that young people may relate is if they wanted to start a new friendship with someone who was not in their circle of friends, or religious or ethnic group. They may be more comfortable journaling than speaking aloud about this.

Creative exploration

- **Research stories about individuals** who have made great personal changes in their lives that saved themselves or others (e.g., Studs Terkel's book on former Klan members. See the end of the chapter.)

- **Creative adaptation:** The story has a strong metaphor about letting go of the old and familiar in order to move forward. Encourage the students to write stories in which the main character uses this type of action to solve a problem, and how the character is transformed.

Turning the story ideas into action

- **Discussion and promoting new ways of being:** This is a story about thinking outside the box and being observant. Have a discussion with the class about situations in their lives, in the school, community, and world in which this kind of thinking is needed to abolish prejudice and hate crimes. Brainstorm ways that the students could encourage people in their community to reach outside of their comfort zone to get to know new people.

The Monk and the Scorpion

Once upon a time, a Zen Buddhist monk and his student sat at the edge of a great river in quiet meditation, watching the water flow by. After a while, a large scorpion came ambling along the bank, slipped on loose sand, and fell into the water at their feet. Without any hesitation, the monk reached into the water and lifted it out and set it back higher up on the bank. As he did, the scorpion stung his hand.

They sat again in silence for some moments as the scorpion made its way back down the bank toward the river, until it again slipped into the water. Again, the monk reached in and retrieved the struggling insect, and again was stung as he set it on the bank. This happened a third time, but this time the student could not restrain himself.

"Master," he said, "why is it that you keep trying to save that wretched insect? Can you not see that it is just going to sting you?"

"Of course I know it is going to sting me," the master replied with a smile. "It is the nature of a scorpion to sting. But it is my nature to save."

With that, the two went back to sitting in silence, watching the river flow.

India

Grades 6+

THEMES: Passion, commitment to values, integrity, courage, sacrifice, risk taking

SOURCE

Doorways to the Soul: 52 Wisdom Tales from Around the World by Elisa Pearmain (Cleveland: Pilgrim Press, 1998).

Tips for the telling

This story is so short that, like many teaching tales, its ending takes us by surprise. It is helpful to notice if your audience needs a closing sentence, or if they are content with the silence that you have created to signal its end. You may want to have a way to end it that signals that it is over, such as, "And for all we know, they may be sitting there still. The end!"

You may want to be sure that all of your students are familiar with scorpions, and the fact that they sting rather than bite. They should also be familiar with what a Zen Buddhist monk is.

This may be a good place to discuss metaphor. Developmentally many middle school students will still be grappling with the concept.

Follow-up activities
Tip for retention

• Such a short tale should be remembered with ease at this age level.

Making a personal connection

• **Questions and discussion:** Why did the monk continue to save the scorpion, even when it meant being stung? What are the things that are your "nature" to do? Another way to put this might be to discuss what your student's fierce beliefs are about what is necessary behavior and/or what they feel so passionate about as to put up with a sting.

• **Discussion:** The scorpion in the story can be seen as a metaphor for those things or people in life that hurt or threaten to hurt us. After discussing this, ask the students to make a list of potential scorpions in their lives. Examples could be people who they think might make fun of them, or those who are particularly critical. It could be a peer, a parent, a coach, a teacher, or themselves. Have a discussion about how these people have kept them from doing things they might have felt strongly about doing. After hearing this story once, a woman told me that it made her want to quit an office job in which there were "just too many scorpions."

• **Story sharing:** What are examples of things you have done that took courage, even when you knew it might not go well? Examples might be asking someone to dance, trying out for a team, submitting a poem for a contest or the school newspaper. Even speaking out strongly for something that you believe in that might not be a popular view. Encourage stories of times that "fear of the sting" stopped you from trying something that you really wanted to do.

Creative exploration

• **Literature share:** Talk about fictional books each has read about characters that took risks despite a potential "sting."

• **Research characters** in history that took unpopular stands. Examples could be Pee Wee Reese's story of standing up for Jackie Robinson, the only African-American player on his team, when fellow players were discriminating against him. Another example is the non-Jews who aided their Jewish neighbors during the Holocaust.

- **Journaling:** Ask students to notice when in their days they have the choice to do something difficult that might involve a "sting." Have them write these down in journal format. Have them share these the next day.

- **Brainstorm** types of situations that may be scary for people. Examples could be telling someone about your political beliefs, standing up for a person who is unpopular, or even wearing something new to school. Make a list and see if it does not generate some new empathy. Have the class make posters or write something for the school paper about what they learned.

The Leopard's Revenge

Africa

Grades 4-8

Themes: Courage, revenge, listening, respect, honesty

Once a leopard cub strayed from his home and ventured into the midst of a great herd of elephants. His mother and father had warned him to stay out of the way of the giant beasts, but he did not listen. Suddenly, the elephants began to stampede, and one of them stepped on the cub without even knowing it. Soon afterward, a hyena found his body and went to tell his parents.

"I have terrible news," he said. "I've found your son lying dead in the field."

The mother and father leopard gave great cries of grief and rage.

"How did it happen?" the father demanded. "Tell me who did this to our son! I will never rest until I have my revenge."

"The elephants did it," answered the hyena.

"The elephants?" asked the father leopard, quite startled. "You say it was the elephants?"

"Yes," said the hyena. "I saw their tracks."

The leopard paced back and forth for a few minutes, growling and shaking his head. "No, you are wrong," he said at last. "It was not the elephants. It was the goats. The goats murdered my boy!"

And at once, he bounded down the hill and sprang upon a herd of goats grazing in the valley below, and in a violent rage, he killed as many as he could in revenge.

SOURCE

The Book of Virtues, edited with commentary by William J. Bennett (New York: Simon & Schuster, 1993).

I suggest telling this simple tale in a straightforward manner. You will want to think about how much emotion you put into the telling and how you leave your audience in the end. The ending is quite disturbing; you might want to soften it a bit in the telling.

Tips for the telling

Follow-up activities
Tip for retention

- **News reporter retelling:** Small groups retell with individuals taking roles of a newspaper journalist, a surviving goat, elephants, leopard, and the hyena.

Making a personal connection

- **Story dissection:** Retell the story from the start as a group, asking students to yell "Stop" whenever they encounter an error in judgment, or have a question. For instance: Why didn't the leopard cub listen to its parents? Why did the elephants stampede without even knowing they had killed the cub? Why did the leopard insist that the goats had killed his son? Why did he attack them instead of the elephants?
- **Discussion and story sharing:** Have you ever felt like taking revenge on someone who hurt you or someone you care about? Why did you think it would help you to feel better? Did it? What were the repercussions? Why do people seek revenge?

Creative exploration

- **Creative adaptation:** Retell this story imagining how the father leopard could express his anger without endangering himself or others. Modernize the story: Older students will enjoy putting this story in a modern setting and imagining that the animals are people. I would urge them to change the problem too, from someone dying to perhaps someone being hurt. What would be a situation that people get into in which a person feels like taking revenge against someone but instead picks on someone weaker? Share these tales with one another.
- **Dramatic discovery:** Set up a classroom drama experience in which you select several students to be goats, one judge, two leopards, several elephants, the hyena, and a jury. Let them have a trial to decide the guilt or innocence and the punishment of the leopard.

Turning the story ideas into action

- **Class play:** Have your students perform this story for other classes as part of a bullying prevention program. Let them design and initiate a discussion with their audiences to talk about why certain people are picked on and why others bully.
- **Brainstorm:** Have small groups brainstorm anger-management strategies. Let groups share and come up with one list of skills to display, role play and practice in and out of the classroom.

Favorite picture books

Rainbow Crow, by Nancy Van Lann (New York: Alfred A. Knopf, 1989). In this beautifully illustrated retelling of a Lenape Indian folk tale, a crow of many colors finds the sun and brings back its fire to warm a dying earth that has a never-ending winter. It loses its colors in the process, but gains the respect of humans who do not hunt it to this day.

The Monster That Grew Small, by Joan Grant Marshall (New York: Lothrop, Lee & Shepard, 1987). This Egyptian folk tale tells the story of a boy who is full of fear, and with the help of a rabbit is set upon a journey to overcome his fear by meeting the fear monster. The monster appears smaller the closer the boy gets to it, and he learns in this way that he can face his fears when he meets them directly.

The Banza, a Haitian folk tale retold by Diana Wolkstein (New York: Dial Press, 1981). In this lovely story, a small goat plays his guitar and sings a song to keep up his courage and outsmart a hungry, mean tiger. As he plays, his courage grows.

The Story of Ruby Bridges, by Robert Coles (New York: Scholastic, 1995). The true story of Ruby Bridges, the first African-American girl to integrate an all-white school in New Orleans in the early 60's, and how she found the strength to walk to school each day past groups of angry adults.

See Studs Terkel's interview with C.P. Ellis, the former Ku Klux Klan member who tore up his Klan card and became a civil rights supporter. His friendship with African-American civil rights activist Ann Atwater inspired a book called *The Best of Enemies: Race and Redemption in the New South*, by Osha Gray Davidson (New York: Scribner, 1996). Terkel's interview also spawned a short documentary film called *An Unlikely Friendship*, by Diane Bloom, 2002.

www.oshadavidson.com—*The Best of Enemies*, how to order, chapter selections.
http://myhero.com—On Studs Terkel's work
www.filmakers.com—*An Unlikely Friendship*, how to order the film

Diversity
Appreciation

THE UNITED STATES IS A HIGHLY DIVERSE NATION. It is probably safe to say that we have people of more different religions and cultural and ethnic groups than any other nation. This diversity is part of our heritage. It is something to celebrate and capitalize on to the benefit of all.

While we have become more accepting and tolerant of differences pertaining to culture, religion, race, and physical challenges, there is still a long way to go toward full appreciation of our similarities and differences, and toward wiping out prejudice, fear, and even hatred. Change is happening slowly as we live and work side by side and get to know one another as human beings, but we also need to take conscious action to build bridges and heal old wounds.

We are diverse in countless ways, from our appearance, likes and dislikes, left- or right-handedness, strengths, and challenges. In every classroom, there is a wide diversity of learning styles. If we consciously respect and celebrate all of our unique differences in the classroom, students will feel validated and safer to be themselves.

It may be human nature to evaluate other people. Early humans had to make quick judgments for reasons of safety and survival. We still need to be safe, but most of our judgments now are not about safety or survival. Some of our judgments serve no useful purpose at all, and are just plain mean. Most of us make thousands of snap judgments and comparisons each day as we interact with others. We compare ourselves for intellectual capacity, attractiveness, power, values, income, and friendliness. These habits of judgment cause much of the fear and strife in the world, as we focus on how we are different, rather than looking deeper to discover our shared humanity. If we allow ourselves to override a fear of "difference" and stop our judging minds, we open ourselves to the possibility of deep friendships, vast learning, and a fuller experience of life.

Many young people feel the need to shore up their sense of identity by closely associating with certain groups of peers, and excluding, criticizing, and even bullying others. This is the source of much of the pain that young people experience in schools today. When we judge people for single issues, or based on appearances, we lose the richness of connection that our diversity offers. We lose, too, because when we are so critical of others we usually apply the same rigid standards to ourselves and come up wanting.

Stories can be bridges to help young people be more tolerant and appreciative of differences of all kinds. Helping students to know the stories of their own ethnic backgrounds is a crucial step in building acceptance of ethnic and cultural differences. We all have ethnicity. We all come from cultural groups. Stories allow students to walk in the shoes of others, to empathize with their experiences, and to discover the many things they share. Stories also foster self-awareness and honesty about our own biases and judgmental thoughts, and they offer new models of behavior.

Issues related to diversity that are addressed in the following stories are valuing each person's unique strengths, inclusion/exclusion, questioning prejudicial notions passed from one person to another, teasing, bullying, making false assumptions, power over, and self-acceptance.

The Butterfly Friends

Once upon a time, in a hollow tree at the edge of a meadow, there lived three butterfly friends. One had great big red wings, one had medium-size yellow wings, and one had tiny paper-white wings. Now just across the meadow and over a green lawn, there was a beautiful flower garden. The three butterflies loved nothing better than to flit over that garden, enjoying the colors, smelling the fragrances, and tasting the delicious nectar.

One day they were having such a good time that they forgot to check the weather. By the time they looked up, big rain clouds had rolled in and raindrops were falling on their wings.

"We must get out of the rain before our wings are tattered!" they cried.

"I have an idea," the red one said. "We can ask the flowers to open their petals and let us hide inside until the rain is gone!"

"Great idea," the others agreed. They began to fly about over the flowers calling to them, "Please give us shelter from the storm! Inside your petals it is dry and warm."

Before long, a big red tulip opened her petals. She saw the red butterfly and said, "You are just like me. Come in. Come in." But to the yellow and white butterflies she said, "You two are different. I'm afraid of things that are different. Go away. Go away."

Butterfly red looked at her two friends and said, "I don't want to go where my friends aren't wanted. No thanks, tulip."

But now it was raining even harder and the butterfly friends' wings were getting heavier and heavier. So again, they sang out, "Please give us shelter from the storm! Inside your petals it is dry and warm."

Soon a great yellow tulip opened her petals. She saw the yellow butterfly and said, "You are just like me. Come in. Come in." But to the red and white butterflies she said, "You two are different. Go away. Go away."

Butterfly yellow looked at her two friends and said, "I don't want to go where my friends aren't wanted. No thanks, tulip."

On they flew, their wings getting heavier and heavier as they cried, "Please give us shelter from the storm! Inside your petals it is safe and warm."

The same thing happened with a great white lily. She welcomed butterfly white, but told her friends to go away. Do you think butterfly white went inside without her friends? No way!

But now the rain was pouring down and the three butterflies could not fly at all.

They sank down onto the ground beneath the flowers. There they heard a small voice.

Germany

Grades Pre-K-3

THEMES: Inclusion/exclusion, diversity of appearance, fear of difference, loyalty, perseverance, kindness

It was coming from a patch of red clover weeds at the edge of the lawn. "Our flowers are not big like the tulips and lilies, but you can hide under them until the rain is gone." The three friends thanked the flowers and climbed up their stems under the puffy blossoms.

Now the sun had been watching through a crack in the clouds. She had seen how the three friends stuck together, and she was moved by the kindness of the clover plants. She pushed back the clouds and shone down on the garden. The butterflies climbed onto the clover blossoms and dried their wings in the sun. With a "thank you," they flew on home.

After that day, the butterfly friends still liked to play in the flower garden, but they never forgot the kindness of the red clover plants. And if you want to be sure of seeing a butterfly, walk out into a wildflower meadow and you will see them, flitting from clover to clover in the sun.

So, no matter what people look like, or what they like to do, be kind to everyone, and it all comes back to you.

This is my adaptation of the story. In the version translated from German, there is no clover plant. The sun simply shines on the butterflies and they fly home, happy again.

See source notes. See my adapted version in rhyme for older audiences in *Ahhhh! A Tribute to Brother Blue and Ruth Edmonds Hill* (Somerville, Mass.: Yellow Moon Press, 2003).

SOURCES

"The Three Butterfly Brothers," in *Easy to Tell Stories for Young Children*, by Annette Harrison (Jonesborough, Tenn.: National Storytelling Press, 1992).

"The Three Butterflies," in *My First Story-book*, by Richard Bamberger, translated by James Thin (London: Oliver & Boyd, 1960).

This story lends itself beautifully to audience participation and drama or puppetry. The first time through you can invite your audience to make the rain with you. I suggest **practicing various rain sounds** in advance so as not to interrupt the flow of the story. I do this in four parts:

1. Snapping their fingers and/or making a drip drop sound by clicking their tongues, makes a nice beginning-to-rain sound.
2. Rubbing their hands together makes a wonderful sound of rain falling in sheets, but it only works if you have a large enough group participating.
3. Hitting two fingers against the palm makes a harder rain sound.
4. Slapping their hands against their thighs very fast makes a pouring rain sound.

Butterfly movements: Students like to make the movements of a butterfly by putting their two wrists together and putting the hands together and apart.

Singing the repeating refrain: The next great place for participation is to have the children sing the repeating refrains when the butterflies are calling out to the flowers to open their petals.

With small groups of young children, I have had them simply act out the parts of the story I am telling, and they love to flit around the room. I have used parents or teachers to be the flowers and the clover in the story. In a classroom situation, I would tell the story first, and then act it out together, in large or small groups depending on the age. If you bring scarves, it can add to the drama as they dress in different colors.

• Before the story, you can review what the students know about butterflies—what they eat, their role in transporting pollen, and what happens if their wings are damaged.

• **Acting it out as a group:** Retell with puppets, or dramatize as above.

Follow-up activities
Tip for retention

Making a personal connection

• **Questions and discussion:** Are there situations in which your students act together, or where one or another is left out? Can you share a story about this without including names? Brainstorm with the students situations in which people can be included or excluded. You might suggest some scenarios and ask if the students think this is fair or unfair exclusion. Have the students write letters to one of the butterflies telling of a time when they felt left out, or when their friends included them. These can be shared with the group.

• **Personal story sharing:** The flowers were afraid of the butterflies that did not look just like them. Their fear caused them to exclude the butterflies that were different. This is a very important awareness for everyone to examine. When have they felt afraid of someone who was different? Have they ever felt like excluding someone because they were different? Did they discover that someone really was not so different after they have gotten to know them? Telling the stories of how we overcome our fears and recognize the similarities between others is a crucial step in learning to see beyond one another's differences.

Creative exploration

- **Story adaptation:** Have students create original stories in which characters act similarly to the butterfly friends. Perhaps they change the main characters to different animals and/or change the settings. With younger students, I would suggest the class make up a story as a group and then act it out together. They can also perform it for other classrooms.

Turning the story ideas into action

- **Brainstorm** a list of places where exclusion and inclusion happens in the school or community. Ask the students what they can do about exclusion in the places they have noticed it, and commit to practicing inclusion. This might look like inviting someone new to join them at a game at recess, to sit with them at lunch, or to share a game at a play center in the classroom.

- **Visual representations:** Have the students make posters of the butterfly friends with captions that remind people to be inclusive and accepting of differences. These can go up around the classroom and or school. Examples could be butterflies and bees in the cafeteria lunch together, or butterflies at recess inviting bumblebees to play tag.

Frog Child and Snake Child

Africa (Ekoi)

Grades K-5

THEMES: Learning fear and prejudice from others, accepting, enjoying and overlooking differences; tolerance, inclusion, learning from others

Once upon a time in the forest, a little Frog child wanted to go out to play. "Be careful," said his mother. "Don't go too far from our home, and don't talk to strangers."

"OK, Mama," said the Frog child as he hopped happily away.

Meanwhile a Snake child also wished to play outside. "Be careful," said his mother. "Don't go too far from home, and don't talk to strangers."

"OK, Mama," said the Snake child as he slithered happily away.

Soon the two met on the path. "What are you doing?" asked the Snake child as he watched the Frog child hop happily to and fro.

"I'm hopping! That's what frogs do," answered the Frog child. "What do you do?"

"I like to slither," answered the Snake child. "That's what snakes do! I can teach you to slither, if you teach me to hop."

"Good idea," said Frog child. "Just watch what I do." Frog child began to hop as high as he could. Snake child tried to hop, but there was just too much of him—if one part went up, another went down. It sure felt funny. He began to laugh and Frog child laughed too. "Don't worry, you'll get better at it," he said.

Then Frog child began to try to slither. He ended up rolling over several times and landing in a bush. "Ouch!" he called, and then they both started to laugh. All day they spent in the sun together, hop-slithering, slither-hopping, and mostly laughing.

Finally, it was time to go home. "See you tomorrow?" asked Frog child.

"Yes," said Snake child. "I want to play some more."

The two friends each went home, hop-slithering and slither-hopping right down their respective holes to their waiting mothers.

"What on earth are you doing?" asked Frog's mother when her son came rolling in.

"I met a new friend today," said Frog child excitedly, "and he taught me how to slither."

Frog's mother turned pale. "What is your friend's name?"

"His name is Snake," Frog child replied.

"Oh no!" shouted Frog's mother. "You must never play with Snake child again! Snake people are bad. They are our enemies. They eat us! Besides we don't slither, we hop!"

At the same time, Snake child hop-slithered down into his cozy home.

"What are you doing?" asked his mother.

"I met a knew friend today," said Snake child excitedly," and he taught me how to hop."

"What is your friend's name?" she asked.

"His name is Frog," Snake child replied.

"Frog," smiled his mother. "We do not play with frogs, we eat them! Next time you see your friend Frog, you must eat him!"

"But if I eat him," Snake child said sadly, "I won't be able to play with him anymore."

"Frogs and snakes are not friends, and that is that. And furthermore," said his mother, "snakes do not hop!"

The next day Frog child and Snake child met on the path. They stopped some distance away and looked at each other. "My mama says that I can't play with you anymore," said Frog child sadly. "You are my enemy."

"Yes," said Snake child, "My mama says I'm not supposed to play with you anymore either. I'm supposed to eat you."

"I guess I better go home now," said Frog child sadly. He hopped away as fast as he could.

Snake child stayed, still watching Frog child hop away. Frog child did smell good to eat, but he would miss playing with his friend.

They never played together after that day, but you can sometimes see them sitting alone by the path, remembering the day they spent together as friends.

SOURCES

This tale was originally published in *In the Shadow of the Bush*, by P. Amaury Talbott (London: Heinemann, 1912) as a brief eighteen-line tale. Ashley Bryan turned it into a long and rhythmical story called "Why Frog and Snake Never Play Together" in *Beat the Story-Drum, Pum-Pum*, (New York: Simon & Schuster, 1980). Margaret Read MacDonald includes the story in her book *Shake-It-Up Tales! Stories to Sing, Dance, Drum and Act Out* (Little Rock: August House Publishers, 2000), retold by Storyteller Jim Wolf as "Little Boy Frog and Little Boy Snake." Her book offers ideas for making the story participatory and telling it with a partner.

PICTURE BOOK

You can also find an illustrated version in *The Children's Book of Virtues*, by William Bennett (New York: Simon & Schuster, 1995).

This is a very physical story, with lots of wriggling and sliding and hopping for the younger audience and more thoughtful listening and imagining for the older. Decide how you want to depict the hopping and slithering, whether with your hands, arms or whole body, and then invite the students to join you. You can also stop the tale and ask volunteers to demonstrate what would happen if a frog tried to slither, and if a snake tried to hop. Make sure you do this on a carpeted area with plenty of room to avoid injuries!

The story has a sad ending. Leave a little time to sit in the sadness that follows before jumping into discussion.

Tips for the telling

- **Whole-group dramatization:** If you have a large space you can act this out with the whole class or a few students at a time, with you as narrator. They will love to hop and slither about. Divide them into two groups of frogs and snakes and have one from each group be the "mother." For older students, let them act this out without full body movements, as they choose.

Follow-up activities
Tip for story retention

This is a story about animals in which one is a predator and the other prey, so it makes sense that they be taught not to be friends. However, it is also a model of how human beings have behaved down through history. All too often people only associate with others who look, talk, and act most like themselves. It is in branching out that we are challenged to grow and come more into our full selves. The two characters teach each other something new, and they find enjoyment and new possibilities for themselves in the process. They can laugh at themselves together and look forward to new learning.

Making a personal connection

- **Questions, discussion and story sharing:** I suggest starting the discussion by asking your students how the story made them feel. There are a number of possibilities in their responses, and all should be accepted. What would have happened if the mothers had not told them that they could not be friends? Have you ever been told that you could not be friends with someone because they were different? Tell about a time that you made friends with someone who seemed different from you in some way and what you learned from each other. It is also important to lead a discussion about why people are afraid of people that they think are "different," and how to move beyond that.

- **Biographical stories:** You might relate a story from Martin Luther King Jr.'s childhood. Until the age of six, he played every day with two white boys who were his neighbors. When he reached grade school, the boys' mother told him that they could not play together anymore because he was colored and they were white. This experience was the first of many that set him on his path for civil rights. See the picture book *My Brother Martin—A Sister Remembers*, by Christine King Farris (New York: Simon & Schuster Books for Young Readers, 2003).

Also see *Teammates*, by Peter Golenbock (San Diego: Harcourt, Brace and Jovanovich, 1990). In this true story, baseball player Pee Wee Reese stands up for Jackie Robinson, the first African-American player in the major leagues, when other players are ostracizing him.

- **Connecting to the characters:** Play "hot seat" and choose one student to come up and pretend to be one of the characters. Let the other students ask him or her questions. Alternatively, pair up the students and let them pretend to be frog or snake and interview each other.

Creative exploration

- **Creative adaptation:** Have students make up their own versions of this story using different animals, and coming up with different more satisfying endings. Older students could make modern versions in which students from different cultures discover that they can be friends even when others tell them they are not supposed to. What might they learn from one another?

Turning the story ideas into action

The best way to overcome fears and prejudices is to get to know other people that you think of as "different" to discover what you have in common and to experience their humanity.

- **Have a "mix it up" day** in which you encourage each child to spend some time getting to know someone new. You can try it in different ways, one day specifying only that the "new" person be someone that they do not consider a friend already. The next time it could be someone from a different ethnic group or social group. You might have them eat lunch together, or just get to know one another, or teach each other something, and then share it with the group.

- **Visual representations:** Encourage your students to make posters to remind them and others of the joy of making new friends, and reaching out to those who seem "different."

Anansci and His Gifted Sons

Once upon a time in Africa, Anansci's wife gave birth to a baby boy. "How strange he looks," Anansci said. "His eyes are too big. People will laugh at him." His wife, Aso, said, "Do not judge him harshly. His eyes will serve him well." Soon it became apparent that with his eyes, this son could see for miles and miles. Anansci named him See Far.

Not long after, another son was born. "How strange he looks," Anansci said, "His mouth is too big. People will laugh at him." Again Aso said, "Do not judge him harshly. His mouth will serve him well." Indeed, it was not long before they realized that this son could drink up a whole pond. They named him Drink Up the Waters.

Soon a third son was born. This one had huge muscles throughout his whole body. Again, Anansci worried that people would laugh, but his wife again reminded him that good things would come of it. Soon they realized that this son was so strong that he could pull huge tree trunks up and clear a forest in no time. They called him Forest Clearer.

Then came the fourth son. He too had big muscles, but only in his arms. Soon they saw that he could throw a stone with great speed and strength and it would land a mile away. They called him Stone Thrower.

Next came a son with unusually large hands and long sharp nails. Anansci was sure that he would be laughed at too. Soon they saw that with those hands and sharp nails he could skin a fish or a jaguar in no time. They called him Skinner of Game.

Finally, they had one last son. This one was enormous. He was as round as he was tall. Anansci worried that people would laugh at him. One last time Aso reminded him that good things would come of his size and shape. They called him Large as a Bed because he looked like one and the children liked to jump on him.

One day Anansci went for a journey to sell some wares. However, after a few weeks, he had not returned. Aso asked her son See Far to look and see if he was in trouble. See Far climbed a tree and saw his father some miles away, deep in the jungle in the middle of a deep lake in the belly of a huge fish. Then Aso called the others together.

"I will clear a road through the jungle so that we can rescue him," Forest Clearer said. Quickly he cleared the trees one after the other and the rest of his family followed behind.

When they reached the lake, they saw that the water was very deep, and they could not get to the fish. "I will drain the lake," said Drink Up the Waters. He crouched at the water's edge and began to drink until the lake was dry. There they found the huge fish.

Africa (Ashanti)

Grades K-4

THEMES: Respect, diversity, appreciation of difference, individual strengths, cooperation, non-judgment, loyalty

Now it was Skinner of Game's turn. He skinned the huge fish with several swipes of his hands, and out jumped Anansci. No sooner had they hugged him than a giant hawk swooped down and grabbed him up, so weak and thin was he. He flew up into the sky out of reach.

Now it was Stone Thrower's turn. He found a big stone and, taking aim, he let the stone fly high into the air until it struck the bird in the head. Down, down fell Anansci. "Oh, my husband! He will die!" cried Aso.

"No he won't, Mother," said Large as a Bed. He lay down on the ground and cushioned Anansci's fall, so that he did not hurt himself at all. Anansci and his family returned home.

Some time later, when Anansci was walking in the woods, he found a beautiful large white ball that glowed like a gem. He decided that he wanted to give it to one of his sons. He asked Nyame the Sky God to hold it for him until he had decided which of his sons had done the most to save his life. Nyame held the beautiful, glowing white ball in the sky for all of them to see. Anansci listened as each son argued as to why he had done the most to save his father. The sons argued and argued and could not agree. Finally, Anansci grew tired of listening. He decided that everyone had helped equally and that the gem needed to be shared. He told Nyame to keep the beautiful white ball, so that all beings could share in its light. That is why the moon resides up in the sky to this day.

As for Anansci, he loved all of his sons, and he never judged anyone for their different qualities again.

SOURCES

Anansci the Spider, retold in picture book form by Gerald McDermott (New York: Holt, Rinehart and Winston, 1972).

"Anansci," in *Moon Tales: Myths of the Moon from Around the World*, by Rina Singh and D. Lush (London: Bloomsbury Children's, 1999).

"Anansci's Rescue from the River," in *A Treasury of African Folklore*, by Harold Courlander (New York: Marlowe & Co., 1996).

This story has some unusual names. It is worth learning them, or changing them to ones that you can remember. This can be a fun one to act out with the class, giving small groups responsibility for coming up with a movement and sound for each son. There is also the repetition of Anansci repeatedly worrying that people will tease his odd children, and his wife repeatedly reminding him that some good shall come of it. For brevity, I have not repeated Aso's lines each time here, but with a group of younger students I would repeat them and have the students join me. This repetition reinforces the idea of non-judgment, and that good things come from our differences.

Tips for the telling

- **Round-robin retelling:** Sit in a circle and have each child add in a small part of the story, asking for help if they forget the sequence.
- **Draw the story:** Get the children into groups of six. Have each child make a picture of one of the brothers. Then have them put the pictures into the correct order to be able to retell the story using the pictures.

Follow-up activities
Tips for story retention

- **Questions, discussion, and story sharing:** Tell their own stories about ways in which they think they may have been teased for unusual qualities and how these might serve them. Tell about a time that they helped to solve a problem. It will help if you give some ideas, and share a story of your own first.
- **Acknowledging our own special qualities:** Let everyone in the class make up a name for themselves of what they do best, and what skill or talent they bring to the group. Display the list.

Making a personal connection

- **Create a class story** in which the list created above of everyone's special skills is used to solve an imaginary problem.
- **Creative adaptation:** Have the students each make a card with a character and a unique trait that they can do (e.g., a person with ears that stick up like a fox can hear people talking a mile away). Have the students put the cards in a hat and each pull out a different one. They then can make up a story with the same structure as the Anansci tale with five other students that use that character and its skill in solving the problem. I suggest that you read or tell the story of the Six Chinese Brothers (Cooperation) first so that they have more ideas to go on and a firmer sense of the story structure. Have the groups share their tales for one another.

Creative exploration

- **Share this story as a play with other classes:** Have your students reenact this story in small groups and take it on the road to other classrooms. Have them initiate discussion after the play about diversity.
- **Honoring one another's gifts:** Have students in the class pick one person and tell the class something special about them.

Turning the story ideas into action

The Lions and the Tree Sprites

India (Buddhist)

Grades 2-8

THEMES: Diversity appreciation, tolerance, broad thinking

Once upon a time in a certain forest, there dwelt two tree sprites. Also living in this forest were several large and fierce lions. The lions had a fearsome roar that frightened the animals of the forest and the people who lived on the edge of the forest. They preyed on the animals and any people that dared to enter the forest and then left the bones lying around for all to see.

One day, one of the tree sprites said to the other, "I am so tired of listening to those lions roar and of seeing the other animals run in fear—and oh, all of those unsightly bones they leave lying around! I think I will scare them away and they can live in some other forest."

The other tree sprite shook her head. "Yes, it is true that they are loud and fierce and they do leave bones everywhere. But it would not be wise to send them away. They have always been here and they have a part to play here."

But the other sprite would not listen. She had made up her mind that the forest would be better off without the lions. So, she spent her days plotting ways to get rid of them.

Finally, one day she changed herself into a huge, terrifying monster, much larger than the lions, with a roar much louder than theirs. She roared into their cave, and told them to leave or she would eat them up. The two lions ran from their cave with the monster chasing them all the way out of the forest and into another land.

The next day it was very quiet in the forest, and the day after that. No new bones appeared on the forest floor. Then one day, the people from the nearby village tiptoed into the forest. "Are the lions gone?" they asked one another. "We no longer hear their roars. Perhaps it is safe now for us to come in." And so they did. They began to cut down the trees. Now the forest was filled with a new sound, that of trees falling to the ground, and the sound of new houses being built in the forest.

The tree sprites saw their beloved trees being cut down and they were terrified. "This would not have happened if the lions were here," said the foolish sprite. "Now I see why they were important to the forest." The tree sprites watched sadly as the trees were cut down, one after the other, and the animals and birds fled. Finally, all the trees were gone, and the two sprites had to leave in search of a new forest: a forest to protect by accepting all of its creatures.

SOURCES

Jataka Tales: Fables from the Buddha, edited by Nancy DeRoin (New York: Dell Publishing Co., Inc.).

I Once Was a Monkey: Stories Buddha Told, by Jeanne M. Lee (New York: Farrar, Straus, and Giroux, 1999).

The Jataka, or Stories of the Buddha's Former Births, edited by E.B. Cowell (Cambridge, England: The University Press, 1885).

You might start by telling the audience that this is a story from India about tree sprites. You can tell the class that they are perhaps like fairies that protect the trees. You might ask them to describe what they would look like before the story begins.

This story has several repeating sounds in it that could be used for audience participation: The repeated roaring sound of the lions, and then the crashing of trees. The quiet in the middle of the story could be used dramatically, as you portray the sprites, animals, and villagers listening for the lions' roars.

Tips for the telling

- **Round-robin retell:** Sit in a circle and let each child add a bit until the story is told.
- **News reporter retelling:** Put the students into groups of four and let the reporter interview the two sprites and the lions.

Follow-up activities
Tips for retention

- **Questions and discussion:** This is a powerful story for promoting protection of wildlife. It can also help us to be more tolerant of people we do not understand or fear. It can also help us to remember to stand back and look at the bigger picture before taking action or making judgments. Are there animals in the area where your students live that they are afraid of, or that are endangered?
- **Story sharing:** Do you ever wish that certain people were not around, or do you judge other people for behaving strangely, only to discover that they had good reasons for doing what they did? We cannot always know the reasons that people behave as they do. For instance, someone may appear cold or unfriendly, when actually they are terribly shy. Share stories about how first impressions are often wrong.

Making a personal connection

- **Story adaptation/creative writing:** Have the students make up a similar story as if they were the sprite responsible for a certain environment, whether it is natural or human made. Something in the environment causes problems, and what they do as the sprite changes the environment for the worse.

Creative exploration

- **Research:** This story has obvious environmental implications. You can research how endangered animals have changed the environment in your area, or how the introduction of a new animal or insect has affected the environment.
- **Brainstorm** ways to celebrate the diversity in the school population. You might focus on ethnic diversity and have each child do a short presentation on his or her cultural background by bringing in food, music, objects or clothing, or telling a story from his or her culture.
- **Journaling for self-awareness:** Have students keep a journal in which they notice and challenge their fears and assumptions about others who appear different. You may want to keep these confidential between student and teacher and then have them process what they have learned together in the end.

Turning the story ideas into action

The Lost Ax

China

Grades 4-8

THEMES: Cultivating a nonjudgmental mind, mindfulness

One morning a farmer stepped outside of his door to begin his wood chopping. He reached for his ax on the hook where he always kept it, but it was not there. "Wife, did you take my ax?" he called.

"No, dear," she answered.

Why wasn't it there, he wondered. Did someone else take it? He said, "Someone has stolen my ax!"

He looked over at his neighbor's yard. There was his neighbor. The farmer noted that today the neighbor looked as if he had something to hide. "He is avoiding my eyes," he thought. "He knows I am here, but he is not looking at me. Oh now he even turns his back." He noted too that the man was moving about in a nervous, shifty manner.

The farmer went back into the house and told his wife, "That no-good neighbor of ours has stolen my ax."

"Maybe, dear," she cautioned, "but look around more before you accuse him."

So the man walked around his yard, grumbling and turning often to watch the neighbor, who clearly seemed to have something to hide. Then at the far edge of his property, by the tree that he had been cutting the day before, the farmer found his trusty ax, lying where he had left it when he had suddenly been called away.

The man looked over at his neighbor. He was still working in his yard, concentrating so hard on his task that he did not look up. The man was busy, and he moved quickly and carefully. "What a good and hard worker my neighbor is," thought the man, lifting his ax to his shoulder and heading off to begin his day's work.

SOURCES

"The Stolen Ax," in *Wisdom Tales from Around the World*, by Heather Forest (Little Rock: August House Publishers, Inc. 1996).

"The Missing Ax," in *Favorite Folktales from Around the World*, edited by Jane Yolen (New York: Pantheon Press, 1986).

This is a very short tale, which is over almost as soon as it begins. You may want to draw it out, adding more humorous examples of what the judgmental man notices about his neighbor. You can give it a little more introduction as to place and character if you wish. Think of how you end the story so that the audience knows it is over—maybe saying "The end"—and have just enough imagery and feeling to want to dwell contentedly there for a time.

- **Police investigation retelling:** Get students into groups of four: a police person, the old man, the old woman, and the neighbor. Have them pretend that the man called the police to report his ax stolen and his suspicions about the neighbor. Then before the police arrive, he finds his ax. The policeman asks questions of the others to get to the bottom of what happened.

- **Questions and discussion:** This story can help us to be more aware of how quickly we rush to judgment about others, and how often we are wrong.

- **Perspective changes:** Let the students retell it to one another as if they were various characters, such as the man, the wife, the ax, and the neighbor.

- **Telling personal stories:** Share stories together about times when you rushed to judgment about another person, or had someone accuse you of something you did not do.

- **Creative adaptation:** Invite your students to make up versions of this story in which the main character accuses someone of something and then turns out to be wrong, with interesting consequences. You may want to start by brainstorming a list of the kinds of assumptions we make about people that turn out to be wrong.

- **Sharing the story:** Have small groups dramatize their version of this tale with other classes, and then have them generate a discussion about how we judge people quickly and often find ourselves to be wrong.

- **Look at stereotyping and name-calling:** This happens around ethnicity, and "typing" one another into certain groups. Brainstorm types of judgments that are made in the school community and how these hurt people. Discuss ways to bring people to greater awareness about this.

- **Visual representation:** Generate some posters to urge people not to stereotype or judge others.

Once Upon a Time...

Wisdom of the Elders

Rumania, Japan,
and Russia

Grades 3-8

THEMES: Forgiveness,
wisdom, courage, respect
for the elderly, caring

Long ago in a small village in Rumania, the people believed that when people got old and could no longer work, they were no longer useful. At one time when food was scarce, it became the custom that families would put their old people on a sled and leave them at the top of the mountain to die, so that they would not have to feed them. Though this seems terribly sad and cruel, it happened in different parts of the world long ago.

Now there was a man who lived with his wife and son and his aged mother on a farm. His mother had become too old to work, and she sat by the stove each day and talked with her family. Her hands shook too much to even sew or cook. The farmer knew that his mother had reached that age, but he said nothing. He could not bear to lose her. However, neighbors were starting to stare. One day the mother said, "Son, it is time to take me to the mountains."

So early the next day, the man put her on a sled and began to set off up the mountain path. His small son begged to be allowed to come on the journey, to be able to say goodbye to his beloved grandmother. The man agreed. When they reached the mountaintop, the man hugged his mother and turned to go.

The boy called after his father, "Father, do not leave the sled—I will need it to carry you up the mountain when you are old."

The man stopped in his tracks. How could he expect his son not to do the same to him as he had done to his mother? He picked up the rope of the sled and began to tow his mother back down the mountain. After thinking a great while, he spoke. "Now we must keep this a secret, but we will keep grandmother in the cellar. We will feed her and visit her every day. That way she will be well, and we will not have to be without her." And so it was that under the cover of darkness they returned the old mother to the house and made a place for her in the cellar.

Not long after this, there was a terrible famine in the land. No rain fell and the crops did not grow. For seven years, the harvest was very poor. The people had so little food that they ate all of their wheat and rye down to the very last grain. The next season when it was time to plant, they had no seeds to plant. No one knew what to do.

The old woman had been noticing that every night the pieces of bread they brought her were smaller and smaller and were no longer of wheat, but hard barley. "My son," she said, "I do not want to complain, but I notice that you bring me less and less bread each night, and now you bring me barley bread. I would eat it if I could, but it is too hard for this old mouth with few teeth left. Is there no more wheat bread?"

114

ONCE UPON A TIME

"No, Mother," he replied. "There is a terrible famine and we have eaten even our wheat seed. Now there is nothing to plant and almost nothing to eat. We shall surely starve next year, unless a miracle occurs."

"I do not think you will need a miracle, son," she said. "Is there any thatch left on the roof of the barn?"

"Yes, mother," he replied.

"Go and take the thatch from half of the roof and thresh it," she suggested. "You should find enough grain to plant."

The farmer did as his mother suggested and, sure enough, there was enough seed in the thatch of the roof that he could plant his fields. When he returned and thanked her, she suggested that he take the thatch from the other side of his roof to save for eating.

When the farmer's neighbors saw the man planting, they asked him how he had managed to find seed. He told them that his wise mother had told him what to do.

"But you took your mother to the mountain years ago," they said.

"No, I hid her in the cellar, for I could not bear to have her die. Now I see that it was wrong to think that she had no value in her old age. It was her wisdom that saved me, and you too may be saved."

Never again in that place did they think that people had no value when they grew old, for they had learned that the elderly keep the wisdom, just as the thatch keeps the seeds.

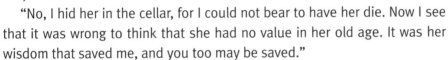

SOURCES

"Grandfather's Sled," in *Thirty-Three Multicultural Tales to Tell*, retold by Pleasant DeSpain (Little Rock: August House, 1993).

"Grandfather's Advice," in *More Tales of Faraway Folk*, by Babette Deutsch and Avraham Yarmolinsky (New York: Harper and Row, 1963).

"The Land Where There Were No Old Men," from *Rumanian Folk Tales*, by Jean Ure (New York: Franklin Watts, Inc., 1960).

CULTURAL VARIANTS

Japan: "The Wise Old Woman," from *The Sea of Gold and Other Tales from Japan*, adapted by Yoshiko Uchida (New York: Charles Scribner and Sons, 1965).

Italy: "The Wooden Bowl," in *Old Italian Tales*, by Domenico Vittorini (New York: David McKay and Co, 1958).

Nepal: "The Doko," retold by Barbara Lipke in *Spinning Tales, Weaving Hope: Stories, Storytelling, and Activities for Peace, Justice and the Environment*, edited by Ed Brody, et al. (Philadelphia: New Society: 1992).

Tips for the telling

You will have to think of how you will present the idea that long ago in a number of cultures, older people were not valued and were sometimes taken or left to die when they reached a certain age or level of incapacity.

The tale can be told in a very straightforward manner, or from the perspective of one of the characters, such as a grandson or daughter.

Follow-up activities
Tip for retention

- **Gossips:** Have partners pretend to be the town gossips telling each other what has happened.

Making a personal connection

- **Questions and discussion:** What questions did the story evoke in your students? What part, phrase, or image stuck in their minds?

- **Personal experience stories:** Who do the students know who is elderly? What have they learned from them? Tell about a time spent with a grandparent or older person. What wisdom or skill do they have that the students do not have?

Creative exploration

- **Creative adaptation:** Modernize this story. What if a law were passed decreeing that all persons over the age of 70 were taken off to "Isle of the Elders"? What types of knowledge would be lost, and what problems might arise? Create a hero or heroine who would be brave enough to go and ask for help from the elders and to free them.

Turning the story ideas into action

- **Interviewing elders:** What information do elders have that a younger person would not? Have students go and talk to an older person to find out what they can learn from them that someone younger would not know.

- **Group projects:** Elders in today's society often feel left out and left behind. How can your class help the elders in your community to feel appreciated and needed?

The Blind Men and the Elephant

Once upon a time six blind scholars heard that an elephant was in the town square. They decided that they wanted to experience it for themselves. They were led to where the elephant stood.

The first man stepped forward and grasped the elephant's long, smooth, and pointed tusk. "So long and smooth and sharp! This elephant is like a sword!" he said.

The second blind man stepped forward just as the elephant swung out its long trunk. He touched the trunk all up and down, and exclaimed, "This creature is like a giant snake!"

The third man stepped forward and touched the broad side of the elephant. "So big, so wide, this creature is like a wall!" he declared.

The fourth man, quite taller than the rest, stepped forward and touched the elephant's ear. He said, "So flexible and thin, and how it moves about. This elephant is like a fan!"

The fifth man, a bit shorter than the others stepped forward and touched the elephant about the knee. "So sturdy, so strong, this elephant is like a great tree trunk," he announced.

Finally, the sixth man stepped forward, though he was actually standing at the elephant's rear, and was quickly struck by the elephant's tail swishing this way and that. "So long, and thin. This elephant is like a rope!" he added.

Then the six men went and sat in the teashop, drinking their favorite tea and debating about the nature of an elephant. Was it like a wall, a fan, a sword, a rope, a snake, or a tree? They will never say, because they could not agree!

India

Grades 3-8

THEMES: Judgment, points of view or perspective, stereotypes, the need for broader awareness before making decisions

SOURCES

Buddhist Parables, translated from Pali by Eugene Watson Burlingame (Delhi: Banarsidass Publishers, 1991).

PICTURE BOOKS

The Six Blind Men and the Elephant: A Traditional Indian Story, retold by Claire Boucher (Cambridge, Mass.: Candlewick Press, 2000).

The Six Blind Men and the Elephant, retold by Karen Bachstein (New York: Scholastic 1992).

Tips for the telling

In order to remember the sequence of elephant parts, you may want to imagine how the blind men start at the head of the elephant and walk around its head and finally end up at the tail. However, the sequence does not matter at all! The more you can include mime and description, the more your students will picture the elephant parts as you describe them.

Follow-up activities
Tip for story retention

- **Group retelling:** Divide the students into six groups, each representing one of the blind men. As you retell the story, call on each group in turn to act out feeling that part of the elephant, and then as a group deciding and telling the audience what the part is. This will get many laughs, while reinforcing the ideas and sequence.

Making a personal connection

- **Questions and discussion:** This story offers a great opportunity to raise awareness about prejudice and assumptions people make about one another based on very little information. You might ask the students to reflect on the saying, "Don't judge a book by its cover," and how this relates to this story, and then to experiences they have had in life.

- **Personal story sharing:** Try to come up with some examples of times when you saw something from one perspective and then learned to see the larger picture. Do your students ever feel that people have judged them wrongly? Let them share these stories.

Creative exploration

- **Creative adaptation:** What else could you use besides an elephant to tell this tale? Could it be Martians coming to earth and seeing a car and thinking it is a house until it drives away? Have students write and share personal stories about a time when they made assumptions about someone or something and then learned that there was much more to them.

Turning the story ideas into action

- **Story sharing:** Invite students to share this story as a play with other classes, whether in original or modernized adapted form. Older students can then lead a discussion with peers about how the story relates to their lives and issues around diversity.

- **Reflect on prejudice and judgment in the school community:** Brainstorm about ways and places in which students judge one another and put one another into groups based on certain characteristics. This could begin with noticing who sits with whom in the cafeteria, if there are groups of students that are given names. Are students are given a descriptive name by others, such as "nerd" or "jock"? How does this limit them?

- **Create opportunities to break stereotypes** and get to know one another. Brainstorm ways in which students can break out of groups and get to know others as full people. Try a lottery system in which everyone picks a name out of a hat and gets to know that person for one hour. Then students write something about what they learned about their match. Helpful guidelines could be to have them tell each other stories about special times in their lives, favorite activities, books, etc.

- **Journaling** can help students to see when and how they prejudge others, and to help them to step back from it.

Switching Jobs

Once upon a time in the foothills of Norway, in the middle of a field, there stood a farmhouse. In that farmhouse lived a man and a woman and their little baby. Now every day the man went out and worked in the fields and chopped wood for the fire, while the woman stayed in or near the house and cooked and spun and took care of the baby. The man was frequently in a bad temper when he returned home at the end of the day. "Why do I have to do all of the hard work?" he would grumble. "I come home and you are whistling in the kitchen or sitting by the fire rocking the baby."

"I have just as much hard work to do as you, dear," his wife would say.

"Oh no, you don't!" he would grumble.

Finally, one day the wife grew tired of this talk and she said, "I have a fine idea. Why don't you stay home today and do my share of the work and I will do yours."

"Huh! A fine idea indeed," her husband replied. "We'll see how you like it! You've got to plow the main field and bring in enough wood for the evening."

"Fine," she said. "You've got to bake the bread, cook the soup, tend the baby, churn the butter and take care of the cow."

"Child's play," he laughed and waved her off.

The next morning, the wife went off to work in the field. The man decided that the first thing he should do was to bake the bread. He stoked up the fire and made the dough. He had never actually made bread, but he had watched his mother do it dozens of times. Still he forgot the yeast, but into the oven it went. "While the bread bakes," he thought, "I'll churn the butter so that we can have some warm bread with butter on it." He started to churn the butter, but it was hard work, and he soon decided that he wanted a drink of cold ale. He ran down into the cellar and was just filling his mug from the big barrel, when he heard a thud and a cry. He ran up the stairs to find that the baby had knocked over the urn and was sitting in a puddle of cream. He began to clean up the mess when he remembered that he had left the spigot to his ale barrel open. He ran into the cellar to find that all of the ale he had brewed was spilled on the floor. Again, the baby was wailing so he ran upstairs. He cleaned up the baby, but she continued to cry.

"You must be hungry," he said. He looked at the bread in the oven but it was flat and burned. He got the pot for porridge. "I need some more cream," he thought and went to the creamery and found more cream. Then the baby began to cry again because she had not been fed any breakfast. "OK, I'll make you porridge. I just need to get some water from the well."

He decided that he should not leave the urn full of cream on the floor as he did the last time, so he fastened it on his back with a rope. Then he went

Norway

Grades 2-8

THEMES: Appreciation of the work of others, judgment, walking in another's shoes, respect, diverse strengths

to the well for water, but when he leaned over the well, the cream in the urn on his back flowed down his neck and into the well, turning the water a creamy white.

"Unbelievable!" he said. "I'll bet the wife is even more exhausted than I am by now. She's probably half dead being dragged by the horse through the freshly plowed earth." Thinking of the horse dragging his wife reminded him that the cow had not been fed or watered at all that day. He went to the barn and gave the cow a drink. Then he decided that rather than taking her all the way down to pasture while he had so much still to do, he could let her graze on the roof, which was covered with thick grass. He took two planks of wood and, resting them against the hill at the back of the house, he pushed the cow onto the roof. Then, thinking that he did not want the cow to run off, he took the rope around her neck, dropped it down through the smoke hole of the house and, when he got inside, tied the other end around his waist. "I'll bet the wife never thought of this!" he laughed. Again, he began to churn the butter, realizing that he had not stopped for a bite to eat or to rest for one minute and that he was exhausted.

The cow was not accustomed to grazing on the roof and soon wandered to the edge and fell off. When she did, the rope attached to the man inside the house was suddenly pulled tight. Down he fell and he was quickly pulled upside down halfway up the chimney.

Sometime later, the wife finished her work in the field and gathered some wood for splitting. She was carrying it home to split when she heard a terrible sound coming from behind the house. There she saw the cow dangling off the roof, mooing piteously. She grabbed the scythe and cut the cow down. As she did, she heard a thud and a yell in the house as the husband fell into the ashes of the fireplace. The baby was crying with hunger and covered in a sticky cream. There was no bread, no soup, and no butter.

"Did you have a nice day, dear?" she asked pleasantly. "Shall we do it again tomorrow? I'm tired, but think I could get to like this."

"No, that's all right, dear," he said, as he picked himself up, dusted off the black soot that covered him head to toe, and went out back to wash up. As you can imagine, the man went quietly back to the fields the next day and never was heard to grumble about who had the harder work again.

SOURCES

Maid of the North: Feminist Folk Tales from Around the World, by Ethel Johnston Phelps (New York: Henry Holt and Co., 1981).

"The Husband Who Was Never Pleased," from *French Folktales,* by Henri Pourrat (New York: Pantheon Books, 1989).

"The Old Man and Woman Who Switched Jobs," from *Favorite Folktales from Around the World,* edited by Jane Yolen (New York: Pantheon Press, 1986).

This tale was obviously written during a time when there was a clearer division of work in the home. Now most men and women share in more of the housework and cooking, and many women work outside of the home. Still I think it is widely appreciated that women are especially good at multitasking, which is what the man in this story found so impossible to do. I include this tale not to cause male listeners to feel put down, but because I believe the story is useful in helping us to appreciate all kinds of work, and that we should not be quick to judge someone else's work as easier or worth less. It can help us to be more respectful of what others do to help our lives to run more smoothly. It can help us to be more inquisitive into the work of others.

In one version of this story, in *Maid of the North: Feminist Folk Tales from Around the World* by Ethel Johnston Phelps, the story ends with the man and woman agreeing to share both jobs, alternating several days a week. It would be interesting to let the students decide what ending they would find most fitting and fair.

The story is meant to be humorous, with a chain of events that goes from bad to worse in quick succession. You want to learn the order well enough to be able to reel them off and to picture them in your head so that you can imagine how the farmer looked more and more rattled and messy as the story unfolds. If you want to add audience participation, you might have the man repeatedly ask the audience, "What was I supposed to be doing?" or "Where was I?" He could also say, "I'll bet the wife never thought of that," as he tried one or more of his harebrained schemes.

- **Group retelling with student drawings:** Have the students draw pictures depicting various scenes in the story. Then sequence the pictures for a group show and retelling.

- **Group retelling with drama:** Older students will enjoy depicting various scenes through skits in small groups.

- **Questions and discussion:** This story can help to build an awareness and appreciation for types of work that are undervalued in terms of pay, and often in the minds of others. Many people work very hard for low pay to clean our buildings and to provide us with basic services and goods that we take for granted. It is also a place to have a discussion about the value of the job of housewife. I suggest generating discussions about different types of chores or work that students have engaged in, and what they found most difficult. You might also remind them of the saying, "Do not judge a person until you have walked a mile in his moccasins." It will have greater meaning.

- **Personal story sharing:** Students will relate to this as a story about siblings and chore loads, or about what they notice about the division of labor between their parents. They could have fun retelling it as if it were happening at their house.

Follow-up activities
Tips for story retention

Making a personal connection

Creative exploration

- **Creative adaptation:** Let the students modernize the tale. Suggestions could be to make it a tale between siblings, or between a highly paid executive and the secretary, a doctor and nurse, or the people in the maintenance department and the principal.

Turning the story ideas into action

- **Research:** Let the students go and interview and or follow people (walk in their shoes) who do different jobs in the school and/or community and come back and tell the story of what that person does in a day. What were their assumptions before they observed the work, and what did they learn?

- **Begin a tradition** of celebrating each different member of the school staff by honoring the hard work that they do individually.

- **Journaling** to gain awareness of the judgments we make about other people without walking in their shoes.

Sir Gawain and Lady Ragnell, or the Loathly Lady and the Loyal Knight

Celtic

Grades 5-adult

THEMES: Loyalty, tolerance, courage, friendship, respect

Long ago in the days of King Arthur, there was one knight who stood above all the rest for his courage and his loyalty to the king. This was Gawain, the king's own nephew.

The story began in the fall of the year when the leaves had turned gold and lay upon the ground. King Arthur and his men had gone out on the hunt. When they returned in the late afternoon, the King was not with them. Gawain waited for him at the gate.

Late in the evening, the King returned alone. He was pale and visibly shaken. Gawain pressed him. "What happened, my lord? You look terrible."

"The strangest thing happened, Gawain. I was out on the hunt, when I fell behind the others. Perhaps I was dilly-dallying or fell into a daydream. Suddenly a huge buck leaped across the path in front of me. I followed naturally into the thick of the forest. I shot one arrow after the other as we wove in and out of the trees. Finally, we reached a clearing. I had but one arrow left. The deer stood directly in front of me. I took aim and shot. Just as that arrow should have pierced the deer's heart, it vanished. Then suddenly from behind me, I heard the sound of thundering hooves, and I turned to see a large gray horse bearing a knight in full armor. He raised his sword as if to strike."

"Who was this knight?" Gawain asked.

"He said that he was Sir Gromer, and that he sought revenge for our taking of the Northlands. He said he wished to kill me, but saw that I was not armed and that it would not be a noble killing. He told me that he would give me a chance to live. 'Come back in one year's time,' he told me, 'with the answer to this riddle and I will spare your life. Answer wrongly and I will gladly kill you then.'"

"What was the riddle, sire?" Gawain asked.

"That was the strangest part. For he asked me what a woman most desires and deserves in the world."

"Well this should be easy, sire. There are thousands of women in the kingdom and at least one of them has to know. We will send riders to every home, we will find the answer. Do not fear."

The next day and every day after for many months, riders traveled to every home in the kingdom asking the women what they most desired and deserved. They went to the home of a newlywed, who answered, "Children."

Others said, "Wealth," "Wisdom," "Beauty," "Love," and "Good Health." Everywhere they went, they seemed to get a different answer.

Three hundred and sixty-four days went by. The leaves had again turned gold upon the trees. King Arthur rode out of the palace gates on his horse. His head was down as he thought about how he must face Sir Gromer with an answer the next day, and how none of the answers had seemed quite the truest of all. Suddenly his horse reared up, as there in front of them at the crossroads sat a beast upon the stone wall. She was in human form, but barely. A bag of bones she was, with a bald head, sporting several spikes of coarse hair and red bulging eyes. Her lips hung low and great horse-like teeth protruded. She was hunched and her head cocked to one side.

"Look at you, King Arthur," she said. " All depressed because you don't know the answer to the question."

"It's none of your business if I do or don't," he answered and turned his horse to go.

"Well, I do know the answer," she spoke again, half laughing.

"Oh," the King answered, "how is it that you know?"

"My name is Lady Ragnell. Sir Gromer is my stepbrother, and I know everything in his foul and simple mind."

The King got down off his horse and knelt before her. "I would give you anything—silver or gold—for the answer."

"I have no need for silver of gold," she laughed.

"Then you name the price, my lady."

"I wish to marry Sir Gawain." She smiled and sat back.

"Gawain! Well he is not mine to give away. I couldn't," the King stammered.

"That's right. If you want the answer, he must freely ask for my hand."

The King was so flummoxed that he paced back and forth on the road, unable to speak. At last, the loathly lady stood up and spoke. "I'll be here tomorrow if you make up your mind. My name is Lady Ragnell." Off she moved into the forest.

King Arthur rode back to the palace slowly. He wanted to live, but he was not willing to force Gawain to marry a barely human beast. He decided not to mention his meeting. However, when he returned, there was Gawain waiting for him. He could easily see that the King was upset and badgered him until the King told him of the beastly woman who knew the answer, and her price.

"Uncle," Gawain said, "if the answer she gives you spares your life, I will gladly marry her." No description the King gave, however vivid, could change his mind.

And so the next day, the two of them rode out to that place at the crossroads. There sat the beastly Lady Ragnell. She laughed loudly, "I knew you'd be back."

Gawain got down on one knee and took her bony, hairy hand in his. "My lady," he said, "if the answer you give spares my uncle, I will gladly marry you this very eve."

"Fine," said Ragnell. "You are a man of your word." She gave the answer to the King.

King Arthur rode alone to that clearing in the forest. No sooner had he stopped his horse than he again heard the thundering hooves and saw the knight with his sword held high.

"All right, King Arthur. Let's hear the answer that you do not have."

King Arthur spoke clearly and slowly. "What a woman most desires and deserves in the world is sovereignty, the ability to be the ruler of her own life. To decide who she will be, how she will live, and whom she will love."

There was a moment's silence as the knight turned a deep shade of red and began to tremble in his armor. "You didn't think of that yourself. It was my trouble-making stepsister, Ragnell. ARRRRGGGHHH!" He galloped out of the clearing, and King Arthur's life was spared.

King Arthur rode back to the crossroads where Gawain and Ragnell waited. When Gawain saw his uncle alive and well, he formally asked for Ragnell's hand in marriage. She accepted, and he helped her up onto his horse. They rode back to the palace.

That evening the wedding was held in the chapel, and there was a celebration in the great hall. All of the guests were silent or whispering, "How could he? She must be very rich." Only Ragnell smiled and laughed the night away. Finally, when the last guest had left, Gawain escorted Ragnell to his chamber and they were alone.

"My husband, you have been good to me so far. You have not shown pity or revulsion, and so I have decided that I would like to be kissed."

Gawain took a breath. "Yes, my lady, it is your right." Closing his eyes, he placed a kiss on those horrid lips. He felt a strange sensation and opened his eyes.

The beastly Ragnell was gone, and there in front of him stood a lovely young woman! She had long brown hair and flashing green eyes.

"What kind of sorcery is this?" he asked, shaking.

"It is sorcery indeed," Ragnell answered. "You see, my stepbrother hated me because I would not bend to his will. I would not be who he wanted me to be, or act as he thought I should act. And so, with the help of my stepmother, they cast a spell on me. A spell that said that I would remain in the beastly form until the finest knight of England would marry me of his own accord."

"We have broken the spell," cried Gawain, grabbing her hands and dancing her around the room.

"Well kind of," she answered. "You see, I can only stay like this half of the time, either as a beauty for you when we are alone in our room at night, and a beast for the world to see during the day—or a beauty for the world, and a beast when we are alone. You decide, but think carefully."

Gawain bowed his head, as if to think, but the first thing that came to him was the answer to the riddle. "My lady," he spoke, "this is not an answer that I can give. You must decide how you would be. Beauty by day or beauty by night—whatever you decide, I will abide."

A smile spread on Ragnell's face and she took Gawain's hands and danced him around the room. "You have answered well! For the answer you give breaks the spell completely. For the spell said that if the finest knight would not only marry me of his own accord, but if he would also let me choose how I would be, I would be truly free. I think that we are both free!"

The happy couple took hands and danced around that room until the sun came up in the sky. There began the truly happy marriage of Sir Gawain and Lady Ragnell.

SOURCES

You can find versions of this tale in many sources, including *The Canterbury Tales* by William Chaucer.

"Gawain and the Lady Ragnell," in *Maid of the North: Feminist Folktales from Around the World*, by Ethel Johnston Phelps (New York: Henry Holt, Co., 1981).

"What Women Most Desire," in *Happily Ever After*, edited by Melissa Bunce (Little Rock: August House Publishers, 2003).

PICTURE BOOK

Sir Gawain and the Loathly Lady, retold by Selina Hastings (New York: Mulberry Books, 1987).

This is a longer tale, taking approximately 12 minutes if told as it is written here.

Be sure that your audience is ready to sit. They will be engrossed by this one. I suggest that you have a large sign with the word "sovereignty" written on it to show to the group, as many students are not familiar with it. I always give more of a definition in the story, as I have done here, so that audience members are not confused and taken out of the story. You could teach them the word first, but that would give away the answer. A good story often has an element of suspense.

In this tale, there are opportunities to stop and contemplate the answer to the riddle when it is first put forth, and to consider how Gawain should decide at the end. You may stop the story and ask students to talk with a partner or write down their answer. You can then share them on the spot, or at the end.

I suggest practicing this tale and developing the characters. If each has a distinct voice and manner it will be more effective.

- **Gossips:** Have small groups of students pretend to be gossips among the castle's workers who retell what they know about the story to one another.

- **News reporter retelling:** Put the students in groups of five and having four of them each choose a part from the four main characters. The fifth will be newscaster interviewing them to get the story down for prime time TV.

- **Questions and discussion:** Why did Sir Gromer cast a spell on Lady Ragnell? How do you think Ragnell felt being in the beastly form? Why was it so important for her to have control over her own life? How was Sir Gawain able to make the decision to marry the beastly Ragnell? How would you have answered the first and second questions in the story?

- **Discussion:** Sir Gromer is a bully. He cannot tolerate Ragnell being different than he wants her to be. He makes her ugly in the eyes of the world. How do bullies try to make people who they think are different "ugly"? You can posit the idea that all of us have some of each of the characters' tendencies in us. Sometimes we may feel more like Sir Gromer, sometimes like Sir Gawain toward others. We also have a Ragnell who wants to be ourselves and not have to be like others. Explore each of these in writing and discussion. Encourage them to notice for a day when each of those voices speaks to them and to write about it at the end of the day. This requires the ability to reflect metaphorically. If you help them, many can do it at the level of grades 6-8. They can tell about these experiences as stories. We have all been bullied, particularly if we have siblings. We have almost all been the butt of a bully's wrath. This exercise can build sensitivity and greater awareness.

  The spell that Gromer casts is an example of a bully's need to feel that he or she has "power over" another. This power-over takes many forms, from physical hurt to threats to exclusion. Help your students to think about how and where they see themselves or others trying to have power over someone else and why.

- **Survey:** Ask all students anonymously what they most desire and deserve in the world. Display these on the wall.

Tips for the telling

Follow-up activities

Tips for story retention

Making a personal connection

- **Connect to the characters:** Play "hot seat," allowing a different student (or teacher) to take a chair as one of the characters in the story and let the class ask questions. This might be especially enlightening for Ragnell and Sir Gromer, who can help explain why bullies pick on others.

Creative exploration

- **Creative adaptation:** Retell the story with different answers to the riddle. Placing the story in a modern setting, such as a school. Many of them will have seen "Shrek," which is sort of a reverse of this story. Let them make their own versions.

Turning the story ideas into action

- **Brainstorm:** Where have bullying and "ugly-spell casting" happened in the class or grade or school and brainstorm ways to stop it. Talk about tolerance and how to let people be themselves. Have students tell each other things about themselves that are different for which they want to be respected. Talk about how we stereotype one another. Examples are nerds, jocks, etc.

- **Make posters** promoting individuality in the many aspects of our lives. Make up skits and stories about individuality, bullying, and tolerance and share them with other classes.

- **Retell as a play:** Act out the story of Gawain and Ragnell as a small play for large or small groups. Have students initiate discussion with the audience about bullying.

Favorite picture books

The Ugly Duckling, by Hans Christian Andersen. Many picture book versions. Pre-K-2.

The Story of Ferdinand, by Munro Leaf (New York: Puffin Books, 1977). This generation of students needs this story as much as previous generations have. Just because of his size, Ferdinand is judged to be a fighter. In the end, he is allowed to be himself, a lover of flowers and peace.

A Bad Case of the Stripes by David Shannon (New York: Blue Sky Press, 1998). Grades 2-5. A tale about a little girl who wants to be different, but feels she can't show her true self without being laughed at. She develops an illness in which she turns into everything she sees until a wise woman helps her to be herself.

Molly's Pilgrim, by Barbara Cohen (New York: Bantam Skylark, 1990). Grades 2-5. A little girl moves from Russia to America and is made fun of for her appearance, accent, and poor English skills. At Thanksgiving, her mom makes a pilgrim for the school diorama in the image of herself, and the students learn that modern-day immigrants are pilgrims too.

Older students Grades 6-8

See Studs Terkel's interview with C.P. Ellis, the former Ku Klux Klan member who tore up his Klan card and became a civil rights supporter. His friendship with African-American civil rights activist Ann Atwater inspired a book called *The Best of Enemies: Race and Redemption in the New South*, by Osha Gray Davidson (New York: Scribner, 1996). Terkel's interview also spawned a short documentary film called *An Unlikely Friendship*, by Diane Bloom, 2002.
www.oshadavidson.com—*The Best of Enemies*, how to order, chapter selections.
http://myhero.com—On Studs Terkel's work
www.filmakers.com—*An Unlikely Friendship*, how to order the film

Empathy

EMPATHY MEANS RELATING TO OTHER PEOPLE in a caring manner, putting oneself in their shoes. In practice, it could be listening to their story and hearing their feelings, then offering concern and support.

Few people value anything more than love and caring—it's a natural human inclination. From the day we are born, and likely before that, we need and thrive on love. Studies show that premature babies who are held have a better survival rate than those that are not. When we are loved and appreciated consistently, we learn to be able to give that to ourselves and to others. When love is withheld or is conditional, we will give it to ourselves only conditionally, or not at all, and then it is difficult for us to give it to others. Studies have shown that people who bully lack the ability to empathize and come from homes where there is little empathy toward them.

To feel empathy and love for others, we must know how to love and nurture ourselves. This is a skill learned mostly at home, where our primary love relationships are formed. It is difficult for a teacher to undo neglect and trauma, but every act of love that a child experiences teaches him or her that love and empathy are possible. Allowing children to experience these emotions through story increases the range of their emotional intelligence as well.

Love, caring, and empathy are driving forces behind so many good works in our world. Cures for disease, laws protecting the vulnerable, wars fought and lives lost to end brutality, and charitable contributions to helping organizations are examples of the impulse of love, caring, and empathy. A lack of empathy can lead to many forms of violence and abuse, including bullying.

Storytelling is a wonderful device for building empathy because it invites us to walk vicariously in the shoes of another. For the duration of the story, and however long it lives in our minds, we feel what the characters feel. We know what it is like to be who they are, experiencing what they are experiencing. Once you have known someone's story, it is difficult not to feel more empathetic toward them. As the Native American saying goes, "Do not judge a man until you have walked a mile in his moccasins." Storytelling allows you to walk that mile almost as closely as with actual experience.

How the Guinea Fowl
Got Her Spots

Africa

Grades K-3

THEMES: Friendship,
kindness, cooperation,
courage, reward,
cleverness

Once upon a time in a village on the edge of the African bush, there lived a cow and a flock of guinea hens. Now back in the old days, guinea hens were all black. They did not have speckles as they do today.

The guinea hen and the cow were friends. They often spent their days at the edge of the river where the grass was greenest and the bugs most plentiful. There they would chat and enjoy one another's company. The river was deep and fast, however, so they were careful not to fall in.

One day the flock of hens was making their way from the village along the edge of the river when they saw Cow quietly eating grass a bit further down the river than usual. Then they saw something else. Hiding behind a tree just beyond the riverbank, crouched low, its tail twitching back and forth, was a lion! The guinea hens looked at one another. That lion wanted to eat their friend Cow!

"We must protect Cow," they cooed quietly to one another.

"But we are no match for the lion!" one of them spoke.

"Together we can stop him so that Cow can run home!" said the third and smallest hen. This little hen took off down the riverbank and the other hens followed, running on their little feet, and making as much noise as they could. "Run, Cow, run!" they cried. But the lion was fast and sprang down onto the river bank, right between the guinea hens and the cow. The birds could feel the lion's hot breath on their faces, he was so close. The littlest bird thought fast. She felt the dry sand of the riverbank on her feet and quickly dropped down as if bowing. But in the next second she began to fan the dry sand into the lion's face. The other birds saw what she was doing and began to do likewise. "Run, Cow, run!" they cried.

"How dare you?" roared the lion as he tried to rub the sand from his eyes and twisted in agony. The birds continued to throw sand into the lion's face until he tried to run away. Unable to see where he was going, he fell right into the deep stream and was swept away.

That night the guinea hens went to visit Cow to see that she had made it home safely.

"I have thought of a way to thank you for saving my life and to protect you at the same time," said Cow. They followed her back to her yard until they came to an old bucket. Cow dipped her tail in the bucket and then began to shake it all over the guinea hens.

"Spread your wings," she said. "That way I can better cover you." The guinea hens spread their black wings as the drops of white milk rained down

130

ONCE UPON A TIME

all over them. When she was done, they looked beautiful—and speckled, just as they are today.

"This is a wonderful reward, Cow," the birds said. "But how does it protect us?"

"Well," said Cow. "When that old lion comes back, he will be angry at you for keeping him from his dinner. He will look for black hens, but he will not find anything but speckled ones. We can tell him that the black hens were so afraid that they ran away and never came back!" And that is what they did.

Those spots still help the guinea hen today, when she needs to hide in the bushes and not be seen by lions, or anyone else.

SOURCE

The Complete Tales of Uncle Remus, retold by Richard Chase (Boston: Houghton Mifflin, 1955/1983).

PICTURE BOOK

How the Guinea Fowl Got Her Spots, retold by Barbara Knutson (Minneapolis: Carolrhoda Books, Inc., 1990).

Tips for the telling

As this is a pourquoi story, it is useful to show a picture of the guinea hen before telling the story. There are lots of movements and some repetitive phrases that the students can learn in advance, or during the story.

Follow-up activities
Tips for story retention

- **Sequencing through drawing:** Have the students divide a large piece of paper into four sections and draw parts of the story in each one. Box 1: how the guinea hen looked before the change; box 2: what happened in the story to cause the cow to want to reward the hen; box 3: hen getting her reward; box 4: the hen with her new spots. Let the students take the four-part picture home to use as a guide as they retell the story to a family member.

Making a personal connection

- **Questions and discussion:** This is a good story to foster a discussion about helping out a classmate who is being bullied. It acknowledges the danger of standing up to someone who we perceive to be more powerful, and it can help facilitate a discussion of why we might not have intervened in the past. It is also a story about cooperation and friendship.

- **Story sharing:** Talk about times when you might have seen a friend or classmate being bullied or teased and wanted to help. What did you do or not do and how did it feel? What could you have done?

Creative exploration

- **Creative adaptation:** This is a pourquoi story, which explains how something came to be. Have the students make up stories about how else the guinea hen could have gotten her spots. This story could also be updated to happen on a modern farm or in a school yard with students. Maybe the students could get some kind of medal for bravery instead of spots!

- **Connecting to the characters:** Let the students pretend to be the brave little hen and retell the story to another group of students. Retelling as a drama will also help.

Turning the story ideas into action

- **Role-playing:** Help your students to practice being brave in situations in which bullying occurs by role-playing scenarios. Have them try out different responses to different types of bullying and discuss the pluses and minuses and feelings of each.

- **Awards:** Have the students create some kind of reward system for the school in which acts of kindness and caring would be reported and rewarded. Some schools have a box and slips by the office that anyone can take and fill out if they see or hear about a positive thing that someone has done. Then in a weekly assembly, or over the loud speaker at morning announcements, you can recognize this act and give the person something tangible to wear or have.

The Legend of the Panda

China and Tibet

Grades K-5

THEMES: Kindness, courage, sacrifice, loyalty, grief

It has been told that long ago in China there were no panda bears. The bears were pure white. A girl named Li Min lived with her mother and father and her four sisters in a forested, hilly area of the country. It was her job each day to take the sheep up into the hills to feed on the green grass. While they grazed, she would pick herbs and flowers to give to the elders to make medicine.

One day as the sheep were grazing, a shy white bear cub appeared at the edge of the forest and watched Li Min. It came again the next day, and the next. Each day Li Min was able to get a little closer to the bear, until at last she was able to sit next to it and to stroke its fur. After a while the bear would even put its soft head in her lap. She saw that it was a gentle creature, eating only the soft, tender bamboo shoots. Soon the sheep befriended it also. It came every day to join the girl and her herd, and it followed her about.

One day as the girl was picking herbs a short distance from the sheep, she heard a growling noise and turned to see a leopard leap from the forest and begin to attack the white bear. Without thinking, she picked up her stick and ran at the leopard. It stopped attacking the bear and turned on the girl. Soon the girl lay dead. When Li Min did not come home that afternoon, the villagers searched the hills until they found her body.

The family decided to bury her on the hillside that she had so loved, and everyone from the village came to the ceremony. As they stood together sadly crying, they heard a noise from inside the forest. There, a whole group of white bears was sitting, wearing black armbands and crying too. As they cried, they hugged one another and rubbed their eyes with their paws. Their hands were covered with dirt from the forest floor and the black dye from the armbands. As they rubbed their eyes, black circles began to form around them.

Those circles, born of their grief and love for the kind girl, remain to this day. We now call the bears pandas. We love them for their gentleness and work hard to prevent their extinction.

SOURCES

The Legend of the Panda, retold by Linda Granfield (Plattsburgh, N.Y.: Tundra Books, 1998).

Once There Were No Pandas, by Margaret Greaves (New York: Dutton, 1985).

Giant Panda, by Karen Dudley (Austin, Tex.: Raintree Stech-Vaughn, 1997). Panda facts, folklore and actions for preventing extinction.

Tips for the telling

Before telling the story, I would ask the children what they know about pandas: Their special features, where they live, eating habits and anything else they may know. Some children may not be familiar with pandas, so it would be helpful to show a picture. The story lends itself to a simple and straightforward telling. You can help the children to imagine the bear by pantomiming the girl patting its fur as it lays its head in her (your) lap.

Follow-up activities
Tips for story retention

- **Flannel board retelling:** Let the students tell you what happened, and take turns moving the flannel pieces around.

- **Drawing:** Have each child draw a white bear. Then have them tell the story to their parents or a reading buddy, and at the end at the appropriate place in the story, have them paint or draw in the black circles around the eyes.

Making a personal connection

- **Questions and discussion:** What feelings did you notice as the story was told? Why do you think Li Min chased the leopard with the stick, instead of climbing a tree or running away? Do you think that that was a good idea? When should we run, and when should we try to help? What questions do you have for the characters? Do you have a favorite pet that has grown to trust you?

- **Story sharing:** Sometimes it is love and passion for a person, animal, or an idea that gives us courage. Generate story sharing in a story circle by telling a story of a time that you did something that you didn't think you'd have the courage to do, because it helped something or someone you loved. The students will want to tell their own stories. You may need to do some brainstorming as a class to make a list of the type of experiences that require courage and empathy in our everyday lives. Examples would be going to school for the first time, making friends with someone new, saving an animal from students that were being mean to it, saving a mouse or bird from your pet cat, or sticking up for someone who is being teased or bullied. See what ideas they have and then encourage them to share their stories. (Note: This story may bring up stories that the children have of losing a loved one. Do not be afraid to let the children speak of their losses. It is a natural and necessary part of the healing process and hearing and telling stories helps to normalize it.)

Creative exploration

- **Pourquoi story:** This is a pourquoi story, which explains how something came to be. Have each child think of an animal that they like and one of its most special characteristics. Have them retell the story, imagining that Li Min befriends that animal. Let them change the ending to explain how that animal got its special characteristic. An example could be the giraffe that hung its head so low in sadness that its neck stretched long. Maybe it could be the owl that goes around calling, "Who, who, who hurt my friend?" Try creating several stories together as a group first.

- **Research:** This is a story about an endangered species. The children could research other endangered animals or homeless pets, then make up and tell stories about them to other children and parents to raise awareness. Through learning about animals in need, the children will be developing empathy. Help them to see that by building empathy, they are more willing to take action to help others.

- **Artwork:** Make posters that describe the love they feel for needy animals.

Talk

Africa

Grades Pre-K-4

THEMES: Empathy, respect, responsibility, leadership

Once, not far from the city of Accra on the Gulf of Guinea, a country man went out to his garden to dig up some yams to take to market. While he was digging, one of the yams said to him, "Well, at last you're here. You never weeded me, but now you come around with your digging stick. Go away and leave me alone!"

The farmer turned around and looked at his cow in amazement. The cow was chewing her cud and looking at him. "Did you say something?" he asked.

The cow kept on chewing and said nothing, but the man's dog spoke up. "It wasn't the cow who spoke to you," the dog said. "It was the yam. The yam says leave him alone."

The man became angry because his dog had never talked before, and he didn't like his tone besides. So he took his knife and cut a branch from a palm tree to whip his dog. Just then the palm tree said, "Put that branch down!"

The man was getting very upset about the way things were going, and he started to throw the palm branch away, but the palm branch said, "Man, put me down softly!"

He put the branch down gently on a stone, and the stone said, "Hey, take that thing off me!"

This was enough, and the frightened farmer started to run for his village. On the way he met a fisherman going the other way with a fish trap on is head.

"What's the hurry?" the fisherman asked.

"My yam said, 'Leave me alone!' Then the dog said, 'Listen to what the yam says!' When I went to whip the dog with a palm branch, the tree said, 'Put that branch down!' The palm branch said, 'Do it softly!' And the stone said, 'Take that thing off me!'"

"Is that all?" the man with the fish trap asked. "Is that so frightening?"

"Well," the man's fish trap said, "did he take it off the stone?"

"Wah!" the fisherman shouted. He threw the fish trap on the ground and began to run with the farmer, and on the trail they met a weaver with a bundle of cloth on his head.

"Where are you going in such a rush?" he asked them.

"My yam said, 'Leave me alone!' Then the dog said, 'Listen to what the yam says!' When I went to whip the dog with a palm branch, the tree said, 'Put that branch down!' The palm branch said, "Do it softly!' And the stone said, 'Take that thing off me!'"

"And then," the fisherman continued, "the fish trap said, 'Did he take it off?'"

"That's nothing to get excited about," the weaver said. "No reason at all."

"Oh, yes it is," his bundle of cloth said. "If it happened to you, you'd run too."

"Wah!" the weaver shouted. He threw his bundle on the trail and started running with the other men.

They came panting to a ford in the river and found a man bathing. "Are you chasing a gazelle?" he asked them.

The first man said breathlessly, "My yam said, 'Leave me alone!' Then the dog said, 'Listen to what the yam says!' When I went to whip the dog with a palm branch, the tree said, 'Put that branch down!' The palm branch said, 'Do it softly!' And the stone said, 'Take that thing off me!'"

The fisherman panted, "And my trap said, 'Did he?'"

The weaver wheezed. "And my bundle of cloth said, 'You'd run too!'"

"Is that why you're running?" the man in the river asked.

"Well, wouldn't you run if you were in their position?" the river said.

The man jumped out of the water and began to run with the others. They ran down the main street of the village to the house of the chief. The chief's servant brought his stool out, and he came and sat on it to listen to their complaints. The men began to recite their troubles.

"I went out to my garden to dig yams," the farmer said, waving his arms. "Then everything began to talk! My yam said, 'Leave me alone!' Then the dog said, 'Listen to what the yam says!' When I went to whip the dog with a palm branch, the tree said, 'Put that branch down!' The palm branch said, 'Do it softly!' And the stone said, 'Take that thing off me!'"

"And my fish trap said, 'Well, did he take it off?'" the fisherman said.

"And my cloth said, 'You'd run too!'" the weaver said.

"And the river said the same," the bather said hoarsely, his eyes bulging.

The chief listened to them patiently, but he couldn't refrain from scowling. "Now this is really a wild story," he said at last. "You'd better all go back to your work before I punish you for disturbing the peace."

So the men went away, and the chief shook his head and mumbled to himself, "Nonsense like that upsets the community."

"Fantastic, isn't it?" his stool said. "Imagine, a talking yam!"

"Talk," is reprinted with the permission of Henry Holt & Co. from *The Cow-Tail Switch and other West African Stories,* by Harold Courlander. Copyright © 1947.

SOURCES

The Cow-Tail Switch and Other West African Stories, by Harold Courlander (New York: Henry Holt & Co., 1947).

Talk that Talk: An Anthology of African-American Storytelling, edited by L. Goss and M.E. Barnes (New York: Simon and Schuster, 1989).

PICTURE BOOK

Too Much Talk, retold by Angela Shelf Medearis (Cambridge, Mass.: Candlewick Press, 1995).

Tips for the telling

This is a perfect story for audience participation. You can add or subtract objects that speak and can simplify as needed for the age group. I usually have the whole class remember all of the parts and repeat them with me, which keeps their attention. I give each animated object a different character, voice, and movement. In this way, they are remembering words, expression, and often movement. Alternatively, you can divide the class into groups and have each group responsible for a part, or have individual students take and remember parts.

I also use this one to teach storytelling skills as the farmer, fisherman, and weaver all become storytellers during the tale, repeating what has happened. After the second time through, when the farmer and fisherman meet the weaver, I let a student, (grade 2+) stand up and pretend to be the fisherman retelling the story. This is fun for them and gives them a highly structured taste of how it feels to be a storyteller. Small groups can then repeat this process together, so that everyone gets a chance.

Follow-up activities
Tip for retention

There is so much repetition in this tale that everyone will have the sequence and what the characters say by the end. Follow the instruction in Tips for the Telling.

Making a personal connection

- **Questions, discussion and story sharing:** This story can help to build empathy by reminding us that others have feelings too, and allowing us to imagine what animals or other people might be feeling. I have found that starting with fun, creative exploration exercises paves the way to talk about how real people feel in hurtful situations, and then to more personal introspection.

Creative exploration

- **Story creation:** Have the students create original stories animating other objects and scenes, such as waking up and having everything in the kitchen come to life, or animals in a zoo, furniture in the classroom, etc. Students can then tell the stories to their peers and families.

- **True-life story scenarios:** Tell your students some story scenarios in which people are bullied or teased. Ask them to be the voices of the victims, imagining what they are feeling, and what they would like to say.

Turning the story ideas into action

- **Service-learning projects:** Have the students think of a project that they could undertake to practice empathy for something that does not have a voice to represent itself. This might be raising money for endangered species, protecting wetlands in their area, or it might involve thinking of people who are in need and finding a way to help.

- **Community building:** Start a "listening project" in which students get to talk to people they do not ordinarily talk to, to see things from their point of view.

- **Develop listening and feelings expression skills:** Create a talking stick (or other object like a shell or rock) for the classroom circle time. Only the person with the talking stick should be talking, while others listen with full attention.

  Have students practice expressing their feelings while holding the talking stick. It can be used as a symbol that someone has something to say that they need everyone's attention for.

The Man in the Moon

China

Grades K-5

THEMES: Kindness, friendship, generosity and greed, lack of empathy, just rewards

Once upon a time in China, a boy and his mother lived alone at the edge of the village. They spent their days searching for food in the forest. Their life was hard, but they had each other and they were happy. Next door in a big house, there lived a rich and greedy man. Although he watched the mother and son work hard day and night, he never offered to help.

One day as the boy and his mother were looking for berries, the boy spied something moving about in the leaves. Looking closer, he saw that it was a bird, trying hopelessly to fly. Its wing was bent at an odd angle.

"Mother, come quick!" he called.

"Oh, my," she cried, "this bird has a broken wing."

The boy pleaded with the mother to let him take the bird home. "If it stays here, it will soon be eaten by a snake or a fox." His mother agreed.

The boy gently picked up the bird. It was shaking, but it did not try to fly away. He carefully carried it home and made a cage for it. He gave it food and water and talked to it gently. Within a few days, the bird was hopping from one of the boy's hands to the other. With a week or so, it had begun to take little hopping flights as the boy held his hands further apart. Soon it could fly short distances and spent much of its time riding about on the boy's shoulders.

Then one day it flew all around the room and nearly hit the window. "I think our little friend is well," said the boy's mother. "It's time to let her go back to her home in the forest."

Although the boy had become very fond of the bird, he knew his mother was right. So the next morning he opened the window, and holding the bird on his palm, told her to go free. The bird looked back, sang its pretty song, and flew away. The next day, however, when the boy and his mother were at breakfast, there came a tapping at the window. The boy opened the window and the bird flew onto his palm. In its mouth was a large striped seed. The bird dropped the seed and flew off.

They decided to plant it right away in their garden. The boy watered it and pulled away the weeds. The next day they were surprised to see that it had already sprouted. The day after, a vine had grown, and in several days small melon-like fruits were growing.

When the fruits looked big enough to eat, the mother brought a knife to the garden and cut one open. To their disbelief, out of the melon flowed gems and silver and gold. They could not believe their good fortune and danced about. They cut open several other melons, and they were also full of riches.

With their new wealth, the mother and son decided to change their lives for the better. They bought some chickens and goats and hired some men to fix their roof. They bought new clothes and rice for the winter.

140

Their neighbor took note of the changes happening next door and came over to inquire. "I see that good fortune has shone upon you. Please share your secret," he said.

"Why, of course, neighbor," the mother replied and told the man about the bird with the broken wing and the seed.

Immediately the man went out into the forest looking for a bird with a broken wing. After several hours, he grew impatient. "If I cannot find a bird with a broken wing," he thought to himself, "I can make one." So saying, he went home and got his slingshot. Though it is cruel to tell, he shot a bird from a branch, and it fell to the ground. The man ran to the bird and picked it up. "I will heal you," he threatened, "if you promise to bring me a magic seed too."

He took the bird home, put it in a cage, and fed it for many days. At last, the bird was fluttering both wings against the cage. The man opened his window and released the bird. "Don't forget my seed!" he called.

The next day the bird was back tapping at his window. It deposited a round white seed in the man's hand and flew away. The man went straight to his garden and planted it. Very soon, his seed had sprouted, but it did not grow a vine. Instead, it had a stalk, as straight as a sunflower. Day after day the stalk went higher and higher. The man did not see any melons on the stalk, but he continued to watch it grow higher and higher every day.

Finally, one night as the greedy man was looking at his plant, he noticed that it had grown straight up to the moon. "Ah ha!" he laughed. "I will climb up to the moon. I will get even better than melons with gems! I will find gold and silver on the moon!" So saying, he began to climb the stalk. He climbed higher and higher, higher and higher—until he was high enough to step off onto the moon. He began to look around on the moon. He did not see any gems, gold, or silver. All he saw was cold, gray moon dust. He turned to look back at the stalk, but it was not there. It had shriveled up and fallen back to earth. That greedy man let out a scream that traveled around the world. It woke up the boy and his mother, who ran outside and looked up at the moon. There they swore they saw the face of a very mad man.

On a full moon night, you can see him. He still doesn't look very happy.

SOURCES

"The Greedy Man in the Moon," from *The Man in the Moon: Sky Tales from Many Lands*, by A. Jablow & C. Withers (New York: Holt, Rinehart & Winston, 1969).

Picture book collection: "The Greedy Man," in *Moon Tales*, retold by R. Singh and D. Lush (London: Bloomsbury Publishing, 1999).

Cultural variant: "The Pumpkin Seed Bird," a Creole version from Martinique, retold by M.J. Caduto in *Earth Tales from Around the World*, (Golden, Colo.: Fulcrum Press, 1997).

Tips for the telling

This fun tale is rich with imagery and ripe for character development. Have fun with both. In some versions, the greedy man's vine produces melons, but when he gets to the moon and picks them, they are full of spiders and worms.

This is a pourqoui story. Sometimes I start it by asking if the children ever see any faces when they look at the moon. I talk about how many cultures have stories about what people think causes the images on the moon. Some say a rabbit, others a hunter. You may want to have several small tales to tell before you get to this one in earnest.

Follow-up activities
Tips for story retention

- **Story drawing for sequencing:** This story makes for beautiful illustrations. Invite your students to draw their most favorite and least favorite scenes from the story (that way you are more likely to get the whole story), and then to sequence them together until the whole story is told through pictures.

- **Storytelling homework:** Have them take this story home with their pictures to retell for family.

Making a personal connection

- **Questions, discussion and story sharing:** This story invites the opportunity to talk about our motivations for helping. The boy helped because he felt for the injured bird. The greedy neighbor healed the bird (after hurting it) so that he could get a reward. Sometimes we help because we are called to do so out of empathy. Sometimes we help because we think it will make us look good. Have your students ever helped a hurt or lost animal? Let them share their tales.

- **Connecting to the characters:** How do you suppose it felt to be the bird in the story? Play "hot seat" and let the children take turns pretending to be the birds in the story. Bird A, who is rescued by the boy, and bird B, who is injured by the greedy man. Where some children have been involved with hurting animals, this is a more gentle way of helping them to gain empathy for other creatures.

Creative exploration

- **Creative adaptation:** This pourquoi story will inspire your students to make up stories of their own to explain what they see on the moon. You can suggest that they include the element of empathy—or lack of it—into their stories. Encourage them to share their tales with classmates and family.

Turning the story ideas into action

- **Volunteering to help others:** There is nothing like engaging in the act of helping others to bring empathy. I suggest exploring local agencies that help animals or people, and ask if someone from the agency would volunteer to come to your class to show and tell what they do.

- **Brainstorming:** Offer the students opportunities to explore what types of situations pull at their hearts. Are there opportunities in school or town where they could experience empathetic helping?

Two Brothers

Jewish

Grades 2+

THEMES: Empathy, caring, generosity, sharing, love, friendship, leadership

Once upon a time in the land of Israel, there lived an old farmer. When he died, the farmer left his land to his two sons. They divided the land evenly and built their own houses on opposite sides. The younger brother soon married and had a family. The older brother did not marry but lived alone. Both brothers remained the best of friends and often helped each other on their farms.

One year at harvest time, both brothers undertook the process of harvesting their crop of wheat. They bundled the stalks of grain into sheaves, counted them, and took them into their barns to store and then to the market to sell. After a long day of work, the brothers usually slept well. But on this night, the elder brother lay awake.

"It is not right," he thought, "that I should reap as much grain as my brother. He has a family to feed and I have only myself." Making up his mind to set things right, he dressed and slipped out to his barn. There he took as many sheaves as he could carry across the field to his brother's barn. Feeling better, he returned to his bed and slept well.

The younger brother also had not slept well that night. He awoke and lay worrying. He too thought of his brother. "It is not right," he thought, "that I should reap as much grain as my brother. I have a family to help me, while he works alone." So saying, he too rose, dressed, and went to his barn, not long after his brother had left. There he took as many sheaves as he could carry and walked across the fields to his brother's barn. Feeling better, he returned to his bed.

The next day the two brothers each went to their barns. They looked and looked again at their grain. There was as much there as there had been the day before. The two brothers worked again in their fields all day and did not speak of what had happened.

The next night they did the same thing. First, the older brother, taking as much wheat as he could carry to his brother's barn, and then the younger brother, narrowly missing him, did the same. Again, the next day both brothers stood in awe and counted their grain, which was as much as before they had given it away. Again, both kept their thoughts to themselves.

Then on the third night, both brothers rose late. The moon had gone down and they went to their barns. Again, they each gathered as much grain as they could carry and headed out across the field to their brother's barn.

"Waaa!" They nearly bumped into one another in the dark. They both fell to the ground and in the dark peered at one another. What they saw made them smile, and then laugh, and then hug one another for a long, long time.

They made a promise to one another that there would always be help and food for each other, no matter what.

It is said that King Solomon, who was the ruler at that time, could understand the speech of the animals. They told him of the two brothers and their tale of generosity. The King was much moved and decided to build a great temple on that spot where the two brothers had met. The temple became the center of Jerusalem. It still stands there today.

SOURCE

This story is retold from the Talmud. Other written sources include:

"Brotherly Love," in *Angels, Prophets, Rabbis and Kings, from the Stories of the Jewish People*, by Jose Patterson. (New York: Peter Bederick Books, 1991).

PICTURE BOOK

The Two Brothers: A Legend of Jerusalem, retold by Neil Waldman (New York: Atheneum Books for Young Readers, 1997).

This beautiful tale deserves to be told with a well-developed sense of place and rich imagery, so that the listener may engage heart, soul, and mind. Think about your use of space, so that you clearly delineate which brother is in which scene, and which way they are sneaking across the fields between their two houses.

Follow-up activities
Tip for story retention

- **Story drawing:** Draw a big rectangle on the board to represent the farm. Ask the students where the houses of the two brothers should be placed. Then let the students take turns coming up and telling through drawing each section of the story. They should use arrows and stick figures rather than artful representations to describe the story's characters and action.

Making a personal connection

- **Story sharing:** This is one of the oldest stories ever to have been written down. Perhaps author O. Henry got his idea for The Gift of the Magi story from it. Sacrifice for another out of love is a beautiful thing. Share stories of times when you and your students have put another's well being first and been willing to sacrifice. If the teacher can come up with a simple, concrete example, it may help, such as like giving up your favorite kind of cookie to someone who lost his or her lunch.

Creative exploration

- **Creative adaptation:** Let your students retell this story in a modern or different setting. Let them try to imagine a scenario in which they would sacrifice for someone else. Have them tell the story.

Turning the story ideas into action

- **Brainstorm** examples of people who might need things that your students have enough of. Develop a project that helps your students to come up with ways to get those things to those people. Examples could be food for the hungry, company for lonely seniors, winter clothing for homeless families, homes for homeless pets. The point is to practice opening our hearts and thinking about what others need, and then to experience the joy of giving.

The Magic Listening Cap

Japan

Grades 2-5

THEMES: Empathy, awareness and respect, courage

Once upon a time in Japan, there lived a poor man who faithfully visited the shrine of his guardian god each day. Every day he left a small gift for his guardian god, usually a bit of food from his own plate. But one day the poor man had no food to feed himself. He went to the shrine and knelt down.

"I have nothing left to give," he said sadly. "Take my life if I may better serve you."

Suddenly he heard a voice. "Old man, you have served me well. Take this magic cap so that you may serve me better, and so that you will no longer suffer." When the old man looked up, there on the ground was a brightly colored cap. He put it on his head. Suddenly he became aware of a conversation going on around him that he had not noticed before. Looking up, he saw two birds on a nearby branch. To his amazement, he could understand every word they said!

"How are you, dear?" said one sparrow to the other.

"I am fine, and you?" said the other.

"Any interesting news from the town?" asked the first.

"Have you heard about the camphor tree under the Mayor's tea house?" the second bird asked.

"Yes, how is she?" asked the other.

"She is worse every day since the Mayor cut her down and built his teahouse over her. He did not cut out her roots, so she is still alive. Her roots keep trying to put out new shoots, and the gardener keeps cutting them down."

"Yes, and I heard that the camphor tree has cast a spell on the Mayor too," said the first bird. "The Mayor will just get sicker as the tree does, and when the tree dies, the Mayor will die too!"

When the old man heard this, he was very upset. He knew that the Mayor lived some distance from his home in the town. He knew that no one else would be able to hear the words of the birds, so no one would know about the dying camphor tree and the spell on the Mayor. He decided that he would have to do something about it. He doubted that anyone would believe that he could hear the sounds of the birds, so he dressed himself up like a traveling fortune-teller and made his way to the Mayor's home.

"Fortunes told! Answers to life's biggest questions sold!" the old man cried as he came to the Mayor's door.

The man's wife opened the door. "Fortune teller, could you help my husband? He has been sick for so long, and none of the doctors can seem to help him. He weakens each day."

"I will try my best," the old man said, bowing. "Let me see your husband."

The old man was taken to the Mayor, who lay in his bed, pale and weak. "Tell me, sir," the old man spoke, "when did you build your tea house? I have a feeling about it."

"The house was built one year ago," the mayor whispered, "just before I became sick."

"Ah," said the old man. "Please allow me to spend some time in your teahouse. Perhaps my answers are to be found there."

The old man went to the teahouse, where he spent the afternoon. He placed the listening cap upon his head. Soon he heard a low, sad, groaning sound. Then there was another voice, "Camphor, are you all right?"

"Is that you, maple tree?" the camphor weakly replied.

"Yes, it's me. How are you today?"

"I am not doing well, dear friend. I feel weaker each day. I know that soon I will die."

Soon the old man heard another conversation, that of two lizards climbing up the wall. "When the camphor dies, the Mayor will die too," one lizard said to the other.

"Yes," replied the other. "If only he would tear down the teahouse and let the camphor live."

The old man knew that he had to act quickly. He removed the cap and ran back to the Mayor's bedside. "Mayor, you must have your teahouse taken down at once, or you will die. Remove it, and restore to health the camphor tree growing beneath it, and you will be well again."

The Mayor, fearing that his end was near, ordered his servants to remove the teahouse immediately. There beneath it were the dying roots of the camphor tree. The gardener then set to work bringing the roots back to life.

Soon new shoots began to grow from the stump. Soon too, the Mayor was able to sit up in bed and to take food, and then, to rise from the bed, a new and healed man. The old man was given a bag of gold, and he went on his way, with his listening cap in his pocket, ready to help others, as he had promised to do.

SOURCES

"The Magic Listening Cap," from the *Magic Listening Cap: More Folktales from Japan,* retold and illustrated by Yoshiko Uchida (Berkeley, Calif.: Creative Arts Books, 1987).

"The Listening Cap," in *Thirty-Three Multicultural Tales to Tell,* by Pleasant DeSpain (Little Rock: August House Publishers, Inc., 1993).

Tips for the telling

Before you start the tale, you might invite your students to imagine that they have found a magic cap. What would that cap allow them to do? This will stir their imaginations and get them ready to listen to this story. This is a listening tale, probably not well suited to audience participation. There is room for expanding the tale, adding details that enrich the sense of place and culture, as well as examples of things that the old man hears while wearing his cap. Students could join in on providing examples of this if the teller wishes.

Follow-up activities
Tip for retention

- **Round-robin retelling:** Have students sit in a circle and pass a cap around. Whoever wears the cap can add in a piece of the story until it is retold. (If you are worried about head lice, you can make a paper hat or skip this part.)

Making a personal connection

- **Questions, discussion and imagining:** This is such a beautiful story about listening and hearing the feelings of those we might disregard. It also illustrates the connections between all beings in a metaphorical way. Ask your students to imagine that the birds and animals were all talking in their neighborhood—what would they say? Ask them to imagine what it would be like if we could hear one another's thoughts and feelings. Do they ever wish that others would know how they were feeling? Would the world be a better place?

Creative exploration

- **Original story creation:** Have your students make a listening cap of their own, whether drawn or from folded paper or cloth. Let them tell the story of what they heard when they put on the cap, and how it enabled them to help creatures or people that they might not have known were suffering. Have them share these stories aloud or in writing with one another.

Turning the story ideas into action

- **Contemplating:** Have your students spend quiet time each day thinking about people who might be being bullied or excluded, and imagining what they might be feeling inside. Have them write in a journal about what they thought about and how it made them feel.

The Seal Hunter

Once Upon a Time...

Scotland

Grades 3-8

THEMES: Empathy, suffering, healing, sacrifice, courage, self-mastery

Long ago in Northern Scotland, there lived a man who made his living from the selling of sealskins. Every day he would go out in his boat to hunt and kill them and then he would sell their skins in the market. One evening, just as he sat for his dinner, he was visited by a stranger on horseback. The man told him that he had come on behalf of someone who wished to make a purchase of a large number of sealskins. He urged the seal hunter to come with him as quickly as possible.

The seal hunter jumped up behind the stranger on his horse, and they rode like the wind to the edge of the cliffs above the sea. Looking around, the seal hunter saw no one else. He was about to inquire about the one they were to meet when the stranger took hold of his hand and plunged them both straight over the cliff and into the cold waters of the sea far below.

Down and down they swam, until at last they came to a great door in the side of the cliff. Entering through it, the seal hunter saw that they were in a huge underground compound, with many apartments and rooms inhabited by seals. At this point the hunter realized that he too had become a seal, as had his guide. They swam through the compound, and everywhere he looked were seals. He noticed that the mood in the compound was very low, and that all of the seals were deeply saddened. He felt this sadness too, as if nothing in the world would be right again.

Suddenly his guide produced a great fishing knife. The seal hunter thought at first that his own life was in danger, but then the guide spoke. "Do you recognize this knife?" he asked.

"Yes," the seal hunter replied honestly, "It is my own. I lost it this morning when I speared a large seal who swam away with it."

"Yes," said the guide, "that seal is my father. He now lies dying, and only you can save him."

They came at this point into a darkened room. In the center of the room on a flat rock was a large seal with a deep wound in his hindquarters. "Lay your hand upon his wound," the guide instructed the hunter.

The seal hunter swam forward, as all around watched. He laid his hand upon the wound. Such a feeling rose up in him as he had never felt before. It was the worst of pain, followed by the greatest of joy. Instantly the wound was healed, and the seal rose up as if he had never been injured. Then there was great rejoicing in the compound.

The guide turned back to the seal hunter. "I will now take you home, but you must first take a solemn oath never to hunt or kill a seal again." The seal hunter did not know how he would make his living, but so full was his heart, that he easily accepted the oath.

And so the guide led him back up through the cold waters of the sea, and up through the air to the cliff top where the horse stood waiting. Back they flew to the man's home. There the guide pressed into his hand a bag full of gold that kept him well, until the end of his days.

SOURCES

The Fairy Mythology, by Thomas Keightley (London: George Bell & Sons, 1882).

Favorite Folktales from Around the World, by Jane Yolen (New York: Pantheon Books, 1986).

This is a quiet, thought-provoking, yet exciting story. It is also a feast for the imagination as the two men ride, leap over a cliff, and plunge into the cold waters around Scotland, entering the realm of the seals. It requires the suspending of disbelief on the parts of the listener and teller. It also requires setting a moods to enter the hall of the seals. There is also a transformation, which needs to unfold in a realistic manner, as the seal hunter comes to understand the consequences of his actions on others. Take your time with the telling, and make frequent pauses.

Follow-up activities
Tips for story retention

- **First-person retelling:** Have students retell to the group or a partner as if they were the fisherman retelling his story. This helps them to step into the shoes of the characters, getting them closer to the feelings.
- **Imagination journey:** Have your students close or avert their eyes, and lead them through a retell in which they picture everything that is happening with all their senses in detail.

Making a personal connection

- **Questions, discussion and story sharing:** The fisherman in this story learned to empathize with the seals he had hunted by becoming one. Through deeply experiencing what they felt, he was transformed. Invite discussion and story sharing of times when your students have gained insight into the experience of another. How did this happen? How did it change them?

Creative exploration

- **Creative adaptation:** Have your students create original adaptations of the story by modernizing it, making it about person-to-person bullying, or some other form of aggression that one group might make against another. Have them share with one another and other classes. Urge them to make the story rich in sensory detail.

Turning the story ideas into action

- **Help your students to design a project** or experience in which they help themselves and/or others to walk in another's shoes. This might include researching about people who have certain kinds of experiences like homelessness, mental illness, or disabilities, and helping others to know what it feels like to be them by writing and telling first-person stories.

Once Upon a **Time**...

The Dervish in the Ditch

Middle Eastern (Sufi)

Grades 6-8

THEMES: Empathy, compassion, far-sightedness, ego control

Once upon a time, a Dervish holy man and his student were walking along a dusty road from one village to the next. Suddenly they saw a cloud of dust rising in the distance. Before they knew it, from around the bend in the road came a fine carriage pulled by six horses, approaching at a full gallop. The two men soon realized that the carriage was not going to slow down or to veer aside to avoid hitting them. It was coming at such a speed that they had to throw themselves from the road, landing quite unceremoniously in a ditch. The two men got up as quickly as they could and looked back at the carriage as it sped off into the distance.

The student began to call out a curse against them, but the teacher ran ahead of him, calling to the carriage: "May all of your deepest desires be satisfied!"

"Why would you wish that their deepest desires to be satisfied?" the bewildered student asked. "That man nearly killed us!"

The old holy man replied, "Do you really think that if all of his deepest desires were satisfied, he would be so thoughtless and cruel as to nearly run down an old man and his student?"

The younger man had no answer, for he was deep in thought. And so, in silence, the two men continued their journey down the dusty road.

SOURCE

Doorways to the Soul: 52 Wisdom Tales from Around the World, edited by Elisa Pearmain (Cleveland: Pilgrim Press, 1998).

It will be helpful to introduce the Dervish as a religious group with its roots in the Sufi tradition, which has its roots in the Muslim tradition. This is a simple tale, with a good deal of action in it, and works best if you capture the fast pacing, and put your full voice into the old man and his student calling out to the driver.

Tips for the telling

Follow-up activities
Tip for retention

- **News reporter retelling:** Get students into groups of three and have them each take a role: investigating journalist, old man, or student. Let the journalist pull the story from the other two.

Making a personal connection

- **Questions, discussion and story sharing:** We can all relate to the problem in this story. We have all had someone do something to us that demonstrated their lack of attention, or downright inconsideration of our feelings or well-being. Most of us would feel like responding as the student did. The student took the affront personally, while the teacher did not. Let your students tell about times when something like this happened to them. Have them imagine that they responded like the student. How do they feel afterwards? Have them imagine that they responded like the teacher. How does that feel? Why did the teacher not feel the need to curse the perpetrator?

Creative exploration

- **Modernize this tale as a group:** If time is short, suggest a scenario: Several students are walking down the hall when a group of older students go by, so involved in impressing each other that they intentionally force the younger students into the lockers, knocking their books to the floor. They do not even stop to help them pick them up. Talk about choices that the victims have. What could they call out that, instead of reflecting their hurt pride, could reflect a wish that the older students could be more self-confident so that they did not need to impress others? Brainstorm scenarios and solutions with your students. Remind them that the point here is not to "get someone back," but to honestly wish them to be in a more aware, thoughtful state of mind.

Turning the story ideas into action

- **Brainstorm wise responses** that students can use when others are inconsiderate or hurtful of them. Practice these together in role-playing. Make visual representations of these as reminders for the classroom.
- **Put the story ideas into practice:** Have students notice situations that happen in the classroom, school, or home, and encourage them try to respond wisely and report or journal on how it felt.

Necklaces

South Africa (Zuni)

Grades 5-8

THEMES: Compassion, bullying, peer pressure, self-care

Once upon a time in an African village, a girl named Nosa walked to the river with her bucket of washing for her mother. There at the edge of the river, a group of five girls was waiting and laughing. They had played a trick on the girl, for they thought that she was different, and that she had a necklace that was more beautiful than theirs.

"Look, Nosa!" they cried, "We have given our necklaces to the goddess of the river so that she won't be angry with us. Don't you want to do the same?"

"What a lovely idea," said Nosa. She immediately took off the necklace that she had been given when she became a young woman and threw it into the river, where a deep pool formed. But as she turned, she heard the girls laughing and saw them digging their necklaces out of the sand. "Nosa lost her necklace!" they called, and ran away.

Suddenly Nosa realized what she had done. Her coming-of-age necklace was lost! She ran to the edge of the river and began to call out to the goddess of the river to help her. Soon she heard a voice that said, "Jump into the river." Jump she did, diving down, down through the clear green water to the bottom of the pool.

There, sitting on a rock at the bottom of the river, was an old woman. Her long hair was like thick, tangled river grass, and she was all covered with open and oozing sores. The old hag turned and called out to her, "Come, girl, wash my sores. I am in great pain." Nosa did not really want to do this, but seeing the old woman in so much pain, and knowing that she was the river goddess, it seemed like the right thing to do. She went hesitantly forward, picked up a cloth, and began to wash the old woman's sores. "Much better," the old woman crooned, and the sores began to disappear like magic.

Soon Nosa began to notice that the current in the river was changing. It was picking up. Small whirlpools were forming in the pool, and the clear water was turning a muddy gray. She looked at the old woman.

"Ah, it is the monster of the river is coming. The monster that eats young women. I will hide you." The old woman hid Nosa within her long hair. The water in the river frothed and spun darker and darker, until at last a great serpent with a mouth as wide and sharp as a crocodile's came thrashing and searching the deep pool. He turned the water into a raging whirl, but he did not find Nosa. At last, he turned and headed back up the river.

When the water at last had cleared and settled, the old woman pulled Nosa out of her hair. "I was hoping you could help me find my coming-of-age necklace," Nosa said. "I lost it into the pool."

"You no longer need that necklace," said the old woman. "I will give you an even more beautiful one, for you have proved yourself to be both wise and kind." She pulled from behind a rock the most stunning necklace that Nosa had ever seen. It was woven of the finest threads and covered with jewels that sparkled in the water light. "Take this and go now," croaked the old woman as she fastened the necklace for the girl. Nosa thanked her, and then pushed off from the river bottom, up through the clear green water to the surface, where she pulled herself out on the bank.

When Nosa returned to the village center, the group of girls were amazed at the beauty of the new necklace, and they swarmed around her like flies, wanting to know how she had come by it. She told the girls how the river goddess had given it to her. Before she could tell them the whole story, they were off to the river like a swarm of bees. They threw their necklaces in the water and then dove down to the bottom as well.

There they also saw the old woman sitting on a rock, her hair like tangled river grass, covered with open and oozing sores. "Wash my sores," she called to them.

"Ewww, gross!" they said. "No way! We just want our beautiful necklaces."

"If you want your lives, you'd better swim away fast," the old woman warned. For she had felt the change in the current of the river. She settled herself on a rock and watched as the water began to churn, froth, and whirl, until the creature of the river came. Thrashing and hunting, he ate one girl after the other, bones and all. Finally, the creature went back up the river, leaving nothing but the old woman and five necklaces lying in the sand.

Nosa had run down to the river, for she was afraid for those foolish girls. She waited, but they never came again. It is said that when she was older, she became the medicine woman of the village and many sought her wise and compassionate service.

(In the original source, the old hag asked her to "lick" her sores, a more powerful meaning, but not something that most modern audiences can tolerate.)

SOURCES

This is a story that I heard told many years ago, and have been telling it since. I find two written sources:

"An African Tale," retold by Helen M. Luke, in *Betwixt and Between: Patterns of Masculine and Feminine Initiation*, eds. Mahdi, Foster & Little (LaSalle, Ill.: Open Court, 1987). Luke states that she heard this tale told by Laurens van der Post, who had heard it directly from a Zulu wise man in Africa. Luke's explication of the story in terms of metaphor and significance for teenage girls is well worth reading for anyone seeking deeper understanding of the power of stories.

Tell It by Heart: Women and the Healing Power of Story, by Erica Helm Mead (Chicago: Open Court, 1995). Helm Meade heard the story from West African Storyteller and Author Sobonfu Some. In her book, Helm Meade describes using the story with teenage girls in a residential center. In the West African version, the jewelry lost in the river is a coming-of-age belt.

Tips for the telling

This is a magical tale that requires suspension of disbelief. I find that when asking a group of middle school students to go to a place of imagination with me, it helps to take my time and use rich sensory imagery. I love to slowly describe the changing of the water in the river, and let it build until the creature turns the pool into a churning whirl of madness. Picture the creature in a way that is most real for you and describe this to your listeners.

Follow-up activities
Tips for story retention

- **First-person retelling:** Let the students pretend to be Nosa and take turns telling the story of what happened to her and the group of girls.
- **News reporter retelling:** Boys may prefer to tell the story as a newscaster interviewing Nosa, the river goddess, and the monster for the story details.

Making a personal connection

- **Questions, discussion and story sharing:** Clearly there is bullying in this story: gang bullying, preying on someone's gullibility, or desire to be a part of the group. This can lead a discussion in itself. Have your students witnessed or been a part of this type of bullying? Why did the girls treat Nosa that way? Why was she so eager to do what they told her they had done? What is it about a group that allows the individual members to do mean things together that they would not do alone?

  On one level this is a basic story in which one person is moved by empathy or compassion to help a sickly old hag and is rewarded, while others who are not willing to help are harmed. This message is clear. Look beyond a person's appearance and empathize with his or her need. How do the students feel about this? When have they been able to do this? You might remind them of Mother Teresa, who worked with lepers and imagined that each one was Christ.

  There is also the deeper metaphor in the story for the victim of bullying, or for anyone who has suffered a loss or depression. In order to heal, we must go deep within ourselves to our wounded self and be willing to pay attention to it, no matter how abhorrent, to clean it, and thus to be able to access the part of our selves that is stronger, more beautiful, and whole. Your students may not be able to get this yet, but it represents a universal task in growing up and healing. Hopefully, they can store the message in their hearts for later. I would work individually to point this out to a victim of bullying rather than in the group.

Creative exploration

- **Bullying:** Have your students modernize the tale, imagining that it took place in their time and place. What kind of group bullying tricks do students play? What kind of a helper could there be? What kind of monster?
- **Change the ending:** The ending is harsh, as is so often the case in old tales. What could happen so that the girls (or boys if they wish to change it) do not die, but are taught a lesson?

- **Research:** Have your students research biographical figures that help those who may be less desirable or attractive. Share these stories with the class.

- **Story sharing:** Have your students share this story or their modernized stories with other students to educate and initiate dialogue about group bullying. Help your students to lead the dialogue.

Turning the story ideas into action

The Tongue-cut Sparrow, retold by Momoko Ishii, translated to English by Katherine Paterson (New York: E.P. Dutton, 1987). An old man cares for an injured bird and is rewarded.

Slop! A Welsh Tale, retold by Margaret Read MacDonald (Golden, Colo.: Fulcrum Kids, 1998). An old couple have dumped their bucket of leftover food over the garden wall every night until a tiny man shows them that they are dumping it right on the roof of his house. The old couple uses their resources to find a new place to dump their bucket, and the tiny man and his wife reward their kindness.

Favorite picture books

The Resource section lists some cooperative games books that suggest many games and exercises that increase empathy, and cooperation in students of all ages.

Other suggested resources

Friendship

WHAT DOES IT MEAN TO BE A GOOD FRIEND? What is the difference between a friend and an acquaintance? Some of the qualities that we value in a friend are as follows:

> We can be ourselves and feel comfortable in each other's presence.
> We enjoy sharing time and interests.
> We can trust each other with our secrets.
> We stick together in good times and bad.
> We will be good listeners for each other.
> We share our things as best as we can.
> We will be honest but gentle with each other.
> We care about each other's feelings and well-being.
> We accept each other for who we are, including our differences.
> We are forgiving.
> We help each other when we can.
> We have an equal give-and-take relationship.
> We are understanding.
> We can compromise our needs so that both of us are happy.

What would you or your students add to this list?

Most students do not reflect on what having a real friend feels like. Ask the students to each write a list, or brainstorm a list together as a class. Exploring qualities of friendship can help us to increase our awareness of how we treat our friends and what we value in a friend. Sometimes children and teens are hung up on being friends with someone who is popular rather than someone who really meets these criteria. It is also common for friends to tease one another without realizing the hurt they are causing. Taking the time to make this list can help them to think about whether they are getting their needs met, and whether they are being good friends to others. They might even like to rate the list in order of importance.

Stories offer wonderful examples of characters interacting in friendly and not-so-friendly ways, in which the above traits are learned or found lacking. Stories can offer examples of forgiveness, working through disputes, and overcoming differences. They are great springboards into discussions, for personal reflection, and for reminding us of our own stories and our own feelings. They can offer new ways for students to see how all of their peers can be friends in various ways.

The Lion and the Mouse

Once upon a time deep in the African savannah, a curious mouse crawled up to a sleeping lion and sniffed at his great face. Suddenly the lion's whiskers tickled the mouse's nose and she sneezed. The lion awoke with a start. Seeing the mouse, he grabbed it up in his mighty paw and looked at it, as one might look upon a soon-to-be-consumed snack.

Aesop

Grades Pre-K-2

THEMES: Loyalty, acts of kindness, unlikely friendships, courage

"Please don't eat me," begged the mouse. "I promise that I will repay your kindness some day."

"How could a tiny mouse help a lion?" the great beast asked lazily.

"I don't know, but I will! I promise I will!" the mouse replied shakily.

The lion was not hungry, and this bold mouse amused him. With a laugh, he dropped the mouse, which scampered away as fast as she could.

Some days later while walking in the forest, the lion was caught in a hunter's trap. Great ropes fell all around him, and he could not free himself. His angry roars filled the forest, scaring the birds from the trees. The little mouse heard the sound and recognized it as the voice of the lion who had freed her. She ran quickly to where the lion lay helplessly entangled in the net. "Don't worry, friend," she squeaked. "I will help you, as I promised."

She began straight away to gnaw at the rope that connected the net to the trees. In the distance, she could hear the sound of the hunters' voices as they ran toward the roaring lion. Ever quicker she gnawed, until she broke the ropes free. The lion bounded off into the forest with the mouse clinging to his back. When they reached a quiet and safe place, the lion again held his small friend in his paw and looked at her, as one looks upon someone who has saved one's life. "Thank you, friend," he said.

And, indeed the lion and the mouse remained friends until the end of their days.

See page 44 for information on Aesop.

Tips for the telling

Take the time to develop the sense of place in the story by describing the lion's home in the African savannah engaging all of the senses. Think about capturing the voices of these two characters, and getting inside their bodies so that they come to life. You may ask the children to help you to roar when the lion is tangled in the nets. You may want to practice this in advance to build anticipation.

Follow-up activities
Tips for story retention

- **First-person retelling:** Have students work in pairs. One will retell the story as if he or she were the lion, and then the other as the mouse.
- **Mixed media representations:** Younger students and those with learning disabilities will benefit from making a diorama of the story with clay and moving the clay figures around as they retell the story. Puppets work well too.

Making a personal connection

- **Questions, discussion and story sharing:** This is a story about unexpected or unlikely friendships. We all experience them, if we allow them to bloom. Share stories about people who have become your friend unexpectedly. It is also a story about small creatures helping larger ones. Your students may have tales about doing something to help someone older or bigger, or even someone frightening. Conversely, it is important to remember that we can be helped by those who seem less powerful than we are. Share these tales as well.

Creative exploration

- **Creative adaptation:** Give your students different animals (e.g., a frog and a bug, or a bird and an alligator) or different settings (e.g., the Everglades, backyard, or zoo) and have them make up a lion-and-mouse-type story. Help them to make dioramas or to use puppets or stuffed animals as they retell their story.

Turning the story ideas into action

- **Brainstorm:** Have students partner with someone that they do not normally play with. Have them act the story out together using a blanket for the net and having the mouse pull the blanket away to save the lion.
- **Visual representations:** Make pictures from the story of unlikely friends and put them on the wall.

The Shepherd and the Goats

A shepherd was tending to his goats on a mountain pasture when a sudden storm blew in. Sensing the danger, the shepherd drove his goats into a cave for shelter. Once inside, he found that there was a wild flock of goats taking refuge in the back part of the cave.

As the shepherd sat looking at the wild goats, a thought came to him. "I can feed these wild goats, then perhaps they will choose to stay with the herd, and it will double in size!" So saying, the shepherd gave the wild goats the best of his grain and hay and made sure that they had water to drink. He had limited food with him, so his own goats received less than their usual ration, only a few handfuls each. They bleated sadly, but he told them impatiently, "This is the way it must be, so please be quiet."

When the storm finally passed, the wild goats ran bleating joyfully out of the cave, clearly not planning to stay with the shepherd.

"Wait!" he called. "After all I gave to you, don't you want to stay with me?"

The goats stopped long enough to reply. "We saw how you treated your own flock. Why would we think that you would treat us differently if we stayed with you?"

So the shepherd made his way home with no new goats, and a flock of disgruntled ones besides.

Aesop

Grades 3-8

THEMES: Loyalty to old friends, leadership, generosity

See page 44 for information on Aesop.

Tips for the telling	You can add to the fun of this tale by having goat voices for the two herds and letting them speak. You might also consider stopping the story before the wild goats speak, and asking the students if they think the wild goats would stay with the shepherd, and why or why not.

Follow-up activities Tip for retention	• **Act out as a group:** With younger audiences you can pretend to be the shepherd; with older groups let a student take this role. Divide the children into two groups, representing the wild and herded goats.
Making a personal connection	• **Questions, discussion and story sharing:** Help students to make connections between this story and how we might treat old and new friends. New friends can be exciting, and sometimes we neglect our old friends, which can hurt their feelings. They will probably have been on one or both ends of this experience. • **Stepping into the shoes of the character:** As you retell this story as a group, stop and interview each group, or reflect on how it felt to be treated as they were by the shepherd.
Creative exploration	• **Creative adaptation:** Make up a group adaptation in which the shepherd goes back out to try to win over a new group of wild goats by showing them how well he treats his herd, and thus they may decide to join him.
Turning the story ideas into action	• **Journaling:** Have students write about old friends and what is special about them. Have them interview their parents about their old friends and why they value them. • **Share the story with other classes** and have your students initiate discussion. Sing the song about old friends and take the story to other classes. ("Make new friends but keep the old, one is silver and the other's gold. Love is a circle, that never ends, that's the way I want to be your friend."— Girl Scout song as I remember it from childhood.)

Two Friends

Once upon a time, two friends went for a walk in the woods. Then suddenly one of them found a bag of gold coins lying in the path. "Look what I have found!" he cried in excitement. "I'm going to be rich!"

"You mean we are going to be rich, right?" asked his friend.

"But I found it. It's mine!" the first man said, pulling the bag of coins close to his body.

Suddenly a group of robbers came running at them, pointing to the man holding the bag. They shouted, "There, there, he took our gold!"

"Oh no," said the man holding the bag, "We didn't steal your gold, we just found it here."

"We?" his friend said, frowning, "A minute ago it was yours. If you wish to share troubles with me, you must also be willing to share treasures."

TWO POSSIBLE ENDINGS:

So saying, the second friend walked away down the road and left his friend to contend with the angry robbers.

Or:

"You are right," said the first friend, "How selfish I was. I am sorry, my friend."

So saying, he handed the bag back to the robber and said, "Let us go, my friend, I do not wish any more trouble on you."

Aesop

Grades 4-8

THEMES: Loyalty, courage, generosity, empathy, forgiveness

See page 44 for information on Aesop.

Tips for the telling

This is a simple tale. You may wish to add a bit more detail to draw in the students. Decide whether you wish to share the story twice with the possible second ending, or to let the class come up with their own alternate endings later.

Follow-up activities
Tip for retention

• **Dramatize:** Let small groups retell this one.

Making a personal connection

• **Questions, discussion and story sharing:** One of the most important qualities of true friendship is loyalty. We need to know that a friend will stick with us in good times or bad. That trust has to be earned. This simple story illustrates reciprocity. When we treat friends well, they will remember that and be there for us in times of trouble. If we are fickle, or "fair-weather" friends, we may find that our friends do not find us trustworthy or deserving of care. Everyone has a story about having, or being a fair-weather friend. A discussion of this story should lead to some inner reflection, perhaps in journal form.

Creative exploration

• **Creative adaptation:** Let small groups retell, modernizing the story and coming up with their own endings. Share these with the class.

Turning the story ideas into action

• **Reflecting:** Help your students to think about ways that they can show loyalty to friends. Have them keep a journal for a week or so, writing down ways that they or others showed good qualities of friendship to one another. Did they have opportunities to share that might have been challenging for them?

• **Performance:** Send your students to other classrooms with their adapted stories to share and talk about the qualities of friendship.

The Legend of the First Strawberry

Long ago when the world was new, the Creator made the first man and the first woman. They lived together as husband and wife, and for a long time they were happy. But one day they quarreled. Their words hurt one another, and the more they argued, the more painful they became. Finally, First Woman said, "You have hurt me. I would rather be alone than continue to be hurt by you." And she walked out of their home and began walking east toward the rising sun.

"I am better off without you as well!" First Man shouted, and he did not try to follow her. But as the hours passed and the sun grew higher, his anger left him and he began to feel lonely without her and to regret the things he had said.

First Man began to follow First Woman, but he could not catch up to her. First Woman was still angry and she was walking fast.

The Creator had been watching, and saw how sad the man was and spoke to him. "Why did your wife leave you?"

"I was foolish and started an argument with her," he replied. "I said unkind things that I did not mean."

"Are you still angry?" asked the Creator.

"No, I am just sad," First Man replied.

"Then I will help you to catch up to her," said the Creator.

First Woman was still full of sadness and walking fast. The Creator wanted to slow her down, so she made some raspberry bushes growing on the side of the path burst into fruit. First Woman kept walking, not even noticing. Next, the Creator saw a huckleberry bush and made that to bloom with hundreds of ripe berries. Still First Woman walked by, brushing them with her elbows, but not noticing. On and on she walked, and everywhere she walked the Creator made bushes of blackberries, blueberries, and trees of apples and pears to ripen before her, but never did she even slow down.

"I have got to create something new, something that she cannot ignore," the Creator thought. "It must grow upon the ground, and must be of a beautiful bright color, and it must smell very sweet." And so, the Creator made the first strawberries, growing low upon the path.

First Woman came charging along and stepped upon a big ripe strawberry. The smell of the sweet fruit burst into her nose and she slowed her step and looked down. There on the ground she saw the most beautiful, heart-shaped fruits, in the color of ripest red. She bent down and picked one. When she popped it into her mouth, she stopped in her tracks. It had the sweetest

Cherokee Indian

Grades 2-5

THEMES: Forgiveness, kindness, sharing, conflict resolution

taste, as sweet as love itself. First Woman reached down and picked another. This one she savored in her mouth. She picked another and another, and as she ate them her anger began to drain out of her and she was filled with peace. She began to think of her husband, and how she wished she could share them with him. She remembered their love and decided to pick some for him.

Just then, First Man caught up to First Woman. He opened his mouth to apologize, and First Woman popped in a strawberry. They did apologize to one another and promised to treat each other with love and kindness ever after. They returned home, their hands full of strawberries. They lived out their days in peace, and ever since, the Cherokee people have considered the strawberry to be the berry of love.

SOURCES

Big Cove: A Collection of Cherokee Indian Legends, by Courydon Bell and John Rattling Gourd (New York: MacMillan, 1955).

"Strawberries," retold by Gail Ross in *Homespun Tales from America's Favorite Storytellers,* edited by Jimmy Neil Smith (New York: Crown Publishers, Inc., 1988).

PICTURE BOOK

The First Strawberries, by Joseph Bruchac (New York: Dial Books for Young Readers, 1993).

Buy some strawberries to share after the story, or to use in the retelling. It can be helpful to remind students of the color and heart shape of the berry.

This is a sensual tale that describes a path with many fruit trees and bushes along the way. Take the time to develop these in your imagination so that the students can also picture them clearly. If the students are not familiar with all of the types of fruits mentioned, you may want to have pictures, or bring a sample of each to class. You can also substitute whatever fruits you wish along the way, or even vegetables!

Tips for the telling

- **Round-robin retelling:** Sit in a circle and invite each child to retell a small portion of the story.

- **Drawings:** Have each child draw his or her favorite scene and sequence them, adding in the missing parts to retell the story.

- **Questions, discussion and story sharing:** In this story, the people disagree, and hurt and angry feelings result. Everyone experiences these emotions. It is good to normalize them by letting the students share stories about times when they fought with someone or felt hurt and angry. This is also a story about reconciliation and forgiveness. Few relationships are without conflicts. It is important to normalize this as well, and to help young people to have the emotional intelligence to navigate them. Help your students to tell or write about a time that they resolved a disagreement or "fight." What did it take to forgive the other person? Are there times when it felt impossible to forgive? This is also a story about saying you are sorry, which is often the first and most difficult step in resolving a disagreement. Share stories about a time when you had to say you were sorry and invite your students to do the same.

- **Creative adaptation:** Let your students each come up with a different fruit or vegetable which to them symbolizes forgiveness or love, and retell the story in their own way, perhaps changing the setting and main characters, maybe modernizing it, having that fruit or vegetable help to save the friendship. See notes on pourquoi stories in the Pre-Story section. Students can also write original stories from personal experience about a time in which they "fought" with someone and how the conflict was or could have been resolved.

- **Visual representations:** Have the students make posters from the story to remind them of how to resolve conflicts with one another.

- **Personal actions:** Have each child think about someone with whom they have an unresolved conflict and whether they would like to offer a "strawberry" or olive branch of some sort to begin the friendship again.

Follow-up activities
Tips for retention

Making a personal connection

Creative exploration

Turning the story ideas into action

The Stork and the Cranes

Aesop

Grades 3-8

THEMES: Wise choices, leadership, judgment, and responsibility

A flock of cranes saw a lone stork nesting in a tree. "Come with us," they called as they flew by. "We're going to a field where there is tender grain to eat, as much as you can hold!"

Eagerly the stork flew with the cranes to the field. But before the birds has so much as taken a single bite, a farmer crept up behind them and threw a heavy net over them all.

"Oh, please," cried the Stork, "I'm a stork, you see, not a crane like the rest. I do not belong to this flock. I didn't know that they were going to do a bad thing!"

"You may be innocent," replied the farmer, "But you kept company with thieves, and now you will share their punishment as well."

See page 44 for information on Aesop.

It might help to show your students pictures of storks and cranes so that they know the difference. I would suggest filling out the story with details and dialogue, such as the stork thinking about whether or not to go with the cranes, or how much he loves the idea of tasty grains to bring the character of the stork to life .

Tips for the telling

- **Dramatic reenactments:** Let small groups or the whole group retell this one together.

Follow-up activities
Tip for retention

- **Questions and discussion:** This is a great story to talk about peer pressure. Every student has or will experience peer pressure in one form or another. There is pressure to conform in many ways of fashion and behavior, pressure to pass on gossip, to exclude unpopular children, to help a classmate to cheat, to disobey parents, and to do things that they know are wrong and would not do by themselves, such as stealing. Brainstorm with your students all of the ways that a young person might feel pressure from peers to behave in ways that are not in keeping with their own preferences or judgment. Discuss with them why peer pressure is so hard to resist, perhaps using specific scenarios to make the discussion more concrete. This story can also be used to discuss bullying situations, and how peer pressure can make it more difficult to stand up for a victim. This is also an opportunity to concretize the sayings "guilt by association" and "you are judged by the company you keep."

Making a personal connection

- **Story sharing:** Everyone has a story about peer pressure. It may be a story about not doing something we wanted to do for fear of social embarrassment, or for doing something we didn't want to do under pressure. It may be a story about being in a group when one person did something wrong and everyone got into trouble, or about getting into trouble for what someone else did. It will help if you tell them a story about a time when you were influenced by peer pressure. It is also important that they share stories about times when they were able to resist peer pressure. This will help them to remember what strengths they drew upon, so that they can be used in the future.

- **Creative adaptation:** Let your students retell this story with their own adaptations: modernizing, changing the characters, and fictionalizing personal experiences. They can also create original stories about characters who feel peer pressure and make good or bad choices, with the resulting consequences.

Creative exploration

- **Visual representations:** Let the students make posters about peer pressure to put up around the school. Use the story title as a catch phrase when issues such of peer pressure come up in class.

Turning the story ideas into action

- **Role-playing:** Help your students to role-play situations in which someone is being pressured into doing something that they know is wrong. You might let them come up with the topics, or assign topics from the list they generated above. Try to include at least one role-play on bullying and bystanding. Help your students to brainstorm ways to resist the peer pressure. Discuss the challenges of resisting peer pressure and the value in doing what they believe is right.

Damon and Pythias

Once upon a time in Greece there were two friends named Damon and Pythias. They trusted each other greatly and always helped each other when the need arose. Now at this time, a powerful and cruel King named Dionysus ruled the island of Sicily. He was greatly feared and despised, and so he was constantly afraid of being assassinated.

Damon could not tolerate how the King abused his people, and he began to make speeches in the town squares, urging the people to rise up and overthrow him. Dionysus soon learned that Damon was speaking against him, and he was captured and thrown into prison. The next day he was brought before King to hear his sentence. Dionysus sentenced him to die at the hand of the executioner.

"I accept my fate," Damon spoke bravely to the King, "but I beg that you allow me one week's time to return home to my village to say goodbye to my parents, and to settle my affairs so that I will not leave them in poverty."

The King laughed. "Why should I trust you to come back? No, you may not go unless someone agrees to take your place in case you do not return."

Immediately a voice rose up from the assembled masses there at the trial. "I will take his place!" It was Pythias. "I will stay in his cell, and if need be, I will die for him."

Again the King laughed. "What a fool you are to trust another man with your life. I will not hesitate to execute you at sunset in seven days." Pythias agreed and was led off to the jail cell.

Meanwhile Damon ran to his home and after two days had arranged for all of his things to be sold. He then took the money and walked to the harbor. He boarded a ship that, after two more days' journey, took him to his parents' home in the village many miles away. Once there, he gave them the money and told them the sad news. They wept bitterly. Their grief was as great as the strong winds that whipped at the house all night long.

It was difficult for Damon to tear himself away from his parents, but the next morning he left their house and ran back to the harbor. There he again tried to board a ship.

"The sea is too fierce," the ship captain told him. "We'll have to wait it out!" Damon's heart dropped. If he were even one hour late, his friend would die in his place. All morning he paced the docks of the harbor until at last the captain was satisfied that the storm was passing. Damon again traveled several days aboard the ship. When he reached the harbor he still had several hours to go to reach the palace, and the sun was going down. Damon ran like the wind.

At the palace, it was the day of the execution. King Dionysus was delighting in the fact that Damon had not returned. He went to Pythias' cell and chided him for trusting in his friend. "You were a fool to trust him. See how he loves his own life more than yours."

"It is not true, Your Highness," Pythias replied. "He must have had some trouble on his journey, but if he can he will come, for he loves me more than his own life."

However, by sunset Damon still had not come, and Pythias was led to the chopping block. "Now what do you say about your so-called friend?" asked the King.

"I trust him still," replied Pythias as his head was put to the block.

The executioner raised his ax and was ready to strike, when there came a cry from the courtyard. "Wait!" Damon gasped. "I have returned! Set Pythias free."

Dionysus watched as the two friends embraced. He found himself strangely moved. He had never seen such a display of friendship, and he could not bring himself to tear them apart.

"Both will live," he proclaimed, "for friendship such as this is rare, and too beautiful to die."

SOURCES

Favorite Folktales and Fables, by Joanne Strong (New York: Hart, 1950).

More Favorite Stories Old and New, by Sidonie Matsner Gruenberg (New York: Doubleday & Company, Inc., 1948).

A Book of Great Old Stories, by Frederick Hoppin (New York: David McKay, Inc., 1931).

This is a suspenseful tale if told well. It is also a tale of great love and courage. You will want to find distinct voices for each character and in particular the two friends and the King. Let it take its time and provide a clear sense of how time is running out for Damon as he takes care of his business.

Tips for the telling

- **Dramatic reenactments:** Let small groups reenact this story for the whole group, putting one person in the role of director, with several assistants to make sure they get the sequence right.

Follow-up activities
Tip for retention

- **Questions, discussion and story sharing:** Have students share about a time that they showed loyalty to a friend, or a friend showed loyalty to them.

Making a personal connection

- **Creative adaptation:** Have small groups make modern-day versions of this tale about two students who stuck together, and how one was willing to take the punishment of the other if necessary. Let them act these out for the class or other classes.

Creative exploration

- **Brainstorm** the qualities of a good friend and examples of loyalty. Have the students make posters from these for the classroom and school corridors.

- **Play trust games** to build trust among all members of the class. See Resource section for books with trust games.

Turning the story ideas into action

Once Upon
a **Time...**

Old Joe and the Carpenter

North American—
Southern States

Grades 3-8

THEMES: Friendship,
forgiveness, creative
conflict resolution,
honesty, leadership

Old Joe lived way out in the countryside all by himself. His best friend was also his closest neighbor. It seemed that they had grown old together. Now that their spouses had passed on and their children were raised and living lives of their own, all they had left were their farms...and each other.

But for the first time in their long friendship, they had had a serious disagreement. It was a silly argument over a stray calf that neither one of them really needed. The calf was found on the neighbor's land and he claimed it was his own. Old Joe said, "No, no! That calf has the same marking as one of my cows, and I say it belongs to me!"

They were stubborn men, and neither would give in. Rather than hit each other, they just stopped talking and stomped off to their respective doors and slammed them shut! Two weeks went by without a word between them. Old Joe was feeling poorly.

Come Saturday morning, Old Joe heard a knock on his front door. He was not expecting anyone and was surprised to find a young man who called himself a "traveling carpenter" standing on his porch. He had a wooden toolbox at his feet, and there was kindness in his eyes.

"I'm looking for work," he explained. "I'm good with my hands, and if you have a project or two, I'd like to help you out."

Old Joe replied, "Yes, as a matter of fact I do have a job for you. See that house way over yonder? That's my neighbor's house. You see that creek running along our property line? That creek wasn't there last week. He did that to spite me! He hitched a plow to his tractor and dug that creek bed from the upper pond right down the property line. Then he flooded it! Now we got this creek to separate us. I'm so darn mad at him! I've got lumber in my barn—boards, posts, everything you'll need to build me a fence—a tall fence—all along that creek. Then I won't have to see his place no more. That'll teach him!"

The carpenter smiled and said, "I'll do a good job for you, Joe."

The old man had to go to town for supplies, so he hitched up his wagon and left for the day. The young carpenter carried the lumber from the barn to the creek side and started to work. He worked hard and he worked fast. He measured, sawed, and nailed those boards into place all day long without stopping for lunch. With the setting of the sun, he stared to put his tools away. He had finished his project.

Old Joe pulled up, his wagon filled with supplies. When he saw what the carpenter had built, he couldn't speak. It wasn't a fence. Instead, a beautiful footbridge with handrails reached from one side of the creek to the other.

174

ONCE UPON A TIME

Just then, Old Joe's neighbor crossed the bridge with his hand stuck out and said, "I'm right sorry about our misunderstanding, Joe. The calf is yours. I just want us to go on being good friends."

"You keep the calf," said old Joe. "I want us to be friends, too. The bridge was this young fellow's idea. And I'm glad he did it."

The carpenter hoisted his toolbox onto his shoulder and started to leave.

"Wait!" said Joe. "You're a good man. My neighbor and I can keep you busy for weeks."

The carpenter smiled and said, "I'd like to stay, Joe, but I can't. I have more bridges to build." And he walked on down the road, whistling a happy tune as he went.

SOURCE

Thirty-Three Multicultural Tales to Tell, by Pleasant DeSpain (Little Rock: August House Publishers, Inc., 1993). For more resources by this author, see the Resource section of this book.

Tips for the telling

This tale touches each reader and teller uniquely. Read it though, and tell it to someone you trust. Then discuss what you like about it. Make sure to draw out this aspect in your telling. This tale is a lot of fun to tell with character development. You could tell it from the perspective of the main character, the friend, or the carpenter. You might think about changing the gender of the main character to "Old Josephine," a crusty old farm wife. The key is to build up the tension between the two friends to show what would bring them to the point of never wanting to speak to one another again. I also draw out the feelings of loneliness that the main character has after he and his friend are estranged. (This helps strengthen what is lost when friends break off.) The trickiest part is how to not give away too soon the fact that the carpenter has built a bridge. Usually someone in the audience will know, and if you do not want them to shout it out, you might want to specify that.

Follow-up activities
Tip for retention

- **Dramatization of the story:** Have your class retell the story spontaneously as a play. Give out the parts of cows, old Joe, his neighbor, the carpenter, and narrator (or keep this part for yourself). Let several other students be the directors.

Making a personal connection

- **Questions, discussion, and story sharing:** Who among us has not had a disagreement with a friend, and not felt like talking to him or her? What does it feel like to be fighting with a friend? What does it feel like to forgive someone who has hurt your feelings or your trust? What is forgiveness, and how does it happen? Let students share their stories of times when walls were built between friends and times when bridges were built, and how these felt. This story offers older students a great opportunity to work with a simple metaphor.

Creative exploration

- **Alternate endings:** Have your students imagine other ways that Old Joe and his neighbor could have handled their dispute. What if the carpenter had not come along? What if the carpenter had built the wall? Make your own ending in which the two reconcile.

- **Creative adaptation:** Tell a modern-day version with two students who live next door to one another and are best friends. What would they do to get back at one another, and who could help solve their problem?

Turning the story ideas into action

- **Conflict resolution:** Imagine that your students take turns being conflict solvers in the classroom or school. Does your school have a conflict-mediation team? Students can be trained to mediate and help solve conflicts that come up in the school setting. I highly recommend *The Kids' Guide to Working Out Conflicts*, by Naomi Drew (Minneapolis: Free Spirit Press, 2004).

- **Visual images:** Have your students make posters of people building bridges rather than walls.

- **Journaling:** Have your students keep a journal to notice over a period of several days when they build walls from others and when they build bridges, and how both feel. Allow them to share, as they feel comfortable. Look at how language can be a means for building walls or bridges. The word "whatever" is another way of saying, "Who cares?" although the person saying it rarely feels that way. It is a defense, a wall against saying what we really feel. The words "I'm sorry" can be bridges.

Favorite picture books

Toad for Tuesday, by Russell Erikson (New York: Dell Publishers, 1974). This wonderful chapter book can be read to the younger child or read alone by the child grade 3+. In this story, an owl captures a toad that was skiing to his aunt's home to bring her a Christmas present. The owl holds him hostage and plans to eat him on Tuesday, which is his birthday. The toad and the owl end up sharing tea and having nice talks in the evening. Finally, the toad escapes and saves the owl from a fox. The owl has meanwhile decided not to eat the toad, because he has learned to value his friendship more than a short meal!

The Cat's Purr, retold and illustrated by Ashley Bryan (New York: Atheneum, 1985). In this story, a cat and rat are the best of friends. The cat is given a tiny drum that makes a purring sound. Her uncle tells her that only she may play the drum. Her friend rat tricks her and plays the drum. She becomes so upset she chases rat. In his fear, rat throws the drum into kitty's huge mouth, and she swallows it, thus getting her purr. Many issues that present in friendships can be discussed from this story, including sharing, honesty, and trust.

See the suggestions for Cooperative Games books in the Resource section. These books have many games and exercises for building trust and friendship in groups.

Generosity

SHARING IS CHALLENGING AT ANY AGE. It does not come naturally, even though our parents are constantly modeling it. "Mine" may be the word most frequently heard in a play group of two-year-olds, but you will still hear, "This is special to me" between second and third graders! As we get older, we do not use those words, but we still may struggle when someone asks for a bite of our precious chocolate chip cookie, or to drive our new car, or to borrow a favorite necklace. Luckily, the advantages of sharing grow more evident as we grow older. Young school-age children can see how sharing brings friendship. As they age, students who have acted generously toward others can feel the satisfaction of helping.

How can storytelling help to cultivate a feeling of generosity and a desire to help? The generous instinct vs. the self-centered one is one of the most popular themes in folk tales from all around the world. Giving to and/or helping others builds trust. Through generosity, characters are aided in overcoming their obstacles. When you give a piece of bread to the old woman on the path, she gives you guidance or tools that help you to receive a pot of gold. When you spurn her, you end up with a pot full of snakes and spiders. This theme is so prominent in folk tales because when stories were the dominant source of information, this idea was one of the most important to the people who were telling them. In addition, the generous impulse that helps many others is rewarded. Raven brings light to all. Coyote frees the water. The generous impulse is a major quality in heroism. It is also a major quality in the process of spiritual transformation. The joy of sharing is a very popular theme in literature. It is worth writing about.

Many of the folk tales tell about the consequences of greed. There are plenty of examples of this in real life, too. Just look at the newspaper. Any war or act of aggression by one people on another usually has an act of greed at its heart. Fueling greed is fear. It is worth following this cycle to its beginning, as in the story of King Solomon and the Otter (see page 310). Stories can teach us a lot about human motivation and choice.

Hearing stories about generous acts can remind us of our own experiences with generosity and greed. When we act generously to others, it usually feels good and often leads to more consequences that are positive. Reminding us of these experiences helps retain their value.

Gratitude is a precursor to generosity and is a wonderful quality to develop in your students and children. Going through life with the attitude that the cup is half full will bring an entirely different experience than imagining it to be half empty. Hearing stories about people who were or were not thankful for what they had can be great food for thought. Honoring the big and small gifts in our everyday lives can make the difference between greed and generosity, bitterness and peace of mind.

Sweet and Sour Berries

China

Grades K-3

THEMES: Generosity, sacrifice, honesty, empathy, courage, love

Some two thousand years ago, in a village along a river, in a cottage near the woods, lived Tsai Shun and his mother. Although Tsai Shun was only a little boy, he worked hard to help his mother. Every morning, he fed the chickens, cut firewood, drew water from the well, and lit the stove to make breakfast. The rest of the day he worked in the fields with his mother.

The year Tsai Shun turned eight, there was no rain for several months in the area where he and his mother lived. Nothing grew in the fields. Food became scarce. Starved and worried, Tsai Shun's mother became ill. She lay in bed most of the time.

One morning, Tsai Shun went to the fields hoping to find some wild cabbage. He returned home disappointed. As he entered the courtyard, he knew something was wrong. All the chickens were gone. The door of the cottage was wide open and inside, the tables and chairs were overturned. Clothes, pans, and broken pots were scattered everywhere.

Tsai Shun found his mother lying on the floor in the bedroom. "Mama, what happened?" he asked.

"Some highwaymen ransacked out cottage! I tried to stop them, but a big man struck me down." Mrs. Tsai choked on her tears as Tsai Shun helped her get back into bed.

Tsai Shun went into the kitchen. He checked the rice jar—not a grain of rice was left. He was very sad because he was hungry, and he knew that his mother was hungry too. "Mama," he said. "I am going into the woods to see if I can find any wild berries. If I do, I will bring them home for you."

Tsai Shun took a basket from the kitchen and went into the woods. He did not find any wild berries, so he kept on walking. Finally, he saw some wild berries on a tree. They were dark and shiny. He plucked one and put it in his mouth. It was sweet and juicy. He ate another, and then another.

Then he stopped. "Mama is still hungry. I must pick some berries for her." As he was picking, he made up a little song:

One for Mama, one for me!
One for Mama, one for me!

Tsai Shun went home with a basket full of berries. "Mama!" he cried as he ran into the cottage. "I brought you some berries!"

Mrs. Tsai sat up slowly. She took a berry and put it in her mouth. It was delicious. She ate one after another, until she was no longer hungry. "My dear child," she said. "You are so good. I am feeling much better now."

"Mama," said Tsai Shun, "I am going back to the woods tomorrow to pick some more berries. Then we won't have to worry about food for a while."

The next morning, Tsai Shun took two baskets and went into the woods for the second time. But when he came to the tree from which he had picked the berries the day before, he burst into tears. The berries left on it were hardly enough to fill one basket!

Then he saw some berries on another tree. They were red. He plucked one and ate it. It was sour! "What shall I do?" he said to himself. "There are not enough sweet berries for both of us."

Then he had an idea. "I will put all the dark shiny berries in a basket for Mama, and put the red ones in another basket for me." As he did so, he sang a little song:

Sweet for Mama, sour for me!
Sweet for Mama, sour for me!

When the two baskets were filled, Tsai Shun headed home. "Sweet for Mama, sour for me! Sweet for Mama, sour for me!" he sang happily as he walked home.

All of a sudden, he was startled by a loud cry. A man dressed in black leaped out of the bushes. He was wearing a black mask. It was a highwayman! "You must pay for using my road!" the man demanded, pointing a knife at Tsai Shun.

Tsai Shun began to cry. "I don't have any money. Please don't kill me!" he begged as he tried to hide the two baskets behind his back.

The man would not listen. "You're lying. What do you have behind your back?"

"Only two baskets of berries," Tsai Shun replied.

"Give me the baskets," the man ordered.

Tsai Shun laid the baskets down before the man. The man picked up a red berry and put it in his mouth. It was sour! He spat it out. "How can you eat something like this?" he yelled.

Then he picked up a dark shiny berry and tasted it. It was very sweet. He ate another, and then another.

Tsai Shun began to cry again. "You are eating all my mama's berries! She is ill. We are hungry. We don't have any food in the house."

The man stopped eating. "Stop it. Big boys don't cry. I don't believe a word you are saying. If you are hungry, you can't be happy. But you don't look unhappy at all. I heard you singing just now."

I was singing to remind myself to give all the sweet berries to my mama," said Tsai shun. "The sour ones are for me."

"I've never heard of anyone doing something like this," said the man. "Why should I believe you?"

"I am telling the truth," cried Tsai Shun. "I never lie."

The man was silent for a moment, and then he said, "Let me hear you sing the song once more." So Tsai Shun sang again:

Sweet for Mama, sour for me!
Sweet for Mama, sour for me!

A big tear ran down the man's cheek. "Why are you crying?" asked Tsai Shun. "Big boys don't cry."

"I just thought about my mother," said the man sadly. "I left her many years ago, when I ran away from home." He wiped his eyes with his hand and then pointed to the basket. "You may go home now. Take your berries with you."

Tsai Shun picked up the baskets and ran home. He gave his mother the berries and told her about he man he had met in the forest.

That night, Tsai Shun and his mother were awakened by some footsteps. Somebody was coming to their door! They held their breath as they listened to the rustling sounds outside. But soon the footsteps went away. Tsai Shun and his mother waited in the dark all night; they could not go back to sleep.

The next morning, when Tsai Shun opened the door, a large bag of rice covered the threshold. A note was attached to the bag. It read:

> I hope this bag of rice will help you and your mother get through the hard times.
>
> —*Your friend from the woods.*

The highwaymen never came to that village again.

"Sweet and Sour Berries" by Storyteller Linda Fang is reprinted here from *More Ready to Tell Tales from Around the World*, ed. David Holt and Bill Mooney (Little Rock: August House Publishers, 2000) with permission from the author.

SOURCE

More Ready to Tell Tales from Around the World, edited by David Holt and Bill Mooney (Little Rock: August House Publishers, 2000). Storyteller Linda Fang includes musical notation for the song and follow-up thoughts in this publication. Her web site is www.chinesestorytellerlindafang.net

This is a sweet and straightforward tale that will surely stir the empathy of the listener. As it is a tale for younger children, I suggest that you put yourself as much as possible into the shoes of Tsai Shun and let him tell the story. Imagine his delight in eating the wild sweet berries and the face he must have made when he ate the sour ones. Imagine his fear in meeting the highwayman. Let us hear the emotion in his voice as he sings the song and asks the highwayman not to kill him. Imagine how he would have picked the berries—stylize the movements so that your students can join you in the picking as they sing with you. You will also be likely get some laughs and some spine-tingling if you exaggerate in the right places. Let the funny faces be bigger, and the voice of the highwayman be as fierce and deep as your students can tolerate.

I suggest that you think about how you deliver the line "Big boys don't cry." This is a message that many of us would like to change. I would be inclined to leave it out, if the story did not include the irony of the highwayman crying. Be sure to cover this as a discussion point. It is a place to do some dispelling of myths and to offer some new perspectives.

Tips for the telling

- **Sequencing ideas:** Bring in two baskets. Write "Sweet" on one and "Sour" on the other. Ask the students to draw one picture representing a part of the story that was "sour" or sad, and one picture to represent a part of the story that was "sweet" or happy. Take the pictures and sequence them together to tell the story.

- **Retelling ideas:** Have a basket and a sack that could be full of rice. Invite the students to take turns coming up and telling the story as if they were Tsai Shun (holding the basket) or the highwayman (holding the sack of rice).

Follow-up activities

Tips for story retention

- **Questions and discussion:** What made Tsai Shun decide to eat the sour berries? Why did the highwayman change his mind and give Tsai Shun's family rice?

- **Story sharing:** Teachers can tell a story about a time in which you chose to give something that was important to you to someone else. Perhaps your dad won two tickets to a ball game and you let your sister go. Maybe you had something that one of your friends really wanted and you gave it to him or her. Ask your students: Did you ever give something better to someone and take the smaller or less valuable part for yourself? Be sure to discuss the feelings associated with this kind of sacrifice. Often we are unable to share something we treasure with others. It is important to acknowledge the difficult feelings here as well.

Making a personal connection

- **Small-group reenactments:** Four students to a group can retell this story for other classes.

- **Creative adaptation:** Guide your students in adapting this story by setting it in the present day, or in a forest with animals instead of people. Ask each child to change one thing but leave the message the same. Share

Creative exploration

stories with one another. Have the students make up stories about a bully who learns to be nicer from someone else's example.

- **Personal story book:** Make a book of "Sweet and Sour Berry Stories" in which each child tells of a true experience of generosity.

Turning the story ideas into action

- **Practice sharing:** Help the class to practice the trait of generosity demonstrated so well in this story. Maybe you could make cookies in the class. Make enough so that each child gets two. Then invite another class in, have your students act out the story, and then each give one of their cookies to another child. Maybe they could even try giving the bigger cookie. Afterwards discuss how it felt with your students.

The Legend of the Big Dipper

Once upon a time, a little girl lived with her mother in a small village at the edge of the mountainside. Now there came a time when no rain fell, and the land grew dry. The streams dried up, and the crops did not grow well. Many people grew weak, including the little girl's mother.

One day when the mother was too weak to rise from the bed, the little girl determined to go in search of water. She took her mother's old tin cup with the long handle and began to walk away from her village, up the hill towards the mountainside. As she walked, she thought about how much she wanted to find water to help her mother to feel strong again.

As she walked up among the rocks on the mountainside, she heard the sound of water trickling. She found a place where a small spring came out from under the cool rocks and earth and dropped down into a stream bed. The little girl sat down beside it and waited patiently as the tin cup filled slowly, drop by drop. It was some time before it was full. When the cup was full, the little girl got up and began to walk slowly back down the hill, careful not to spill a drop. She was thinking all the while about how she wanted her mother to drink the water so that she would feel better.

As she neared the village, the little girl heard the sound of whimpering. There under a tree lay a little dog. He too was so weak, he just lay there panting. "Poor little dog," said the little girl. "I will give you some of my water. It is meant for my mother, but she would want you to have some too." So saying, she poured some water into her hands and let the dog lap it up. The dog was so grateful that it got up and wagged its tail. The little girl was so busy smiling at the dog's newfound energy that she did not notice that her tin cup had turned to silver, and was full again!

The little girl continued toward her village, carefully holding the cup so that it would not spill. As she entered her village, she saw an old man leaning against a stick, trying to find something to eat in his garden. She could see that he was barely strong enough to stand. "Here, old man," she said. "Have a drink from my cup. It will give you strength."

The old man drank from the cup and then sighed a big sigh. "You are very kind," he said. "I feel so much better now. Thank you, my child." The little girl felt so happy for the old man that she did not notice that the long-handled cup had turned gold, and was full again. She carefully made her way home, holding the cup so that it would not spill.

There was her mother lying in the bed, weak and pale with her eyes closed. "Mother," she called, "I have brought you some water. Let me help you to drink. I had to give some away, but I think there is enough to help you a bit." She helped her mother to sit up, and watched as she began to drink

Probably European Origin

Grades K-4

THEMES: Generosity, compassion, reward

from the cup. At last, her mother looked at her and smiled, "I feel so much better, dear," she said, "and I have saved the last little bit for you." But just before the little girl could drink, there came a knock at the door.

The little girl went to the door to see a woman she had never met before, looking very weak and covered in dust from the road. "Would you have a bit of water for a tired traveler?" she asked through parched lips.

The little girl stepped outside. "Of course, ma'am," she said. She handed the woman the cup. But the woman did not drink from the cup. She lifted it high up into the air. Suddenly the little girl saw that her long-handled cup was now made of beautiful sparkling crystals. The woman turned it upside down and the last drops spilled onto the ground. Where they landed a spring burst forth. The woman then turned and hurled the long-handled cup high into the air—so high that it never came down.

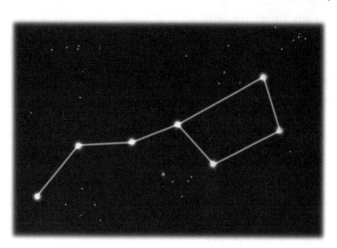

That night as the townspeople gathered to wonder at the new spring, they looked up overhead and saw the girl's long-handled crystal cup shimmering in the sky. It is there to this day, and we call it the Big Dipper.

SOURCES

I first heard this story told by Storyteller Marni Gillard and have loved it ever since! "The Star Dipper," in *The Road to Storyland*, edited by Watty Piper (New York: Platt and Munk, 1952).

"The Legend of the Dipper," retold by J. Berg Esenwein and M. Stockard in *The Book of Virtues*, edited by William J. Bennett (New York: Simon & Schuster, 1993).

This tale is rich food for the imagination. Take the time to picture the girl's journey in vivid detail with all of your senses before telling it. Picture also the cups as they transform. You may wish to talk about the Big Dipper constellation before starting the story.

- **Draw the sequence:** Have students divide a piece of paper into four equal parts. Have them write "tin cup" at the top of the first square, "silver cup" at the top of the second, "gold cup" at the top of the third and "crystal cup" at the top of the fourth. Then have them draw what is happening in each of the boxes based on what type of cup she has. They can take this paper home and retell the story using it as a guide.

- **Gossips:** Older students can retell as townspeople spreading the story of how the spring appeared and how the Big Dipper got into the sky.

- **Questions, discussion and story sharing:** This story is about transformation. The changing of the cup may signify the changes in the girl as she shares the water with more and more people. The water refills in the cup as our sense of inner joy is refilled when we help others in need. Ask your students what it means to them. How does it change us when we are kind and generous? How do we become more beautiful inside? Help them to remember and share times when they have shared with someone else and felt good about it afterwards.

- **Creative adaptation:** This is a pourquoi story in which something is created due to kindness and generosity. As a class, see if you can make up a similar story in which something else is made because of generosity, such as the moon, stars, or clouds. Change the story so that there is no food and the little girl or boy searches in the forest for food and then shares it on the way home and what happens to reward the child.

- **Experiencing generosity and helpfulness:** Have the class brainstorm ways in which they could practice acts of generosity and helpfulness. Have everyone commit to practicing these in their own way, and then report to the group about how it felt. You can also have a box marked "Generosity and Helpfulness." The teacher or students can put notes in the box about good deeds that students and classmates have done.

- **Visual representations:** Have the students make a large dipper cup out of paper and masking tape. Put it somewhere in the room and when someone reports an act of kindness or generosity, let the students add a sparkly sticker. When the dipper is covered with sparkles, hang it up on the ceiling to signify all of the kindness that has come from the class.

Why the Sea Is Salty

Norway (variants also found in Japan)

Grades K-4

THEMES: Generosity, greed, family loyalty, wisdom and stupidity, fair trade, listening

Long ago when the world was newer and the sea water was sweeter, two brothers lived upon a hill on the coast of Norway. The older brother lived on one side of the hill in a great big house all by himself, and the younger brother lived on the other side in a small cottage with a large family. The older brother was very rich, but he did not like to share his wealth with his younger brother, who was a fisherman.

One year the younger brother had had bad luck at fishing and did not have enough food to feed his family. His wife begged him to go to his rich older brother to ask for some money to buy some bread and milk. So the younger brother crossed the hill and went to his elder brother's home.

"I cannot always be paying for your large family's food!" the rich brother replied to his brother's request. "You will eat me out of house and home. I will give you this piece of bacon, but don't come back again!"

So saying, he slammed his door, and the poor brother began his journey back home. Great was his sorrow as he stopped by a tree to sit and think of what to do to help his family. He was muttering sadly to himself when he heard a rustling in the bushes. He jumped up to see an old man standing there smiling at him.

"What is wrong?" asked the old man. The poor brother explained about his problems and how he had only this small amount of bacon to feed his family.

"I will tell you what to do, young man," said the old one. "Do you see that cave in the rocks over yonder? Knock at the entrance to the cave. The old people inside have a magic mill. They will want your piece of bacon more than anything, for it is hard to come by in these parts. Do not give it to them unless they hand you the mill behind the door. Take it home and your poverty will be over."

So the poor brother knocked at the entrance to the cave and soon a number of small old people came and ushered him inside, all staring intently at his piece of bacon.

"Give us the bacon, please give us the bacon!" the old people called to him, more and more of them gathering round, like bees to a hive.

Remembering what the little old man had said, the brother said, "I will part with the bacon only if you will give me the mill behind the door."

At first the old people shook their heads, "No, no, it is not possible." But the longer they stood gazing at the large piece of bacon and smelling it, the more their hearts could think of nothing else. "All right, take the mill," they cried. "Give us the bacon!"

So the poor brother found himself on the path again, mill in hand, heading for home. Soon he met the old man again. "Do you know how to use the mill?" he asked.

"No, they didn't tell me." The old man told the brother how to start and stop the mill and sent him on his way.

When the younger brother got home, his wife was upset to see that he had brought no food with him. "Be patient," he told her. "Let us see what this mill can do." He set it on the table and spoke, "Mill, oh mill from behind the door, grind me a fine meal!"

The mill began to grind, and out came a fine porridge, bread, meat, vegetables and pies. When enough was there, the brother called, "Mill, oh mill from behind the door, thank you for grinding—grind no more." The mill stopped. The wife and children were so happy at their good fortune that they danced and danced round the table. They soon found that the mill could grind them anything they needed: clothing, coins, plates, and shoes. They knew that their lives would be much easier now.

Soon the rich brother, feeling guilty about his harsh words, went to visit his brother. He saw that the brother's life had changed and wondered at his good fortune. The brother showed him the magic mill and said, "Mill, oh mill from behind the door, grind me a fine meal."

The older brother was astounded, and a great sense of envy came over him. He was so busy thinking about how he deserved to have a magic mill that he did not listen when the younger brother said the magic words to make it stop. The older brother began to beg the younger to sell the mill to him. Day after day, he harangued him, until at last the younger brother agreed to sell it to him for $300.

The older brother took the mill home, thinking all the while of all the things that he wanted to mill to grind, such as herring, porridge, and wine, and coins, fine clothing, and jewels. "I will sell what the mill produces and I will be even richer!" he chuckled to himself. "Mill, oh mill from behind the door, grind me a fine meal of herring and vanilla pudding!" The mill began to grind and grind out herring and pudding; it overflowed his bowls, and began to spill out on the table.

"Stop, mill!" he commanded. But the mill kept on grinding. He ran around the room trying to pick up the fish and to contain the pudding, but it flowed out into the other rooms of his house. Soon the food overflowed out of the house, sending the rich brother into the streets and running down the road. He ran all the way to his brother's house. "Help! Please tell me how to stop the mill!"

"Give me back the mill and I will tell you!" the younger brother said.

"Agreed! Just make it stop!" So the younger brother ran over to his brother's house and said the magic words, "Mill, oh mill from behind the door, thank you for grinding—grind no more."

So once again, the mill belonged to the younger brother. He kept it for many years as his family grew. He shared its wealth with everyone in his village, until everyone was comfortably off and he began to grow old. One day a sea captain visited the town and heard about the magic mill. He made his way to the younger brother's house and saw the mill for himself. "Can it grind salt?" he asked.

"It can grind anything you wish," said the brother.

"I must have this mill," the sea captain said. The younger brother was not at first interested in parting with it. Still the sea captain begged, offering him more and more money until he had offered him thousands of dollars. The younger brother began to think, "I have enjoyed this mill for many years, and my life is now very comfortable. Perhaps it would be wise to share it with a sea captain who can take it all over the world."

The younger brother at last agreed to sell the mill for a huge sum. The sea captain was so excited that he thrust the money into his hands, grabbed the mill, and ran away before the brother could change his mind. He knew how to make it run, but he did not know how to make it stop.

The sea captain ran straight down to the sea and got into his boat. He headed out to sea. Once the small town was safely out of sight, he pulled out the mill and said, "Mill, oh mill from behind the door, grind me salt, so that I may enjoy my meal." The mill began to grind salt. Soon the captain found that he had enough. He called, "Mill, oh mill from behind the door, stop!" Nothing happened—the mill kept on grinding. "Stop!" he yelled as the salt began to overflow from his plate onto the table. "Please stop!" he screamed. Still the salt began to flow down from the table onto the floor. "Stop, mill!"

But the mill kept on grinding. It ground and ground out salt until it made a huge pile and the ship began to tip, and to sink, and to tip, and to sink, until it tipped right over and sank, captain and all, to the bottom of the sea.

The magic mill lies on the bottom of the ocean to this very day, grinding away and churning out salt. That is why the sea is salty!

SOURCES

Best Loved Folktales of the World, edited by Joanna Cole (New York: Doubleday, 1982).

The World's Best Fairy Tales, edited by Belle Becker Sideman (New York: Readers Digest Assn., 1967).

CULTURAL VARIANT

"The Magic Mortar," in *The Magic Listening Cap: More Folk Tales from Japan*, retold and illustrated by Yoshiko Uchida (Berkeley: Creative Arts 1987).

PICTURE BOOK

Why the Sea Is Salty, retold by Wesley Porter (New York: A Westport Group Book, 1979).

I have added the starting and stopping chant to the story. I did not find one in any traditional versions. You can feel free to change it to suit your students. Your students will learn it quickly and want to repeat it with you. Have fun making up things that people in the story could wish for the mill to grind out for them. Add their suggestions right into the heart of the story when you are talking about how the brother used the mill. You may need to explain to the students that herring and pudding are traditional foods of Scandinavia where the story is from.

Tips for the telling

- **Drawing the sequence:** Younger students—Draw a picture from a favorite part in the story. Sequence them together. Older students—Divide students into three groups. Ask those in group number one to draw a scene from the beginning of the story. Group two can draw a scene from the middle, and group three from near or at the end. Then ask each group to sequence, and then sequence them with all three groups.

- **Questions, discussion and story sharing:** This story offers an opportunity to talk about a number of feelings and experiences, including sharing and feelings of jealousy, envy, and greed. We all have those feelings at some point. Identifying them can help children to recognize them without having to act on them. How did the rich brother and the sea captain's greed get them into trouble? Have they ever had trouble sharing with someone else? What would your students do if they got a magic mill? Would they use it to help others? If so, how? When they had all they needed, could they give it away?

- **Creative adaptation:** This is a pourquoi story that explains how something came to be. Have the students tell a similar version in which they keep the basic idea of generosity or greed, but change what the mill produces and what happens when the stopping verse is not known. Let them tell these stories to one another. You might start by making one up together.

- **Explore cultural variants:** Share the Japanese version of this story with the class, as a way of showing how cultures share ideas and values, and how individual cultural traits can be learned and appreciated by hearing multicultural tales.

- **Brainstorm:** It is not likely that any one of us will find a magic mill. That should not stop us from being generous to others. Put the saying, "Practice random acts of kindness" on the board. Let the students brainstorm some random acts of kindness that they can perform even without a magic mill. Let them report on acts of kindness and generosity that they practiced or noticed throughout the day.

- **Random acts of generosity box:** Have a box in the front of the room with slips of paper next to it. Let students report acts of generosity that other students do, and then celebrate them once a week. This can also be applied to acts of kindness, helpfulness, honesty, or hard work.

Follow-up activities

Tip for story retention

Making a personal connection

Creative exploration

Turning the story ideas into action

The Goose and the Golden Eggs

Aesop

Grades K-4

THEMES: Gratitude, satisfaction, greed, impatience, shortsightedness, just rewards

Once upon a time, a farmer went out into his goose yard to collect his eggs. There, among his dirty brown eggs, a beautiful golden egg sparkled in the sunlight. When he picked it up it felt heavier than any egg he had ever held. When he took it to town, the jeweler told him that this egg was made of the purest gold and paid him a handsome price for it.

The next day the farmer was delighted to find another golden egg, and the next day he found another. The farmer watched his geese until he knew which one was responsible. He put a red sash around her neck and, for a while, he lavished her with the finest foods. Every day he found a new golden egg, and every day he was richly rewarded.

Soon the farmer was rich, but he was not satisfied. Now he wanted more and more things—things that he could not buy with a single golden egg. He fed the goose more and more, but still she only produced one egg a day.

Then one day as the man was thinking of what he wanted to buy, he had an idea. "Why wait for one egg a day? I could kill the goose and collect all of the eggs that are inside her at once!"

Wasting no time, he got his ax and went to the goose yard. Then he took off the red ribbon and killed the special goose. He took her into his kitchen and cut her open, grinning with anticipatory delight. But when she was opened up, there was not a single egg inside her. Not a single egg. In addition, he never found another golden egg in his goose yard ever again.

See page 44 for information on Aesop.

This is my simple adaptation of this short fable. I suggest that you develop the setting as it feels right for you. Decide how much to emphasize the farmer's growing greed. Develop his changing personality from a grateful man to a greedy, impatient one if you choose.

You may also use this opportunity to talk about how eggs develop inside chickens and geese. Children often have questions around whether there is a baby chicken in the eggs we eat. A little information may help the children to see why there would not be a storehouse of golden eggs inside the goose.

- **Gossips:** Put the students into pairs and have them retell the story pretending that they were other geese in the yard watching the story unfold and telling each other what they saw and thought. Let volunteers share their retelling with the whole group.

- **Questions, discussion and story sharing:** This story helps us to look at the fear of not having enough, feelings of greed in which we always want more, and the difficulty of delaying gratification. It can also be about gratitude for what we do have. It will be important for the teacher to give some personal examples of situations where she has faced these feelings. Encourage the students to share as is developmentally appropriate. It may be as simple as eating more than your share of brownies at snack and then feeling mad because your mother would not let you have one after dinner with everyone else.

- **Character perspective:** Process the student's feelings from when they told the story from the perspective of the geese in the yard.

- **Creative adaptation:** Read your students "The Golden Goose" from India that follows and discuss the differences. Then let your students make up their own versions of this story in which something gives a gift, one day at a time, and the owner loses patience and loses out in the end.

- **Gratitude list:** Brainstorm with your class things for which the students feel grateful. Make a nice long list and leave space for people to add more things. Talk about taking things and people for granted, and think of ways that they could express their gratitude to those people and for those things. Display this list and let them add to it as they will and to report to the class.

Follow-up activities
Tip for retention

Making a personal connection

Creative exploration

Turning the story ideas into action

The Golden Goose

India (Jataka)

Grades 2-8

THEMES: Love and
gratitude, compassion,
greed and fear,
lack of forethought

Once upon a time a man died, leaving his wife and two daughters in great poverty. They had to beg for food and clothing and only survived thanks to the kindness of neighbors. One day as the family sat drinking their thin broth, they watched as a beautiful gold-colored goose flew in through the window and lighted on the beam above them. As they stared in awe, the goose shook its wing, and a feather of pure gold dropped upon the table with a delicate clatter.

The goose spoke to them, telling them that he was the reincarnation of their husband and father come to care for them. (Truly, he was the Buddha). He promised that whenever they were in need, he would appear and would drop them a golden feather. The family was overjoyed and was able to live comfortably after that. They counted their blessings each day, and always the girls would leave crumbs of bread for the goose outside the house.

But after a time the mother grew worried. "What if the goose doesn't return to us one day?" she asked her daughters one evening. "We would be poor again."

"He will always return, Mother," they assured her. "Do not worry for tomorrow, be glad for today."

But the mother did not cease her worrying, and one day she said, "I say that the next time the goose appears, we catch him and pluck all his feathers. That way we will be assured a happy future." The girls, thinking of the welfare of the goose, were horrified and begged their mother not to consider such a thing.

One day when the girls were not at home, the woman had her way. She called out in need to the bird, and when it appeared, she captured it and plucked out all its feathers. Not wishing her daughters to see what she had done to the bird, she took him outside and set him down far from the house. When she returned to count her golden feathers, she cried out in horror. For there in the basket were only soft golden brown feathers, no different from any other goose! Not one of them was gold at all. And though the mother cried out her need ever more, the goose was never seen again.

SOURCE

The Fables of India, by Joseph Gaer (Boston: Little Brown and Co., 1955).

194   ONCE UPON A TIME

This story has a wonderful fairy-tale quality to it that is worth capturing. If you like, you can have the daughters repeat the refrain to their mother, "Do not worry for tomorrow, be glad for today" each time she worries. The children may ask what would have happened to the goose, so you should think about how you will answer that one! Because it is a magical goose, you can say that it went back to where it came from, which is a mystery to everyone!

Tips for the telling

As above in the first version of the Golden Goose.

Follow-up activities

The Hodja's Feast

One hot day, Nasrudhin the Hodja was working hard in his garden. It was late afternoon and yet he worked on, hoping to finish a large pumpkin patch before sundown. Suddenly his friend called to him, "Nasrudhin, have you forgotten Halil's feast? It is starting in five minutes—we will be late!"

Nasrudhin knew that there was no greater insult to Halil, the rich man in town, than for one of his invited guests to arrive late. There was no time to go home and wash and change into his dining clothes. So Nasrudhin hurried out of his garden, throwing some water in his face and hands, and went along with his friend to the party.

When they arrived at Halil's fine home, the other guests were already seated and talking together. Nasrudhin noticed that no one called out hello or turned to ask his opinion, as they so often did. Halil himself did not greet Nasrudhin, but waved for him to be seated at the farthest place from him, near the kitchen door. When the servants brought the platters of meat around, they did not stop at Nasrudhin's side, but passed him by.

Soon Nasrudhin was smiling to himself and shaking his head. Without a word, he slipped out of the side entrance and hurried home. "Fatima, come quickly," he called to his wife. "I need help with a bath and my finest clothes and my new expensive coat!"

"Are you meeting a king?" she asked. But Nasrudhin just smiled and said he would tell her the whole story later.

So, freshly scrubbed and dressed in handsome trousers, his most elegant turban and vest, and his new expensive coat, Nasrudhin walked back to Halil's residence. As he entered the feast hall, all eyes were upon him. Halil rose quickly and came to his side. He was given the seat right next to Halil this time, and everyone wanted his attention. Fine trays of food were passed to him piled with every kind of delicacy.

When his plate was full, Nasrudhin began to pick up one piece of food at a time and to stuff it into the many pockets of his coat. Some meat in this one, a piece of garlic and onion bread in that one. Squash and eggplant were smooshed into the hem of each sleeve, and fruits were tucked in any little fold he could find. Halil and his guests looked on in astonishment. All the while Nasrudhin was speaking, "Feast, my fine coat. Eat your fill."

Halil's face had turned red, and he rose in astonishment. "Hodja, why are you not eating this fine food? What on earth are you doing?"

"Well, my fine host, I am feeding my coat. When I arrived earlier after a long day at work, you gave me no notice and told your servants to pass me by with their trays of food. Now I return in my finest clothing and you lavish me with attention and treat me as the guest of honor. Since I am still Nasrudhin, I can only surmise that it is my coat that you wish to honor and feed, and not me." So saying, he popped a grape into his buttonhole.

Halil, the rich man, was greatly embarrassed. He promised Nasrudhin that from that day on he would judge a person by his character, and not the clothing upon his back.

SOURCES

This tale is widely told and published in collections of Nasrudhin tales, including *Watermelons, Walnuts and the Wisdom of Allah, and Other Tales of the Hoca*, by Barbara Walker (New York: Parents Magazine Press, 1967).

Once the Hodja, by Alice Geer Kelsey (New York: David McKay Co., Inc., 1967).

PICTURE BOOK

The Hungry Coat, retold by Demi (New York: Margaret K. McElderry Books, 2004).

Tips for the telling

A wide range of ages can enjoy this story. It does not lend itself particularly well to participation. The story is easily told from different points of view, including that of the selfish rich man, the guests, servants, Nasruhdin, or even his wife Fatima. It is worth reading a number of Nasrudhin tales and becoming familiar with his character. I suggest miming the use of the coat rather than actually wearing one.

Follow-up activities
Tip for retention

- **News reporter retelling:** Divide the students into groups of five. Let them choose the parts of news reporter, Nasrudhin, the rich man, Fatima, and a servant. Let the reporter ask them questions as if the event had recently occurred, and let each tell a bit of the story from their point of view.

Making a personal connection

- **Questions and discussion:** If we are not careful, we are likely to make a number of snap judgments about someone based solely on a quick look at his or her appearance. Frequently, when we have a chance to get to know someone, we revise our judgments, but we do not always get this chance. This story can generate discussion about the focus on appearance so common in middle and high school. What would it be like if your school had a school outfit? Do you think the saying is true that you cannot judge a book by its cover? Have you ever judged people harshly based on their appearance, only to discover more about them later?

- **Personal story sharing:** Let students share their personal stories in writing, or orally if they are comfortable, about making friends with someone who on first sight they thought they would have nothing in common with. Let them share stories of a time when they felt judged by their appearance.

Creative exploration

- **Creative adaptation:** This is a fun story to modernize or to tell from different perspectives. They can also come up with alternate endings. Let the students write and tell their own modern versions, setting the tale in another place and time, such as Washington, D.C. or Hollywood. Let the rich man be a politician, or a rock or TV star. Let them share their versions with each other to perfect them, and then take them on the road.

Turning the story ideas into action

- **Visual representations:** Have the students make posters representing the idea of not judging others by their appearances and treating everyone equally.

- **Practice making second impressions:** Give your students the assignment to notice all day when they are judging someone and suggest that they say to themselves, "judging" when they notice themselves doing it. Have them make a conscious effort not to judge. Remind them of the Golden Rule, and that they do not want to be judged either. Check in to see how they did, and have them reinforce this by making posters.

- **Fundraiser:** Let the students make the story into a play and ask people to bring food or money to get in. Donate the proceeds to a food bank or kitchen.

The Baker's Daughter

Once upon a time in a small village in England, a baker had two daughters. Now these daughters were as different as night and day. One daughter was kind, generous, and loved to laugh, while the other was mean, stingy, and always seemed to wear a scowl upon her face. She too loved to laugh, but her laugh was often at another's expense.

Early one winter morning, long before the sun had risen, the kind daughter was working in the bakery preparing for that day's bread, when the shop door opened. In came a withered and bent old woman with nothing but a threadbare shawl wrapped about her bony shoulders. She made her way to the counter and croaked, "Can you spare a wee bit of dough, and could you put it in the oven for me?"

"Why of course, granny. Sit a spell, and while you wait, I'll make you a cup of tea," the daughter answered.

The old woman went and sat at a corner table and sipped her tea, while the girl took a bit of the fresh dough she had been kneading and put it in the oven. After a time, the smell of freshly baked bread filled the bakery. The young woman opened the oven and cried out in surprise. "Why that little bit of dough I put in has doubled in size!" She brought the bread to the old woman, who smiled, threw back her shawl, and rose up as a beautiful shining woman.

"Your bread has doubled in size because you have shown to have such a grand and generous heart. From now on, everything you bake will double in size." She kissed the girl on her forehead and nearly flew out of the door.

A few days later the stingy daughter was working, preparing the bread in the wee hours of the morning. The old, ragged woman again visited the shop, shivering in her threadbare shawl. She made her way to the counter and again asked for a bit of dough, and if it could be popped into the oven to warm her bones.

"I'm really busy, you know," said the girl. "I can't just be giving things away for free." But she remembered that her father had told her to be kind to beggars. Reluctantly she took a tiny piece of dough and put it in the oven. The old woman went and sat in the corner.

Soon delicious smells filled the store, and the stingy daughter opened the oven door. She too saw that the bread had doubled in size. "Well this is too good for her," she pouted. So saying, she put the bread aside and put an even tinier piece of dough in the oven. Soon this bread was done too. When the girl looked at it, she was shocked to see that dough had quadrupled in size, to be bigger than the first loaf. "This is too good for a beggar woman," she said. Now she put the tiniest piece of dough into the oven, no larger than a bean.

England

Grades 2-8

THEMES: Generosity vs. greed, rewards of generosity, empathy

At last, the old woman stirred from the corner and asked, "Is my bread ready yet?"

The girl went to the oven and nearly shrieked as this tiny piece of dough had grown to nearly fill the oven. "No, old woman, your bread has burnt! There is no more for you, whoo whoo whoo!" She howled with malicious laughter at her good fortune.

"Is that all you have to say to me, young woman?" asked the old woman.

"Whoo whoo whoo!" laughed the girl. "That's all!"

"Well, then, whoo whoo whoo is all you will ever say!" The old woman threw back her shawl and became the shining beautiful woman again. She touched the stingy daughter on her forehead and she turned into an owl, soaring out into the night, calling, and "Whoo whoo whoo."

SOURCES

Clever Gretchen, retold by Alison Lurie (New York: Thomas Crowell, 1980).

Children Tell Stories, by M. Hamilton and M. Weiss. (Katonah, New York: Richard C. Owen Publishers, Inc., 1990).

Take the time to capture the sense of place and time in this magical story. The events unfold in the wee hours of night before dawn, in the dead of winter. It also takes place in a bakery. Let them smell the smells, feel the heat of the oven, and hear the sounds of the dough being kneaded. You will also want to find the two distinct characters of the daughters. This will help you to find two voices, and especially practice the mean laugh of the selfish daughter. Create a laugh that easily melds into the calling of an owl.

Tips for the telling

- **Gossips or news reporter retelling:** Get students into pairs or small groups and have them retell as if they were townspeople passing on the story of what happened to the selfish daughter.

Follow-up activities
Tip for retention

- **Questions, discussion and story sharing:** In this story a good deed multiples itself, while a selfish action causes a punitive reaction. Mother Teresa was quoted as saying she "treated each person she met as if they were Jesus Christ." I believe that this helped her to feel blessed in doing the work she did. Share stories of times when your students treated others kindly, and how it felt.

Making a personal connection

- **Research:** Send your students to the library to research stories about individuals who acted with great generosity. Have them share the tales with one another. Alternatively, they can go home and interview an adult family member or neighbor about a time when they acted out of generosity and how it felt. These too can be shared.

Creative exploration

- **Brainstorm opportunities** to act out of generosity with your students. Start with opportunities in the classroom, school, town and beyond. Have your students make posters about these opportunities and/or choose a class project to practice this generous urge.

Turning the story ideas into action

Dinner with Fox and Stork

Aesop

Grades 2-5

THEMES: Generosity vs. greed, envy, cleverness, revenge, manners, just rewards

Once upon a time, a fox was envious of a stork. Ever since she had moved into his neighborhood, his children kept remarking how elegant and graceful she was. The fox, who was very vain, decided to play a trick on her so that his children would consider her foolish. One day as the stork was feasting at the water's edge, the fox approached.

"My dear neighbor, Stork. It is long past time that I welcomed you to our neighborhood and invited you to dinner. Would you join me at my house at six o'clock this evening?

"Why, how kind," answered the stork. "I would be delighted."

But, when the stork arrived at the fox's table, all he offered her was a shallow bowl full of broth. Though she was hungry, the stork could not eat from a shallow bowl, as her bill was far too long. She watched as the young foxes lapped greedily at their bowls and whispered about her from one to the other. The stork said nothing, and pretended to enjoy the meal.

At the end of the meal, she said to the fox, "Thank you for your generosity. I would love to return the favor. Won't you and your children dine at my home tomorrow evening?"

The fox was thrilled, as he loved a good meal, and knew that storks were excellent fishermen. So the next night the fox family trotted over to the Stork's nest in the reeds by the river.

"Welcome, and do have a seat at my table," said the stork. "I have made a lovely fish stew with many chunks of fish for your enjoyment." The foxes sniffed the delicious smell and hurriedly sat at the table. But soon they gasped when they saw that the stork had served each one of them with a tall and very thin glass jar, just wide enough for a stork's bill to slip down, but far too long for a fox's tongue to reach any food.

The fox was outraged. "How can you invite me to dinner and serve me in a container that I cannot reach?"

"Now, dear neighbor," the stork said. "Do not be angry. I am sure that you will enjoy your dinner at my home just as much as I enjoyed yours."

Have fun miming how each animal tries unsuccessfully to eat from the other's dishes. I suggest having pictures of the two animals in the story to help make clear the problems the stork and foxes faced. Try to find unique voices for both fox and stork, which reflect their characters.

- **Partner retelling:** Let the students retell to one another in pairs with one as the fox and one the stork.

- **Questions, discussion and story sharing:** This simple story provides food for thought on a number of issues, such as jealousy, dishonesty, and revenge, or in softer terms, giving someone a taste of their own medicine. Help them to tell stories about times when they have grappled with the above issues, either feeling jealous, being tricked, or wanting to take revenge.

- **Relating to the characters:** Let them take turns sitting in the "hot seat," taking questions as both the fox and stork about their choices.

- **Compare and contrast** this tale with variants from other cultures, such as "Anansci's Visitor." See page 205.

- **Creative alternatives:** We often feel like taking revenge when people hurt us. Stork finds a way to teach fox the error of his ways without publicly embarrassing him, or hurting him. Ask your students to think of alternative endings to this story.

- **Brainstorm real-life scenarios** in which someone may hurt or embarrass us, and come up with ideas for taking action without seeking revenge.

The Doorbell Rang, by Pat Hutchins (New York: Mulberry Books, 1989). A mother bakes cookies for her child. Friends keep coming over and they keep dividing the cookies—an opportunity to practice simple division and sharing.

The Legend of the Bluebonnet: An Old Tale of Texas, by Tomie de Paola (New York: Scholastic, Inc. 1989). This is a Comanche legend in which a girl sacrifices her doll (her only tangible connection to her dead relatives) so that rain will come. She is rewarded with rain and the deep love of her people.

Mufaro's Beautiful Daughters, by John Steptoe (New York: Scholastic, Inc., 1989). A variation on the Cinderella story—a kind and a selfish daughter both want to wed the king, but only one has unknowingly befriended and helped him. The other has unknowingly hurt and ignored him through her greed.

The Baker's Dozen: A Colonial American Tale, retold by Heather Forest (San Diego: Gulliver Books, 1988). In this Christmas tale, a baker becomes greedy, and his business declines. An old woman teaches him about generosity, and the term "baker's dozen" is born.

The Old Woman Who Lived in the Vinegar Bottle, retold by Margaret Read MacDonald (Little Rock: August House, 1995). An old woman is granted wishes by a fairy and she moves from a vinegar bottle house to bigger and bigger houses, but she is never content.

See *Gluscapi and the Four Wishes*, retold by Joseph Bruchac, described under Self-Mastery.

Honesty and Fairness

MANY INTERESTING ISSUES ARE RAISED when we talk about honesty and fairness as characteristics of a person, citizen, and friend: Why is it important for each of us to be honest? What happens when we tell a lie to someone else? What happens to us? What happens to our relationship? How does the other person feel? Why is it so hard to tell the truth sometimes? What can you do to make up for having told a lie? Are there big lies and little lies? Can we be too honest? When does honesty require tact and sensitivity?

Honesty is an important issue in the classroom. Issues of honesty arise around stealing, testing, homework, sharing equally on the work of a cooperative project, resolving conflicts that arise, and taking responsibility for one's actions as they affect others.

Fairness and justice are cousins to honesty and trustworthiness. We will not respect a leader, parent, or teacher who does not treat everyone fairly, nor a system that does not hand out equal justice for all. We will also be left feeling uneasy if we receive better treatment than another does. We know that the tables could turn. Children are keenly aware of what is and what is not fair.

Much can be taught about the importance of fair laws, equal rights, and the justice system through folk tales. Stories offer examples of the rewards of honesty and the ramifications of dishonesty. The basic formula of a folk tale—characters facing and resolving conflicts—make them the perfect tools for teaching students to think about issues of honesty and fairness. Students will readily evaluate the rightness of a character's honesty and will be eager to hand out just punishments for dishonesty.

Anansci's Visitor

One hot day in the late afternoon old Turtle came lumbering up the dusty path by Anansci the spider's door. He had been traveling all day and he was tired and hungry. There was still a long way to go before he would reach his own home under the river.

There were delicious smells coming from Anansci's house. Anansci loved to eat. He had been cooking all day and was about to sit down to a sumptuous feast when Turtle knocked upon the door.

"Hello, Anansci," said Turtle. "I am tired and hungry. Could I please come in and share your dinner with you?"

When Anansci saw Turtle, his joy turned to anger. He did not want to share his meal with Turtle, but it was the custom in that part of Africa that if a visitor comes to your house, you must share your meal. "Come in, Turtle, I am just sitting down to dinner," Anansci sighed. Turtle entered the house to see a full tray of every delicacy of the jungle on Anansci's table.

"But wait!" Anansci smile returned, "It is customary in my part of the jungle that you must wash your hands before eating. Look at you, all covered with dust!"

"Very well," said Turtle, turning and heading down the dusty road to the river. There he carefully washed his hands and feet and headed back up the dusty path to Anansci's home. When he entered, again he could see Anansci at the table, the tray of food now half gone.

"Come and sit," said Anansci. "Oh, but Turtle, look at your hands," he sighed in mock dismay. "You will have to wash them again."

"But Anansci, the path..." Turtle began, but Anansci cut him off.

"Now, now, Turtle, it is a custom in my part of the jungle that a person may not come to dinner with dirty hands."

So Turtle headed back down to the river and washed his hands again. This time when he walked back to Anansci's, he stayed on the side of the path and trod on the leaves and plants. His hands were clean when he got to Anansci's home. However, there was not a drop of food left.

"Oh, I am so sorry, dear Turtle!" said Anansci. "You will have to be quicker next time."

"Yes, indeed," said Turtle. "Well, never mind, Anansci. Why don't you come to my house for dinner tomorrow evening?"

Anansci's stomach shivered with delight. "I should love to."

"I live around the third bend, at the bottom of the river," said Turtle as he started for home.

The next day Anansci washed at the river, dressed in his best suit coat, and headed to Turtle's home. He did not want to arrive late. He reached the bend in the river where Turtle lived and stopped. A question formed in

Africa

Grades K-4

THEME: Generosity vs. greed, dishonesty, just rewards, manners, respect

Anansci's mind. "How do I get to the bottom of the river? Well, if Turtle can do it, so can I," he thought. He jumped into the water, where he floated like a water bug. "Hmm. I shall have to get some more momentum," he thought, walking away from the river. He then ran forward, gave a great leap and disappeared under the water. Pop! Within seconds, he had popped back up again.

Anansci sat on the bank of the river, thinking. He had glimpsed a bit of Turtle's dinner. It looked so good. Water shrimp salad was his favorite! Soon an idea came to him. He began to fill his pockets full of pebbles. Pebbles here and pebbles there—he had done it! Anansci stepped back and jumped straight into the river. This time he sank all the way down and landed at Turtle's table.

"Good evening, Anansci," said Turtle, smiling. "You are just in time for dinner. Do have a seat."

"Yes, yes," said Anansci, reaching for a piece of fresh water lettuce.

"Oh, not so fast, Anansci," smiled Turtle. "We have a custom in my part of the jungle. You must remove your jacket before eating a meal."

Anansci's smile faded. Turtle was resolute. So Anansci began to slowly take off his jacket. First one sleeve—he floated half out of his chair—then the other. He began to float away. He tried to reach out for some water shrimp salad, but it was too late, he was rising higher and higher, until pop! He was on the surface again.

Anansci walked home with no dinner that night. That is what he got for tricking his visitor Turtle.

SOURCES

"Anansci and His Visitor Turtle," in *African Village Folktales*, by Edna Mason Kaula (New York: World Publishing Co., 1968).

The Cow-Tail Switch and Other West African Stories, by Harold Courlander and George Herzog (New York: Henry Holt & Co., 1947).

"Hungry Spider" in *Thirty-Three Multicultural Tales to Tell*, by Pleasant DeSpain (Little Rock: August House, 1993).

This story is best suited as a listening tale, as it is not long on repetition. It has many opportunities for depicting the actions, such as turtle walking slowly to the river, washing his hands, and returning slowly, and Anansci trying to sink below the surface.

Follow-up activities

Tip for story retention

- **Group retelling with pantomime:** Let each student pick a favorite part of the story, retell without words, and have the others guess what was happening in that part. Then have them sequence themselves correctly. You could also write different parts of the story on slips of paper and ask each child to depict one without words. Then have them tell in the correct order.

Making a personal connection

- **Questions, discussion and story sharing:** This story contains lots of food for thought. It is difficult for Anansci to share. He knows the "rules" of proper conduct, but finds a way around them. Why did Anansci's culture have rules about sharing with visitors? What rules do your students know they must follow? Why are they important? What rules do they wish other students would follow? Have they ever been tricked and wanted to take revenge as Turtle did? What is the difference between revenge, and giving someone a taste of their own medicine?
- **Talking to the characters:** Pretend to be Anansci and let the students tell you what they thought of your actions. Pretend to be Turtle and let the students tell you what they thought of what you did in return.

Creative exploration

- **Compare and contrast** this tale with variants from other cultures, such as "Dinner with Fox and Stork."
- **Creative adaptation:** Have students make up their own version of this tale with creative lessons at the end.

Turning the story ideas into action

- **Brainstorm real-life scenarios** in which a person might be hurt or embarrassed by someone's dishonest action. Come up with ideas for teaching the dishonest person a lesson, without seeking revenge.
- **Visual representations:** Have the students make posters based on the story and the "rules" they think are important as brainstormed above.

The Magical Ax

China and Aesop

Grades K-4

THEMES: Honesty, greed, just rewards

Once upon a time, a woodcutter found his way into a new part of the forest. The sun was hot, and he rested for a while beside a cool, deep pool of water in a stream that came down from the mountains. He drank and washed his face, and then closed his eyes and rested for a spell. He heard a noise and he jumped, knocking his old wooden ax into the pool. He knelt and felt into the pool, but realized that it was very deep indeed. He was just removing his shirt to dive in and search for his ax, when he heard a splashing sound. He jumped back in shock to see a water sprite swimming in the center of the pool.

"Did you lose your ax?" she asked him in her sing-songy, watery voice.

"Yes, my dear ax that I need to make my living has fallen into your pool. I was just going to dive for it."

"I will get it for you," she said, and disappeared into the pool. A moment later, she resurfaced. However, what she held in her hand was not the man's old wooden ax. A beautiful silver ax sparkled in the sunlight. "Is this the ax that you lost, woodcutter?"

"Oh no, my ax was just a simple wooden ax, with an old handle and a well-used blade," the man replied.

"Very well," she said, and dove down into the deep. Soon she reappeared with an ax even more resplendent. For this one had a handle of pure glittering gold. "Is this your ax?"

"Oh no, my ax is made of simple wood, carved with my father's own hands."

"Very well," she said, and disappeared again. The third time she reappeared, she had the old wooden ax in her hands. "Is this your ax?"

"Yes! Oh, thank you so much."

"You are welcome, woodcutter. For your honesty, I will give you the other two axes that they may help to make your life easier in old age."

"Oh, thank you! Thank you!" said the woodcutter in disbelief. The water sprite disappeared, and the woodcutter picked up the three axes and carried them straight home.

When he arrived home, he called his family and friends together, fed them a good meal, and told them the tale of his amazing good fortune. His neighbor listened carefully and well. The next day he too set out with his wooden ax to find that mountain pool in the forest. He too drank and washed, and rested in the shade. Then in a sudden move, he threw his wooden ax into the center of the pool, pretending to exclaim with dismay. He too removed his shirt and made as if ready to dive into the pool to search for his ax. Soon enough the water sprite appeared.

"Did you lose something?" she asked.

"Yes, my beloved ax."

"Let me find it for you." She reappeared with the golden ax. "Is it this one?" she asked.

"Oh yes, that is it!" he exclaimed, reaching to put his rough hands upon it.

"Oh, no," she said. "I have dropped it!" She dove down and down, and finally reappeared. "It has fallen into a crevice, where I cannot reach it, right next to an old and probably useless wooden ax. Surely, you do not need that one, if you can afford a golden ax. Goodbye, woodcutter."

The greedy woodcutter went home that day with neither new wealth nor gold, but hopefully a little wiser.

SOURCE

"Mercury and the Woodman," from *The Aesop for Children Children's Press Choice* (Skokie, Ill.: Rand McNally, 1984).

PICTURE BOOK

Chen Ping and the Magic Axe, by Demi (New York: Dodd & Mead, 1987).

Tips for the telling

This story is best suited as a listening tale, as there is not much repetition of movement or language. Try to find a unique voice for each character and to use rich sensory imagery to create the feel of the forest and the cool, watery pool.

Follow-up activities
Tip for retention

- **Small-group retelling:** Divide the students into pairs, with each person taking the part of either the first or second woodcutter and telling what happened. Ask volunteers to tell to the whole class.

Making a personal connection

- **Questions, discussion and story sharing:** Have you ever wanted something that did not belong to you? Have you ever been given something such as a prize, or an award, which really belonged to someone else? What did you do? Have you ever found something that you wanted that belonged to someone else? What did you do? Tell a story about a time when you were able to be honest about something that was difficult for you. These questions will invite story sharing.

Creative exploration

- **Group story creation:** Have the class make up real-life scenarios that are similar to the story. Maybe you can start by giving out suggestion slips, such as someone finds a wallet in the school parking lot, or someone is given an award for winning a race when he knows he accidentally tripped someone who might have won. Brainstorm scenarios with the class and let them pick. Small groups can create/write the stories and act them out with follow-up discussion. Remember to have the students think about different ways in which we are rewarded for honest behavior, and the possible consequences of dishonesty.

Turning the story ideas into action

- **Story presentations:** Take your students on the road, sharing their group stories with other classes and inspiring follow-up discussions with other students.

- **Journal keeping with older students:** Have your students keep an honesty journal for a whole week, noticing situations in which they found it easy or difficult to be honest, and what they did. This will help to build awareness.

- **Puppet sharing with younger students:** Create a water sprite puppet that could hear their stories and give them encouragement. In circle time invite them to share with the puppet something that happened within the past few days when they had to decide whether to be honest or not. The puppet can help them to talk about how it is difficult sometimes to tell the truth. She could make up a story about a time when she broke a friend's toy and was so scared that she hid it and ran home instead of telling the friend. This would invite honest discussion about fears and challenges with honesty.

The Emperor's New Clothes

Many years ago there lived an Emperor who loved fine clothing more than anything else. He spent most of his money on fine new clothing. He did not spend money on his soldiers, or for keeping his country beautiful, and he only went out to show off his new clothes. He had a robe for every occasion. He spent most of his time changing his clothes and admiring himself in the mirror.

One day two swindlers came to town. They pretended to be weavers and said that they could weave the finest cloth imaginable. "The colors and patterns are exceptionally beautiful," they said. But what is more extraordinary is that the material has the magical quality of being invisible to any man or woman who is bad at their job, or who is very foolish."

When the Emperor heard about the magical, beautiful cloth, he wanted it right away. He wanted everyone to see him in the beautiful clothes, and he wanted to know if any of his servants or advisors was unfit for their jobs, or truly foolish. "Yes," he cried, "I must have this cloth woven for me without delay!" He gave a lot of money to the two swindlers in advance, so that they should set to work at once. They set up two looms and pretended to be very hard at work. They asked for the finest silk and the most precious gold; this they put in their own bags and pretended to work at the empty looms until late into the night.

"I should very much like to know how they are getting on with the cloth," thought the Emperor after a few days. However, he felt uneasy when he remembered that no one who was not fit for his office could see it. He believed, of course, that he had nothing to fear himself, yet he thought he would send somebody else first to see how matters stood. Everybody in the town knew of the magical property the cloth possessed, and all were anxious to see how bad or stupid their neighbors were.

The Emperor sent his most trusted Minister to see how the cloth was coming along. When the old man entered the weaver's workshop, he was embarrassed. He could see nothing but two men working away at empty looms. "Oh no," he thought. "Am I unfit for my job, or hopelessly foolish? I mustn't let on!" So he stepped forward and pretended to look upon the cloth. "How beautiful it is, indeed," he lied. "I will report to the Emperor at once." The two swindlers requested more gold, silver, and jewels, which they said they would put into the cloth they were weaving.

The Minister reported to the Emperor and told him how beautiful his cloth was. The Emperor grew more impatient by the day. Soon he sent his second top advisor to check the progress of the cloth. Like the first man, he too saw nothing, but in his shame he pretended to see glorious cloth and reported

Hans Christian Andersen

Grades K-3

THEMES: Honesty, greed, courage, leadership

the same thing to the Emperor. Person after person went to view the cloth, and each saw nothing, but each was too ashamed to admit it, fearing he would look bad.

Finally, the two swindlers announced that the magical clothing was ready. The Emperor announced that he would wear it in a parade for the whole town to see. Then he could notice who was a good worker and who was not.

The swindlers pretended to bring the clothing to the Emperor's chamber. They pretended to hold up each piece in turn for him to see. "Is this not the most magnificent clothing you have ever set eyes on? Do you not wonder at the colors, the sparkle of the gems?"

The Emperor concealed a gasp. He saw nothing, nothing! Did this mean that he was not qualified for his job? Did this mean that he was a fool? "Quite beautiful indeed," he stuttered.

The swindlers began to help the Emperor into the imaginary clothes, one piece at a time. "Here are the trousers, your majesty. They are as light as cobwebs. You will hardly feel them at all." As they spoke the Emperor's attendants all pretended to swoon over its great beauty. All the while, they were thinking that they must be the only ones not to see it at all.

When the swindlers declared that the Emperor was fully dressed, they motioned to two attendants. "Come," they said, "pick up the Emperor's train. Be gentle, it is of the most delicate cloth." The two men came awkwardly forward and pretended to pick up the cloth that they could not see or feel. The procession began to wind its way out of the palace and through the streets.

The whole kingdom had come out to see the Emperor's new clothes. As he began his procession down the main street of town, the onlookers' eyes grew wide. For all they saw was their Emperor in his underwear, marching down the street as proud as a peacock. But everyone thought, as the Emperor's advisors had, that they could not see the clothes because they were not good enough or smart enough. So they too pretended to be in awe of the beautiful clothing.

"Isn't it amazing? Truly he has outdone himself this time!" they exclaimed to one another as he passed by.

Suddenly a small child stepped out from the crowd and pointed at the Emperor. "But he has no clothes on!" the child cried. "The Emperor is only wearing underwear."

Soon other children began to join in the chorus. "He's not wearing anything at all!" Soon the adults were looking at one another.

"Do you see any clothes?"

"No, I don't either."

By now the Emperor himself was becoming self-conscious. People all around him were whispering that he was not wearing anything at all. He feared that they were right, but he thought to himself, "I must keep up the procession. I must not let on that I have been misled." And so, he walked past all of the crowds, wearing nothing but his underwear, as his chamber-lains continued to carry his train, which was not there at all.

The swindlers disappeared with the gold and jewels and were never seen again.

SOURCE

Fairy Tales by Hans Andersen, by Hans Christian Andersen (New York: Weathervane Books, 1932).

PICTURE BOOKS

The Emperor's New Clothes, A Tale Set in China, adapted by Demi (New York: Margaret K. Celery Books, 2000).

The Emperor's New Clothes, Hans Christian Andersen (New York: Michael Nergebauer Books, 2000).

Tips for the telling

This is a fun story that can have meaning for all ages. It lends itself to pantomime as the swindlers pretend to weave, and as the emperor tries on his clothing and the servants carry his train. It lends itself to participation as person after person sees nothing at all. You can have them all stifle a gasp, or say to themselves, "Oh no, not a thing do I see! What does that say about me?" Alternatively, you can create one phrase for everyone who pretends to find the cloth beautiful as they describe it to the Emperor.

Follow-up activities
Tip for retention

- **Gossip or newscaster retelling:** Put the students into small groups and have them retell the story together as if they were the Emperor's advisors retelling the tale to one another. Younger students will enjoy acting this out as a whole class.

Making a personal connection

- **Questions, discussion and story sharing:** This story has characters who are thieves and liars, and many characters who are afraid of telling the truth. Only the children were able to speak the truth. Students will have many questions about this story. This is a place to discuss the concept of tactful honesty. Have they ever been afraid to tell the truth because they thought they would get into trouble, hurt someone's feelings, or be embarrassed? Let them share their stories.

Creative exploration

- **Class retelling:** Make the story into a play for your class to retell for other classes or parents. During the rehearsal process, ask the students in character to explain why it is hard for them to be honest.

- **Creative adaptation:** Have students modernize this tale in small groups as if it happened in their town or country. Share with classmates.

- **Make a new ending:** Let the students create an ending with examples of the Emperor behaving more responsibly and the people being more honest.

Turning the story ideas into action

- **Practicing courageous honesty during lessons:** Students of all ages are often reluctant to raise their hands when they do not understand what is going on in class because they do not want to appear dumb. Usually they are not the only one who is lost or confused. Try to equate the timid people in the story with timid students and urge them to act like the brave child who trusted his own judgment and did not worry what others said. Have a contest as to who can raise his or her hand with the most questions about a subject (things they really are confused about) in one day.

The Theft of Smell

There once lived a poor student who got by on bits of rice and whatever he could beg. It so happened that the student rented a room with several friends upstairs from a small restaurant. Every day at lunchtime the young man would go and sit by the window and smell the delicious smells coming from the kitchen below. When his friends complained to him of how hard their lives were subsisting on rice alone, he laughed. "Why, I have a gourmet diet!"

"How?" they gasped. "You are as poor as we!"

"Yes," he said, "but each day when I take my lunch break and eat my rice, I sit at the open window and smell the delicious smells coming up from the kitchen. In this way my rice is mixed with fish and delicious sauces, tempura vegetables and spices."

Now it just so happened that the greedy shopkeeper who lived below happened to be standing out in front of the shop. He heard this conversation coming from the open window. "Thief!" he called up to the window. "Now I know that you are stealing my smells. You must pay for this!"

The young man came to the window. "How can you ask me to pay for something that is free? Anyone may smell anything they wish."

"We'll see about that," yelled the man, now purple with rage. "I'm taking this to the judge!"

And that was just what he did. The shopkeeper took his complaint to judge, who presided over the town. In those days, the court was an open and public place, and the many spectators laughed when they heard the man's charges. They knew that judge was fair and were sure he would send the man packing. Instead, however, he merely shook his head and agreed to hear the case. The poor student had to come and stand next to the shopkeeper before the judge.

After the judge had heard all of the evidence, he frowned. "This student is guilty of taking the shopkeeper's property. Why should a smell be treated any differently than any other thing that a person makes?"

The crowd was stunned. The poor student could not believe his ears or eyes as the judge beckoned him forward to hear his punishment. "How much money do you have, young man?" he asked.

"Only five small coins, and it must last me until next month. I will not be able to pay my rent or eat at all."

"Show me your money," the judge ordered.

Japan, Italy, and Mexico
Grades 3-8

THEMES: Fairness, greed, empathy, wisdom

The young man held the few coins in one hand. The judge ordered that he drop the coins from one hand to the other five times. Everyone sat in stunned silence listening to the clinking of the coins as they went back and forth.

"There!" said the judge to the shopkeeper. "You have been paid!"

"But he did not give me the money!" the shopkeeper said.

"That is right," said the judge. "The punishment should always fit the crime. You have been paid for the theft of your smells with the sound of his money. If he can grow fat on the smell of your food, then you shall grow rich on the sound of his coins. Case dismissed!"

SOURCES

Ooka the Wise: Tales of Old Japan, edited by I.G. Edmonds (Hamden, Conn.: The Shoe String Press, 1994).

Old Italian Tales, retold by Domenico Vittorini (New York: David Mckay and Co., Inc., 1958).

PICTURE BOOK

The Fence, A Mexican Tale, by Jan Balet (New York: Delacorte Press, 1969).

Have fun with this story. Create characters for the shopkeeper, the student, and the judge. Let the audience be the crowd gathered to hear the case. You can encourage them to laugh, to shake their heads in disbelief, and to clap at the justice in the end. You may even choose to bring some coins and to ask one child to come forward to pass the coins back and forth five times, or you can do it yourself.

- **Gossip or newscaster retelling:** Put the students into small groups and have them retell the story together as if they were bystanders in the courtroom, or bystanders being interviewed by the local news station later that day.

- **Questions, discussion and story sharing:** This is a story about fairness, something that young people are keenly tuned into. Let students talk and write about times when they witnessed or heard about something that felt very fair or unfair to them. You might start by brainstorming situations in which fairness issues often arise.

- **Creative adaptation:** Share cultural variants of this tale with students. Then have students make modern version of this tale to tell to other classes.

- **Act it out:** Imagine that this story had happened today, and that either side had to get a lawyer. Put students into small groups and have them pick a lawyer for either side, a person to be each character, and a judge. Let the rest of the students be jurors who decide the case. They can share their verdict with the other groups.

- **Brainstorm:** Have the students talk about and survey other students about fairness issues that come up in school.

- **Conflict mediation:** Create a conflict mediation group with your students in which they take turns acting as fair mediators in situations of conflict in the classroom. Have them make a list of conflicts that might come up, and role-play ways of solving them. This puts the students in role of mediator, which will help them to think more objectively. This will require reading some basic material on students as conflict mediators. Many schools now have these groups.

For conflict resolution and mediation curriculum in the classroom, this site has many links: www.peaceeducation.com/cgi-bin/links/show

The Kids' Guide to Working Out Conflicts, by Naomi Drew (Minneapolis: Free Spirit Publishing Inc, 2004).

Follow-up activities

Tip for retention

Making a personal connection

Creative exploration

Turning the story ideas into action

Resources

King Solomon and the Baby

Jewish

Grades 3-8

THEMES: Honesty, empathy, love, wisdom, leadership

Once long ago a man had two wives, but only the younger one had given birth to a son. To protect him from his stepmother, who was very jealous, the younger woman gave the boy to the older wife to raise as her own. The father died when the boy was still young, and the two women began to fight about who would own all the things that the boy had inherited. They could not solve their problem on their own, and so they took the problem to King Solomon, the wise judge.

King Solomon looked at both mothers and asked who the true mother was. When both women declared themselves such, the King told them he would have to resort to a contest of strength. He called the small boy into the room, and told each woman to take hold of one of his arms. Then he told the mothers that whoever could pull the boy to her first would win. He gave the signal, and instantly the poor boy cried out in pain. Just a second later he was lying in a heap on top of his stepmother.

"Now we know who the true mother is," the King stated. "The boy shall go to live with the younger wife, and she shall inherit with him."

"But I pulled harder!" cried the older wife. " I won the contest!"

"Yes," sighed the King, "but as soon as her son cried out in pain, his true mother, unable to cause him suffering, let go of her grip, while you, thinking only of profit, held tight. He will go with his true mother, and the inheritance is hers to divide as she sees fit." And so it was.

For a second clever ending see: *Ooka the Wise: Tales of Old Japan*, edited by I.G. Edmonds, (Hamden, Conn.: The Shoe String Press, 1994). In this version, Ooka tricks the mothers in a different way, revealing the step-mother's greed.

SOURCES

God's People: Stories from the Old Testament, retold by Geraldine McCaughleen (New York: Margaret McElderry Books, 1997).

Moses' Ark: Stories from the Bible, by Alice Bach and J. Cheryl Exum (New York: Delacorte Press, 1989).

Stories to Solve: Folktales from Around the World, told by George Shannon (New York: Beach Tree Books, 1985).

It is good to give some background about King Solomon. Many of his stories are very short, and several can be shared at one time to illustrate how wise he was, and how often he was called upon to solve problems and riddles. This is a fun one to act out. I would suggest calling three volunteers up from the audience and having them pretend to be the mothers and the boy. Choose people who will not pull too hard!

Follow-up activities
Tip for retention

- **Small group retelling:** Put students in groups of four to act this out together.

Making a personal connection

- **Questions and discussion:** This story is about determining honesty and intention in a dispute. The king is very clever in discovering who the true mother is. However, it is less black and white than some cases, as some would say that the stepmother should have some of the inheritance, as she was the one who raised the boy. Let the students debate this among themselves. This story may hit close to home for those children whose parents have divorced, and who feel caught in the middle of their fighting. The children can literally feel pulled in two directions. This story can provide a way for the children to put into words what they have been feeling, and to realize that they are not alone. These are two key ingredients to healing.

Creative exploration

- **Creative adaptation:** Have your students imagine themselves to be King Solomon. Let them come up with a list of scenarios and take turns to solve them. For other examples of wise judges and to get ideas for clever and fair solutions, read other King Solomon stories, *Ooka the Wise* from Japan, or *Old Italian Tales* (see sources and variants from "The Theft of Smell," above), and "Judge Rabbit" tales from Cambodia. They can also have fun modernizing the tale.

Turning the story ideas into action

- **Learn and practice conflict-mediation skills** together and take turns mediating real and imagined disputes that happen in the classroom or school. See the previous story follow-up for suggested resources for conflict mediation training.

Once Upon a **Time**...

Truth in a Peach Pit

Korea, Japan and China

Grades 4-8

THEMES: Honesty with others and with oneself, justice, choices, fairness, cleverness, change, leadership

Once upon a time in a city, maybe near and maybe far from here, there lived a thief named Han. He was raised on the streets as an orphan, and there he had learned from the best of the thieves how to steal a loaf of bread or a piece of fruit for his meal. Han learned to be clever too, living by his wits, and he had never been caught. Then one day he fell in love. The young woman loved him too, but required that he reform his ways and live an honest life. Han was glad to do this, but there was first the problem of a wedding ring. He would steal a ring for his beloved, and then start a new life. Unfortunately Han's desire for the perfect ring had shrouded his keen instinct for danger and he was caught. Han was thrown into jail, where he would likely spend out his whole life.

Day after day, he sat in the jail cell thinking and thinking of how to escape. The walls were strong, and the jailers never left their posts. They did not even open his cell, but passed food in to him. Though his mind kept churning for answers, his hope was growing dim.

Then one day as he mulled over his simple lunch, an idea came to him. The prisoners had been given the customary meal of rice, a very small portion of fish, and a piece of fruit. Today it was a peach. The peach was delicious and reminded him of the beautiful peach trees blossoming outside of the city where the rich men lived. After eating the peach, he carefully wrapped the peach pit in a piece of cloth and called the guard to him.

"Please tell the head jailer that I must see the Emperor. I have a very important present to give to him." The guard laughed. However, each day Han kept at him with the same request until at last he was brought before the Emperor.

"Your Highness," he said bowing very low. "I have brought a great present to you." Han handed the Emperor the piece of cloth. The man opened it and turned red with anger. "How dare you take my time and insult me with a peach pit? Did you think you would escape somehow? You are a thief, and you belong in jail!"

"Your Highness," Han went on, still bowed low, "this is no ordinary peach pit that I bring to you. I beg you listen, for this is a magic peach pit, given to me many years ago. When it is planted it will bear fruit of purest gold."

"If this is so, why did you not plant it yourself, thief!" scowled the Emperor.

"Ah, Your Highness, that is the catch," Han said humbly, "for the man who gave me this seed told me that it would only yield golden fruit for an honest person who has never stolen or cheated. For those who have, it will give only

220

ONCE UPON A TIME

regular peaches. Therefore, as you can see it would be wasted on me. I have been waiting to find the perfect person to whom to give it. These many days spent in prison have given me time to realize that you are that person."

Instead of glowing with excitement, the Emperor grew redder than ever. While more honest than most men in high places, he could not help remembering how in his younger days he had once lied and cheated another man out of his chance for a high-ranking position, while he himself had risen in power. "No, no I couldn't accept it," he murmured into his beard. "There may have been something in my youth that I no longer remember. I believe it should go to my Prime Minister."

All eyes turned to the Prime Minister, who had also gone red with embarrassment. "Oh no, I am afraid that I am not the right person either," he stammered, knowing full well that he regularly accepted bribes from people who wished him to influence the Emperor in their favor. "I suggest the Commander of the Army."

Then it was the Commander's turn to blush and stammer and mumble, for he had even had a man killed once in order to secure his place in the government. He demurred to the Governor, who also could not accept the magic seed, as he had grown immensely wealthy on the hard labor of peasants who remained terribly poor.

This went on and on down the line of noble officials who had audience to the Emperor. Finally, there was no one left in the room to take the magic seed, as each had used their position of power to cheat or steal. The room was silent.

Slowly the Emperor began to smile. "You are a clever man, Han. You have showed us that your crime has cost you dearly, while for our own we go free. I think you have served enough time in prison. Return to your life as an honest man, and please let none of us steal or cheat again.

And so Han put the peach pit into his pocket and left a free man. Free to choose to change his life for the better. He kept the peach pit in his pocket all of his life, and he passed it on to his children. It helped him to remember that when all is said and done, honesty yields gold, and that gold is freedom.

SOURCES

Best Loved Folktales from Around the World, by Joanna Cole (New York: Doubleday, 1983).

Tales the People Tell in China, by Robert Wyndham (New York: Julian Messner Pub., 1971). In this version, it is a pear seed.

Tips for the telling

This is a tricky story in that it deals with a main character whom we empathize with, and yet he has made poor choices, including stealing. I see it as a good opportunity to talk about the reasons that some people resort to stealing, but how it never pays in the end. It is a good opportunity to talk about justice and fairness in terms of crimes and punishments. I feel good about sharing this story in that it ends with the main character learning a lesson and keeping a reminder of it with him through his life.

Have fun creating the different characters and inventing crimes which they have committed in their lives. Who among us would be able to plant the peach pit and reap golden fruit?

There are a number of cultural variants of this tale from Asia, involving the same basic story, but different fruits.

Follow-up activities
Tip for retention

- **News reporter retelling:** Divide students into small groups. Have one be the news reporter, one the prisoner, one the jailer, one the Emperor, and several other men in his court. Let the reporter interview each to retell the story.

Making a personal connection

- **Questions, discussion and story sharing:** Divide students into two groups to debate the outcome of this story, with one side arguing that the thief should not be let out from jail and the other that he should. Students can share their stories of times when they felt that they were punished fairly or unfairly. What would the golden peaches represent if one could plant the pit?

- **Dramatize as a group,** pretending that each one in the class is offered the peach pit in turn. Are there any who feel that they have never been dishonest, never lied, cheated, or stolen? Let each tell or opt to pass in telling their dishonesty story. Do not let them tell on each other. Process this afterwards in journal writing or orally.

Creative exploration

- **Research current events and literature:** Have your students go to their parents, to the library, or online to find examples of situations through history or in literature in which there was inequity of punishment. Examples could be the number of minority prisoners who get the death penalty vs. white prisoners for the same crime, and in blue vs. white-collar crime, and how it is punished.

Turning the story ideas into action

- **Dramatic retelling:** Have your class act this story out for other classes and follow it with a discussion to help other people to have an increased awareness about themselves and the small "crimes," they may try to get away with.

- **Visual representations:** Have students make a giant peach pit that they place on a pedestal (out of clay or other materials they choose) to keep in the classroom to remind them about honesty, and about not casting blame and judgment on others until they have decided whether they could plant the pit themselves.

The Wise Teacher's Test

Once upon a time, in an old temple on the outskirts of a big city, a Buddhist Master decided to teach his young students a lesson. "My dears," he said looking at them through sad eyes. "As you can see, I am getting on in years. The time has come where I can no longer provide for all of the needs of our temple. I know that I have not taught you to work for money, and so there is only one thing that I can think of that can keep our school together." The students listened with wide eyes.

"As you know, the nearby city is full of wealthy people and shops that do a good business. I need you to go into the city several days a week and to steal the things that we need from the shops, or to snatch the purses of the rich people as they are passing by. That way we can keep our school together."

The students looked at their Master in disbelief. "But Master, you have taught us not to steal," one young boy stammered.

"Indeed I have," the old man replied, "and it would be wrong to steal if it was not absolutely necessary. You must only take what we need. That way no one will suffer. In addition, there is one other thing: You must not be seen! If anyone sees you or catches you stealing, you must not bring the stolen object or yourself back to the temple. It would ruin our reputation. Do you understand?"

The students looked nervously from one to the other and then at their Master, whose old eyes shone back with intensity of purpose. They sadly shook their heads.

"Good," he said. "Now go into the city and get the things that I have written on these lists. Just remember, you must not be seen!"

The students took the lists with lowered heads and began to shuffle out of the temple. The old Master walked slowly to the door and watched them go out of the gate. When he turned back inside, there was one student still standing quietly in the corner of the room.

"Why did you not go with the others?" the old man asked. "Don't you want our school to continue?"

"I do, Master," the boy said quietly. "But you said that we had to steal without being seen, and I know that there is no place that I would not be seen, for I would always see myself."

"Aha!" cried the Master in delight. "That was the lesson that I wanted to teach, and only you have seen it. Run and tell your friends to return to the temple before they get us into trouble."

The boy ran and got his friends. When they returned, the Master told them of the words the boy had spoken, and they all understood the lesson.

India (Jataka)

Grades 4-8

THEMES : Honesty, self-awareness, self-mastery, making wise choices, integrity, responsibility

There is a Christian version, which is retold in *The Children's Book of Virtues*, by William J. Bennett (New York: Simon & Schuster, 1995), in which a father tells his daughter to stand guard in a field while he steals wheat. He tells her to call out if anyone sees him. She keeps calling out, "Someone sees you," even though no one is there. Finally, he asks her what she is talking about, and she says, "Someone from above sees you."

SOURCES

Kindness: A Treasury of Buddhist Wisdom for Children and Parents, by Sarah Conover (Spokane, Wash.: Eastern Washington Univ. Press, 2001).

Wisdom Tales from Around the World, by Heather Forest (Little Rock: August House, 1996).

Twenty Jataka Tales, by Noor Inayat Kahn (London: George G. Harrap and Co., 1939).

This story is tricky, in that it involves a teacher pretending to condone stealing. As parents or teachers telling the story, you are put in the position of pretending that this is all right, until the story is resolved. My experience is that students with sufficient developmental maturity can handle this dilemma with no difficulty, and will explain to you why the teacher used it as a test. It does generate much discussion, which is a good thing! I would not tell it to students under about the 4th grade for this reason.

You want to think carefully about how you set the story up. I think it is helpful to tell the students in advance that Zen teachers often use a trick or riddle to make a point that really hits home. This will ease them in to understanding how this man could do such a thing. It also helps to have the students in the story be very confused by the teacher's request.

I like to pull up a chair when telling this one. From this vantage point I can best characterize the old teacher, and to imagine that my audience are the teacher's students. I characterize the young boys in the story with body language and a simple change of my voice tone.

- **Class reenactment:** Assign two directors, a wise teacher, the thoughtful student and the rest of the students. Let the students retell this story to you in improvised drama.

- **Questions and discussion:** You may want to ask the following questions to be sure that your students are not confused about the story message: Did the old Master really think that it was OK to steal? (Your students will want to discuss this!) What was the old Master trying to teach his students? Why did most of the students obey the Master when he told them to do something that they knew was wrong? What would you have done in that situation? Turn the idea of being seen by ourselves on its head, and ask your students to think about whether they do good things because they know or hope that others will recognize them, or because they feel that they should. Put this quote on the board and let the students think about, and then write or share their answer for homework. "The measure of a person's real character is what he would do even if he knew he would never be found out." (Adapted from a quote by Lord Macaulay.) The idea is not what negative actions we would take, but what positive ones.

- **Story sharing:** Have you been in this situation where you had to decide whether to do something based on your own conscience? Talk about what it means to have a "conscience."

- **Dramatic reenactment with different scenarios:** Have the students imagine what would have happened if none of the students had guessed the right answer to the Master's test.

- **Creative adaptation:** Have the students make up modern-day versions of this story. Use some of the situations that you brainstormed in the exercise below.

Turning the story ideas into action

- **Brainstorm** a list of other examples of situations in which even if nobody else sees us, we still see ourselves. These might include cheating on schoolwork, breaking something and not telling anyone, lying to someone, taking more than our share of a tasty treat, not recycling or cleaning something up because we are feeling lazy.

- **Journal reflections:** Have students reflect in journals on their actions for that day and anything they wish they had handled differently.

Favorite picture books

The Empty Pot, by Demi (New York: Henry Holt & Co.,1990). This is a powerful story about honesty, self-respect, courage, and perseverance that works with grades K-4. The Emperor sets a test for all the children in China who would like to be the next Emperor. He gives each a seed and asks them to come back in one year with what they have grown. The young hero tries to grow the seed but without success, though not for lack of trying. When he returns he is the only child without a big and beautiful flower in his pot. The Emperor rewards him for his honesty and courage, for all the seeds he had given the children had been cooked, and would not grow a thing.

Pedro and Padre: A Tale from Jalisco, Mexico, retold by Verna Aardema (New York: Dial Books, 1991). In this fun story, a boy named Pedro works for the padre (priest) of a small town. Pedro is very lazy and dishonest and his lies get him into big trouble until he vows never to lie again.

The Cow of No Color: Riddle Stories and Justice Tales from Around the World by N. Jaffe and S. Zeitlin (New York: Henry Holt, 1998). This book is full of short tales that offer students the chance to debate and find solutions.

Leadership
and Citizenship

WHAT QUALITIES DO WE LOOK FOR IN OUR LEADERS? Here are some that I think of: courage, wisdom, humility, vision, equanimity, willingness to sacrifice, optimism, willingness to take risks, integrity (walking the talk), new ideas, passion, empathy for others, justice. What would you add?

What qualities do we look for in a responsible citizen? Here are some that come to mind for me: activism, volunteerism, generosity, vision, caring and empathy, tolerance, appreciation of difference, belief in democratic principles of equal rights and responsibilities. What would you add?

Most of our children will not automatically strive to take on leadership roles in school, but serving in leadership roles helps children to build confidence and empathy. How do we help inspire them?

Students learn primarily by example. They will learn about leadership and citizenship from their parents and teachers. How do you as a parent and teacher model leadership and citizenship in the school and community? Do your children see you voting, volunteering to do charitable work, and working in leadership positions?

Stories can help to expand your students' awareness of the importance of everyone taking on leadership roles and demonstrating citizenship by caring about their school and community.

The Monkey King

India (Jataka)

Grades K-5

THEMES: Leadership, empathy, respect, greed, courage and sacrifice, civic duties

Once upon a time, deep in the countryside of India, there stood a tall, lush tree that was always full of beautiful ripe, red fruits. A large flock of monkeys lived in this tree and ate the delicious fruit. The monkeys had a King, who was far larger than the others were. He looked after them, protected them from danger, and advised them in all matters.

Now the Monkey King told his flock regularly that they must be sure to remove all of the fruits from the branches that overhung the river. For he knew that if the fruit fell into the river and floated down to the city, it would be desired by others and its source discovered, and the monkeys would no longer be safe. So the monkeys spent every evening clearing any new fruit from those branches.

But one time, a fruit hidden by a large green leaf continued to grow until it was ripe and fell into the river. It was carried downstream, where some women who were bathing in the river picked it up. The fruit smelled so sweet that they were tempted to eat it, but they knew that if their King found out that they had tried the fruit and not given it to him to enjoy, he would be angry.

When the King tasted this fruit, he was overwhelmed by a desire to have more of it. He demanded that a boat carry him and his servants up the river the next day to find the source of this fruit. After traveling up the river for some time, the King's party began to smell the sweet, delicious fruit. Looking up on the bank, they saw the great tree, and the ripe, red fruits. But, the King's joy turned quickly to horror as he saw that the tree was full of monkeys who were eating the fruit.

"This is my tree and my fruit!" roared the King. "I will not stand for animals eating my fruit. Archers, prepare your arrows and shoot them all."

The King's archers took aim and began to shoot at the little monkeys in the tree. The Monkey King realized what was going on and thought fast. He climbed to the top of the tree and, holding tight with his feet to the topmost branches, he swung to the nearest tree. He grabbed the top of that tree, making his body into a bridge. "Come, my friends, climb across my back and escape from the tree! Otherwise you will die."

The little monkeys raced to the top of the tree, climbed upon his back, and ran free into the forest. The weight of the monkeys was great, and the two trees pulled against one another. The strain on the Monkey King's back and arms was tremendous. He was about to lose his grasp and fall to his death.

Meanwhile on the ground below, the King became aware of the Monkey King's attempt to save his followers. He stood in awe and watched as the great monkey strained and weakened. "Stop shooting," he ordered. "Save this brave monkey from death. Get a net and catch him before he falls."

The King's servants held a net below the Monkey King and he soon fell into it, exhausted but unhurt. The King rushed to his side. "You are a strong and brave monkey," he said, "but I don't understand your actions. Why would you risk your life to save the lives of your inferiors? They should be saving and serving you!"

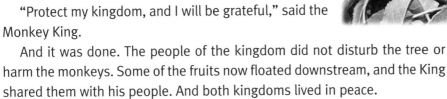

The Monkey King raised his tired head and spoke to the King. "As their King, it is my job to protect and care for them. If I saved myself and thought not of them, they would perish. It is because I love them so well that they chose me as King."

The human King was quiet for a long time. At last he said, "You have taught me well. I have thought that to be King meant that people were responsible to serve me. I see that it is I who am responsible to serve and to love them. How can I repay you?"

"Protect my kingdom, and I will be grateful," said the Monkey King.

And it was done. The people of the kingdom did not disturb the tree or harm the monkeys. Some of the fruits now floated downstream, and the King shared them with his people. And both kingdoms lived in peace.

SOURCES

The Fables of India, by Joseph Gaer (Boston: Little Brown and Co., 1955).

The Jatakamala, by J.S. Speyer, translated by Motilal Banarsidass (Delhi, India: Motilal Banarsidass, 1982).

Stories of the Buddha: Being Selections from the Jataka, translated and edited by Caroline Rhys Davids (New York: Dover Publications, 1929).

PICTURE BOOKS

The Monkey Bridge, by Rafe Martin (New York: Knopf, 1992).

Buddha Stories, by Demi (New York: Henry Holt and Co., 1997).

Tips for the telling

You can introduce the story by explaining the origin of the Jataka tales to your students. (See page 76.) Then tell the story in a straightforward manner. Alternatively, you could tell it in the first person as one of the monkeys living there, or the human king, or one of his servants. This story does not have obvious audience participation. You may want to think about how you will describe the way that the Monkey King stretches his body between the two trees to make it visual. To draw out the theme of leadership, you might want to add some more ways that the human king required sacrifice from his people.

Follow-up activities
Tip for retention

- **Group reenactment:** Have the class retell this by acting it out together. If the students are older, choose several directors to move people around and to give out parts. If they are younger, you can be the director and narrator.

Making a personal connection

- **Questions and discussion:** What would have happened if the Monkey King had fled first into the forest? What kind of leader was the human king at the start of the story? What changes did he probably make after this story?

- **Story sharing:** Help the students to think of times when they had been a leader. Did they assume that it was their job to look after their followers, or to be looked after? Can they think of examples of people in leadership roles in the present or down through history who take either tack? What leaders can they name? What do they do as leaders? What do the students respect about them?

Creative exploration

- **Leadership research:** Older students can research stories from history about great leaders; have individual students tell those stories to the class. Younger students can interview a parent asking them which leaders they most respect and why. Share this information with the class.

Turning the story ideas into action

- **Brainstorm:** Have the class make a list of the qualities of a good leader and the qualities of a person who is a good citizen, or who participates in his community. Invite leaders in the school and community to come in and tell the students what leadership roles they take.

- **Act locally:** Remind your students of President John F. Kennedy's famous quote, "Ask not what your country can do for you, but what you can do for your country." Change the quote to "...what you can do for your school or community," and let the students come up with activities that they could do to be responsible citizens.

Reaching for the Moon

Once upon a time, on the island of the Dominican Republic, there lived a King who was both greedy and foolish. Worse than that, he demanded that his servants and the people of his land do whatever he asked of them, or they would be thrown into his dark and dreary dungeons for the rest of their lives.

One night the King climbed to the topmost turret of his castle and gazed up at the moon. "How I long to touch the moon," he thought to himself. He had had this thought many times, and he had spent much time thinking about how he could reach the moon. Suddenly an idea occurred to him. "I am King and I should be able to get what I want!"

"Servants!" he yelled. "Get the royal carpenter immediately!" Although it was late in the evening, the royal carpenter came quickly.

"Carpenter, I want you to build me a tower tall enough to reach the moon. Begin at once."

"Tall enough to reach the moon, Your Highness?" he stammered. "But, Your Highness, it can't be done. The moon is too far away for such a tower."

"Take him to the dungeon," screamed the King.

"Wait," the carpenter said. "Give me one night to think about it. Perhaps there is a way that I have not thought of yet."

And so the King agreed. The next day the carpenter returned to the royal throne room. "Your Highness, I think I have a plan that will work. I will need to have all of the strong wooden chests in the kingdom. If I pile one on top of the other, we may have enough to reach the moon."

So the King ordered that all of the wooden chests be brought from the people's houses and piled one on top of the other. Soon there were no more wooden chests to be found. The King climbed to the top. He reached up, but the moon was still far away. "I need more wooden chests, carpenter! This tower is not tall enough," he yelled down.

So the carpenter began to build more chests. He employed all of the carpenters in the kingdom. They worked day and night until they had used up all of the wood supplies in the kingdom. Again, the King climbed to the very top. He reached up toward the moon, but he was still far away.

"Get more wooden chests!" he demanded.

"Your Highness, we have used up all of the cut wood in the kingdom. There is nothing left to build houses or furniture or gates," the carpenter explained.

"Then cut down all the trees!" the King said. "I want my tower!"

Dominican Republic

Grades K-5

THEMES: Greed, authoritarianism, foolishness, following unwise advice

So, the carpenter got the woodcutters to cut down all of the trees in the kingdom, and carpenters made wooden chests. They piled the new chests up on top of the tall tower. Again, the King climbed up to the top and again he reached out, but he was not tall enough to reach the moon.

"Carpenter!" he called down angrily. "Get me more wooden chests!"

"There aren't any more, Sire," he called back. "There is no more wood to be had in our whole kingdom."

"I must reach the moon. I must!" he said to himself. Then an idea came to him. "Take a wooden chest from the bottom and bring it up to the top," the King called down. "Then I think I shall reach the moon."

"It can't be done, Sire," the carpenter yelled.

"Can't, can't! All you say is can't! Guards, take him to the dungeon!"

"All right," sighed the carpenter. "I will do it."

He grabbed the wooden chest on the bottom of the tower and pulled and pulled. All the other carpenters pulled with him, and finally out it came. And with it came all of the other wooden chests, tumbling down. Down too came the King.

You could say it was his downfall.

SOURCES

Magical Tales from Many Lands, retold by Margaret Mayo (New York: Dutton Books, 1993).

Ride with the Sun: Folk Tales and Stories from All Countries of the United Nations, edited by Harold Courlander (New York: McGraw Hill Book Co., 1955).

Folk Tales of Latin America, adapted by Shirlee P. Newman (Indianapolis: The Bobbs-Merrill Co., Inc., 1962).

CULTURAL VARIANT

"Reaching for the Moon," from *Tibet in Peace Tales* by Margaret Read MacDonald. A monkey king demands that his people make a chain of their bodies hanging from a tree so that he can reach into a pond to rescue the moon, which he thinks has drowned. They all fall in and drown.

This tale is meant to be humorous and lighthearted in its telling. The more outrageous you can make the king, the better. Most of the story is told with the king high up on the tower calling down to the carpenter, and the carpenter calling back up to him. You can easily show this with your body. The students can join you as the carpenters in making chests, or you can add in a participatory movement to show the king climbing up the tower.

Show the students where the Dominican Republic is on the map. The Dominican Republic shares an island with the country of Haiti. Sadly, Haiti has nearly deforested its side of the island after many years of poor management and leadership. In the fall of 2004, Hurricane Jeanne hit the island. More than 900 people and countless more animals drowned, partly because of deforestation.

Make sure everyone knows what a wooden chest is or substitute the term "wooden boxes." In some countries and in early times people stored most of their things in wooden chests rather than closets.

- **Small-group retelling with props:** This is a fun story to retell with wooden blocks at a drama or block area of the room. If they like they can use small figures made of clay to represent the characters, or simple small plastic figures that you may have in the room. Let the students retell as they use all of their blocks to build the tower. See what happens when they remove the bottom block.

- **Questions and discussion:** Have you ever wanted something that you just could not realistically have? Share your answers. The king wanted to touch the moon, but it meant taking everyone's wooden chests, and eventually cutting down all the trees. Do you think the king was a responsible leader? What would happen if all of the trees were cut down in an area?

- **Creative adaptation:** Younger students can make up a new version of this tale, changing the way that the king goes about trying to reach for the moon. Older students can modernize the tale, setting it in a country they can relate to, and choosing something that a leader might want that would be greedy or damaging to the people or environment, and how it comes back to haunt him in the end.

- **Change the ending:** The carpenter, who is a much wiser leader, realizes that the tower will fall if he takes out the bottom box, so before he does, he devises a plan to catch the king. See if the students can come up with such a plan, and what they would demand of the king if they did save his life.

- **Practicing leadership:** Help your students to take a leadership role at home and in school to protect the environment. Have your students investigate ways at home and in the school to be more energy efficient and to do more recycling. If the students are younger, you can make it concrete, focusing on recycling paper or plastic shopping bags. Have the class pick a resource to research and come up with suggestions for ways to save and recycle more. Have students be leaders in their family by teaching everyone how to take new steps for the environment.

Follow-up activities

Tip for retention

Making a personal connection

Creative exploration

Turning the story ideas into action

The Father, the Son and the Donkey

Aesop and Buddhist

Grades 2-8

THEMES: Thinking for oneself, self-respect/ confidence, worrying about others' opinions, wisdom

One day a farmer decided that his young donkey was fat enough to sell in the market. He called to his son and told him to bring two poles. "We will carry our donkey to market on these two poles so that she will not get too thin from walking the long distance," he said.

So they tied the donkey to the poles, hoisted the poles on their shoulders, and headed off down the road to market. The donkey hung upside down between them, braying in dismay.

Soon they came to a group of people coming the other way on the road. The people saw them and began to laugh. "Look at the stupid fellows carrying a donkey like a pig! That donkey should be carrying you! Why don't you get on its back and ride it?"

When the farmer and his son heard the laughter and jeering, they were embarrassed. When the people had gone, the farmer said to his son, "I guess we made a mistake. Perhaps we should ride the donkey. But she is too small for both of us to ride, so you ride her, as you are lighter than I am."

So the young man got up on the donkey, the farmer led her by a rope, and they went on down the road. Soon they came to a group of people by the side of the road. Again, these people began to laugh and to point. "Look at that selfish son, riding while his poor father walks and leads the donkey! The old man should ride and the boy should walk!"

When they had passed the group, the farmer said to his son, "It seems as if we have made a mistake again. I guess I should ride and you should walk."

"Yes, father," the young man agreed. So they switched places and started down the road again. Soon they came to the river. They crossed the bridge and entered the outskirts of town. Here there were quite a few young women gathered on the road. Again, they laughed at the boy and his father. "Hey, what is an old, ugly man doing riding when the handsome young man must walk like a servant? The boy should ride like a prince and the old man should walk."

The boy turned toward his father. "Father, have we made a mistake again?"

"Yes, my son. But what can we do? First, they say it is wrong for us to carry the donkey, and then they said it was wrong for you to ride, and then they say it is wrong for me to ride. What if we both ride together?"

So the boy got on with his father, and the two of them rode into the center of town where the busy market was in session. But here again a group of people turned to stare at them.

"How could you be so cruel?" they asked, pointing. "That donkey is barely old enough for one rider and yet you put on two? That donkey is so little you should be carrying her! Shame on you, shame on you!" they cried. More and more people joined the angry mob of onlookers. Their cries were joined by others and they got louder and louder.

The farmer and his son got off at once, but the crowd was so loud that they frightened the donkey, which bucked, and kicked herself free and ran off, never to be seen again.

SOURCES

Doorways to the Soul: 52 Wisdom Tales from Around the World, edited by Elisa Pearmain (Cleveland: Pilgrim Press, 1998).

Cambodian Folk Stories from the Gatiloke, retold by Muriel Paskin Carrison (Rutland, Vt.: Charles E. Tuttle Co., 1987).

Tales of the Hodja, by Charles Downing (New York: Henry Z. Walck, 1965).

Tips for the telling

Tell this story in a straightforward manner, or from the perspective of one of the characters. You can add humor by telling it as if you were the donkey, the farmer, or the son. To add participation, you can give the parts of the people they meet to groups of students. Tell them exactly what to say, or better yet, write down their parts on the board so they are easy to remember. This adds a quality of reality to the story. Have the last group be joined gradually by all the other groups until the jeering is so loud that the donkey runs away.

Follow-up activities

Tips for story retention

- **Act the story out together:** Pick three students to play the father, son, and donkey. Divide the rest of the students into the four groups that criticize the farmer and son. Give them a simple line to say.

- **Retell through drawings:** Have each student draw one scene from the story and sequence them together for a retell.

Making a personal connection

- **Questions, discussion and story sharing:** A good leader is able to think for him- or herself, and can take unpopular stands when he or she believes they are right. It is common for leaders to change their policies and perspectives depending on opinion polls or influence groups. A responsible leader will also be respectful and tolerant of other people's choices, even if they differ from his or her own.

- **Questions for story sharing:** When have you felt like you had to change something that made sense to you to fit in and be accepted? Were you ever laughed at for doing things a certain way? Did you ever criticize someone else for his or her behavior? What do you do that is totally you, even if others laugh at you, or don't understand? How easy is it for people to get you to change your mind? Share a time when you took an unpopular view, or when you dared to do something that other people might think was strange.

Creative exploration

- **Point-of-view retelling:** Let the students have fun retelling this story from different points of view.

- **Modernize the story** and change what is being criticized. Make a list of things that people could or would do to try and fit in: politicians changing their stance on an issue, or students changing clothing style, taste in music, hair color, friends...see what the students come up with. Let them write their own tales and share them with one another. Pick one of two to act out for other classes. Let them act out the original story or their own versions for other classes.

Turning the story ideas into action

- **Visual representations:** Let the students make posters with messages about the value of individuality, thinking for oneself, and not judging others.

- **Common catch phrases:** Help students devise a language to remind each other of the story when they find themselves criticizing someone else's style or choices.

- **Journal reflection:** Have students keep track in their journals of times during their day when they find their decisions being affected by others, and when they can make choices that feel right to them. This can be as simple as a choice of dress or hair, a decision about which elective to join, whom to sit with at lunch, or whether to ask a question in class.

Belling the Cat

Once upon a time, many mice lived in a barn. Their lives were happy and carefree until a large cat moved into the barn and began to reduce their numbers with each passing day. The cat was clever and sneaky, and she often took them by surprise. It got so that they barely dared to leave their holes in search of food.

One day the mice called a meeting. "We must find a way to get rid of this beast!" they cried. Many plans were bandied about, but they all seemed too difficult. Finally, a young mouse stood up.

"I have a plan," he squeaked. "It would not kill the cat, for I do not think we can do that. But it will at least let us know when she is coming, so that we may run and hide." Everyone listened in. "All we have to do is to hang a bell around the neck of the cat. When she moves, the bell will ring, and we will know that our enemy is coming."

The older mice looked at one another. "Why did we not think of this ourselves? Such a simple, but brilliant, plan! We have a new leader!" they called excitedly.

Soon all of the mice were chanting, "Lead us, lead us, lead us" as they lifted the mouse high upon their shoulders and paraded him around. He grinned furiously.

Then the oldest mouse of all stood slowly, leaning heavily on her cane. "It is a good idea, young ones. But tell me, is our new leader brave enough to put the bell on the cat?"

Everyone was quiet. The young mouse's eyes grew wide as he considered the task. At last, he shook his head and said, "No."

"Then who will bell the cat?" the old mouse asked. Everyone else shook their heads. "Good ideas are only good if someone is willing to carry them out," said the old mouse sadly, as she hobbled back to her hole.

See page 44 for information on Aesop.

Aesop Grades 2-8

Themes: Leadership, courage, wisdom

Tips for the telling

This tale can be expanded to include more detail and character development, or kept as a simple and short story.

Follow-up activities

Tip for story retention

- **Dramatize it as a group:** This is a fun story to retell as a short play. Assign someone to be the cat and everyone else the mice, including the young mouse with the idea, and a few elderly mice, including the one with the cane. You narrate as they go through the action. Let the main characters say the lines in their own words, asking prompting questions to remind them if they are stuck. The whole "mouse group" can chant, "Lead us, lead us, lead us!"

Making a personal connection

- **Questions, discussion and story sharing:** It is one thing to come up with a good idea, but leaders should always think about whether they would be willing to carry out their ideas, or if they would expect others to do so. Have you ever had a good idea that you needed someone else to do? Has anyone ever wanted you to do something that they didn't dare to do? What was the outcome? Share these stories with one another.

- **Debate:** This is a good topic for a debate with older students. A good leader can mobilize people to action, but a responsible leader will not endanger others without having a very good cause. Let them imagine scenarios and take opposing sides of this debate. Examples could include the wars of the last two centuries.

Creative exploration

- **Create alternate endings:** The mouse with the good idea could have seized on his new leadership power and demanded that a group of mice go and bell the cat, like soldiers going off to war. Tell this story with possible alternative endings in which the young mouse acts in various ways, as a good and not-so-good leader.

Turning the story ideas into action

- **Role-play** in your classroom based on the story model in which the students identify the biggest problem in the school or town and then go about trying to find solutions. If someone comes up with an idea, call out, "Lead us, lead us," and see if that person can take a leadership role, or if the idea does not seem realistic.

King Solomon and the Hoopoe Bird

Once upon a time, there was a King named Solomon. It was said that he could solve any riddle and that he could speak and understand the language of every animal. It was said that he could summon the animals and tame the wind. News of his power and wisdom spread far and wide. The Queen of Sheba decided to visit the King to see for herself. There are many stories of the riddles she put to him and how cleverly he solved them. When the Queen of Sheba made ready to return to her palace, King Solomon offered to give her a gift. She decided to make this a test as well.

"Any gift?" she asked.

"Any gift," he responded. And so the Queen of Sheba asked King Solomon to build her a palace made entirely of bird beaks.

The King was a bit worried. A palace made of bird beaks would require that every bird in the world give up its beak. But he had made a promise. So he called all of the birds in the world to his palace. Hearing his call, they readily came: large birds, like the eagles and hawks, storks and cranes; and small birds, like the hummingbird, the sparrow and the bluebird; and every bird in between. The sky darkened as all of the birds of the world surrounded his palace. Every bird except one: the hoopoe bird, a small bird with colorful wings and a long pointed beak.

"Where is the hoopoe bird?" the King asked. "It has disobeyed me. Find the hoopoe bird," he ordered his servants. "It will be punished for disobeying the King!"

Soon the hoopoe bird had been found, and was brought before the King. "Why have you disobeyed me? Where have you been?" the King asked.

"Please do not be angry with me, Your Highness," the bird cried. "I have been flying about trying to gain wisdom, so that I might serve you. Please let me prove to you that I have served you well. Let me ask you three riddles. If you can answer them, then you may punish me. If I can teach you something new, please set me free."

"I like riddles and I like to learn new things," the King said. "If I cannot solve one of the riddles, I will set you free."

The hoopoe bird began, "This is the first riddle: How long are the world and its creatures made to last?"

"Hmm," said the King, "the world and its creatures are meant to last a long time." But to himself the King thought, "And here I am changing the birds forever."

Jewish

Grades 2-6

THEMES: Wisdom, flexible thinking, courage, foresight, humility, compassion

The hoopoe bird continued, "Here is the second riddle: What water never rises from the ground and never falls from the sky?"

The King smiled again, for he also knew the answer to this question. "It is a tear, a tear made from sadness." As he answered, he looked around and saw that all of the birds were weeping. "They are crying because I am going to cut off their beaks," he thought.

Now for the third question, the bird continued. "What is gentle enough to feed the smallest baby, and yet strong enough to bore holes in the hardest tree?" For a third time the King smiled. He also knew the answer to this question. "It is a bird's beak!" he shouted triumphantly. But as he looked around at all of the birds with their heads sadly bowed, he thought to himself, "And I am going to take those beaks from the birds. How will they survive, for they also use them to build their homes and defend themselves."

The hoopoe bird bowed its head too. "Your Highness, you have indeed answered all of my questions correctly. You may punish me as you wish." But for a fourth time King Solomon smiled.

"I may have known the answers to your riddles, little bird, but I did not have the wisdom to see how my actions would affect others. You have shown me that. I will not build the palace of bird beaks. It would not be fair to hurt the birds just to show that I could give any gift asked of me. You will not be punished, hoopoe bird, you will be rewarded. From now on, you will wear a crown of golden feathers upon your head." With the wave of his hand, the hoopoe had a beautiful golden crown, which it wears to this day.

He then turned to the Queen of Sheba. Now it was her turn to smile. "This was my final test, King Solomon. Not only are you clever, but also you are wise and compassionate. You can admit when you are wrong, and you can reward others for their wisdom. That is the greatest gift of all."

SOURCE

"The Palace of Bird Beaks," in *The Diamond Tree*, by Howard Schwartz and Barbara Rush (New York: HarperCollins Publishers, 1991).

PICTURE BOOK

The Wisdom Bird: A Tale of Solomon and Sheba, retold by Sheldon Oberman (Honesdale, Penn.: Boyds Mill Press, Inc., 2000).

Another story of King Solomon and the hoopoe can be found in "How the Hoopoe Got Its Crown" in *And It Came to Pass*, by Hyman Nahman Bialik (New York: The Hebrew Publishing Co., 1938).

This may be your students' first introduction to stories of King Solomon. You may want to have other stories on hand, such as "King Solomon and the Bee," an example of one of the tests put to him by the Queen of Sheba. I suggest telling this tale in a straightforward manner, allowing for the emotion that the King and birds feel to come through.

- **Group reenactment:** I would suggest having the class retell this story with everyone involved. You can be the narrator, or with older students, appoint a director and narrators.

- **Questions, discussion and story sharing:** King Solomon promises to give the Queen of Sheba whatever gift she wants. He does this because he is so powerful that everything bows to him. What makes him break his promise? Have you ever felt that you were more powerful than someone else? How did this affect how you treated that person? Have you ever had to break a promise? Did you ever feel that someone else was hurting other people or animals because they could get away with it? A good leader can admit when he or she has made a mistake. This can be a rich area of story sharing.

- **Creative adaptation:** This is a pourquoi story that explains how the hoopoe bird got its crown. What other gifts could the Queen of Sheba have requested, and how could another animal teach the king that it is not wise to sacrifice others to show power? Make up a story as a group and or let the students create their own adaptations.

- **Modernize:** This story offers an opportunity to teach about the concept of "power over," and how bullying often happens when one student discovers that he or she can be more powerful than another, whether mentally, physically or due to popularity. I suggest that you guide your class in reshaping a modern-day version of this story as if it were about a bully who bullied because he or she could (maybe on a dare) and then learned a lesson. Retell the modernized story to other classes and initiate discussion about bullying and leadership qualities.

- **Self-reflection:** For older students invite them to be aware of when they feel they have the power to do something that might not be nice to a sibling, neighbor, or peer, and to try to practice restraint.

Favorite picture books

Brer Tiger and The Big Wind, retold by William J. Faulkner (New York: Morrow Junior Books, 1995). Faulkner heard this version of the tale from an African-American gentleman named Simon Brown, who worked on his grandfather's farm. I like this version for the purposes of leadership studies as the main character enlists the help of everyone in the community to solve a problem, giving them encouragement and hope. The problem is solved by group action and creativity rather than force.

The Legend of the Bluebonnet: An Old Tale of Texas, by Tomie de Paola (New York: Scholastic, Inc., 1989). This is a Comanche legend in which a girl sacrifices her doll, (her only tangible connection to her dead relatives) so that the rain will come. She chooses her people over her personal needs. She is rewarded with rain and the deep love of her people.

"Yertle the Turtle," from *Yertle the Turtle and Other Stories*, by Theodore Geisel and Audrey Geisel (New York: Random House, 1950) Yertle the Turtle wants to be king of all he can see. He cannot see much from his pond so he keeps demanding that his turtle subordinates make a higher and higher pile so that he can see more and more. Finally, someone in the pile burps and down goes Yertle and his rule.

The Boy Who Dreamed of an Acorn, by Leigh Casler (New York: Philomel, 1994). In this literary tale, a boy goes on his rite-of-passage vision quest hoping to have a vision of a powerful animal to bring back to his people. Instead of these, he dreams of an acorn. He is ashamed of this vision and lack of physical strength. The wise man convinces him to plant the acorn in his village and to stay near it to watch it grow. The tree grows and becomes a center for both animal and village life. As the boy grows into a young man, more and more people congregate around the tree and seek his advice, and in time, he becomes the wise man of the tribe.

Web resource

www.civiced.org—Curriculum and resources for teaching civics in schools and communities nationally and internationally.

Perseverance

PEOPLE WITH CHARACTER DO NOT GIVE UP EASILY. If they believe that achieving a goal is important, they will persevere until they succeed. What does it take to persist despite difficulty? Some of the ingredients are faith in yourself and often something greater than yourself (spiritual faith), courage, patience, and a passionate belief in what you are doing. If you look at the stories of those who have had great successes, you will find that many, many failures preceded the successes, and these failures were necessary for them to learn what they needed to do. Persevering means not giving up. It means working hard at your task and giving it your all for as long as it takes.

Perseverance and diligence are required in school. Students are repeatedly required to stick at things, from practicing musical instruments and athletic skills, mastering mathematical concepts to making it through grueling tests.

Patience is a necessary skill for success. Our modern culture has an "everything now" quality to it, in which young people get the message that anything can be had with the swipe of a credit card or swallowing the right pill. As a whole, we have become less and less patient with waiting, hard work, and unknown outcomes. Patience is a very important quality of character for meeting the challenges of life and for working with others.

Folk tales are replete with examples of how perseverance, diligence, and patience pay off in the end. Our ancestors who created and told the tales clearly felt that these lessons were valuable. Hearing the stories of how others persevered can help us to have the patience and faith to do the same in times of adversity and challenge. Stories are excellent food for the future. Like fat, we store them in our memory cells, and call on them in lean times.

The Crow and the Vase

Aesop

Grades K-3

THEMES: Perseverance, cleverness, diligence, hard work, patience

It had been a long dry summer. No rain had fallen on the land and the rivers and streams had dried up and gone beneath the ground. The animals were thirsty. Two crows out in search of water spied a pitcher of water behind a house. They flew over the yard and landed on the pitcher's brim. Peering into it, they saw water, but it was so low down that their beaks could not reach it.

Together the crows tried to tip the pitcher over, but it would not budge. They tried holding each other as they leaned over the side, but it was no use. It was too narrow to reach. "This is impossible," cackled the first. "Let us not waste any more time here."

"Wait, friend," said the second. "I know we will think of something if we try." Not wanting to give up with water so nearby, the second crow sat and looked at the water and thought and thought. Suddenly she cawed with delight and flew off a short distance to the road. There she picked up a pebble in her beak and flew back to the pitcher. She dropped it in, and a splash of water hit her face. "Look!" she said. "If we fill the pitcher with stones, the water will rise."

"Oh, no," said the first crow, "That's hard work, and it will take all day. I'm going to go and find me a nice cool stream." He flew off.

The second crow kept up at her idea. She flew to the road again and dropped another pebble in, with the same reaction. Repeatedly she flew to the road and back until at last she had filled the bottom of the pitcher with stones. The water level rose and rose until finally when she threw in a pebble, it was not a drop of water that hit her beak, but the surface of the water itself. The crow had a nice long drink. As for her friend, he flew back later, tired and thirsty, to find his friend happy and refreshed.

See page 44 for information on Aesop.

This is a short and straightforward story that lends itself well to a demonstration. I suggest telling the story once through and then letting the students try it out for size. You can also use the props the first time through. All you need is a pitcher half full of water and some pebbles or marbles. I like to emphasize the difference between the crow who did not have the patience to wait and the one who did. You should decide at what point the lazy crow would fly off. I wait until the resourceful crow had thought of her idea, so that it is clearly a matter of being willing to work hard, rather than lack of brains.

Tell this story as a riddle and do not reveal how the first crow was able to drink. Change the story so that the lazy crow decides to fly off when he cannot drink from the vase. Have the other crow stay and fly back and forth from the road for several hours until she is able to drink. Ask your students what the clever crow did. Then demonstrate!

Tips for the telling

- **Retell with props:** This short tale should not require much going over. Have a number of pitchers half full of water and some pebbles at various tables or stations so that small groups can try it out. They can also estimate how many pebbles or how long it will take, or what kind of objects will cause the water to rise most quickly and effectively. (You might also have sand, straw, and other things on hand.) Have them go home, tell the story, and do the demonstration for their family members.

Follow-up activities

Tip for story retention

- **Questions, discussion and story sharing:** Did you ever have to do something that took a lot of work but had a great result? Did you ever give up on something only to have someone else follow through and get the reward that you missed? Did you ever put your all into something and feel very proud? What kinds of things do you do that require constant practice or work to see an improvement? What makes it easier for you to persevere?

Making a personal connection

- **Teacher tells:** Can you think of some examples of projects that you have worked hard on and received a reward, such as learning to play an instrument, excelling at a sport, or staying in school. Share these with your students. They will make an impression and help the students to think of times when they have worked hard or stuck with something difficult.

- **Creative retells:** Have groups of three retell the story with props, making it their own by changing it in small or not-so-small ways.

Creative exploration

- **Visual representations:** Have the students make posters of the story, including captions, to put up in the room to remind them to stick with something until it is completed.

Turning the story ideas into action

- **Brainstorm** ideas for a simple project they can stick with until it is complete, and do it together with a nice reward afterwards. Examples could be making rock candy, a papier mâché piñata or puppets, or something else that takes several days and stages.

The Grasshopper and the Ants

Aesop

Grades Pre-K-3

THEMES: Working hard for future reward, planning, concentrating on a task, persisting when it would be more fun to stop and play, kindness

Once warm summer day, a Grasshopper was sitting in the shade of a tree playing his fiddle and hopping from foot to foot in a happy dance to his own tunes. As he played, a line of ants marched by carrying grains of wheat bigger than their heads in their mouths.

The Grasshopper stopped his tune and called out to the ants to come and dance. All of the ants ignored him, except the last ant in line, the youngest, who looked longingly at the Grasshopper having fun. "I'd like to dance and play, Mr. Grasshopper," she said, "but my family needs to build a new home and to gather food for the winter."

"Winter is far off, my friend," the Grasshopper laughed. "Come and play now, work later."

The little ant smiled at the happy Grasshopper, but shook her head and kept on working.

All summer the Grasshopper played his fiddle and danced, and every day the ant family passed by. Every day he called out to them to stop and play

with him, and every day they shook their heads, and the littlest ant told him that they had to prepare for winter.

Finally, the summer passed to fall. The nights grew chilly and frost covered the ground. Now the Grasshopper sat by the tree and shivered. He was hungry and cold. He saw the ants go passing by one more time, and he followed them. When he reached their door, he knocked. "May I come in? I'm so cold and hungry."

"No," said the ants. "All summer you played while we worked. Now you will face the consequences."

"Bu-bu-but, I'm freeeeeezing and huuuungry," stammered Mr. Grasshopper.

"Go away!" the ants cried and closed the door. The Grasshopper slumped down against the door feeling very cold, very hungry, and very sad.

Suddenly the door came open and the littlest ant called out, "Mr. Grasshopper! We worked hard all summer, and now we can rest. If you will come in and play your fiddle for us, we will share our food with you. But next summer you must gather your own food."

"Thank you, little friend," said the Grasshopper. "I promise I will. I've learned my lesson." He slipped inside, glad for a second chance.

See page 44 for information on Aesop.

This is my version of this short fable. In the more traditional version, the ants do not let the grasshopper in, and tell him only that "since he sang all summer, he can dance all winter." I like a version that offers the grasshopper a second chance and that acknowledges that it is challenging to keep your nose to the grindstone, especially when others are playing. You might want to explore different versions and adapt the one that feels right for you.

This is a fun story for audience participation. The grasshopper can have a song and a dance. The ants can also have a marching song and movement if you wish. You can add more information about how ants can carry things that weigh more than they do! You can have a repeating reframe for the big ants, and one for the little ant.

As an artist, I take some offense at this story for not valuing the role of the musician. I like the story *Frederick* by Leo Lionni (New York: Knopf, 1967), in which a poetic little mouse sits and gathers colors, sounds, and feelings all summer while his brothers and sisters work. Then he entertains them all during the cold winter. This offers a better balance, as it values all different kinds of work.

- **Group retelling:** Act this one out as a class. Pick a couple of directors, or with younger students, ask them what parts are needed and take volunteers. Act as narrator to keep the action going, or ask the directors what happened first, then what? You will want to create a marching movement and song for the ants to keep them organized.

- **Questions, discussion and story sharing:** Children can all relate to the frustration of having to work hard at something when they would rather be playing. What are activities in our own lives that we have to work hard at when we'd rather be playing? (Examples: Homework when other neighborhood children are outside playing, practicing a musical instrument or for a sport or dance, and helping with family chores.) Share the stories of times we have worked hard and received a positive result, making the work worthwhile.

- **Add a new ending:** Tell the next chapter of the story in which the grasshopper learns to do some work for the next winter and still finds time to play his violin.

- **Make up original tales:** Remind the students of the Three Little Pigs and how similar it is to this story. Encourage them to make up their own tales in which someone works hard while others play, and how they all benefit from the work of the one who planned ahead and persevered.

- **Referring to the Story:** Anytime your class has to do something that they don't want to do, like cleaning up or learning some basic skills, remind them of the story and how they are like the ants—storing up information or cleaning up, so that they can enjoy the next thing as the ants did. Maybe they could even sing the ants' marching song as they clean!

Follow-up activities

Tip for retention

Making a personal connection

Creative exploration

Turning the story ideas into action

The Tortoise and the Hare

Aesop

Grades K-3

THEMES: Perseverance, slow and steady wins the race, patience, non-judgment

Once upon a time, a Hare was always boasting about his great speed. He bragged to all of his friends and he always teased the Tortoise because he was so slow.

One day the Tortoise got tired of hearing the Hare brag about his speed. "You say you are so fast, Hare, and I am so slow. Why don't you and I have a race? I bet I can beat you, but if I do, you will have to promise not to brag any more."

The Hare fell on the ground laughing with glee. "Race you, Tortoise? I'd love to race you, and when I'm done, I'll have even more to brag about!"

And so, the race was planned—from one side of the forest to the other, with Owl giving the official start signal and the sparrows setting up the finish line.

"On your mark, get set, go!" hooted the owl, and the race was off!

The Hare bounded down the road and was soon far out in front of the Tortoise, who lumbered slowly along the road, putting one foot in front of the other. "Why should I be working up a sweat, when I could take my time?" thought the Hare. "There is no way the Tortoise can catch up with me. In fact, I think I'll take a nap!" So saying, the Hare lay down against the tree and was soon fast asleep!

Meanwhile Tortoise kept lumbering along, one foot in front of the other, along the dusty road. He passed by the sleeping Hare and just kept on going. The sun began to go down, and Tortoise kept on moving.

Finally, the Hare woke up. When he looked down the road, he could not see the Tortoise, so he began to hop as fast as he could toward the finish line. There in the distance was the finish line, and there was Tortoise about to cross it! Hare ran as he had never run before, but he could not overtake the Tortoise. Tortoise, who kept going, slow and steady, had won the race.

See page 44 for information on Aesop.

248

ONCE UPON A TIME

This is a well-loved story that every child should know. You can tell it straight out with character development and movements that the students can do along with you. You can also tell it with a flannel board to show the progress of the two animals in a visual way.

Tips for the telling

• **Flannel board retells:** Let young audiences take turns retelling this story using a flannel board, puppets, or stuffed animals in front of the class and then at stations when everyone has heard it a few times. Older audiences can act it out in small groups.

Follow-up activities
Tip for retention

• **Questions, discussion and story sharing:** This story offers hope to everyone who thinks they are slower or smaller than someone else is. It also reminds us that it is not how fast or strong we are, but that we put out a good effort and do not give up. Have your students tell stories about times when they have stuck with a project or task until it was done, and how they felt afterwards. Help them to remember from experience that it is not always about winning, but the satisfaction of finishing and doing your best.

Making a personal connection

• **Draw and tell:** Have your students draw a picture of the story, then go home and tell the story to their parents using the picture as a guide. Have the children ask their parents to tell them about a time they worked hard, "slow and steady," to accomplish a goal. Have them share these in class.

Creative exploration

• **Incorporate the story ideas into your classroom** by making "Slow and steady wins the race" into a classroom catch phrase that you and your students can use to remind one another to be patient and to persevere. If you display some of their story pictures, you can point to them as reminders too.

Turning the story ideas into action

• **Projects:** Remind them of the story of the Three Little Pigs. Have them make the three houses. First let them quickly make houses out of straw. Then have them quickly make houses from sticks. Finally have them work carefully and slowly to make houses of bricks (sugar cubes or clay). Then let them try to break them as the wolf did and take pride in their work. Those who work the longest will have the strongest houses.

Once Upon a Time...

Never Give Up!
A Tale of Two Frogs

My adaptation of a Russian folk tale (also attributed to Aesop)

Grades K-8

THEMES: Perseverance, positive attitude

Once upon a time on a farm way out in the country, a farmer's wife milked the cows, poured all the milk into a tall pitcher, and went to find her eldest son to carry it into the house. But in the house, there were all kinds of trouble. The baby was crying, the fire had gone out, the bread she had put into the oven was ruined, and her son was nowhere to be found. So the pitcher full of milk sat unattended and unremembered.

Not far from the barn, in the cow pasture pond, lived two speckled frogs. On this particular day, these two frogs had decided to go on a little journey to see what was inside the barn. They hopped this way and that until they hopped off a shelf and straight into the pitcher of cow's milk.

The sides of the tall pitcher were straight and slippery. The frogs could not touch the bottom. They could not jump out.

"We are doomed, brother," cried the frog named Cronk.

"Keep swimming," cried his brother Gronk. "Sooner or later something will happen." However, the farmer's wife did not come back, and the pitcher sat unattended.

The two frogs swam and swam. Finally, Cronk said, "I can't take it anymore. It is just too tiring. I'm giving up! We'll just die trying." So saying, he flopped onto his belly and sank into the deep creamy milk, never to be seen again.

His brother Gronk cried with dismay, but there was nothing he could do. He could not hold his brother up in the milk. But he did not give up. He swam and he swam, splashing his webbed feet round and round. Every time he got discouraged, he would sing one of his favorite songs. Then he made it a game of swimming ten times round each way and switching. "If I keep going, something good will happen," he kept telling himself. Hour after hour, the tired frog swam in circles, beating the creamy milk.

All of sudden, when his strength was nearly gone, his foot struck something solid. Was it Cronk? No, it was butter! Gronk had churned the milk into butter! He continued to swim and swim until the entire pitcher was full of firm white butter. Then with a tremendous burst of energy, Gronk leapt from the pitcher onto the barn floor, just as the farmer's wife was returning.

"Oh, what a day," she was muttering to herself. "It's nearly noon and I haven't even churned the butter."

The little frog hopped away, relieved to be alive, but sad that his brother had given up. Meanwhile the farmer's wife got two surprises that day!

Alternative ending: You can spell her surprises out if you think the students want it so (as my eleven-year-old did). I would suggest letting the students tell you what her two surprises were.

SOURCES

Baba Yaga's Geese and Other Russian Stories, retold by Bonnie Carey (Bloomington: Indiana University Press, 1973).

Tales from Central Russia, retold by James Riordan (Harmondsworth, Middlesex: Kestral Books, 1976).

Tips for the telling

The story lends itself to movement with the frogs swimming and Gronk singing. I have not yet made up a song, but rather sing little snippets of favorite songs. A song about not giving up would work nicely and could be referred to later. Maybe taking off on the Peter Pan song, "I won't give up. I won't give up. I don't want to sink and die. I don't want to sink and die." (I am sure you can do better than that!) Try telling this story from the perspective of Gronk as he holds his granddaughter Gronkel on his knee and tells the tale of the day he did not give up. You could use a frog puppet. You might consider having a pitcher of creamy milk on hand to demonstrate the process of churning butter from milk, or at least letting the students take turns whipping cream. If you cannot stand the idea of one of the frogs dying, you can simply eliminate that part and let it be about one frog who did not give up.

Follow-up activities

Tips for story retention

- **Retell in character:** Let the students get into small groups and retell as if they were Gronk as an old man telling the story to his grandchildren. Have one child be the teller and the others pretend to be the grandchildren, but let them pipe up if the grandfather forgets a detail.
- **For younger students:** The teacher retells as Grandfather Gronk and intentionally makes mistakes or leaves things out, pretending that his or her memory is not so good any longer. Let them correct you.

Making a personal connection

- **Questions, discussion and story sharing:** Ask the children to share about a time when they had to keep doing something hard, and what helped to keep their spirits up and to keep going. It would be helpful if you shared a story on this subject first.

Creative exploration

- **Group retelling with creative adaptations:** As above, let the students think up songs or activities that Gronk could do while he is trying to keep his spirits up in the milk pail. Have them retell the story in one large group as if they were all in the pail, and invite them to take turns showing what they would do to keep afloat. Have everyone join them in that movement or song.

Turning the story ideas into action

- **Brainstorm** other activities (at home or at school) besides churning milk into butter that take time but yield ultimate rewards. Help the children to think about how to help make such tasks easier to bear. Next time you find the class struggling with a project, remind them of the story and talk about how to make the task easier.
- **Visual Representations:** Have the students make posters about Gronk to remind them not to give up.

The Little Bird's Rice

There once was a bird that lived on a mountainside. She had four little babies in her nest. Every day she would fly about gathering seeds for them to eat. One day she found only one grain of rice and she was flying home to give it to them, when it fell into a crevice in a wooden log that a carpenter was sawing.

The little bird asked the carpenter to please cut the grain out of the log, but he refused.

She asked the king to order the carpenter, but he refused.

She asked the queen to persuade the king to order the carpenter, but she refused.

She asked the serpent to bite the queen, so that she would persuade the king, so that he would order the carpenter, but it refused.

She asked the stick to beat the serpent, so that it would bite the queen, so that she would persuade the king, so that he would order the carpenter, but it refused.

She asked the fire to burn the stick, so that it would beat the serpent, so that it would bite the queen, so that she would persuade the king, so that he would order the carpenter, but it refused.

She asked the water to quench the fire, so that it would burn the stick, so that it would beat the serpent, so that it would bite the queen, so that she would persuade he king, so that he would order the carpenter, but it refused.

She asked the elephant to drink the water, so that it would quench the fire, so that it would burn the stick, so that it would beat the serpent, so that it would bite the queen, so that she would persuade the king, so that he would order the carpenter, but it refused.

She asked the net to ensnare the elephant, so that it would drink the water, so that it would quench the fire, so that it would burn the stick, so that it would beat the serpent, so that it would bite the queen, so that she would persuade the king, so that he would order the carpenter, but again, it too refused.

The poor little bird sat down and began to cry out loud, "Why won't somebody help me? My poor babies are hungry!"

A little mouse heard her crying, and asked how he could help, and the little bird told the mouse her story. The little mouse went to the net and picked up a corner of it in his tiny paws. "Net, oh Net, I will gnaw you to bits if you don't threaten to snare the elephant, so it will drink the water."

The net felt afraid and agreed to go at once to the elephant, and the mouse and bird followed along.

India and Asia

Grades K-3

THEMES: Perseverance, courage, focus, thinking of others

Seeing the net, the elephant agreed to go to the water, and the mouse and the bird followed along.

Seeing the elephant, the water agreed to put out fire, and the mouse, the bird, and the net followed along.

Seeing the water, the fire agreed to burn the stick, and the mouse, the bird, the net, and the elephant followed along.

Seeing the fire, the stick agreed to hit the serpent, and the mouse, the bird, the net, the elephant, and the water followed along.

Seeing the stick, the serpent agreed to bite the queen, and the mouse, the bird, the net, the elephant, the water, and the stick followed along.

Seeing the serpent, the queen agreed to persuade the king. They all went to the king's court. When the king saw all those things and animals in such a grand parade, he stopped what he was doing. The queen ran forward and whispered in his ear. The king called to have the carpenter brought forth. He was ordered to cut down the post and bring out the grain. Before all the court, the grain of rice was given back to the little bird. Everyone applauded as she flew quickly home to feed her hungry children.

SOURCES

The Little Bird that Found the Pea (New York: Holt, Rinehart and Winston, 1965).

"The Little Bird's Rice," in *The Beautiful Blue Jay and Other Tales of India,* by John W. Spellman (Boston: Little, Brown & Co., 1967).

This is a great story for audience participation. You can have all of the children repeat all of the parts. They will quickly pick up the rhythm of the story if you establish it clearly. Alternately, you can have the whole class act the story out. To begin, have the class stand in a circle. This helps to demonstrate how this is a circular tale, keeps chaos to a minimum, and keeps the flow of the story going during the telling. Divide the students into eleven groups (the number of parts in the story, counting the bird). Give parts to small groups or partners. The small groups or partners will then take a few moments to come up with a movement to represent their character and the action it takes. Then as narrator, you tell the story while each group demonstrates its movement and chimes in on its part. This may take a few times to perfect, but when it is done, it can be a traveling tale to take to other classrooms.

- **Sequencing through drawings:** Assign each student a character or part from the story to draw. Then have the class sequence the drawings to retell the story.

- **Questions, discussion and story sharing:** Ask your students to list all of the feelings that the little bird had when she was trying to get help. Did your students ever have those feelings when they were trying to do something important? Tell a story of a time when you kept asking for help until you got it, and encourage them to do the same.

- **Creative Adaptation:** Have the class make up a story about a child who wants something and will not give up asking for help until getting what he or she wants.

- **Story interviewing project:** Send your students out into the school or home to find stories from adults who persevered until they got the help they needed or accomplished something. Do not let them give up until they get a good story! Have them share them with the class.

- **Experiencing the story:** Create a treasure hunt in the school where students have to keep finding different clues or asking different people for help until they find what they were looking for. You might say, "One of the teachers has the clue you need." They must keep asking until they find the answer.

Follow-up activities
Tip for retention

Making a personal connection

Creative exploration

Turning the story ideas into action

The Poor Boy and the Egg

Serbia

Grades 2-8

THEMES: Patience, fantasizing rather than making realistic plans, goal setting

Once upon a time, a poor laborer worked plowing the fields for a rich man who owned a large tract of land. The day was hot and windless, and the boy sweated in the sun. At midday, he was taking a rest under a tree near the barn when he happened to spy a chicken's egg that had rolled out of the chicken coop. He reached for the egg and felt that it was still warm. "Ah, what good fortune!" he said to himself. "I may be able to take this egg home and hatch it." He placed the egg carefully inside his shirt next to his skin to keep it warm.

He sat back down and thought about what could happen now that his fortune had turned. "My chick will grow into a chicken that will lay eggs for me. I will be able to sell the eggs, and I will no longer have to work for the rich merchant. With all of my money, I will buy a cow, and then I will sell milk too.

Soon I will be able to buy land, and have my own farm, and how the young ladies will chase after me! Oh I will go to the dances in town and I will choose the wealthiest young lady and ask her to dance, and of course she will say, "Yes," and I will twirl her around—at which point he lifted his arms as if to twirl a young lady, and squish! He felt a warm liquid seep down his chest. His egg was crushed, and so was his dream of chicks and eggs and cows, fancy women and riches. He set to work again plowing the fields.

This is a short story, but can be quite funny. It allows us to laugh at how much time we may spend in fantasy, rather than working to actually make things happen for ourselves. Take your time allowing the character to delight in the fantasies, letting them get bigger and bigger until he is flailing his arms about and oops!

Follow-up Activities are included after the cultural variants that follow.

SOURCE

"Hatching Boiled Eggs" from *Long Ago in Serbia,* by D. Spicer (Philadelphia: Westminster Press, 1968).

The Milk Maid and Her Pail

Cultural Variant

Aesop

Grades 2-8

THEMES: Patience, fantasizing rather than making realistic plans, goal setting.

One day a milkmaid had filled her pail of milk in the barn and was carrying it to market carefully balanced on her shoulder. As she walked, she thought about how much cream she would get from the milk, and how the butter she would make from the cream would get her enough money to buy a lot of eggs for hatching. Then she imagined her yard full of chicks, and how she would sell them before May Day, and how she would buy a beautiful dress. This she would wear to the fair. Oh, wouldn't the young men be crowding around, asking her to the dance, and for walks around the fair grounds! However, she would not be too quick to give in. No, she would send them away with a quick toss of her head.

Caught up in her fantasy, she tossed her head, and that pail of milk fell from her shoulder and drained onto the ground. There went all of her dreams—of cream and butter, chicks, fine dresses, and handsome young men.

See page 44 for information on Aesop.

The Jar of Rice

Cultural Variant

Laos

Grades 2-8

Themes: Patience, fantasizing rather than making and carrying out realistic plans, goal setting.

Once there was a man who was too lazy to work. He survived only by begging his relatives to feed him. One day someone gave him a large sack of rice. He went home and put it into a large clay pot and set the pot on the foot of his bed. Then he lay down on his bed and began to fantasize.

"I will hold onto this jug of rice until there is a famine. Then I will sell it for a high price. With the money, I will buy a pair of cows. Soon the cows will have calves. I will sell the calves and buy a pair of buffalo. When the buffaloes have calves, I will sell them. With that money, I will be able to find a wife and pay for a great wedding. After our children are big enough to walk around on their own, I will send my wife out into the fields to do the work. Ah, she might not like to work in the fields. What if she protests? Well, if she protests, I will kick her." So saying, he struck out angrily with his foot, knocking the jar onto the floor. It cracked in two, spilling the grains of rice, which ran down between the floorboards and under his house, where his neighbor's pig promptly ate each and every one. The lazy man was left with nothing—no cows, no buffalo, no wife, and no rice—nothing but a broken jar and a hungry belly.

SOURCE

"The Beggar and the Rice" in *I Saw a Rocket Walk a Mile: Nonsense Tales, Chants, and Songs of Many Lands,* edited by Carl Withers (New York: Henry Holt, 1965).

Tips for the telling

This story has many cultural variants. To research others see *The Storytellers' Sourcebook*, by Margaret Read MacDonald (motif index numbers J2050-J2199). I suggest that you give a variant to a small group of students and have them tell it to the class. Then compare them and talk about the theme, which is identical in each.

Aesop's tale finishes as usual with a moral, in this case, "Don't count your chickens before they hatch." You may want to include this, start the story with this, or write it on the board after the story. I prefer the latter, if I use it at all. You may want to skip it altogether so that the students can come to their own conclusions. On the other hand, stories can be a great way to give lasting meaning to the many sayings we share as a culture.

Follow-up activities
Tip for retention

• **Read cultural variants and retell:** Let the students read and retell the different versions of this tale found here or from your own research. They can each retell one to a partner, miming the action.

Making a personal connection

• **Compare and contrast:** Have your students compare and contrast the versions they have shared with one another.

• **Personal stories:** Let them make and tell personal stories of what they would fantasize about, and then discuss how they could really make their fantasies into reality.

Creative exploration

• **Creating original versions:** Once they have read a few different versions, they will be ready to create their own, based either in their modern lives or in different cultures that you may be studying. Alternatively, they could create tales of how the characters in the story could have successfully fulfilled their dreams.

Turning the story ideas into action

• **Visual representations of the story:** Have your students make posters with captions to remind them of the story's wisdom.

• **Practice goal setting and planning:** Invite your students to set an attainable goal and to make a plan for how to reach it with a number of small steps. Help them to keep track of how they are doing in reaching their goals, and help them to acknowledge their successes and learn from their missteps along the way. Starting small and seeing positive results is the best way.

The Buried Treasure

Once, an aging farmer lay upon his deathbed and worried about the fate of his lazy sons. Near his final hour, an inspiration came to him. He called his sons around his bedside and bade them draw in close. "I am soon to leave this world, my sons," he whispered. "I want you to know that I have left a treasure for you. I have hidden it in my field. Dig carefully and well and you shall find it. I ask only that you share it amongst yourselves evenly."

The sons begged him to tell them exactly where he had buried it, but the father breathed his last breath and spoke no more.

As soon as he was gone, the sons took up their pitchforks and shovels and began to turn over the soil in their father's field. They dug and dug until they had turned over the whole field twice. They found no treasure, but they decided that since the field was so well dug up they might as well plant some grain as their father had done. The crop grew well for them. After the harvest, they decided to dig again in hopes of finding their buried treasure. Again, they found not a treasure, but a field prepared for sowing. This year's crop was better than the one before.

This went on for a number of years until the sons had grown accustomed to the cycles of the seasons and the rewards of daily labor. By that time, their farming earned them each enough money to live a happy life. It was then that they realized the treasure their father had left for them.

Numerous sources and variants, including Italy, Aesop, American Indian, Middle East

Grades 4-8

THEMES: Hard work, patience, cooperation

SOURCES

Doorways to the Soul: 52 Wisdom Tales from Around the World, edited by Elisa Pearmain (Cleveland: Pilgrim Press, 1998).

"The Magic Box," a folk tale from Italy in *Way of the Storyteller*, by Ruth Sawyer (New York: Penguin Books, 1942).

"Wink, the Lazy Bird" in *Skunny Wundy: Seneca Indian Tales*, by Arthur C. Parker (Chicago: Albert Whitman, 1970).

The Tiger's Whisker and Other Tales and Legend from Asia and the Pacific, retold by Harold Courlander (New York: Harcourt, Brace & World, 1968).

Tips for the telling

This story lends itself to straightforward telling, though you can have fun developing the characters if you wish, drawing out their laziness and greed and the transformation that happens over time.

Follow-up activities
Tip for retention

• **News reporter retelling:** Divide the students into groups of four. Have one be an investigative reporter, and three others are the sons. Have the reporter interview the sons about what happened and what they discovered. Encourage them to give the characters personality.

Making a personal connection

• **Questions, discussion and story sharing:** This is a story that speaks to the desire or dream in many of us to find a treasure to make life easier, without having to go through the process of working for it. It also speaks to the rewards of labor. It can also help us to develop a vision to support us in our hard work—the vision being the treasure we desire, whether it is monetary reward, recognition, mastery, success, or happiness. Encourage your students to share about dreams or visions they have and times when they have worked hard to succeed at something.

Creative exploration

• **Writing their own story:** Have each child identify something that they wish to succeed at and write a buried-treasure type story in which they are told there will be a treasure if they practice or work hard in some way, and what the treasure turns out to be if they follow through.

• **Explore cultural variants:** Have the students research or read the variants listed above and present them to the class.

Turning the story ideas into action

• **Class project:** Help your students to brainstorm a class project that they can work on together that will have a positive reward at the end. Set goals and encourage them to "keep digging" until they succeed. Examples could be to have everyone raise their grade one point, or to build something for the school out of Legos, or to raise a certain amount of money to benefit a cause, or to buy something for the classroom.

The Lion's Whisker

Ethiopia, Korea

Grades 5-8

THEMES: Patience,
trust, love, perseverance,
friendship

Long ago in Ethiopia, a young woman married a widower who had a son. Her joy was great when she went to live in the home of her new husband, for she had longed for a child. However, the boy refused her affections, saying, "You are not my real mother." He pushed away her cooking, tore her mending, and turned away from her kindness.

After some time, the sorrowing woman's friends suggested that she seek the help of a wise hermit who lived on the mountain. She climbed the path alone to his hut. "Please," she begged timidly, "make me a potion so that my stepson will love me."

The hermit looked at her without smiling. "I can make you a potion," he said. "But the ingredients are very difficult to obtain. You must bring me the whisker of a living lion."

The young woman went away in great distress but she was determined not to give up. That night, while her family slept, she crept out of the village to the edge of the desert carrying a bowl of meat. She knew that a great lion lived near some rocks quite a distance away. She walked under the night sky as close to the rocks as she dared. Hearing him roar, she dropped the bowl and ran back home. Again the next night, she sneaked from the house with the bowl of meat. She walked further into the desert until she could see the form of the lion on the distant rocks. She set down the bowl and ran home.

Every night she drew closer to the lion before setting down the bowl and fleeing for home. Every night the lion came closer until he was eating her food. Finally, one night after many weeks, she put down her bowl and stepped back but did not run. She watched the huge lion come slowly forward and eat from the bowl. The following night, she put down the bowl and did not move away. The lion came slowly forward and began to eat from the bowl. She reached out and stroked his fur. He made happy sounds in his throat. "Thank you, dear friend," she said, and carefully snipped a whisker from his chin. She moved slowly away and then ran all the way to the hermit's hut. The hermit was sitting before his fire.

"I've brought you the whisker of a living lion!" she announced breathlessly. He took the whisker and examined it closely. "You have indeed," he said, and dropped the whisker into the fire.

"What have you done?" she cried. "That was the whisker for the love potion. You do not know how hard it was to obtain. It has taken me months to win the trust of the lion."

"Can the trust of a child be harder to obtain than that of a wild beast?" he asked her. "Go home and think on what you have done."

The young woman returned home, thinking about the hermit's words. Slowly, with love and patience, she cared for her stepson, until at last he would eat her food and listen to her stories. Then one day after many months, as they returned from market together, he took her hand, and she smiled.

SOURCES

Doorways to the Soul: 52 Wisdom Tales from Around the World, edited by Elisa Pearmain (Cleveland: Pilgrim Press, 1998).

"The Lion's Whisker" in the *Lion's Whisker: Tales of High Africa*, by Brent Ashabranner and Russell Davis (Boston: Little, Brown & Co., 1950).

African Village Folktales, by Edna Mason Kaulu (New York: World Publishing Co., 1968).

PICTURE BOOKS

The Lion's Whisker, retold by Nancy Raines Day (New York: Scholastic, 1995).

Korean variant: *The Tiger's Whisker*, by Harold Courlander (New York: Harcourt, Brace & World, 1968).

Students often ask if there are any "nice" stepmother stories. I am always glad to be able to share this tale. I will sometimes even preface the story this way.

Take the time to imagine the setting and emotions clearly in your mind and heart so that you can set the scene, and move your listeners. The story unfolds over many months. Think about how you will convey the slow development of trust and passage of time in the telling.

- **News reporter retelling:** Put students into groups of five—news reporter, young woman, stepson, hermit and lion—and let the reporter gather the story from the other four.

Making a personal connection

- **Questions, discussion and story sharing:** Your students may want to respond to the positive stepmother image in this story, as compared with most fairy tales. They may also wish to talk about times when they have learned to slowly trust someone, or had to win someone or something's (a pet's) trust. Our modern culture promises us magic potions and instant solutions for almost any challenge we face, such as weight loss surgery, instant tans, wrinkle-removing cream, Internet degrees, and instant wealth. The virtues of patience and hard work are not often championed, and we have few models in the media for examples of slow and steady work toward goals. Let your students brainstorm examples of quick-fix "potions" advertised today. Teachers, share personal stories of times when you have worked hard to reach a goal.

Creative exploration

- **Personal story sharing:** Encourage your students to write stories of their experiences in which they have worked hard to reach goals that once seemed impossible. They can also collect these stories of perseverance and patience from family members or biographical sources. Share the stories in class.

- **Creative adaptation:** Help your students to create modern versions of this tale, either individually or in groups, and to present these to the class.

Turning the story ideas into action

- **Goal setting:** Encourage your students to tell the class of an individual or group goal that they have, and how they plan to it meet step by step. Brainstorm and practice ways of cultivating patience, such as relaxation exercises, and visualizing the final goal fulfilled. Have the students keep journals to remark on the progress of the goal. Share these reflections now and then with the group.

- **Trust building:** You can play trust-building games in your class, particularly at the beginning of the year to create a more cohesive classroom. One example of a trust game is to pair the students. One is blindfolded, and the other must carefully guide the partner through an obstacle course, trying to avoid any collisions. See the books listed in the Resources section for many other excellent trust and cooperative game suggestions.

- **Replicate the story:** Have students pair up with someone that they do not know well and set a goal of building trust. Students should keep a journal to reflect on what they did to build trust, how it felt, and how they knew trust had been increased.

Fairy Tales about Perseverance for Grades 5-8

Fairy tales are filled with examples of characters that persevere against all odds, and despite a lack of strength or financial resources. Students should be read or told these more complex fairy tales well into their teen years to relax into their imaginations, while being treated to rich tales that offer many examples of courage, perseverance, honesty, and wisdom. These stories live deep in the psyche and offer food for thought and action in years to come. I will paraphrase several of my favorites here with sources. I will offer only one set of follow-up activities that can be generalized with any of them.

Scandinavia

This story follows the same pattern initially as Beauty and the Beast.

East of the Sun, West of the Moon

Once upon a time, the youngest daughter of a poor woodsman has to go and live with a bear that promises to make her father rich. She is alone in a lovely palace by day and is visited in the dark of night by a kind and gentle lover whom she is forbidden to look upon. Her family convinces her to take a candle and gaze upon him at night. When she lights the candle and gazes upon him, she sees not a monster, but the loveliest prince, with whom she falls instantly in love. When she bends to kiss him, and three drops of wax fall onto his shirt and he is burned. He awakes and tells her that if she had but waited until the end of that year, the spell would have been broken, and they would have been free to marry, but now he must go East of the Sun and West of the Moon to marry a horrid troll's daughter.

The girl determines to find her lost prince and she travels over many months and miles, searching for this place called East of the Sun and West of the Moon. She meets all kinds of helpers until she at last reaches the place where the prince is held prisoner awaiting his wedding day. The girl uses the gifts she has been given along the way to gain access to the prince. Together they hatch a plan and in the end are able to get away together and to live happily ever after.

SOURCE

This fairy tale is found in many collections of tales, both general and specific to Scandinavia, including *Best Loved Folktales of the World*, edited by Joanna Cole (New York: Doubleday, 1982).

The Six Swans

The Six Swans is a lengthy fairy tale in which a girl has six brothers who are turned to swans by an evil queen. The girl sets out to break the spell, which involves six years of silence and knitting six sweaters from the thorny starflower plant. She succeeds through many trials and her brothers are released.

SOURCE

Most fairy tale collections. My favorite is *Grimm's Tales for Young and Old*, translated by Ralph Manheim (New York: Doubleday, 1977). A shorter variant on this is "The Seven Ravens" in the same collection.

The Water of Life

Variants of this tale are found in many cultures. In this story, three sons set out to find the water of life, which is the only thing that can save their father from death. The older two act selfishly and end up lost. The youngest endures many trials, but sticks to his values of honesty and kindness. In the end, he is rewarded by his father's good health and respect, and a bride with a heart as big as his own.

SOURCE

Sources include *Grimm's Tales for Young and Old*, translated by Ralph Manheim, (New York: Doubleday, 1977).

Tips for the telling

These tales take longer to learn and tell. Make sure to explore the imagery thoroughly in your own imagination so that you can convey the settings and characters effectively through the telling. The stories can also be effectively read to the class if you read them through beforehand and take your time with pauses and expression.

Follow-up activities
Tip for retention

• **Round-robin retelling in small groups:** These are longer tales and students will benefit from outlining and retelling exercises to cement the sequence and rework the themes.

Making a personal connection

• **Questions, discussion and story sharing:** What lessons do you take from the story? What images or parts of the story stuck out for you? Who was your favorite character? Why? What helped the hero or heroine to reach their goal? For what goals or causes have you persevered?

Creative exploration

• **Write their own fairy tale:** Let your students write their own fairy tale in which the main character perseveres and succeeds in a nearly impossible goal. Write the following elements on the board: Hero or Heroine, Setting, Problem to be solved, Magical Object or element, Antagonist, Helping Character. Brainstorm examples of these first in the story, and then in other fairy tales with which they may be familiar. Then ask them to write a story of their own that includes the above elements of a story. Have them share the stories in small groups for feedback, including the discussion of how their character perseveres and what helps in this process. Then have them develop them for telling to the whole group. (See the How to Tell a Story section on helping students to be storytellers.)

• **Research biographical stories** of people who have persevered through difficult life circumstances to meet challenges. Share these with classmates.

Turning the story ideas into action

• **Journal reflection and autobiographical story making:** Ask your students to keep a journal to notice the things in their lives that are most important to them, and the ones for which they will persevere. What are the challenges they face as they work toward their goals? What helps them to persevere?

Favorite picture books

Something from Nothing, by Phoebe Gilman (New York: Scholastic, Inc., 1992). A tailor keeps making smaller and smaller items out of a special piece of cloth until he is left with a story.

The Little Engine That Could, by Watty Piper (New York: Platt & Munk, 1976). This classic tale in which the smallest engine succeeds in pushing a big train over a hill by saying, "I think I can, I think I can." Every child should know this tale.

The Name of the Tree: A Bantu Folktale, retold by Celia Barker Lottridge (New York: Margaret C. McElderberry Books, 1989). There is a great drought and the animals have no food. Only one tree has fruit, but its branches are too high to reach. The tree will only lower its branches if the animals can remember and say its name. Lion tells the big, strong, and fast animals the name of the tree, but one after the other they all forget. Slow turtle tries the hardest to remember and succeeds.

Respect

RESPECTFUL BEHAVIOR IS AT THE HEART of safe schools, bullying prevention, and self-esteem. Respecting oneself, respecting others, and respecting the planet are essential ingredients for the harmony and future health of this earth and all people on it.

Self-respect means accepting yourself as you are, including your gifts and your imperfections. It means taking good care of your body and your spirit, and developing yourself to your highest potential. Having self-respect means not speaking disparagingly of yourself, or allowing others to do so. Self-respect involves honoring the fact that your feelings do count, your ideas are important, and your voice should be heard.

Respect for others means respecting people's wishes, and respecting other people's boundaries for physical and psychological privacy, It means respecting different opinions, religions, cultural lifestyles, likes and dislikes, and appearances. It means respecting our elders, listening to other people's opinions and needs, and treating everyone equally. To be respectful of others means not judging them prematurely, or hurting them through gossip, rumor, or criticism. It means being respectful of their property, including school and public property.

Respecting the earth means, first and foremost, being appreciative of the incredible home we all share, and not taking it for granted. Respecting the earth means acknowledging that the earth is a large ecological system that is subject to degradation by our actions, and that our actions affect the system as a whole. Respecting the earth means being aware of and taking responsibility for the consequences of our actions as individuals and nation states, and acting in ways that are conducive to long-term sustainability of the planet. Respecting the earth is a way of respecting the lives of future generations who must live on the planet we have left them.

The Secret Heart of the Tree

Africa (adapted)

Grades K-8

THEMES: Respect for others, good manners, honesty, greed, empathy

It was a scorching hot day in the African bush. Rabbit had gone looking for food, but within a short time she had but one thing on her mind—shade! In the distance, she saw a large old mango tree, with its crown of leaves making a nice pool of shade around its base. Rabbit hopped to the edge of the mango tree, and being polite, she asked the tree's permission to enjoy its shade. The tree spoke, "Of course, my friend."

Rabbit plopped herself down in the shade and said, "Oh, grandfather tree, thank you so much! Your shade is just what I needed." This time the leaves of the great mango tree shivered as if with delight, and down from its branches dropped a huge, ripe mango. The rabbit thanked the tree profusely. Sometime later, Rabbit felt an itch in her back, right in that place that is so hard to reach. "Dear grandfather tree," she asked, "would you mind if I used your bark to scratch my back? I have a most terrible itch." Again the leaves of the seemed to smile as it answered, "Of course, dear one." Again, Rabbit thanked the tree.

The tree was still for some time, and then it spoke. "Rabbit, you are the first creature to show me such respect and appreciation. I would like to show you something in return. I will show you my secret heart if you wish. I only ask that you not touch or take anything."

"Why of course. Thank you," answered Rabbit, her tail quivering with anticipation.

Suddenly a crack appeared in the trunk of the tree. It grew and grew into two doors, which opened to Rabbit. She stepped inside. Immediately she was standing in the most beautiful garden she had ever seen. It was filled with a radiant soft light. A stream ran through it, and its bed glittered with gold and silver gems and rings. On the trees grew magnificent fruits, and from the bushes jewels of every color sparkled. Rabbit wanted so much to touch the gems and to eat the fruit, but she did not. Instead, she sat down in the grass and drank in the beauty of the secret heart of the tree. All was peaceful.

Finally, the tree spoke, "Friend, you have shown me that you can keep your word. Therefore, I would like to give you a gift. Take any small gem you see." Rabbit hopped about until she decided on a simple gold ring to wear on her tail. She thanked the tree and left, promising not to tell anyone what she had seen.

On her way home, Rabbit was ambushed by Hyena. Hyena saw the ring on Rabbit's tail, and threatened to kill rabbit if she did not tell him where it had come from. Rabbit, afraid for her life and her babies, told Hyena how she had obtained the ring.

The next day Hyena went to the tree, and in his most polite manner (which isn't very), asked to sit, "Hey big tree, mind if I catch some shade—heeheehee?" Sometime later, he remembered that he was supposed to say, "Thanks, big tree, heeheehee." When no fruit dropped down, he asked for the fruit, and remembered some time later that he was supposed to say, "Thanks, tree—heeheehee." He scratched and remembered some time later to say thank you. After begging the tree repeatedly, "C'mon, I won't touch nuttin'," he was admitted to see the secret heart of the tree. As soon as those doors opened, Hyena bounded inside and set about eating the fruit and stuffing the gems into sacks that he had brought in his pockets. The beautiful light began to fade inside the tree and the doors began to close. Hyena saw that the doors were closing and began to run towards them. The doors were closing fast, and he was unable to run fast enough with his heavy load. He dropped everything and sprinted towards the doors.

The way the tale came down to me, it ends with the doors of the tree closing before Hyena could escape, and Hyena is never seen again. It was also said that the trees have never shown their secret hearts to anyone again, as a sacred trust had been broken. In the French translation of this tale, the hyena is expelled without the treasures.

My ten-year-old hated the first ending described above. There was not enough punishment for the Hyena. She wanted the doors to open a crack at the last second, and to have Hyena catapulted out and far away across the bush, perhaps into a thorn bush, never to bother anyone again.

Some adult listeners have said that they prefer the latter ending. The first ending is disturbing to me in that the tree must endure the Hyena inside itself, in some form or other, for a long time. However, I also find this to be a fitting metaphor for what happens when our trust is broken and we are traumatized. Often we do retain bad memories and bitterness toward our abusers, as if a piece of them were still in our hearts or bodies, holding us captive.

When I tell this story as a tale of earth stewardship, I end it this way:

It is said that after that the trees never showed anyone their secret hearts, as a trust had been broken. However, the trees still do share many of their gifts with us, and their well being is still in our hands. It is a sacred trust, and one that our lives depend on.

I would ask you, the reader, to decide on how you feel the story should end. I might suggest that it have several endings, depending on who your audience is, on how you feel, and what discussions you are trying to generate.

SOURCE

I first read this story in *The Moral of the Story Folk Tales for Character Development* by Bobby and Sherry Norfolk (Little Rock: August House, Inc., 1999). It was told to them by Allan Davies, who heard it first from Sally Pomme Clayton of The Company of Storytellers. Pomme Clayton first heard the tale told by the well-known French storyteller Abi Patrix, who thinks he found it in a French collection of African folk tales, "Contes D'Afrique." There are many similarities, but as I mentioned the ending is different. Thanks to Aleksandra Petrovic for translating the French version for me.

Tips for the telling

This story works well with audiences of all ages. With young audiences, I invite them to join the tree in shaking with delight, and the rabbit and hyena in scratching their backs. With older audiences, the participation comes at the finish of the story, where I invite them to tell me how they think it should end.

Use a unique voice and mannerisms for each of the characters. I imagine rabbit as nervous and quick. Hyena is always laughing, a bit slow in the head, and rude to boot! Tree is, well, a nice, calm old tree. How do you imagine them?

Follow-up activities
Tip for retention

- **Round-robin retell:** Sit in a circle and let each child add a bit to the retelling. Alternatively, you can invite children to come up and tell a short section of the story for the class.

Making a personal connection

- **Questions, discussion and story sharing:** This is a great story to introduce the ideas of respect and personal boundaries. It is a good place to talk about relationships and trust and to acknowledge that we all have "secret hearts" that deserve to be protected and respected. Students may have stories about times when they trusted someone, only to feel taken advantage of. Hopefully they also have stories of times that they felt respected. Teens and preteens need help identifying what is appropriate and inappropriate touching from others, and learn ways to stand up for themselves.

- **Stepping into the shoes of the characters:** Let your students get into small groups of three or four. Have them choose parts: the tree, the rabbit, the hyena and narrator. Have them act out the story, switching parts until everyone has been in each role. Then have a large-group discussion in which you ask how it felt to be each part. Identify the word respect and ask them when they felt respected, and when they felt like they were being respectful during the drama.

Creative exploration

- **Creative adaptation:** Let your students come up with their own visions of what the secret heart of the tree looked like and what should happen with hyena in the end. Let them retell to parents, classmates or other students. Older students can modernize this one, making it into a story about people who treat each other with or without respect. Changing the tree into a person would allow them to address those issues effectively.

Turning the story ideas into action

- **Brainstorm** a list of respectful behaviors for the classroom and school with your students. Have them **make posters** of these to put up on the walls. Identify times and places where students may feel more or less respected, and talk about what can be done about these.

- **Practice respectful behavior:** Using the above list and new insight into when and where respect is most needed, encourage your students to show utmost respect to everyone and everything they encounter for a day, in and out of school. Then reflect upon how it felt, individually and as a group. What was hard about it? What felt good? Let the parents know that this is happening and encourage them to try it too!

Once Upon a Time...

How Beetle Got Her Colors

Long ago in the Amazon rain forest, there lived a common everyday brown rat. A rat who talked like she was all that! She talked loud, she drew a crowd. She teased, and poked, she made rude jokes. "You call yourself a frog, I call you bump on a log!"

Some animals thought she was cool, but it looked more like cruel. One day, for example, she came upon Turtle ambling down the path towards the river. "Hey, moving house, the minimum speed limit's five miles per hour!" When Turtle didn't move fast enough, she flipped him off the road, and he lay on his back, his legs flailing.

Or if Mouse was going by with dinner in his hand, she'd say, "I'll take that, and don't say nothin', or they'll find your head over my fireplace, full of stuffing."

When someone starts bullying, those who don't want to get teased do one of two things: they either get as far away as they can, or as close as they can—both ways hoping to avoid abuse. Well pretty soon, some of the other animals were vying for Rat's attention. "I'm vice-rat of this gang. Hey, I'm her spokesrat!"

Rat loved the attention. She soaked it up. But secretly she wished that she were not a rat at all, but something much bigger, say a cat or a leopard. Yes, a leopard, with spots, or a jet-black panther. And lose the pointy nose; she wanted a snub nose and night vision. Oh man, she would be the queen of the jungle!

But every morning when she woke up and looked into the reflecting pool, she was still a brown rat, and so she just kept on tormenting the smaller animals. Her gang followed behind, laughing at her jokes and helping in her antics.

Now one day, Rat and her gang spied a little brown beetle coming down the path. "Well, what do we have here?" Rat said, laughing. "A little brown tank with sticks for legs. Hey if you rub those stick legs together, can you get fire?"

"Rat-a-tat!" Rat's gang laughed. "Oh, but look, your hard back is so shiny, I can see myself in it. Don't look too bad today," she said, looking away quickly. She felt that old feeling of wishing that she were bigger, with a glossy coat and spots! This made her mad, so she threw Beetle aside like a Frisbee.

Now in that part of the rain forest, there lived a wise and magical parrot that had been listening to Rat for long enough. He knew that inside every big shot, things are not so hot. Parrot flew down and helped Beetle to get right side up again.

"Rat, I am sick of your mean titter tat!" he said. "Why don't we have a contest and settle things once and for all? Whoever wins will get to choose a new coat of any color or texture. Whoever loses will be more respectful of the other animals. I will decide the contest. You shall race from this tree to the big kapok tree on the other side of the forest."

Rat could hardly believe her ears: a new coat! Her prayers were going to be answered! Yes, she could see it now—even if she wasn't as big, she would be

Brazil

Grades K-7

THEMES: Respect, bullying, judgment, empathy

STORYTELLING TO TEACH CHARACTER AND PREVENT BULLYING

271

the most beautiful rat this side of the rain forest. Why even the big animals would respect her.

"Yeah, a race. Are you ready, little bug? Better do some deep stick bends—hah! Too bad you can't lose the tank. It sure will slow you down!"

Rat began to stretch her massive calf and thigh muscles. Beetle loosened up her shoulder muscles and closed her eyes.

"Are you ready, little Beetle?" Parrot asked.

"Yes, oh wise one," Beetle answered.

"Are you ready, Rat?"

"Am I ready? I'm not even going to get sweaty! Let's go…"

"On my signal." Then the parrot gave the cry, "Go!"

Off went Rat. She turned and looked back. "I don't even see that little tank, left in the dust. Hey, if it sits too long, it just might rust. This is sort of like that tortoise and the hare thing, only I ain't stupid enough to go to sleep. But I can dream a little."

Rat ran along, fantasizing about how she was going to look. "Jet-black fur or spots? Hey, I don't have to decide! I can have jet-black fur, and one spot right in the middle of my face. Take the emphasis off the shnoz."

Rat was coming up to the finish line and looked back. "Still no sign of the tick! Here I come! Everyone is cheering, and I can hear them. Here I come. I'll give it a little spurt. Hey, why aren't they looking at me? Huh?"

There was Beetle, sitting on the other side of the finish line, doing a delicate bow.

"You didn't pass me. How'd you get here?" Rat shouted.

"I flew," Beetle said quietly.

"I didn't know you could fly."

Parrot flew to a branch just above the ground. "There's a lot you don't know about Beetle, or any of the other animals that you tease, Rat," said Parrot. "All animals have special gifts. But you don't know about them, because you don't ask. You give them a two-second look and make a lifetime judgment."

"And now, dear Beetle, what would you like for a coat?" asked Parrot.

"I will keep my hard shell, for it helps me to fly and offers protection, but I would like some colors, please. Blue, like the sky, and green like the trees—and could they be shining and shimmering, like the water?"

"Your wish is granted," said Parrot, spreading his wings.

That is why to this day, one species of beetle in the rain forest is a beautiful shimmering blue-green. It's also why rats look pretty much as they always have, though they don't pick on others so much. They mind their own business, making the best of their gifts like everyone else, scurrying around the jungle floor.

SOURCES

Folk Tales from Latin America, adapted by Shirlee P. Newman (New York: The Bobbs-Merrill Co., 1962).

Multicultural Fables and Fairy Tales: Stories Activities to Promote Literacy and Cultural Awareness, by Tara McCarthy (New York: Scholastic Inc., 1992).

How & Why Stories: World Tales Students Can Read and Tell, by M. Hamilton and M. Weiss (Little Rock: August House Publishers, 1999).

The version of the tale printed here is my adaptation. I have added quite a bit of detail to draw out the bullying aspects. If you wish to tell a more simplified version, go back to the How to Tell a Story section for ideas on how to outline a story. Make an outline of the basic story sequence and then retell it as feels right to you. I find that students are quiet for this story. Sometimes they will laugh at the mean antics of Rat, but this is always tempered. I try to capture separate voices for Rat, Beetle, and Parrot.

- **Small- or large-group retells,** depending on their age.

- **News reporter retells:** Have students make groups of four with a news reporter, parrot, beetle and rat. Let the news reporter pull the story from the other three.

- **Questions, discussion and story sharing:** This story contains many examples of bullying behaviors. I always start the discussion by asking students to identify what different types of bullying they noticed in the story. Usually they will be able to identify teasing, name-calling, physical violence, stealing, and group harassment. Sometimes I have to point out the threatening behavior, which is so common to bullying, "Don't tell or I'll..."

  Next, I ask the group to raise their hands if they have ever witnessed bullying and then if they have ever been bullied. Almost every hand goes up to both questions. The third question is whether they were able to stand up to a bully who was picking on or hurting someone else. Usually a few students will raise their hands and we will give them applause. At this point, I open the floor to hear their stories. Many of them will be sibling, cousin, and neighborhood stories.

  The other dominant message in the story is one of judging others without getting to know them. Here is a good place to teach the meaning of stereotyping and prejudice. When I ask them if they have ever made friends with someone that they at first thought they could have nothing to do with, many raise their hands. This lesson is worth exploring through personal story sharing. They can also go home and ask their parents to tell a story about a time when they judged a person to be a certain way and learned that they were very different.

- **Creative adaptation:** This is a pourquoi story that explains how something came to be, and it will inspire your students to make up tales about other animals who are bullied, who have special skills, and as a result of the story gain a new color or ability. Retell the story, changing the animals in the habitat you are studying. Make note of each animal's gifts. What are some gifts that an animal might have that another animal would overlook?

- **Stepping into the shoes of the characters:** This is a crucial step in building empathy for the victim of bullying. Play "hot seat" and let students take turns being questioned as they pretend to be Beetle or Rat.

Follow-up activities
Tips for retention

Making a personal connection

Creative exploration

Turning the story ideas into action

- **Visual representations:** Help your students to think of a symbol to remind one another not to judge by appearances. This could be a giant beetle that they make together out of papier mâché and hang from the ceiling as it flies to the finish line.

- **Personal research:** Have your students find out about someone that they did not think they had anything in common with in the classroom or school, and share what they learned with others. The focus could be on special gifts or interests.

- **Bullying prevention:** Have the students make lists of bullying behaviors on poster board. Put them up on the walls of the school and classroom serve as reminders, and to make it easier to identify bullying when it happens.

Feathers

Long ago in Poland, in a little Jewish village, the people loved their Rabbi. The Rabbi was the most important person in the village because he took care of the people in so many ways. The Rabbi officiated over Temple services and religious holidays. He was also the town judge, and everyone took his or her conflicts to him. He was also the counselor, listening to people's pain and offering clever advice.

One year in this village, the Rabbi noticed that many villagers were coming to him with the same complaint about a man in the village named Chaim. "Chaim is a gossip," the people told the Rabbi. "He is spreading stories that hurt us!"

"He's mean," others said. "His sharp tongue cuts like a knife!"

One woman came to the Rabbi in a frenzy. "Rabbi," she said, "Chaim spread a story that he saw me talking to a strange man in the marketplace. I was only giving directions. Now my husband is angry with me."

The baker said, "Rabbi, when Chaim came for his bread the other day, I gave him the wrong change by mistake. Now he is telling everyone that I am a cheat, and my business is off!"

Another woman came to the Rabbi. "Rabbi, you know I've had a bad back since my fall three years ago. Chaim says I'm a fake, and that my back isn't really bad. He told my friends that he saw me dancing in my living room."

On and on, the complaints came, until the Rabbi decided that he had to take action. He called Chaim to his home. "Chaim," he said, "many people are coming to me, saying that you've been telling stories about them that aren't true and speaking badly of them. Chaim, you are hurting your fellow villagers with your words."

"Oh Rabbi," said Chaim, bowing his head. "I'm sorry. I didn't mean any harm. They are only words. I'll go and take them back and apologize. Everything will be all right after that."

"It's not so simple, Chaim. Once you start your stories, you cannot take them back," the Rabbi said.

"Oh sure I can, Rabbi, you'll see," Chaim repeated.

"Chaim," the Rabbi sighed, "I need to teach you something. Tomorrow morning, come to the village square and bring your best feather pillow."

Chaim agreed and went home, thinking that he had not gotten off badly with the loss of one feather pillow.

The next day Chaim met the Rabbi in the town square. The Rabbi had a pair of scissors in his hands. He took Chaim's pillow and cut open the top. "Chaim," he said. "I want you to take all of the feathers out of the pillow and throw them into the air." Chaim looked at the Rabbi and then began to take

Jewish Tale from Poland

Grades 1-8

THEMES: Gossiping, empathy, honesty, care of others

the feathers out of the pillow and to throw them into the air. Some of them fell to the ground. Others caught the wind and flew up into the sky, catching on the trees and the rooftops. Some flew away altogether.

When all of the feathers were gone from the pillow, the Rabbi made another request. "Now, Chaim, I want you to put all of the feathers back in the pillow."

Chaim looked at the Rabbi as if he were crazy. "Rabbi, that's not so simple!" Chaim complained. "How could I get all of the feathers back? They have gone everywhere, up in the trees, the rooftops, and some have gone away completely. I would never be able to find them."

"You are right, Chaim," the Rabbi said, smiling. "And your gossiping words are just like those feathers. Once you say them, you cannot control where they go or whom they hurt, and you certainly cannot take them back. Do you understand, Chaim?"

"Yes, Rabbi." Chaim hung his head. "I will not gossip again."

Chaim went home and tried his best not to speak unkindly or untruthfully against others. Just to be sure that he remembered the lesson, the Rabbi nailed a feather to Chaim's front door.

SOURCES

Doorways to the Soul: 52 Wisdom Tales from Around the World, edited by Elisa Pearmain (Cleveland: Pilgrim Press, 1998).

"The Gossip," retold by Marcia Lane in *Spinning Tales, Weaving Hope: Stories, Storytelling, and Activities for Peace, Justice and the Environment*, edited by Ed Brody, et al. (Philadelphia: New Society Publishers, 1992).

Younger children's version: "The Gossipy Child," in *Easy to Tell Stories for Young Children*, by Annette Harrison (Jonesborough, Tenn.: National Storytelling Press, 1992).

This story is told in the traditional fashion, which is geared for grades 5+.

It is possible to adapt this story to hold the interest of younger grades by placing it in the classroom or playground, and making the gossiping and teasing relative to the age group and environment. See Annette Harrison's book listed above for her clever adaptation for young children, set in a classroom, in which a teacher serves as the wise one. You can also change the feathers to other objects that disperse and cannot be returned, such as bubbles. The examples of gossip in this story are my own invention. Feel free to change them to anecdotes that fit your listeners.

Note: The character's name is pronounced "Hy-am" or "Ky-am." The Ch is actually an aspirated K and sounds like something in between the two.

Tips for the telling

- **Gossip (ironically):** This is a great story for acting out in small groups. Have your students pretend to be other townspeople telling about how Chaim had stopped gossiping.

- **Questions, discussion and story sharing:** Whether you tell the traditional version for older students or adapt it for younger, the students will want to respond to the behavior of the gossiping and bullying student, as most have been on at least one side of this experience. They need a chance to reflect on what behaviors fall under the heading of gossip, and the different ways that it happens today. Have the students ever had a rumor made up about them? Have they ever started a rumor? Have they ever refused to pass on a rumor?

- **Creative dramatics:** Imagine scenarios in which people are saying something mean about someone. People in the receiving line can decide what to do, whether to pass the message along, to change it, or tell the messenger not to gossip. It takes courage to not pass on a mean message or to tell a friend to stop certain behaviors.

- **Games:** Play "telephone" with your students. Start sending a message around the circle of students by whispering a sentence in one student's ear. Have each student pass it on, and have the last person share it out loud. Note how it changes as it is passed around. This demonstrates how words and their meanings change as they are passed from one person to another. Emphasize that if you start a rumor, you cannot control how it changes.

- **Visual representations:** Have the students make feathers and keep them on their desks or lockers. If something happens that reminds them of gossiping, or talking behind someone's back, the students could put the feather on the board to start a discussion.

- **Act this story out for other classes:** When this story was told to one half of a seventh grade at a large middle school, the students who had heard

Follow-up activities
Tip for retention

Making a personal connection

Creative exploration

Turning the story ideas into action

it insisted that the students in the other team hear it too. It was clear to the teachers that the students felt safer knowing that every kid had had a chance to hear and reflect on this story.

- **Journal reflection:** Have older students keep a log for a week, noting times when gossiping happened and what role they took in it. At the end of the week, have them reflect on their learning. Did their understanding of gossiping change? Were they more careful about what stories they passed on about others?

The Stonecutter

China, Japan, and India

Grades K-6

THEMES: Self-respect, self-acceptance, strengths, power dynamics

Once upon a time in China, a stonecutter lived on a mountainside. Every day he took his ax and went to the mountain to cut pieces of stone. He was very strong and talented. He sold his stones for walkways and grave-stones, and he carved beautiful statues for rich people's gardens. Though he was strong and talented, he was never content with his life. He always looked at other people and wished that he could be like them.

One day when he was bringing some stone to the market to sell, he saw a crowd of people gathered. He pushed through them to see what they were looking at. There, the Emperor was parading along. His servants were fanning him and feeding him fruit.

"Oh, how powerful he is," thought the stonecutter. "Look at how everyone bows to him. I wish I were the Emperor."

Now the stonecutter did not know it, but there was a spirit on the mountain that looked out for him. She had heard him making wishes such as this for so long that she decided to grant this wish to see if it would really make him happier. She bowed low and said, "As you wish, it shall be."

Suddenly the stonecutter found that he was being carried through the crowd, and that the people were bowing to him! "Huh! I have done it!" he said. "This is great. Look at how everyone bows to me. I am the most powerful person in the world." Or so he thought.

For after a while he began to notice that despite the fans, his skin was being burnt, and his throat was dry and he was sweating. He looked up at the sun. "I thought that I was the most powerful thing, but I see that the sun is more powerful, for it can burn even an Emperor. I guess I do not really want to be an Emperor—I want to be the sun!"

The Spirit of the Mountain heard him again and smiled. "I will let him have his wish and see if he is happier." Again, she bowed. "As you wish, it shall be."

Suddenly the Emperor found himself high in the sky! He was on top of it all! He could reach down, burn the people, burn the crops, and dry up the rivers. And he did. "I've really done it now," he said to himself. "I know that I am the most powerful thing in the world." Or so he thought.

For one day as he was trying to burn the earth, a cloud passed in front of his rays.

"What is this?" He scowled. "A cloud can block my rays. But I thought I was the most powerful thing in the world. Perhaps I do not want to be the sun. Maybe I really want to be a cloud!"

Again, the Spirit of the Mountain heard his wish. Again, she bowed and smiled, saying, "As you wish, it shall be."

Suddenly the stonecutter found that he was a great rain cloud floating in the sky. He rained down on the earth until the waters began to flood, as the rivers overflowed. "I have really done it this time," he said to himself. "I am the most powerful thing in the world!" Or so he thought.

For one day, something began to push him this way and that, pulling him apart, until he was many little puffs, and then mere wisps in the air. "What could be doing this to me?" he asked. Soon he realized it was the wind. "Can it be that the wind is more powerful than the clouds? Because it can tear me apart into nothing, I guess I do not want to be the clouds. I want to be the wind."

Again, the Spirit of the Mountain heard his wish. She bowed and smiled, saying, "As you wish, it shall be."

Suddenly the stonecutter found that he was the wind, blowing the things of the earth this way and that. He blew on the water, making great waves. He blew on the land, bending and breaking the trees. He blew in the air, making terrible storms. "I know I have done it this time," he bragged to himself. "Finally I am the most powerful thing in the world!" Or so he thought.

For one day, he came to something that he could not move. It was a mountain. He blew and blew against that mountain, but it did not budge. "I thought I was the strongest thing in the world," he yelled, "but I cannot move this mountain even a little. I guess I do not want to be the wind. I want to be a mountain!"

Again, the Spirit of the Mountain heard his wish. She bowed and smiled, saying, "As you wish, it shall be."

Suddenly the stonecutter found that he was the mountain, sitting so majestically on the land, towering over everything, so strong, so unmovable. "I have truly done it!" he bragged. "I am really the most powerful thing in the world. Nothing can touch me." Or so he thought.

For one day, the stonecutter felt a terrible pain down near his base. Gazing way down his mountainside, he saw that someone was chipping away at his body and pieces of himself were rolling away on the ground. Do you know who was doing this? Yes, a stonecutter!

"Can it be," the stonecutter asked in amazement, "that a stonecutter is more powerful than a mountain? Because he can reduce it to a pile of pebbles, I guess I don't want to be a mountain. I want to be a stonecutter."

[At this point, I stop and ask the audience if they think that the Spirit of the Mountain should grant this last wish. We take a poll, and talk briefly about why or why not.]

The Spirit of the Mountain decided that the stonecutter would learn more and would probably be happier if he could go back to being who he was, but this was his last wish. She bowed, smiled, and said, "As you wish, it shall be."

And, suddenly the stonecutter found that he was a stonecutter again, chipping away at the mountain, in the sun and the wind and the rain. They say that he almost never wished to be any one else again. When he did wish to be someone else, he would remember that he was perfect and powerful in his own way, just the way he was.

SOURCES

"The Stonecutter," in *Favorite Folktales from Around the World*, edited by Joanna Cole (Garden City, N.Y.: Guild America Books, 1982).

PICTURE BOOKS

The Stonecutter, by Demi (New York: Crown Publishers, 1995).

Cultural variant: *The Mouse Bride, a Mayan Folk Tale*, by Judith Dupre (New York: Alfred A. Knopf, 1993).

The Stone Cutter: An Indian Folktale, by Patricia Newton (New York: Putnam, 1990).

The Two Stonecutters, a Japanese tale retold by Eve Titus (Garden City, N.Y.: Doubleday & Co., Inc., 1967).

Tips for the telling

This story lends itself beautifully to participation. I suggest telling it in the round, as it is a circular tale. Have your students stand in a circle. Divide them into six groups. Assign each group a character: the stonecutter, the emperor, the sun, the cloud, the wind, and the mountain. Instruct them to come up with one group movement and sound to express that character, which they will show and teach to the whole group. Give them a minute or two to work together. Then get everyone back into the circle and explain that you will be the narrator and will call on them to show their parts at the appropriate time. Tell the story and let each group introduce the character and their movement when they come up in the story. Let the rest of the group join in and try that group's actions and sounds briefly. There are many other ways to let the group participate as well. You can ask one child to come up to represent each character, or simply take on all the characters yourself and invite them to mimic you. There are many repeating phrases that they can join in on.

Follow-up activities

Tip for story retention

- **Visual sequencing:** Have your students draw a comic strip of the order of events by dividing a large piece of paper into eight squares. Square numbers 1 and 8 will be pictures of the stonecutter before and after the sequence of events, and 2-7 will contain drawings of the six characters the stonecutter becomes. The students can then take these outlines home and use them to retell the story.

Making a personal connection

- **Questions, discussion and story sharing:** This tale can help to foster self-respect in each student as they place greater value on their uniqueness. They develop trust that they will be most powerful when they accept themselves for who they are and develop their own strengths. We are all like the stonecutter, in that we often undervalue our own skills and self-worth and envy the lives of others. Students will be able to think and talk about times when they had wished to be like someone else. Have they ever wished to be like someone else, only to discover that they are better off being themselves? Have their wishes of what they want to be changed over time? What are their strengths? When do they feel most powerful? What does power feel like? What is the difference between having a power over others, and a power that makes us feel good inside for doing our best?

Creative exploration

- **Explore cultural variants:** See picture book versions listed above.
- **Creative adaptation:** Have your students make a modern-day version of the story, choosing their own main character. Alternatively, they could each write or tell an autobiographical story in which they, like the stonecutter, wished to be all manner of different people and things and discovered that they, too, were powerful and important just as they are.

- **Retell as a play** to perform for other students. This story is well suited to a production in which one third of the class does musical accompaniment, one third portrays characters, and one third takes turns narrating. You may also include movement to portray the characters. For such an elaborate production, you would probably need help from the music teacher, though simple percussion accompaniment is easy to arrange. You can also simply take the original story, with teacher as narrator, and share that with other classes, followed by a discussion.

- **Identifying each child's "power":** Help students in your class to identify and develop their own strengths and experience feeling powerful for doing their best without having to hurt or put others down. You could make a class poem with younger students. Older students can journal and come up with ways to develop and enjoy their strengths and uniqueness.

Turning the story ideas into action

The Cracked Pot

India

Grades 7-8

THEMES: Self respect, self-acceptance, positive philosophy

Once upon a time, there was a man whose job it was to bring water from the stream to his Master's house. The man carried the water from the stream in two clay pots. He hung the pots on each end of a pole, which he carried across his shoulders, and walked to and from the stream many times a day.

One of the clay pots was perfect in every way for its purpose. The other pot was exactly like the first one, but it had a crack in it and it leaked. When the water bearer reached his Master's house, the perfect pot was always full, and the cracked pot was always half full. The poor cracked pot was ashamed of its imperfections and was miserable that it could only accomplish half of what it had been made to do.

One day the cracked pot said to the water bearer, "I want to apologize to you. Because of my cracked side, I have only been able to deliver half of the water to your Master's home, and you don't get the full value from your efforts."

The water bearer smiled on the cracked pot and with compassion, he said, "As we return to the Master's house, I want you to notice the beautiful flowers along the path."

Indeed, as they climbed the path from the river to the Master's mansion, the cracked pot took notice of the sun warming the beautiful flowers along one side of the path, and it felt somewhat brighter. But when they had reached their destination and the meager contents of his pot were poured out, his sadness returned.

"Thank you for trying to cheer me up with the beautiful flowers, water bearer," the pot said. "But I still must apologize for my failure."

The water bearer said, "Dear pot, you have not understood what I was trying to show you. Did you notice that the flowers only grew on your side of the path? That is because of your crack. I planted flower seeds on your side of the path, and every day as we walked from the stream, the water that leaks from your pot has watered them. I could have gotten a new pot, but I have preferred to gather the flowers and, with them, to bless many tables."

SOURCES

This story was first introduced to me on Storytell listserv by a fellow storyteller named Rocci Hildrum. She had heard the story through the oral tradition and could not name a written source. If you know of one, I hope you will pass it on to me. You can find her version and written comments for therapeutic use on www.healingstory.org.

As this is a story for older students, I tell it in a straightforward manner.

- **Draw an image:** As this is a short and easy-to-remember tale, have students draw a picture of the part of story that stands out for them. Have them take it home to share with parents as a homework assignment.

- **Questions, discussion and story sharing:** Have you ever felt like a "cracked pot"—as if you are not as good as others are in some way? Did you ever discover that your "cracks," or challenges, could be advantages, or could allow you to learn something new or unexpected? Have students identify an aspect of themselves that felt "cracked," or imperfect. Tell a story about something you learned because of a challenge or disability you faced. Encourage students to think about and tell a story from their own experience.

- **Poetry or story writing:** Have students write a poem or story expressing their feelings about this story, and what it reminds them of in themselves or someone else. Let them share as they are comfortable.

- **Research biographies** for stories of how others turned challenges and imperfections into gifts and advantages. Share these.

- **Sharing our beauty with the world:** The cracked pot unknowingly watered the flowers along its daily path. We too have daily opportunities to help make the world a more beautiful place. Encourage students to think of ways that they and their fellow students already do this, and new, positive ways that they can use their resources. Each student could write an anonymous note to another classmate telling him or her one way that they make the classroom a better place.

Owl

Haiti

Grades 4-8

THEMES: Self-respect, fear of being judged, low self-esteem, friendship

Owl thought he was very ugly. But one evening he met a girl and talked with her and she liked him.

"If it had been day," Owl thought, "and she had seen my face, she never would have liked me." Still she had liked him.

So Owl went to her house the next night. And the next. And the night after that. Every evening he would arrive at the girl's house at seven, and they would sit outside on the porch steps, talking together politely.

Then one evening after Owl had left, the girl's mother said to her, "Why doesn't your fiancé come and visit you during the day?"

"Mama, he explained it to me. He works during the day. Then he must go home and change and he cannot get here before seven."

"Still, I would like to see his face before the marriage," the mother said. "Let's invite him to our house for a dance this Sunday afternoon. Surely he doesn't work on Sunday."

Owl was very pleased with the invitation: a dance in his honor. But he was also very frightened. He told his cousin, Rooster, about the girl and asked him to accompany him to the dance. But that Sunday afternoon, as Owl and Rooster were riding on their horses to the dance, Owl glanced over at Rooster. Rooster held himself with such assurance, and he was so elegantly and fashionably dressed that Owl imagined the girl seeing the two of them and was filled with shame.

"I can't go on," he said. "You go and tell them I've had an accident and will be there later."

Rooster rode to the dance. "Tsk, tsk, poor Owl," he explained. "He has had an accident, and he has asked me to let you know that he will be here later."

When it was quite dark, Owl tied his horse a good distance from the dance and stumbled up to the porch steps. "Psst," he whispered to a young man sitting on the steps. "Is Rooster here?"

"Well now, I don't know," the man said.

"Go and look. Tell him a friend is waiting for him by the mapou tree."

Rooster came out. "OWL!"

"Shhhhhh—"

"Owl, what are you wearing over your head—I mean your face?"

"It's a hat. Haven't you ever seen a hat before? Look, tell them anything. Tell them I scratched my eyes on a branch as I was riding here and the light— even the light from a lamp—hurts them. And you must be certain to watch for the day for me, and to crow as soon as you see the light, so we can leave."

"Yes, yes," Rooster said. "Come in and I shall introduce you to the girl's relatives."

Rooster introduced Owl to everyone, explaining Owl's predicament. Owl went around shaking hands, his hat hung down, almost completely covering his face. Owl then tried to retreat into a corner, bur the girl came over.

"Come into the yard and let's dance," she said.

Dong ga da. Dong ga da. Dong ga da, Dong.
Dong ga da, Dong. Eh-ee-oh.

Owl danced. And Owl could dance well. The girl was proud of Owl. Even if he wore his hat strangely and had sensitive eyes, he could dance.

Dong ga da. Dong ga da. Dong ga da, Dong.
Dong ga da, Dong. Eh-ee-oh.

Rooster was dancing too. When Owl noticed that Rooster was dancing instead of watching for the day, Owl was afraid that Rooster would forget to warn him, and he excused himself to the girl. He ran out of the yard, past the houses to a clearing where he could see the horizon. No, it was still night. Owl came back.

Dong ga da. Dong ga da. Dong ga da, Dong.
Dong ga da, Dong. Eh-ee-oh.

Owl motioned to Rooster, but Rooster was lost in the dance. Owl excused himself again to the girl, ran to the clearing; no, it was still night. Owl returned.

Dong ga da. Dong ga da. Dong ga da, Dong.
Dong ga da, Dong. Eh-ee-oh.

Owl tried to excuse himself again, but he girl held on to him. "Yes, stay with me," she said. And so they danced and danced and danced.

Dong ga da. Dong ga da. Dong ga da, Dong.
Dong ga da, Dong. Eh-ee-oh.

The sun moved up in the sky, higher and higher, until it filled the house and the yard with light.

"Now—let us see your fiancé's face!" the mother said.

"Kokioko!" Rooster crowed.

And before Owl could hide, she reached out and pulled the hat from his face.

"MY EYES!" Owl cried and, covering his face with his hands, he ran for his horse.

"Wait, Owl!" the girl called.

"Kokioko!" Rooster crowed.

"Wait, Owl, wait!"

And as Owl put his hands down to untie his horse, the girl saw his face. It was striking and fierce, and the girl thought it was the most handsome face she had ever seen.

"Owl—"

But Owl never came back.

The girl waited. Then she married Rooster. She was happy, except sometimes in the morning when Rooster would crow, "Kokioko-o-o." Then she would think about Owl and wonder where he was.

"Owl," reprinted from *The Magic Orange Tree* (New York: Alfred A. Knopf, 1978) with permission from the author, Diane Wolkstein.

SOURCE

The Magic Orange Tree, by Diana Wolkstein (New York: Alfred A. Knopf, 1978). Diana collected this story in Haiti. She is the author of many collections and picture books of folk tales. www.dianewolkstein.com.

Straightforward telling works with this age group. My fifth grade students in the Boston Public Schools enjoyed dancing in the story when the characters dance. Teach them to freeze when you give them the signal, such as hitting a bell or saying "stop." The story has a very sad and somewhat unexpected ending. It is important to talk about the ending. You may even say, "This is the ending that I heard. How would you choose to have it end?" and let them finish the story.

• **Dramatic retelling:** After a straight-through telling, let your students retell, acting out the parts and dancing.

Follow-up activities
Tip for retention

• **Questions, discussion and story sharing:** Owl was so sure that others thought he had an ugly face that he would not risk showing it under any circumstance. He did not even turn around when the girl called his name after seeing his face. Have you ever felt that some characteristic about you would make you unlovable? Have you ever thought that people would judge you in a certain way, only to be surprised when they did not? Have you ever tried to hide an aspect of your appearance or personality? Teachers can help to open the risk taking by sharing a personal story. Students will most certainly want to talk about the ending.

Making a personal connection

• **Creative adaptation:** Let students make and tell their own versions and endings of this story in which Owl learns that he cannot know how others see him, and that people like him for more than his looks.

Creative exploration

• **Dramatic reenactment for other classes:** This story has a lot to teach us about the value you we put on personal appearance and the assumptions we make about how others see us. It would be a good one to have the students share with other students.

Turning the story ideas into action

• **Journal reflection:** Students can benefit from keeping a journal, noting if there are parts of themselves that they find more or less acceptable, questioning these and imagining that they, like Owl, can't know how others perceive them, and thinking about how to be more self-accepting. This is especially true for girls, who frequently have body images that are out of keeping with reality.

Once Upon a Time...

The King Who Wore a Turban

Ethiopia, Burma, and
North Africa

Grades 3-8

THEMES: Loyalty,
keeping secrets,
self-esteem, respect

Once upon a time, there was a King whose ears were quite a bit larger than normal. This embarrassed him greatly, and he kept his head and ears covered at all times with a turban. Once a month, however, he had to have his hair cut. The King had a barber that he trusted greatly. He had ordered the man to keep silent about his ears on pain of death. The barber agreed.

After a time the barber grew ill and died, and a new man took his place. The King told the new barber, "If you ever speak a word to anyone about the size of my ears, I will have you put to death!" The new barber promised and swore never to speak of it. For a time all went well. But gradually, the new barber found it increasingly difficult to keep this secret to himself. It began to burn inside him like a hot coal. Each day he felt more and more strongly that he must tell someone, he must say it out loud. At last, he sought counsel with his wise mother.

"Do not risk telling this secret to any person," she warned him, "for the King might find out, and then you would be put to death. Why not go out into the forest and dig a hole in the ground to say it, or shout it into a hole in a tree."

The barber thought that this was sound advice. The very next day, ready to burst with his secret, he walked into the forest. He was about to begin to dig a hole when some hunters came by. So on he walked until he came to the river. He was about to dig by the river when some women came to wash clothing. Again, he ran into the forest. About to burst, he noticed a huge and sturdy tree with a big hole just as high up as a man's head.

"This is it," he said. "I can hold this secret in no more!" He leaned his head into the hole in the tree and shouted at the top of his lungs, "The King has great big ears! The King has great big ears! The King has great big ears!" Oh, he felt so much better. He was able to walk home with a quiet mind, and he returned to his work as a barber with no problem.

One day however, the King decided that he needed to have a new ceremonial drum made for his son's birthday. The old drum was cracked and worn. He sent his drum makers into the forest to find a good and sturdy tree from which to make a new drum. The drum makers searched and searched until they found a huge and sturdy tree with a big round hole, just as high as a man's head. They cut it down and made a new ceremonial drum and brought it to the prince's birthday celebration.

The drummer began to beat the new drum, but a hush came over the crowd. They did not hear the sound of a drum. The only sound that came

290

ONCE UPON A TIME

booming from the drum was, "The King has great big ears! The King has great big ears! The King has great big ears!"

The King jumped up from the throne and shouted, "Who said that?"

"No one, Your Highness," said the drummer. "It is coming from the drum itself."

The King left the room and called his barber to him. "You have told my secret and now you must die!" he shouted. The King told him of how the new drum had beat out his words.

"I told no one, no one, Your Highness. I swear." But the barber confessed that he had gone into the woods and shouted the secret into the tree.

The King could see that the man was sincere. He realized that no one could keep a secret forever, for even the trees talked. He spared the man's life and did a bold and daring thing. Rather than let the people talk and wonder, he removed his turban for all to see. "Perhaps you will no longer respect me," he said. "If so, I shall pass the throne on to my brother."

The people looked at him, and said, "Yes, you have great big ears, it is true. But you are still our King, and we like you."

From that day on, the King did not worry so much about his unusual ears. He knew he was respected for who he was, great big ears or not. And that made him happy!

SOURCES

"The Enchanted Flute," in *When the World Began: Stories Collected in Ethiopia*, by Elizabeth Laird (Oxford: Oxford University Press, 2000).

"The Goat Ears of the Emperor Trajan," from *The Violet Fairy Book*, edited by Andrew Lang (New York: Dover Publishing, 1961).

"The King Who Ate Chaff," from *The Tiger's Whisker*, edited by Harold Courlander (New York: Harcourt, Brace and Co., 1959).

Tips for the telling

This is a humorous tale and works best when told lightly. Have fun playing up the barber's increasing difficulty in keeping the secret. Perhaps toward the end as he runs through the woods he has to keep a hand over his mouth to hold the words in. Also, be sure that the way you describe the tree both times is the same, so that listeners know right off that it is the same tree.

Follow-up activities
Tip for retention

- **Gossips:** Let small groups of students pretend to be people in the King's royal court retelling the story to one another, interrupting and adding details.

Making a personal connection

- **Questions, discussion and story sharing:** This story is about two separate themes, loyalty and self-esteem. Why is it sometimes hard to keep a secret? Have they ever felt like the barber did? Have you ever told someone a secret that you were supposed to keep to yourself, only to have that person tell someone else? The story also talks about wanting to hide parts of ourselves and worrying that people will not accept us for them. Why did the king think that no one would accept him? Have you ever felt that you had to hide a part of yourself from others?

- **Connecting to the characters:** Play "hot seat," letting the students take turns pretending to be the king and the barber and asking them questions.

Creative exploration

- **Creative adaptation:** Help students to make up their own creative versions of this tale in which a character has some characteristic that they try to hide from the world. Let them think of creative ways that their secret gets told without anyone hearing. Sharing some of the other versions listed above this will spur your students' creativity.

Turning the story ideas into action

- **Visual representations:** Have your students make posters from the story with captions that either remind us to respect ourselves as we are, or to be a good friend and keep secrets to ourselves.

- **Practice keeping secrets:** Have students make up secrets that they give to one other person to hold all week. (Make sure they aren't secrets about other people.) See how many people can keep the secret to themselves, and how many scream them into their pillows at night.

Favorite picture book

The Boy Who Dreamed of an Acorn, by Leigh Casler (New York: Philomel, 1994). In this literary tale, a boy goes on his rite-of-passage vision quest hoping to have a vision of a powerful animal to bring back to his people. Instead of these, he dreams of an acorn. He is ashamed of this vision and lack of physical strength. The wise man convinces him to plant the acorn in his village and to stay near it to watch it grow. The tree grows and becomes a center for both animal and village life. As the boy grows into a young man, more and more people congregate around the tree and seek his advice, and in time, he becomes the wise man of the tribe.

Responsibility

"As you sow, so shall you reap."
"By your actions you will be known."

RESPONSIBILITY IS A CORNERSTONE TRAIT in any character education program. It means we act for a greater good than our immediate wants. It helps us to recognize that we are part of a larger community than our own family or best friends, and our actions, both large and small, affect those around us. Those of us who act responsibly are capable of making moral decisions on our own. Taking responsibility for our actions requires self-awareness, courage, and honesty.

There are many ways that students learn and demonstrate responsibility in the classroom and school. They work on group projects and are expected to do their share. They are asked to volunteer for or are assigned jobs and need to know others depend on them to complete them. Students act responsibly when they follow school rules. They act responsibly when they clean up after themselves (and recycle), are respectful of other's feelings, or tell the teacher if they break something by mistake. As students get older, they can be given opportunities to be responsible for the care of younger students. They can learn to be a dependable member of a sports team, and they can help to make their community a better place through volunteering. All of these behaviors can be encouraged through the activities and discussions that follow the stories in this section.

How do stories help us to become responsible beings? Stories are distillations of life experiences, pleasantly packaged in manageable doses of cause and effect. In a single story we can see a cycle of dilemma, choice, action, and consequences. Stories offer many examples of people who have acted responsibly, and also those who have taken responsibility for their mistakes and worked to right them. Through these stories, the listener can understand that one person's actions can change everything, and that inaction is an action, and that it too has consequences.

Stories demonstrate a range of ways that a person can act responsibly. Once students hear and contemplate a story about responsibility, it remains in their minds as a guide for their future behavior.

The Little Red Hen

Traditional
North American

Grades Pre-K-2

THEMES: Diligence, perseverence, working for one's livelihood, responsibility, cooperation

Once upon a time the Little Red Hen was pecking about for seeds when she discovered some ears of wheat on the ground. "Well," she thought," if I plant them, we can make something good to eat." Then she called to her friends in the barnyard. "Who will help me plant this wheat?"

"Not I," said the cat, snoozing on the step.

"Not I," said the dog, lying in the shade of a tree.

"Not I," said the pig, lounging in a deep, cool mud puddle.

"Well then, I shall have to do it myself," said the Little Red Hen, and she set to work. She dug up the ground and raked it. She sowed the wheat seeds and watered them, and then she kept the weeds away every day. After many days, the grains had grown to tall stalks of golden wheat.

"Who will help me cut the wheat?" called the Little Red Hen.

"Not I," yawned the cat.

"Not I," sighed the dog.

"Not I," groaned the pig.

They all rolled over and went back to sleep.

"Very well then, I shall have to do it myself," said the Little Red Hen, and she set to work. She cut the wheat with a sharp sickle. She threshed it until she had collected a sack full of golden grain.

"Now the grain must go to the miller and be made into flour," said the Little Red Hen. "Who will help me carry it?"

"Not I," said the cat, lifting a paw to bat a butterfly.

"Not I," said the dog, his tail twitching away a fly.

"Not I," said the pig, chomping at a bee as it flew past.

"Very well then, I shall have to do it myself," said the Little Red Hen, and she set to work. She lifted the sack of grain onto her back and trudged all the way to the miller's. The miller ground the wheat into flour. He gave the Little Red Hen a sack full of clean white flour, and she carried it all the way home.

"Now it is time to bake a cake!" said the Little Red Hen. "Who would like to help me cook?"

"Not I," said the cat, rolling over on her side.

"Not I," said the dog, disappearing up under the porch.

"Not I," said the pig, sinking up to her nose in the mud.

"Well then I shall have to do it myself," said the Little Red Hen, and she set to work. She got some milk, some salt, and some sugar and butter and raisins and mixed them together in a great big bowl with the flour. She greased the pan and poured in the cake batter, and then put it in the oven.

Soon a wonderful smell began to fill the kitchen. It drifted out of the window and onto the porch. It drifted off of the porch and across the garden.

"Now it is time to eat," said the Little Red Hen. "Who will help me eat?"

"I will!" said the cat, jumping up onto the window sill.

"I will!" said the dog, rushing up the front steps.

"I will!" said the pig, shaking off a great quantity of mud and hustling across the pen.

"Oh no, you won't!" said the Little Red Hen. "You didn't help me to pick, or plant, or harvest, or carry, or bake. I alone will eat the cake!" And she did!

SOURCE

You can find this story in almost any collection of children's folk tales.

PICTURE BOOKS

The Little Red Hen, retold by Paul Galdone (New York: Seabury Press, 1973).

"Not I, Not I," by Margaret Hillert (Chicago: Follett Publishing Co., 1981).

Tips for the telling

This is a story that lends itself to participatory storytelling. There is so much repetition and familiarity established that the youngest listener can join in. I would suggest starting by establishing some animal voices and practicing saying, "Not I." Either have the whole group practice making cat, dog, and pig voices, or break them up into three groups, each responsible for one voice. They can also join with you in saying, "Well, I will have to do it myself!" in a henny voice. Groups can also practice making up a movement to go with the activities that the Little Red Hen does, such as picking, sowing, harvesting, carrying, baking, and eating. The audience will also be happy to mimic any movements that you initiate for these activities.

Follow-up activities
Tips for story retention

- **Visual sequencing:** Have students draw a picture of one scene in the story. Sequence them together as a class.

- **Dramatic reenactment:** Retell the story as a whole group, acting out each character and part. Try this in an open area where you can encourage full-body expression.

Making a personal connection

- **Questions, discussion and story sharing:** Ask your students to talk about things they love that take a lot of steps to make, like making playdough out of flour, making cookies, raking leaves so that they have a pile to jump in, or making a snowman. Have they ever felt like any of the characters in the story? Invite them to tell a story of a time that they felt like the Little Red Hen—or one of the characters that didn't feel like helping.

Creative exploration

- **Creative adaptation:** Make up a story as a class about someone who was making something good, like a little girl who wanted to make cookies, and discuss all of the steps involved and how her brother and sister kept saying they didn't want to help at each step, but then wanted to eat them in the end.

- **Cooking lessons:** This story could be a whole integrated lesson in how bread or cake is made (from wheat to table, if you can find a flour mill and buy some whole wheat grains at the natural food store).

Turning the story ideas into action

- **Brainstorm** together activities that work better when everyone helps. Put the list on the board. Invite the students to think about something that their parents do for them at home, and suggest that they offer to help next time and to report back on how it felt. You can even send a letter home with suggestions, such as doing the laundry, cooking, or cleaning.

- **Class Projects:** Make something together as a class and have everyone take part in helping, then enjoy the fruits of your labors in a party. Examples would be making cookies, or a clean-up of classroom or play-ground.

Why the Sky Is Far Away

Long, long ago when the world was newer than it is now, the sky was very close to the ground. You could reach right up and touch it. The sky was also the place where the people found their nourishment. All the food they could ever want was right up within arm's reach in the sky. All you had to do was to reach up and break off a piece of sky and eat it. With life so simple, the people did not have to work for their food.

For many years, this arrangement between people and the sky worked just fine. The people would break off just what they needed and would eat it all and go on their way. But after a while, people started to break off bigger and bigger pieces. They would eat what they felt like eating, and then would just throw the rest on the ground, where it would lie rotting. The people didn't think that it mattered because the sky seemed to have an endless supply of food.

The sky, however, did think that it mattered. The sky did not like to look down and see big pieces of itself rotting on the ground. It made the earth look ugly too. The sky waited patiently for the people to see the error of their ways, but they just seemed to do it more and more. Finally one day she spoke up. There was a great rumbling, and all of the people stopped what they were doing and looked up and listened.

"Listen up, people of the earth," she boomed down, "I'm tired of watching you take more sky than you need. I'm tired of watching you throw pieces of me onto the ground. I'm tired of watching myself rot there like garbage. You have to stop that now if you want me to feed you. Do you understand?"

The people looked at one another, then looked back to the sky. They were shaking. They all said, "Yes, Sky. We understand, Sky. We promise." And for a long time they were careful again—careful to only take what they needed, careful never to leave any garbage behind.

But time passed, and again people began to forget their promise, or to think that it wasn't important if they took a little bit more than they needed, because if it was just them, the sky wouldn't be likely to notice. But she did notice. One day a man walked up to the sky. He felt as hungry as a horse. He broke off a piece that was way more than he could eat by himself. He took a few bites and then heaved the rest behind a rock, looking sheepishly around to make sure that no one had seen him.

But the sky had seen him. She began to shake in anger. She began to rumble and roar. She began to pull herself up, higher and higher away from the earth. The people felt the rumbling and heard the roaring. They ran outside and looked up at the sky. They reached up their arms, but they could

Nigeria

Grades K-4

THEMES: Responsibility, consequences, respect, good citizenship, awareness, following rules

no longer reach the sky. They climbed up on their roof tops, but the sky kept pulling further and further away. They climbed trees, but the sky kept pulling away.

The people stood and looked up at the sky, now high above them. They realized what had happened. They realized that they could no longer rely on her for food. They began to cry and cry. As the day wore on, their bellies began to grumble. They were hungry and scared. The sky took pity on them.

She rained down seeds. She rained down water. She rained and rained until the seeds sprouted and plants began to grow. Then she said to her people, "These plants will feed you now. But you must plow the earth, and you must hoe and water, so that the plants will continue to grow year after year."

And that is why the people have to work for their food.

SOURCES

The Origin of Life and Death: African Creation Myths, edited by Ulli Beier (London: Heinemann, 1966).

Black Folktales, by Julius Lester (New York: Richard. W. Baron, 1969).

PICTURE BOOK

Why the Sky is Far Away, A Nigerian Folktale, retold by Mary-Joan Gerson (Boston: Little, Brown and Company, 1992).

This is a fun tale for the students to act out as you tell. Have them reach up and pull down pieces of sky. Let them tell you what the sky looked like and tasted like. Let them mime the characters throwing extra food away, and trying in the end to reach up and grab the sky as it moves away. The more the listener feels in the shoes of the story characters, the more easily they will internalize the ideas and feelings in the story.

- **Physicalizing the story:** Have small groups come up with a stylized movement for a certain section of the story. Retell the story as each group teaches their movement. This could include reaching for and eating sky, throwing away extra sky when full, sky growing angry and talking to people, people promising to be good, man taking too much and hiding it, sky pulling away, people reaching and crying, sky raining seeds and plants growing, people working to make the plants grow into food.

- **Questions, discussion and story sharing:** This is a story about respecting the earth, and it can be a lead-in to discuss many aspects of environmental protection, pollution, or climate change. Do we take certain things for granted in our environment? What happens when we throw something away? Where does it go? What happens to the paper, cans, etc. that we recycle? What happens to the pollution that goes into the air and water? Let them share stories about ways in which they respect the earth.

- **Stepping into the shoes of the characters:** Have students retell the story to a partner or small group (or whole class if appropriate) as if they were the sky, or the man who tries to get away with discarding his sky food in the story. How does this feel?

- **Creative adaptation:** Have your students make up stories similar to this one, but substituting the ocean, forest, or some other element for the sky as the source of food, housing, or warmth. How do careless actions cause them to have to work for those things? You can either have them brainstorm ideas, or to save time, have story starters on strips of papers, such as "Once the trees would open themselves up and people could go inside and have a warm place to live" or "Once the sea was so shallow that the people could walk across it to visit friends on the other side of the ocean." Older students could also research some aspect of pollution and how pollutants move through the environment, and what can or is being done to stop it. An example would be petroleum-based emissions that cause global warming. We all will feel the effects of climate change.

- **Brainstorm:** The man in the story thought that it would not matter if he didn't obey the rule the sky had given him. He felt that one person's actions would not affect the whole world. Make a list of other situations in the world where people think that their individual actions don't make a difference. Share examples of rules that we all should obey to keep the world a safe and healthy place. Make a list of actions in the classroom and school that will assure the safety and health of the school environment if each person does their part.

- **Focus on an issue:** Pick one issue, such as recycling used paper in the classroom, and make a project in which each student commits to doing their part. Have students research what happens to recycled paper vs. paper going to the landfill and give a report.

A Drop of Honey

Once a King stood on his balcony eating honey rice cakes with his chief advisor. As they ate, they gazed down on the street below. The King was in good humor that day, and as he laughed, a drop of honey fell from his rice cake onto the railing.

"Sire, you have spilled a drop of honey," observed his advisor. "Why don't I call a servant to come and clean it up?"

But the King replied, "A drop of honey is not our concern. The servants will clean it later. I do not wish to be disturbed right now."

They went on eating and talking as the drop of honey warmed in the sun and began to slowly drip down the rail. At last it fell onto the street below.

"Your Highness," the advisor said, "that drop of honey has now fallen into the street, where it is attracting flies. Shouldn't we call someone to clean it up?"

But again the King replied, "A drop of honey in the street is not our concern. Someone will deal with it later."

Suddenly a lizard darted out from a crack in the building below and began to catch the flies on his tongue. Then a cat sprang from the baker's shop and began to bat the lizard back and forth like a toy. Just then a dog charged from the butcher's shop and began to bite the cat on the neck.

"Your Highness," the advisor implored, "now the insects on the honey have attracted a lizard, who attracted a cat, who is now being attacked by a dog. Shouldn't we call someone to stop the fight?"

But again the King yawned and said, "A little animal fight is not our concern, dear advisor. Someone else will see to it."

Well the baker did see to it. She saw a dog attacking her cat and ran out with her rolling pin and began to hit the dog. The butcher saw someone hitting his dog and picked up his broom and began to hit the cat. Soon the two people were hitting each other. Then the neighbors joined in taking sides. Then some soldiers showed up, but as they each knew the butcher or the baker, they took sides and soon there was a large battle being waged in the streets. People were throwing rocks through windows, tipping over carts. Someone picked up a torch and threw it through a window. Fire raged, and eventually it spread to the palace. Next thing they knew, the King and his advisor were being escorted down a ladder from the balcony because the palace itself was in flames.

Burma and Thailand

Grades K-8

THEMES: Responsibility, self-mastery, non-violent conflict resolution, leadership, good citzenship

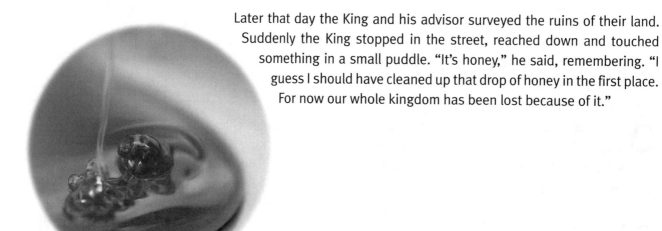

Later that day the King and his advisor surveyed the ruins of their land. Suddenly the King stopped in the street, reached down and touched something in a small puddle. "It's honey," he said, remembering. "I guess I should have cleaned up that drop of honey in the first place. For now our whole kingdom has been lost because of it."

SOURCES

A Kingdom Lost for a Drop of Honey and other Burmese Folktales, by Maung Htin Aung and Helen G. Trager (New York: Parents Magazine Press, 1968).

"Not Our Problem," retold by Margaret Read MacDonald in *Peace Tales* (Hampden, Conn.: Linnet Books/Shoe String Press, 1992).

"A Drop of Honey," retold by Elisa Pearmain in *Doorways to the Soul: 52 Wisdom Tales from Around the World* (Cleveland: Pilgrim Press, 1998).

This story lends itself to participatory telling. The repetition of the king's phrase, "It is not our concern" can easily be picked by the audience. You might also consider telling it from the perspective of one of the characters: the king or his advisor, or add in the king's wife or one of the servants. I have found that by telling it as the advisor, I am able to add a second aspect to responsibility. The advisor notices the problem, but waits for the king to take action, rather than simply doing something about it himself. How often do we think that a problem is someone else's responsibility, only to realize later that our inaction has consequences?

Tips for the telling

- **Round-robin retelling:** Sit in a circle and let each child tell part of the story.

- **Dramatic reenactment:** Divide the students into several groups so that each one has a role. Total number of characters in my version of the story is around 12: narrator(s), king, advisor, fly, lizard, cat, dog, baker, butcher, soldiers. You can always add characters, such as multiple flies, servants, and soldiers. You may wish to be the narrator with younger children, or initially with older children. I would suggest stylizing the street fighting so that no one gets hurt. An example would be to have everyone put their fists in the air, or to point and to yell, "It's your fault!"

Follow-up activities
Tips for story retention

- **Questions, discussion and story sharing:** Have you ever thought that some issue was not your problem, only to discover that you were affected by it? Have you ever had some small problem grow into something bigger than you expected? Have you ever thought, "Someone else will deal with it? It's not my concern"—only to discover that if you had dealt with it, it could have turned out much better?

- **Teacher shares personal stories:** I like to offer examples from my own experience for the class, such as not cleaning up my car, only to have someone need to ride in it and being embarrassed that it smelled like rotten banana. I also tell a story to fifth grades and up about a time when I was in the sixth grade, and I did not help to "clean up a drop of honey" in a bullying incident.

    A friend, whom I will call Jane, called another friend of mine, whom I will call Leah, a religious/ethnic slur. Jane was sent to the principal's office. I did not have the courage to speak up and to tell Jane that what she did was wrong, even though I knew it was. I was afraid that she would get mad at me and not want to be my friend. I realize now that because she valued my friendship, she would have listened to me. I also did not tell Leah that I was sorry for what had happened. I felt uncomfortable and didn't think that I needed to apologize for Jane, because I wasn't involved. But looking back, I can see that I was involved. By keeping silent, I gave the impression that the name-calling was all right with me. I can see that two drops of honey were allowed to fall there, and that I might have been

Making a personal connection

able to avoid these two results: 1) Jane was allowed to become more bigoted and mean, and 2) Leah grew more angry and hurt at not being supported.

After I tell this story, it generates discussion about particular situations in which we have a choice to be responsible or not. Students want to talk about the risks involved in speaking out against bullying, as well as the rewards and long-term effects. Peer pressure can be a good discussion related to this topic: Why is it so hard to tell your friends when you think they have acted meanly? Why do students say mean things to other students, and why do the bystanders laugh? Students often prefer to write about personal experiences of this kind, so that they have the option of sharing them with the class. It helps if you can think about a time when you witnessed bullying and were or were not able to help. You can also use my story as an example.

Creative exploration

- **Creative adaptation:** Retell the beginning of the story, but stop at the part when everyone is fighting. Have the class discuss what is going on and what "should" happen next. They could create an imaginary court and trace the problem back to the king by asking each player what his role was. You can also address alternative non-violent conflict resolution to talk about how the people in the story could have avoided fighting.

- **Personal story sharing:** Encourage students to write and tell stories of times in which they did not take care of something and it grew to be a bigger problem.

Turning the story ideas into action

- **Classroom props:** Bring in a bear-shaped jar of honey from the grocery store and prominently display it as a reminder of what a drop of honey can do. Let it be used as a prop when someone thinks there is a problem to be dealt with. Children are creative—ask them how the wisdom in this story can best be remembered.

- **Brainstorm** lists of situations in which students and teachers can take responsibility for their actions. Are there roles in the school in which students can have a say about how decisions are made? Are there situations in which drops of honey typically fall and aren't dealt with? Discuss ideas for how these can be turned into action projects: picking up litter on the playground, recycling school papers, or making sure students pick up after themselves in the cafeteria. Projects might also involve intervening when they see bullying happening in the halls or on the school bus. Where does bullying typically happen, and how can each student take a part in reducing it? Older students can stretch the brainstorm to include the town, country, and world.

The Tail of the Linani Beast

Western Kenya

Grades 3-8

THEMES: Responsibility, blaming others, unwise thinking, taking advantage of others, stealing, peer pressure

There was a young man who fell madly in love with a beautiful young woman.

Every day he would go to her house and beg her to marry him. She wouldn't say yes, and she wouldn't say no. She would say something like "You know...I am really thirsty for some coconut water. It would be really nice to have some coconut water right now."

The young man would jump up. "You want coconut water? I'll get you coconut water." He would run to the coconut grove, climb a tree, cut a coconut, bring it back and slice off the top and give it to her. "Here! A coconut."

The next day he would be back again. "Would you marry me? Please?" She wouldn't say yes, and she wouldn't say no. She would say, "Well...I am really hungry for some fresh fish. Some fresh fish for supper would be really good."

That young man would race to the stream. He would spear some fish. He would rush back and lay them before her. "Here! Fresh fish!"

Anything that girl could think of to ask, that young man would provide. Still she would not agree to marry him.

One day he asked her, "Isn't there anything I could bring that would persuade you to marry me? I would bring you anything...anything at all."

She got a faraway look in her eye. "Well there is one thing, but I'm sure you could never bring it—the tail of the Linani Beast. I've heard they are so beautiful, so silky, and so rare. How famous I would be if I owned such a tail."

The young man gulped. "The Linani Beasts live deep in the forest. The Linani Beasts crunch up humans for their dinner."

"I know," the young woman replied. "Any man who brought me the tail of the Linani Beast would be so brave, I would have to marry him."

The young man was inspired. Now he knew how to win this girl. All he had to do get the tail of a Linani Beast, and she would be his! He would go at once! That young man sharpened his knife. He set off into the forest, in search of the Linani Beasts.

The Linani Beasts lived in a grove deep in the forest. All day long they slept. But at dusk, the Linani woke up. Then they went looking for bones to crunch. Preferably human bones. The Linani had learned that humans coveted their tails. So to keep the humans from sneaking up on them, the Linani had developed a strange sleeping habit. While the Linani slept, they would keep opening and closing their eyes. They would really be asleep all the while, even when their eyes were open. And while they slept they would mutter under their breaths. When they closed their eyes they would mutter,

"I'm asleep." When they opened their eyes they would mutter, "I'm awake." But really they were asleep all the time.

When the young man reached the grove of the Linani Beasts, he saw them lying in mounds all over the ground. They seemed at first glance to be asleep. But when he ventured closer he saw they were opening their eyes every few minutes and muttering, "I'm asleep...I'm awake! I'm asleep...I'm awake! I'm asleep...I'm awake!"

"They only sleep for a few seconds at a time," he said to himself. "How will I sneak in and cut off a Linani tail?"

He sat down to observe them. He watched for a long while. He noticed that when the Linani opened their eyes, they never looked around. He noticed that when the Linani said, "I'm awake!" they kept right on breathing deeply as if in sleep. "I believe the Linani are really sleeping all the time," he said to himself. " I don't think they wake up when they open their eyes."

He had to have that tail. So he took the risk. Slowly the young man tiptoed up to the sleeping Linani. He stepped over the first Linani. It spoke: "I'm asleep...I'm awake! I'm asleep...I'm awake! I'm asleep...I'm awake!"

The Linani didn't move. "They are asleep! They are all sound asleep!" he thought. The young man tiptoed through the sleeping Linani, looking for the most beautiful tail. There he saw it—the tail of the chief of the Linani. Long...silky...that was the tail for his girlfriend. The young man pulled out his knife. That knife was so sharp. With one quick slash, he cut the tail right off. It was so quick, and the Linani was sleeping so deeply that it did not even wake up.

"I'm asleep...I'm awake! I'm asleep...I'm awake! I'm asleep...I'm awake!" They muttered.

The young man tiptoed out of the pile of sleeping beasts. He began to run back through the forest with the tail. "Now she will marry me!" he said. "Tonight she will be mine!" But he had a long way to travel yet to reach his village.

Night began to fall. Back at the grove, the Linani began to wake up. "Awwnn! Wake up, Linani! Wake up! Time to go out and crunch some bones!"

The Linani began to stretch and get up. The Linani Beast lying next to the chief sat up. He put his hand on the ground and felt something wet and sticky. It was blood from the chief's tail. "Chief, what is this?" he asked.

The chief put his hand down on the ground. "What? It's blood! My tail! Someone has cut off my tail! Only a human would do a thing like this. Whoever that man is, today he becomes my ENEMY!"

The Linani began to snuffle round that grove. Soon they discovered a trail of blood leading into the forest.

"I go to fetch my tail and our supper," said the chief. He picked up a handful of straw grass and tied it in a magic knot. Holding this knot in front of him, he chanted, "You who became my enemy today, you who became my enemy today, no matter where you go, no matter where you hide, I will find you—speak to me!"

The magic knot of grass drew that young man's voice. Running down the forest path, the young man felt himself suddenly answering. "I...I...I..." his voice burst out. He could not stop it! "I who became your enemy today, I who became your enemy today, I cut your tail."

The magic knot made him say that. Then the young man began to call out, "I didn't mean to do it. I didn't mean to do it. The woman...the woman...the WOMAN made me do it."

The Linani stomped down the path after that young man. The young man ran and ran. Every little while the Linani would stop and call again. "You who became my enemy today, you who became my enemy today, no matter where you go, no matter where you hide, I will find you—SPEAK TO ME!"

And the young man would be forced to stop and call back. "I who became your enemy today. I who became your enemy today, I cut your tail. Oh...but...I didn't want to do it. I didn't want to do it. The woman...the woman...the WOMAN made me do it!"

The young man reached his village. He ran to that girl's house. "Here! Here is your Linani tail! Now will you marry me?"

She was impressed. "The tail of a Linani! How brave you must be! Of course I'll marry you."

"Then hide me!" the young man cried. "The Linani is coming." She covered him with mats. He could not be seen.

The Linani entered the village. He looked around at all of the houses. "He is hiding in one of these," the Linani said. "He who became my enemy today, no matter where you go, no matter where you hide, I will find you—SPEAK TO ME!"

Under the mats, the young man felt his voice coming out of him, "I who became your enemy today, I who became your enemy today, I cut your tail. Oh...no...I didn't mean to do it. I didn't want to do it. The woman...the woman...the WOMAN made me do it."

The Linani followed the sound of that voice. He pushed into that house. There sat the girl, holding his tail. He didn't see the young man anywhere. "He who became my enemy today, no matter where you go, no matter where you hide, I will find you—SPEAK TO ME!"

Under the mats the young man held both his hands over his mouth. But it was no use. His voice came out. "I who became your enemy today, I who became your enemy today, I cut your tail! Oh...but..." He leapt to his feet and begged the Linani. "I didn't mean to do it. I didn't want to do it. The woman...the woman...the WOMAN made me do it."

The Linani stared at the girl. "The woman? The woman? The WOMAN made you do it?" He snatched the tail back from the girl. He turned to that young man. "But the man...the man...the MAN is in charge of his own actions."

He snatched that young man up. He threw him over his back. He marched out of the house, out of the village, and into the forest. That young man was never seen again.

Now in that village they tell the young girls, "If you love a young man, do not ask of him impossible things. Do not do that."

And to the young men they say, "If you love a young woman, no matter what she says, no matter what she asks, remember that the MAN is responsible for his own actions."

This story is adapted here with the generous permission of Margaret Read MacDonald. To read the text as prepared by Margaret Read MacDonald please see *More Ready-To-Tell Tales from Around the World*, eds. David Holt and Bill Mooney (Little Rock: August House Publishers, 2000).

SOURCES

More Ready-To-Tell Tales from Around the World, edited by David Holt and Bill Mooney (Little Rock: August House Publishers, 2000). For more information about Margaret Read MacDonald's resources, see her web site: www.margaretreadmacdonald.com

There is so much repetition in this story that it lends itself beautifully for audience participation with younger students. Have them join you in repeating the Lanani Beast's words, "I'm awake, I'm asleep," as they open and close their eyes. They can also join you on the repetitive words of the Linani Beast and the young man. This story asks for rich characterization, and sense of place. Be aware of building the tension as the Linani Beast nears the man and ensnares him in his magic. Teenaged audiences will usually prefer to just listen as you tell this haunting tale.

Tips for the telling

- **Small-group drama:** Divide your students into two small, and one large group. Assign them to portray one of the three scenes in the story. Scene 1: The young man and the woman. Scene 2: The young man obtaining the tail. (This can involve the large group as most students can be the Linani Beasts.) Scene 3: The young man returning to the woman and the capture by the beast. Let some students in each group be actors and others directors.

Follow-up activities
Tips for story retention

- **Questions and Discussion:** Find out what the students think about the story, and the characters' actions. Why did the young man continue to want the young woman so much when she seemed to be using him? How can you tell when someone really likes you and when they are taking advantage of you? What do they think should have happened to the young man in the end? What about the young woman?

- **Personal story sharing:** How often have you said, "But he made me do it." Tell stories about times when you got into trouble for doing something that was someone else's idea, or to please someone else. Have you ever done something for someone because you wanted them to like you and then found out that they didn't treat you any better afterwards?

Making a personal connection

- **Creative Adaptation:** Let the students change the item that was wanted, and the creatures that had it, and retell the story in their own way.

Creative exploration

- **Working with the moral:** Write on the board the phrase "A person is responsible for his or her own actions." Let your students make posters about it, write an essay, or create an original story.

- **Brainstorm** together places in their lives where this phrase is relevant.

- **Sharing the story with other students:** Let your class dramatize this tale for other classes and then generate a discussion about the lessons.

Turning the story ideas into action

Who Started It?

Hebrew

Grades 2-8

THEMES: Leadership, responsibility for one's actions, cause and effect

King Solomon was known throughout the land for his wisdom, his ability to communicate with animals, and his skill as a fair judge. Once, an otter in great distress came before the King.

"King Solomon," she cried, "you have decreed that all of the animals should live in peace, but I say that decree has been cruelly broken."

"How has this come about?" asked the King with a furrowed brow.

"I left my den for just a short time to hunt for food, and when I returned, my neighbor the Weasel had killed two of my children! I beg you to take justice into your hands and punish the Weasel, or I will do so myself!"

King Solomon called the Weasel to come before his throne.

"Weasel, is it true what the Otter says—that you have killed her children? I have decreed that there shall be peace among the animals."

"It is true that they died by my hand, honorable King, but it was an accident. I was walking by the Otter's den when I heard the Woodpecker sound her drum call to war. I was so terrified that I ran straight into the den and crushed two of her babies. I am truly sorry, and I meant no harm."

"Hmm," sighed King Solomon. "Let us call the Woodpecker."

"Woodpecker, is it true that you sounded the drums of war, summoning the animals to fight? I have decreed that there should be peace among the animals."

"Yes, my King, I confess, I did beat the drums of war, but I had good cause. I saw the scorpion sharpening his dagger and I was very frightened and thought others should be warned."

"Hmm," said King Solomon. "Let us call the Scorpion."

"Scorpion, is it true that you were sharpening your dagger today? You know that I have decreed that there should be peace among the animals."

"Yes, I confess, Your Highness, I was sharpening my dagger, but I had good cause! I saw the Tortoise climbing into her armor. I was very alarmed, as I thought that meant trouble ahead."

"Hmm," said King Solomon. "Let us call the Tortoise."

"Tortoise, is it true that you were climbing into your armor today, as if preparing for war? I have decreed that the animals shall live in peace."

"Yes, Your Highness, it is true, but I had good cause! I climbed into my armor to protect myself when I saw the lobster swinging its great claw as if to attack."

"Hmm," said King Solomon. "Let us call the lobster."

"Lobster, is it true that you were swinging your great claw and scaring the Tortoise? I have decreed that the animals shall live in peace."

"Yes, it is true. I did swing my great claw, but I had good cause, Your Highness. I saw the Otter dive into my home to steal my children, which she has done before I could stop her."

"Oh," said King Solomon.

"Otter, is it true that you have gone into Lobster's home and stolen her children?"

"Yes, it is true, but I only did it to feed my own."

"Well then," sighed the King sadly, " I would say that there has been punishment enough for the crime. For you have started this sad chain of events by angering the Lobster, who scared the Tortoise, who alarmed the Scorpion, who frightened the Woodpecker, who terrified the Weasel, who ran into your home and trampled your children. Perhaps we cannot stop eating one another for food, but let us take only what we really need, and not be quick to cast blame or to take revenge on others."

SOURCE

I was introduced to this story by Heather Forest, who has two lovely versions, one in narrative and one in song with musical notation called "King Solomon and the Otter" in *Spinning Tales, Weaving Hope: Stories, Storytelling, and Activities for Peace, Justice and the Environment* (Philadelphia: New Society Publishers, 1992). I also found a similar version in *And It Came to Pass*, by Hyman Nahman Bialik (New York: Montauk Bookbinding Corp., 1938). Peninah Schram also tells a version called "The Cycle," in *Jewish Stories One Generation Tells Another*, (Northvale, N.J.: Jason Aronson Inc., 1993).

OTHER CIRCULAR TALES THAT RELATE TO RESPONSIBILITY

"Why Mosquitoes Buzz in People's Ears," retold by Verna Aardema (New York: Dial Press, 1975). Picture book.

"Gecko Cannot Sleep," in *Earth Care: World Folktales to Talk About*, by Margaret Read MacDonald (New Haven, Conn.: Linnet Books, 1999).

Tips for the telling

This one has a wide audience. I would tell it with much participation with the younger crowd, and in a simple and straightforward manner with grades 5-8. Anywhere that you find a repeating phrase you can invite your audience to join with you. See ideas for participatory retells which can be adapted for the first telling. My ending here is a bit on the preachy and redundant side. Use any, all, or none of it.

Follow-up activities

Tip for story retention

- **Participatory retell:** Retell this tale with younger students sitting or standing in a circle. Divide the students into six groups and give each group a part: otter, weasel, woodpecker, scorpion, tortoise, or lobster. Have the group come up with a sound or movement to represent what they did in the story. Otter is crying and then stealing, weasel trampling, woodpecker sounding drum, scorpion sharpening dagger, tortoise climbing into armor, lobster swinging his claw. Take the part of narrator and let the groups show their actions and sounds when it comes to that part of the story. If they can, let them tell King Solomon why they did what they did.

Making a personal connection

- **Questions, discussion and story sharing:** Your students may have strong feelings after this story. They cycle of life can seem cruel, and yet most humans are involved in eating animals too. How do people reconcile this? Some of your older students may have started to explore vegetarianism and may want to discuss their choices. What did King Solomon mean by peace among the beasts if he knew that some of them ate each other for survival?

- **Hot seat:** Let the students take turns being in the hot seat as King Solomon, the otter and the lobster. Let the other students ask them questions. Help them to debate whether the otter got what she deserved.

Creative exploration

- **Create an original circular story** with the class about responsibility, in which the character discovers that his or her own actions come back to affect them. You may want to read them several other circular tales as listed above first, or let them read and tell them to their classmates.

Turning the story ideas into action

- **Class project:** Take on a class project to look at some aspect of the physical or social environment and see how humans are responsible and can make change. Once the students have learned about this, have them make a circular diagram, and/or a circular drama explaining how our actions affect the environment and come back around, affecting us. Examples are global warming, air pollution, littering, not recycling, poverty, bullying, violence, war...

Once Upon a Time...

The Children and the Frogs

Once upon a time a group of students ran down to the pond near their neighborhood. There they began a game of skipping stones and throwing rocks across and into the pond. What fun they were having as they searched for more and more stones, and threw them with greater and greater splashes into the depths of the pond.

But underneath the water, the inhabitants of the pond were not having such a fine time. In fact they were being hit by those rocks, their homes were being damaged, and their bodies torn. They trembled at the bottom in fear.

Finally the oldest and bravest frog swam to a lily pad on the surface of the pond, and croaked loudly. The students stopped their games and looked.

"Please children, do stop your terrible game," said the frog. "While it might seem like simple fun to you, it means death for us." And he hopped back into the water.

Did the students stop their games? I hope so. What do you think?

See page 44 for information on Aesop.

Aesop

Grades 2-6

THEMES: Responsibility, thoughtfulness, consequences, sacrifice for others

SOURCE

The Aesop for Children (New York: Children's Press Choice, 1984).

Tips for the telling

This is a very short story, but with a powerful message. We need to think about the larger consequences of our actions before we take them. I would suggest having a personal story to couple with this one, or maybe even to enlarge this one, pretending that it happened to you. You could create a second half of the story in which the students broke into two camps in which some said, "Hey, we should stop" and others said, "Why? They are just stupid frogs." You could leave the ending open-ended, and ask the class how they think it should end.

Follow-up activities

Tip for retention

- **Group dramatization:** Pick a director and let the students choose parts: children, frogs, brave frog, and one narrator. Have the director decide where people should stand. The narrator tells the story and the characters interject as they see fit.

Making a personal connection

- **Questions, discussion and story sharing:** What message did your students take from this story? How did it feel to throw stones before the children knew that they were hurting the frogs? How did that change afterwards? Have you ever done something that seemed fun and innocent until you learned the effects that it had on other people or the environment? What do you do differently now that you are more environmentally aware? There are some people whose spiritual practice includes not harming any living being including mosquitos. What would it be like to live that way?

Creative exploration

- **Creative adaptations:** Have your students make up stories in which someone or a group of people do something that harms people, animals, or the environment. Include how they find out and what they do differently.

- **Research:** What practices that harm the environment are no longer done? Have your students research either at the library, or by asking their parents what changes they know about or have seen in their lifetimes. Are there things that still go on that give pleasure to some and cause pain to others? Examples include greyhound racing, cock fighting, and hunting of animals that are endangered to get certain parts that are worth a lot on the black market.

Turning the story ideas into action

- **Brainstorm:** Make a list of other situations in which we might think that something is fun or profitable, without realizing the harm that it could be doing to other people, animals, or the environment. This can extend to social situations such as teasing or gossiping. Other examples include cosmetic products that are tested on animals or skimobiling in national parks. Create original stories as told from the perspective of the victims, and share them with one another and other classrooms.

The Answer Is in Your Hands

Long ago a wise old man lived alone on the edge of town. His ways were thought to be peculiar and sometimes the children would dare one another to run near to his house or pick a fruit from his trees. The children's parents scolded them and told them that the man was very wise and that they should treat him with respect.

One day a group of older boys and girls decided to draw the hermit out onto his front porch and to see if he really was wise. One child had caught a bird and they carried it to the old man's home. They drew straws and the loser ran up and knocked upon the old man's door. The child with the bird held it behind his back.

"Old man," called the boy with the bird, "they say you are wise. So tell me what it is that I am hiding behind my back." The old man was observant and noticed a small downy feather float to the ground.

"I believe you are holding a bird, young man," he replied.

The children were surprised, but the boy with the bird was not satisfied.

He quickly came up with a new plan. He would ask the old man if the bird was alive or dead. If the old man said, "Dead," he would release the bird and surprise him. If he said, "Alive," he would crush the bird, and prove him wrong again.

"Tell me old man," he spoke boldly, "Is the bird dead or alive?"

The old man looked into the young man's eyes and saw the defiance and danger. "The answer is in your hands, young man," he said slowly. "The answer is in your hands."

All of the children looked at the boy, who brought the live bird forward and released it into the sky.

India

Grades 4-8

THEMES: Responsibility for one's actions, wise choices

SOURCES

I first heard this story from Susan Tobin, who has published it as "The Hermit and the Children" in *Spinning Tales, Weaving Hope: Stories, Storytelling, and Activities for Peace, Justice and the Environment*, edited by Ed Brody, et al. (Philadelphia: New Society Publishers, 1992).

"In Your Hands," retold by Margaret Read MacDonald in *Earth Care: World Folktales to Talk About* (North Haven, Conn.: Linnet Books, 1999). MacDonald describes it as being part of a longer Indian tale in which a riddle is told and solved with another riddle.

Follow-up activities

Tip for retention

- **Small-group retell:** Get the students into small groups and have them retell/act it out together using a prop.

Making a personal connection

- **Questions, discussion and story sharing:** It may (should be) disturbing to students to think that someone would consider crushing a bird to make a point. Let them share their feelings and thoughts. Personal stories of witnessing torture of killing of animals or insects may follow. Help them to think about what things they are responsible for in their daily lives, and how many opportunities there are to make a difference one way or another.

Creative exploration

- **Interviewing adults:** Have your students interview a parent or other adult and ask them to tell about a time that they made a difference by the actions they chose. They might start by sharing this story with the adult. Have them share the stories they gather in class.

Turning the story ideas into action

- **Brainstorm:** What actions are in the students' hands? What things that go on in the world could they make a difference with? Have them make lists and decide if there were small projects they could undertake to help make a difference. Perhaps they could spur a school-wide effort to raise money for a cause and could share this story as a way of introducing their idea as they went from class to class.

- **Journal keeping:** Older students can keep a journal and notice as they go through their day how many opportunities arise in which they have the responsibility to make decisions that affect others. Share these together.

- **Responsibility rituals:** In some Native American cultures as part of the rite of passage ceremony, the girls are required to assume the role of "healers," laying hands on each person of the tribe. Putting the girls in the shoes of someone with responsibility for the well-being of another is very empowering and helpful for the girls in seeing themselves as adult members of the tribe. Can you imagine creating a situation in which your students took responsibility for others? It could be as simple as having one student be blindfolded while the other led him or her on a specific course, or helping with the care of younger students for a day.

Water Not Wine

Once upon a time, the eldest and richest man in the village decided that it would be a good idea to give a feast for all of the townspeople at the start of the new year. He called the council of elders together to plan the event. "I will provide the food," he said, "if you will each bring a jug of wine."

"Of course, of course," they all agreed.

However, as soon as they had parted, the youngest of the group was already cursing himself for agreeing to part with one whole jug of wine. He did not have much wine in his stores, and he did not want to spend money either. "There must be another way," he told his wife. And he sat down to think.

After a while, a smile crossed his face. "The other nine elders will pour their wine into the common pot. Could one jug of water spoil so much good wine?"

"Hardly so, my clever husband," chuckled his greedy wife.

China and Africa

Grades 5-8

THEMES: Responsibility to one's community, greed, small-mindedness, care of others

And so it was that on the day of the feast, this man put on his finest robes, filled his jug with fresh cool water from the well, and went to the party. On his way, he met up with the other elders. The delicious smells of food cooking and the sounds of music playing met them at the door. The host motioned for the elders to pour their jugs of wine into a great clay pot in the courtyard.

First there was dancing and entertainment. Then the bell was rung and the guests were seated. The elders sat together at the head table. The host ordered his servants to fill everyone's cup with the wine. Each of the elders waited patiently for the last guest to be served. They were anxious to taste the fine, refreshing wine. The host gave the blessing and the guests put their cups to their lips. They sipped, and sipped again. But what they tasted was not wine, but water, for each one of them had thought, "One jug of water cannot spoil a great pot of wine." Each had filled his jug at the well.

They looked at each other sheepishly, avoiding the eyes of the guests and the host, and then continued to drink as if it were the finest wine their lips had ever tasted.

That day a new saying arose among the people of that village, a saying that spread far and wide: "If you wish to take wine, you must give it also."

SOURCES

"Water Not Wine," in *Doorways to the Soul: 52 Wisdom Tales from Around the World*, edited By Elisa Pearmain (Cleveland: Pilgrim Press, 1998).

"The Feast," collected from the Bamum tribe, Cameroon, Africa, and published in *The King's Drum*, edited by Harold Courlander (New York: Harcourt, Brace & World, 1962).

"Ten Jugs of Wine," in *Sweet and Sour: Tales from China*, edited by Carol Kendall and Yoa-wen Li (New York: Clarion Books, 1979).

"Share the Wine," in *Earth Tales: World Folktales to Talk About*, by Margaret Read MacDonald (New Haven, Conn.: Linnet Books, 1999).

Tips for the telling

This is a pretty straightforward telling that does not particularly lend itself to participation. If you feel that it is unacceptable to tell a story with an alcoholic beverage in it, then change the wine to lemonade or something else. The point will be the same.

Follow-up activities
Tip for retention

- **Whole-group retell:** Have the students brainstorm how to act this out spontanously as a group. Pick a director, actors, and any props. Including guests, there are enough parts for everyone. It should not take long to organize and retell.

Making a personal connection

- **Questions, discussion and story sharing:** I hope everyone has had the experience of feeling rewarded for contributing to a community or group event. We have probably all had the experience of feeling reluctant to give something that was important to us or in short supply. We may have thought then that our contribution would not make a difference or would not be missed. Share those experiences about times when our contribution—or lack thereof—made a difference, and how we felt no matter what choice was made. You might try the creative exercise below first to remind them of their own experiences.

Creative exploration

- **Creative adaptation:** This story is a natural for modernization. Have the students get into small groups and create an original version set in their school or neighborhood with students as the major players. Have them share with one another.

Turning the story ideas into action

- **Brainstorm** types of experiences where our contribution makes a difference. Make a list and reflect upon it together.

- **Take it on the road:** Prepare your classroom as the feast room from the story. Invite other classes to come to the feast and tell the story. Use lemonade instead of wine and have the students experience tasting the water instead of the lemonade at the end of the story. Let the students generate a discussion with peers about how this story relates to their lives.

- **Visual representations:** Have your students make posters that relate to the final saying that spread around the land. How would they change it? Refer to it when the opportunity arises.

Favorite picture books

Gluskabe and the Four Wishes, retold by Joseph Bruchac (New York: Cobblehill Books, 1995). In this traditional story of the Wabanaki peoples of New England, Gluskabe grants four wishes to four men. Only one man wishes for something that will help others, and only one has the self-control to wait and discover how his wish may be granted, and to learn from his animal teachers.

It Takes a Village, by Jane Cowen-Fletcher (New York: Scholastic, Inc., 1994). In this simple story taking place in an African village, a girl is put in charge of watching her little brother. He gets away from her, and while she is looking for him and worrying about him, many of the villagers have watched, fed, hugged, and sheltered him. The story describes how "it takes a village to raise a child."

Miss Rumphius, by Barbara Cooney (New York: Viking, 1988). In this beautifully illustrated story, Miss Rumphius takes responsibility for making the world more beautiful in her own way.

Self-Control

"No man is free who is not master of himself."
—Epictetus

"Self-discipline is holding your ground when you would rather run away; counting to ten when you would rather lash out; keeping a smile on your face when you'd rather cave in; working hard when you would rather give up."
—Unknown

PERSONS WITH SELF-MASTERY have cultivated all of the qualities of character described in this book, and apply them in their daily life. They have integrity. They walk the talk. For most of us, it is a lifetime's process to gain self-control. It is something to strive and work toward, but this goal must be modeled and fostered.

Before we can truly be the masters of ourselves, we must develop self-awareness skills. Self-awareness can be described as the ability to observe ourselves—our thoughts, emotions, habits, prejudices and actions—and to come to know what motivates us to act the way we do, and to act consciously. Self-awareness teaches us to be mindful of what we are feeling and needing in any given situation, and then to make conscious choices of how to respond. Reacting on impulse and emotion often causes us to do things we regret. Having the self-control to step back and observe our emotional reactions, and then to make choices of how to act gives us the tools to act wisely and for the greater good. We increase our "response-ability." Self-awareness also gives us the tools to be honest with ourselves, and to learn and grow from our mistakes.

Teaching our children self-awareness involves teaching them to be emotionally intelligent. More and more teens are struggling with suicidal, self-harming, and addictive behaviors. The Centers for Disease Control in Atlanta reports that the suicide rate for children between the ages of 10 and 14 rose by 75% between 1975 and 1988. It has continued to rise since then. There are many reasons for this beyond the scope of this book. One reason, however, is the inability to tolerate strong emotions and stress. Emotions of all kinds are an inevitable response to being human on this earth. Stories can help to teach emotional intelligence because they portray human beings having emotional experiences of all kinds. Envy, fear, anger, sadness and loss are often present in stories, as are their opposites—goodwill, joy, peace, and acceptance. Stories allow us to experience emotions vicariously. They can help students to build a wider emotional vocabulary. Stories are full of characters that react out of emotion to various situations. They help us to see that a given experience can elicit different emotions depending on how we frame it. Stories teach us that we have options about to how to express and respond to our emotions. I should add that there can be no self-control without self-acceptance. Experiencing through story how others have stumbled along life's path helps us to accept our own imperfections.

Another aspect of self-control is the ability to use restraint. This is the ability to hold oneself back from following unhealthy instincts or taking unwise action, to have patience, rather than acting impulsively or out of greed, and to delay gratification.

A third aspect of self-control as it relates to character education and bullying is in becoming more aware of when we are acting out of prejudice, bias, or intolerance. All human beings grow up with exposure to some types of prejudice, bias, and or fear of others who look or act in ways different from us. Self-control allows us to look at those prejudices and fears honestly, and to then to move beyond them in a manner that is respectful of all beings.

Self-control is also about cultivating a positive philosophy of life that helps us to tolerate life's inevitable ups and downs and its impermanence. The only thing certain is change. Stories of others who have found peace in the turbulence of life can be guides for us on our own paths.

We carry stories around in us like a bank account. The more rich experiences we have encountered vicariously, the more we are prepared to meet and manage in real life. Every story in this book could fall under the heading of self-control, but I have included some favorites here that did not fit quite so well in any other category. Enjoy!

Habits

Africa

Grades K-5

THEMES: Bad habits,
lack of restraint,
self-awareness,
friendship

Once upon a time in Africa, Monkey and Rabbit were the best of friends. They spent their days together, feasting on the delights of the jungle and sharing tales.

They got on very well, but each found the other to have one very annoying habit. Rabbit was forever twitching, nervously looking from side to side, and turning around as if someone were coming when no one was there. Monkey, on the other hand, could not stop herself from scratching. She scratched her arms, her legs, her head, her chest, and her back. No sooner has she finished scratching one area when she would start on another. The animal friends put up with one another until one day.

"My dear friend," said Rabbit politely to Monkey, "could you please stop scratching for one minute? You're making me itchy, and I can't concentrate on my food when you are always at yourself as if some terrible infestation had taken place."

"Well, Rabbit," Monkey replied indignantly, "you are not one to talk. I was just wishing that you would stop twitching about. You are so nervous that you're making me jumpy, and I can't concentrate on my food when you are always looking as if an enemy were about to pounce on us."

"I can stop this twitching anytime I want," said Rabbit, glancing nervously behind himself. "I'll bet you can't stop scratching."

"Oh yes I can," said Monkey raking her leg with her sharp nails. "I bet I can stop for longer than you!"

"All right," said Rabbit. "Let's have a contest! The loser will have shade the other from the hot sun with a banana leaf whenever we need to cross the meadow."

"That is a good deal! I can't wait to start. I can go forever without scratching."

"And I don't need to look about at all," said Rabbit.

"Ready!" they said to each other. "The first to move loses the bet!"

The two friends sat facing each other in the shade of the gum tree. Rabbit held still, and Monkey did not scratch. It was not easy. Rabbit was very nervous inside, so sure that something was going to sneak up and pounce on him. Monkey felt sure that a band of fleas had just fallen from the tree and landed on her arms and legs. But both sat still. They sat for ten minutes. They tried singing, deep breathing, remembering old stories, but within a few minutes, the situation had become unbearable.

Finally, Monkey had an idea. "Rabbit, old friend. Let's tell each other stories to pass the time."

"Great idea," said Rabbit.

"I'll go first," said Monkey, as she could no longer bear sitting still. "There was a time when I got separated from my mother when I was only a three months old. Terrible things happened to me. It is a wonder I was not killed. First, I was hit on the head with a stick. You should have seen the lump on my head. It was right here..." She began to rub the point on his head, scratching as much as she dared. "Then I ran into a hornet's nest and got stung on my chest, all over here." As she motioned, she scratched. "They stung not only my chest, but my arms, and my back..." Monkey scratched away. "I tried to run away, but tripped over a vine and nearly broke my leg. I had a big swelling right here..." Again, she scratched.

"Good story," said Rabbit, who could not wait to begin. "Let me tell you my story, it is even more amazing. "One night when I was young, my mother went on an errand and told me to keep watch over my many brothers and sisters. It was so dark that even the moon stayed hidden behind the clouds, and I jumped at every jungle sound. First, I heard a twig snap somewhere to my right..." Rabbit looked nervously to the right. "Then I heard a strange cry coming from my left." Rabbit looked left. "Soon a big bird fluttered behind me..." He looked behind. "But just then something fell from above..." He looked up. "Finally there was something slithering on the ground..." He looked all around him, "there, there, there..."

Monkey began to laugh. "You tell a good story, Rabbit. Almost as good as mine, and you are almost as good at hiding your bad habits as I am."

It seems like we don't really want to stop our habits," Rabbit laughed.

"You are right," said Monkey. "I just don't feel right if I'm not scratching."

"And I don't feel right if I'm not twitching nervously about to make sure no one is there."

"Well, I guess we'll have to put up with each other's habits if we want to stay friends," said Rabbit.

"Yes," said Monkey. "And we can take turns holding the banana leaf for each other as we cross the meadow." And they did.

SOURCES

"Who Can Break a Bad Habit?" from *African Wonder Tales*, by Francis Carpenter, (New York: Doubleday & Company, 1963).

"Natural Habits," retold by Pleasant DeSpain, *Thirty-Three Multicultural Tales to Tell*, (Little Rock: August House Publishers, 1993).

More Favorite Stories Old and New for Boys and Girls, by Sidonie M. Gruenberg (New York: Doubleday, 1948).

Tips for the telling

This is a very fun story to physicalize and to tell in tandem. See if you can find another teacher to tell this one with you, each taking one part, the monkey or the rabbit. If you can't, then try to find two distinct characters within yourself. Switching back and forth is fun. When you switch from one character to another, you do not have to move your feet to a different spot. Try instead to change the direction you are inclining your head, so that it is clear who is speaking. Also, have a distinct body for each character, so that the listeners get to know who is who. One may be taller, or one is nervous and quick, and the other is slow for instance.

Another approach is to have the audience join you from the start in depicting the character's bad habits. When you are telling each of their stories, the audience can enjoy joining in.

Follow-up activities
Tip for retention

- **Partner retelling:** Let partners take turns telling to another set of partners or to the whole class. Get two stuffed animals and let the students retell, animating the toys.

Making a personal connection

- **Questions, discussion and story sharing:** Human beings are creatures of habit. Some habits are conscious and others are not. We learn habits and we can unlearn them if we are disciplined. Some habits outlive their usefulness long before we drop them. Some habits established young, help us to live healthy and happy lives.

  Help your students to identify habits that they have. Discuss cultivating healthy habits, like washing your hands after using the bathroom or flossing your teeth. Talk about nervous habits, like chewing on your hair when you have to speak out in class, or not raising your hand in class. Talk about unhealthy habits, like smoking, eating too much junk food, swearing, or staying up too late. Offer examples of both kinds from your own life. Here is an example of mine: I used to say, "Um," before almost anything that came out of my mouth. I also used the words "like" and "you know" very frequently in my sentences. I was not even aware of doing this until a drama teacher pointed it out to me. I thought about why I said these things. They reflected an insecure aspect of myself. Once I became aware of this habit, I started watching myself and catching myself saying, "um," "like," and "you know," and was able to interrupt my habits and to say them less and less.

  Let your students tell one another stories about how they got started with both helpful and not so helpful habits, as well as stories of how they changed unhealthy and/or nervous habits.

Creative exploration

- **Creative adaptations:** Let your students have fun with this story, retelling it with new animals and new habits, and new versions of the story that allow them to interject their own bad habits. They could also make up a dance or a song as an excuse to scratch or twitch.

- **Brainstorm:** Identify habits that the class could cultivate as a group that would allow them to do something better, such as cleaning up more quickly so that there is time for a story at the end of the day, or putting their chairs up so that the janitor doesn't have to do it. Teach good study habits at the beginning of the year and check in with how the students are using and adapting them. Have students identify habits they would like to change, and support each other in making those changes. The class could have a campaign to try to help any parents who smoke to quit.

The Monkey's Heart

India

Grades K-4

THEMES: Wisdom, acting from a wise mind, paying attention to one's motivations

Once upon a time at the edge of a river, deep in the forest of India, there lived a large and strong monkey. Not far from the monkey's favorite tree lived a pair of huge crocodiles. One day the female crocodile saw the monkey swinging from branch to branch above the river.

"Oh, husband," she crooned, "look at that enormous monkey! I have not had monkey's heart in so long, and that monkey must have a huge and delicious heart. I feel that I shall die if I don't eat that monkey's heart."

"But wife," the husband crocodile groaned, "we live in the river, and the monkey lives high above in the trees. How am I to get you that monkey's heart?"

"You are clever, dear," she said, feigning sickness. "You'll find a way, and I think you'd better do it soon—I feel weaker by the minute."

The crocodile knew that once his wife got an idea in her head, she would keep pestering him until he had gotten her what she wanted, so he began to think of how he could trick the monkey. One day when the monkey had come down to the water's edge for a drink, the crocodile appeared in the water a few feet away. The monkey sprang back and jumped up into the branches of a nearby tree.

"Dear friend," said the crocodile, in his sweetest voice, "do not run away in fear, for I have come to give you some very good news. I see that your mango trees are running low and that the fruit is small this year. But across the river where the sun shines brighter, there are many trees bearing many kinds of fruit, and the fruit is bigger and better, and so plentiful."

"That is very nice to hear, Crocodile," said the monkey. "But you know very well that I cannot swim across the river."

"I would be happy to carry you across on my back, dear Monkey," said the crocodile with a wide, tooth-filled grin.

"You will try to eat me," said the monkey.

"I will not eat you, I promise," said the crocodile—all the while thinking that he was not really telling a lie, because it was his wife who would do the eating.

"Well, all right," said the monkey, who was thinking greedily of the delicious fruits across the river.

The crocodile swam to shore and turned so that the monkey could easily climb onto his back. Then he set off across the river. But when he reached the deepest part, he began to dive down under the water.

"Wait!" screamed the monkey. "What are you doing? You promised you would not eat me."

"I won't eat you," said the crocodile. "But I have promised my wife that I would bring her your heart. She says she will die if she does not eat your heart."

"Well, why didn't you tell me that when we were back on the bank?" said the monkey, thinking fast. "Your wife would be very mad at you if you brought me down to her under the water and she saw that I had not brought my heart with me."

"What do you mean?" said the crocodile, looking worried.

"Do you think I take my heart with me wherever I go?" asked the monkey. "I do not! The way I jump around from tree to tree, my heart would be knocked to bits! I keep my heart up in that tree, over there with the other monkey hearts." He pointed to a fig tree where bunches of figs hung closely together.

"Just bring me your heart then," begged the crocodile, "and I will not drown you."

"That is fair," said the monkey, "but you must carry me safely back to shore, with no funny business."

"I promise," said the crocodile anxiously. "But don't try to trick me by giving me anyone else's heart. My wife will know the difference."

"I promise," said the monkey. "I will not give you any other monkey's heart."

So the crocodile swam back to the place on the river where he had first met the monkey. The monkey ran from his back and up, up, up into the fig tree as fast as he could.

"Are you coming down?" called the crocodile.

"No," replied the monkey. "Do you really think that a monkey can take out his heart and leave it hanging in a tree? Here take this back to your wife." So saying, he picked large fig and threw it down to the crocodile.

The crocodile disappeared sadly into the deep of the river, and the monkey sat on the branch and watched him go. Neither of them had acted very wisely that day, but luckily, the monkey's brains had saved him in the end!

SOURCES

Jataka Tales Fables from the Buddha, edited by Nancy DeRoin (New York: Dell Publishing, 1977).

I Once Was a Monkey: Stories Buddha Told, by Jeanne M. Lee. (New York: Farrar, Straus, and Giroux, 1999).

The Jataka, or Stories of the Buddha's Former Births, edited by E.B. Cowell (Cambridge, England: The University Press, 1885).

| **Tips for the telling** | Have fun with the characters, creating a unique voice for each crocodile and the monkey. |

| **Follow-up activities** | • **Retelling in pairs:** Let the students retell this in groups of four, with one taking the role of narrator and the other three speaking for the characters. |

Tip for retention

| **Making a personal connection** | • **Questions, discussion and story sharing:** This tale reminds us of how easily people can be lured by the promise of things that they think they need or can't resist. The monkey's greed overruled his discerning mind temporarily and almost cost his life. Have you ever acted like the monkey—doing something that you knew was unwise, even though you knew the possible consequences? What was it and why did you do it? They may prefer to answer this is writing anonymously. You might start by sharing a story from your own experience. |

| **Creative exploration** | • **Creative adaptation:** Students can create their own adaptations of this story, changing the main characters, creating different challenges, or different endings. |

| **Turning the story ideas into action** | • **Brainstorm** examples of actions that students might take because they wanted something, even if they knew that there was a danger. The more examples they can think about, the more likely they will think twice if they are ever in this situation.

• **Visual representations:** Have the students make posters from the situations they brainstormed above, with captions to remind them of the story's message of thinking clearly before we act. An example could be a stranger offering a child candy, and then saying no and running away. |

Once Upon a Time...

It Could Be Worse

Once upon a time in Poland, a farmer lived in a little house with his wife, his parents, his six children, and brand new baby girl. Every day he would come home from work and he would sit down after his dinner and try to take a nap. But the kettle on the stove would hiss, and the fire would crack, and the children would run around the room fighting and laughing, and the baby would cry and the grandparents would snore, and his wife's knitting needles would be click, click, clicking.

"It's too noisy in here! Things could not be worse!" The farmer would cry. However, that did not seem to change anything.

One day the farmer complained to a friend about how noisy his house was. The friend suggested that he go and seek the advice of the Rabbi. "Perhaps he can help you solve your problem, as he has always helped me with mine." So the farmer went into town and knocked at the Rabbi's door. The old man smoothed his beard as he listened to the farmer describe his noisy house, in which the kettle hissed, the fire cracked, the children fought and laughed, the baby cried, the grandparents snored, and the wife's knitting needles went click, click, click. At last he spoke.

"If you do as I say, your situation will improve." The farmer agreed to do as the Rabbi said.

"Tell me," said the Rabbi, "do you have any chickens?"

"Yes, I have chickens," the man said.

"Go home and bring the chickens inside your house."

It sounded like a crazy idea, but the Rabbi was supposed to be so wise, so the farmer brought the chickens inside the house. That night, the kettle hissed, the fire cracked, the children ran around the room fighting and laughing, the baby cried, the grandparents snored, while the wife's needles went click, click, click, and the chickens went cluck, cluck, cluck, and their feathers flew everywhere.

The poor farmer cried out, "It's too noisy in here. Things could not be worse!" The next day he went back to the Rabbi.

"Rabbi," he said, "it's worse than ever. Last night the kettle hissed, the fire cracked, the children ran around the room fighting and laughing, the baby cried, the grandparents snored, the wife's knitting went click, click, click, and the chickens flew about calling cluck, cluck, cluck! Help me!"

"Hmm, let's see," said the Rabbi, stroking his beard. "Do you have any pigs?" "Yes, I have pigs," the farmer answered.

"Go home and bring the pigs into the house."

It sounded like a crazy idea, but the Rabbi was supposed to be so wise, so the farmer brought the pigs inside the house. That night, the kettle hissed, the fire cracked, the children ran around the room fighting and laughing, the baby cried, the grandparents snored, while the wife's needles went click, click, click,

Jewish

Grades K-4 (can be adapted for older students)

THEMES: Patience, positive attitude, creative problem solving, tolerance

and the chickens went cluck, cluck, cluck, and the pigs went oink, oink, oink, and made a terrible smell to boot.

The poor farmer cried out, "It's too noisy in here. Things could not be worse!" The next day he went back to the Rabbi.

"Rabbi," he moaned, "it's worse than ever! Last night the kettle hissed, the fire cracked, the children ran around the room fighting and laughing, the baby cried, the grandparents snored, the wife's knitting went click, click, click, and the chickens flew about calling cluck, cluck, cluck, and the pigs went oink, oink, oink. Help me!"

"Hmm, let's see," said the Rabbi, stroking his beard. "Do you have any cows?"

"Yes, I have cows," the farmer answered.

"Go home and bring the cows into the house."

It sounded like a crazy idea, but the Rabbi was supposed to be so wise, so the farmer brought the cows inside the house, too. That night, the kettle hissed, the fire cracked, the children ran around the room fighting and laughing, the baby cried, the grandparents snored, while the wife's needles went click, click, click, and the chickens went cluck, cluck, cluck, and the pigs went oink, oink, oink, and the cows went moo, moo, moo and took up a lot of space.

The poor farmer cried out, "It's too noisy in here. Things could not be worse!" The next day he went back to the Rabbi.

"Rabbi," he cried, "it's worse than ever! Last night the kettle hissed, the fire cracked, the children ran around the room fighting and laughing, the baby cried, the grandparents snored, the wife's knitting went click, click, click, and the chickens flew about calling cluck, cluck, cluck, and the pigs went oink, oink, oink, and the cows went moo, moo, moo. You have to help me—I'm not getting any sleep!"

"Well," said the Rabbi, who was quiet for a long time. "I think you should go home tonight and take the cows, the pigs, and the chickens out of your house."

"That's it?" asked the farmer.

"That's it," said the Rabbi.

So the farmer trudged home. He shooed the chickens back out to their hen house. He herded the pigs back out to the pigsty. He sent the cows back into the barn. Then he went back into the house and sat down in his rocking chair. The kettle hissed, the fire cracked, the children ran around the room fighting and laughing, the baby cried, the grandparents snored, and his wife's needles went click, click, click. The farmer smiled. "It is so quiet and peaceful in my house without all that clucking, and oinking, and mooing," he said. "It could definitely be worse."

SOURCES

Favorite Folktales from Around the World, edited by Jane Yolen (New York: Pantheon, 1986).
A Treasury of Jewish Folklore, by Nathan Ausubel (New York: Crown Publishers, 1948).

PICTURE BOOKS

It Could Always Be Worse, by Margot Zemach (New York: Farrar, Strauss and Giroux, 1990).
It's Too Noisy, by Joanna Cole (New York: Thomas Y. Crowell, 1989).

This story lends itself especially well to participatory telling. There is so much repetition here that the children will quickly pick up on the lines and will join in. You can also add more or different animals or sounds to your version. The simplest way to tell it with your class is to have them join you on all of the sounds and repetitive phrases and actions as they come up. You can also give certain sounds to small groups to call out each time they come up. The ending to the story works best if you really build the tension of the poor farmer who is dealing with more and more sound and chaos in his home.

For older students I suggest modernizing the tale so that they can imagine it is their own chaotic household, only worse!

Tips for the telling

- **Whole-group retelling:** Your students will want to act this one out over and over and over again. They will especially like to add their own sounds (see Creative Exploration).

Follow-up activities
Tip for retention

- **Questions, discussion and story sharing:** What lesson did they take from this story? How does this remind them of their own home, or the classroom? What sounds would they have in a story based on their own home? Do they ever feel like the farmer? What do they do then?

Making a personal connection

- **Telling the story at home:** Ask your students to tell the story at home with their family. See if they can come back with some unique sounds from home to add to their own version of the story. What could they bring into their home to make it noisier? Have them listen also for peaceful times at home and sounds that are comforting. When is it quiet? How does it sound? Have them report to the class, or draw a picture of either the quiet time or noisy time.

- **Creative adaptations:** Take the ideas they have gathered from home and have them make their own version of the story, where someone in their family goes to some wise person in town and asks for help. Have each student come up with another sound that could add to the noise of the house, and retell the story, letting each student add in his or her noise. Older students can be challenged to make up stories that represent chaotic aspects of their lives and how to gain more perspective and humor about them through imagining them being much worse. Examples could be the bus ride to school, the classroom, or trying to focus during a sports activity with all the noise.

Creative exploration

The beauty of this story in relation to self-control is that it helps us to think about how we look at circumstances unfolding around us. This story reminds us in a humorous way to be grateful for the peace we have, and that things could always be worse. It helps us to laugh at our circumstances instead of complaining. How can you help your students to look with humor at the challenges they face?

- **Visual representations:** Have students draw a picture of a scene from the story with the caption, "It could be worse!" Use them as reminders to find the humor in situations that challenge them, and make it a class catch phrase.

Turning the story ideas into action

The Calabash of Wisdom

Nigeria (Igbo)

Grades 3-8

THEMES: Common sense, wisdom, judging others, greediness

Tortoise knew he was wise, but one day he decided that that was not enough. He wanted to have all of the wisdom in the world. That way the other animals would have to come to him for wisdom, and they would have to pay. He would never have to work again! So Tortoise went about the land gathering up the wisdom in a large calabash, which is a hollowed-out gourd for carrying water. He went here and there seeking out wisdom and putting it into his gourd. Finally, he was sure that he had all of the wisdom. He hung the calabash around his neck with a rope so that it lay on his chest where he could see it and no one could steal it. "But," he thought, "what about when I tuck my head into my shell in sleep? Then someone could steal my wisdom."

Tortoise decided that the safest place to store his calabash of wisdom was at the top of the tallest palm tree in the jungle. As he walked along the path toward the tallest tree, he met Rabbit. Rabbit asked Tortoise where he was going and what he had in the calabash. Tortoise had always thought that Rabbit was just a foolish character with little brains, but he didn't want to take any chances, so he told her that he was carrying palm wine home to his wife.

Rabbit asked, "Why don't you carry the jug on your head, Tortoise?"

Tortoise, growing annoyed with all of the questions, told Rabbit, "Anyone with any brains knows that carrying loads on one's head damages one's brains!" Rabbit shook her head and hopped off into the jungle.

Tortoise came to the tallest tree in the jungle and began to climb. However, it was not easy. With that calabash on his chest, his little short legs could not reach the tree trunk. He jumped up against the tree time and time again, only to fall on his shell. He tried backing up and running at the tree from a distance. That only landed him on his back even harder.

After a time, Rabbit came hopping into the clearing beneath the tall tree. She watched Tortoise for a while and finally spoke, "Tortoise, why don't you try hanging the calabash on your back? It will make it easier to climb the tree."

"What a good idea," said Tortoise, swinging the gourd onto his back, and easily ascending the tree. Tortoise was halfway up the tree when he suddenly stopped and looked down at Rabbit. He said, " Rabbit, how could a simple-minded creature like you have such a good idea, if I have all of the wisdom in the world in my calabash?"

"Well," said Rabbit thoughtfully, "I think that what I told you was just plain common sense, but I guess that is a form of wisdom, isn't it?"

Tortoise held onto the tree and thought a bit. Perhaps, there were different kinds of wisdom. Perhaps it was folly to think that he could own all of it. Perhaps it had not been wise to judge Rabbit so harshly. Tortoise let the calabash crash to the ground, dispersing all of the wisdom he had gathered back out to the world. He walked slowly down to the river, and began to fish for his dinner. That was the wisest thing he had done all day!

SOURCES

The Calabash of Wisdom and other Igbo Stories, collected and translated by Romanus Egudu (New York: NOK Publishers, Ltd., 1973).

How the People Sang the Mountains Up, by Maria Leach (New York: Viking, 1967).

Terrapin's Pot of Sense, by Harold Courlander (New York: Holt, 1957).

| **Tips for the telling** | This is a fun tale to tell with your whole body. Let the audience picture Tortoise trying to climb the tree with the calabash on his belly. |

Follow-up activities
Tips for story retention

- **Retell with clay:** Have pairs of students make a diorama out of clay, forming each character and making a tree out of a stick. Have the partners stand behind their diorama and animate the characters as they retell the story to peers.

- **News reporter retell:** Older students can retell in triads with a reporter, a rabbit, and tortoise.

Making a personal connection

- **Questions, discussion and story sharing:** This story is useful in generating a discussion about wisdom and common sense. What is the difference between the two? How do we gain common sense? Wisdom? Can anyone have all of the wisdom? Why is it a bad idea to judge someone else as having less wisdom than we have? Brainstorm examples of common sense and wisdom, and have the students share examples of times when they have used either or both.

Creative exploration

- **Creative story making:** What would it be like if no one had common sense in this world? Create a story scenario as a group in which people would live without common sense. Have the students create their own stories about this. Create a story scenario in which people had to buy wisdom from Tortoise, who kept it all in a calabash. What kinds of wisdom would they need for life?

- **Hot Seat:** Let your students take turns pretending that they are Tortoise and that they have all of the wisdom in their possession. Have other students go to them and ask for wise advice.

Turning the story ideas into action

- **Journaling or reporting:** Have students keep a journal of all the things they did in a day that required common sense or wisdom. Help them to get started by pointing out how many acts we do each day in which we have to make decisions that are wise or foolish. Have them share with the class. Encourage them to bring dilemmas to the class for help deciding what would be the best decision to make.

The Tailor

Long ago in Poland, there lived a poor tailor named Joseph. Every day he worked hard to make coats and fine clothing for the rich people in his town, but he never had enough money to make himself a warm coat. For years he saved his coins, until he had finally saved enough to buy cloth to make his own coat.

Joseph went to the market and bought a beautiful piece of cloth. It was made of warm gray wool with strands of maroon thread, making it look regal. Joseph took the cloth home to his workshop. In the evening, when his other work was done, he would measure and cut, and stitch and stitch, until finally he had made himself a fine coat.

Old Joseph stood in front of his mirror and put on his new coat. His old shoulders straightened, and a smile spread across his face. "I look like a king in this coat," he said aloud. "I love my coat." And he did love his coat. He wore it everywhere—to the market, to go visiting. He wore it, and he wore it, and he wore it—until he had worn it out.

That was a sad day as old Joseph stood looking at his old coat. It was so worn and frayed around the wrists and elbows. Threads were hanging at the hem. "Old coat," he sighed sadly, "you have made me feel like a king. But there is nothing left." He was about to throw the coat in the rag bin, when he stopped. He began to turn the coat around and around, smiling to himself. "There is something left. Just enough, just enough..." and instead of throwing the coat in the bin, he went back to his workbench. There he began to measure and cut, and to stitch and stitch, until he had made a vest.

It was a beautiful vest. He put it on and stood in front of the mirror. His old shoulders straightened and he smiled. "I look like a prince in this vest." He loved his vest. He wore it, and he wore it, and he wore it—until he had worn it out.

That was a sad day as old Joseph stood looking at his old vest. It was so worn and frayed. There were holes in places, and threads were hanging at the hem. "Old vest," he sighed sadly, "you have made me feel like a prince. But there is nothing left." He was about to throw the vest in the rag bin, when he stopped. He began to turn it around and around, smiling to himself. "There is something left. Just enough, just enough..." and instead of throwing the vest in the bin, he went back to his workbench. There he began to measure and cut, and to stitch and stitch, until he had made himself a cap.

It was a beautiful cap. He put it on and stood in front of the mirror. His old shoulders straightened and he smiled. "I feel like a dapper young fellow in this cap," he said, smiling. He loved his cap. He wore it, and he wore it, and he wore it—until he had worn it out.

That was a sad day as old Joseph stood looking at his old cap. It was so worn and frayed. There were threads hanging from the brim. "Old cap," he

Jewish

Grades K-3 (A version for teens and adults is on my web site.)

THEMES: Resourcefulness, ingenuity, perseverance, recycling, perspective, loss

sighed sadly, "you made me feel like a dapper young fellow. But there is nothing left." He was about to throw the cap in the rag bin, when he stopped. He began to turn it around and around, smiling to himself. "There is something left. Just enough, just enough..." and instead of throwing the cap in the bin he went back to his workbench. There he began to measure and cut, and to stitch and stitch, until he had made himself a bow tie.

It was a beautiful tie. He put it on and stood in front of the mirror. His old shoulders straightened and he smiled. "I look marvelous," he said, smiling. He loved his bow tie. He wore it, and he wore it, and he wore it—until he had worn it out.

That was a sad day as old Joseph stood looking at his old tie. It was so worn and frayed. Threads were hanging from the ends, and there were stains where his soup had spilled upon it. "Old tie," he sighed sadly, "you made me feel marvelous. But there is nothing left." He was about to throw the tie in the rag bin, when he stopped. He began to turn it around and around, smiling to himself. "There is something left. Just enough, just enough..." and instead of throwing the tie in the bin he went back to his workbench. There he began to measure and cut, and to stitch and stitch, until he had made himself a cloth button.

It was a beautiful button. He sewed it on to his coat, and stood in front of the mirror. His old shoulders straightened and he smiled. He loved his cloth button. He wore it, and he wore it, and he wore it—until he had worn it out.

That was a sad day as old Joseph stood looking at his button. It was so worn and frayed. Threads were hanging every which way, and the metal button was showing underneath. "Old button," he sighed sadly, "you have meant so much to me. You were my first beautiful coat, then my vest, my cap, my bow tie, and then my most special button. Now you are all gone. Now there is really nothing left." A tear fell from his eye and hit the bottom of the rag bin. Soon he was smiling again. "There is something left!" he cried. "There is just enough, just enough, just enough to make a story of all the things that I have made with my cloth, and I will tell it to everyone I meet."

Joseph kept the button in his pocket so that he could show it to his listeners when he told them his story. "You see," he would say, "there is always just enough for a story!"

SOURCES

This story was probably first adapted from a Yiddish folk song. I first heard this story from my primary storytelling teacher, Doug Lipman. It is on his audiotape, *Tell It with Me* (Albany, N.Y.: A Gentle Wind, 1985).

Just Enough to Make a Story, by Nancy Schimmel (Berkeley, Calif.: Sister's Choice Press, 1992).

PICTURE BOOKS

Something from Nothing, retold by Phoebe Gilman (New York: Scholastic, 1992).

Bit by Bit, by Steve Sanfield, (New York Philomel, 1995).

On my web site you will find a more detailed version for older students or to tell to adults and elders with a slightly different ending focusing on surviving loss. www.wisdomtales.com/

This is one of the stories that I use to help beginning storytellers learn to tell. There is so much repetition that once you have learned the basic sequence of items of clothing you can easily retell it. In the original versions, a jacket is made between the coat and the vest, but I find that it goes on too long, and I chose to eliminate it. You may add or subtract as you deem appropriate. Your audience will want to tell this one with you. When you first measure the cloth, show your audience a movement to show measuring and ask them to do it with you. Do the same for cutting and stitching. Then every time the words come up again, begin the movement and pause for just a second, giving them the nod and they will join you. Do the same with repetitive phrases such as, "He wore it, and he wore it, and he wore it—until he had worn it out."

Over the years as I have told this story I have begun to make it even more audience participatory by stopping the tale before telling the audience what the Tailor has made this time, and ask them to tell me what he could have made with the remaining cloth. When enough children have had a turn you can say, "All of your answers were things that he could have made, but this time he made a..." They will eagerly await the next opportunity to join in.

Tips for the telling

- **Round-robin retelling:** Your students should have no trouble taking a turn in retelling this story.

Follow-up activities
Tip for retention

- **Questions and discussion:** What lessons did your students find in the story? In today's society, more and more things that we use are made to be "disposable." Discuss with your students things that they use and throw away, vs. things they recycle. What do they do with old clothing? Furniture? Does their family recycle?

- **Show and tell:** This is also a story about the deep significance of personal belongings and the sadness we feel if we lose something or must let it go. Let your students tell stories of belongings that mean a lot to them that may have been worn out, and what they did. See if you can lead with a show-and-tell of something that means a lot to you, such as a quilt, or piece of clothing or a belonging passed down from a loved one.

Making a personal connection

- **Creative adaptation:** This simple bigger-to-smaller story is a natural one to adapt or to set in modern times. Give your students some prompts, such as: Once there was an automobile mechanic who fixed other people's cars but could not afford one of her own. Have them make up a story as a group of things she makes as her car wears out, until perhaps she is left with roller skates, or the rear view mirror to look into to remember the good times as she tells her stories. This process will help them to think bigger to smaller, but also to think about being resourceful, thrifty, and creative.

Creative exploration

• **Personal stories:** Your students may wish to tell personal or family stories from objects of nostalgia that they bring in or describe.

Turning the story ideas into action

• **Recycling objects from home or school:** Invite your children to go home and tell this story to their parents. Then ask them to bring in something that was going to be thrown away that could be made into something else. Have the students bring it to class (if it is too big, they could draw a picture of it). In class let people decide what could be done with these things. Let them see if they can make new things from them (sewing projects, art projects), donate them to others in need, or recycle them.

The Three Wishes

Once upon a time, there lived a poor woodsman and his wife. They lived in a small cottage in the forest and their lives were hard. They both worked from sunrise to sunset. Every day the wife worked the garden and sewed the clothes, while the woodsman took his ax into the forest to cut wood to sell in the town.

One day the woodsman set out into the forest and found a large oak tree that he wished to cut. He readied his ax and was about to strike the tree when there in front of him was a small fairy. "Please, kind woodsman, please do not cut this tree! I am a tree sprite and this is where I live."

The woodsman was so astonished to meet a tree fairy that he could barely speak. At last he said, "Well I suppose there are other trees in the forest. I will do as you wish."

The tree sprite was delighted and decided to reward the man. "To show my appreciation, I will grant you your next three wishes." The fairy disappeared and the woodsman went about his day and nearly forgot about it. When he returned home that evening, he was very hungry. He sat by the fire and asked his wife if the supper was ready yet.

"No, not for while yet, and it's nothing but potato stew again."

"Oh," groaned the man. "How I do wish for a good big sausage." Before he could bat an eye, there before him was a large sausage, all cooked and ready to eat.

"What on earth is going on?" asked his wife. It was then that the woodsman remembered the fairy.

"I didn't believe it was true," he said, "but a tree fairy granted me my next three wishes."

"And you just spent one wishing for a sausage! We could have a fine house, we could have a carriage, and all the money we would ever need! You're such a fool!" she moaned. "I wish that sausage were stuck to your nose!" No sooner had she spoken than the sausage was firmly attached to the woodsman's nose.

"There you've gone and used the second of our wishes, foolish wife!" he cried. "Now come and help me pull this thing off. I'll scare away my customers."

The wife began to pull and to pull, but it just served to make his sausage nose grow longer and longer, and it would not budge from his face. The woodsman was so mad that he opened his mouth to wish that his wife would have a sausage instead of a tongue, but he stopped himself just in time.

Norway, Japan, England

Grades K-4

THEMES: Helpfulness, thoughtfulness, just rewards, greed, poor choices, empathy

The woodsman and his wife sat there looking at one another. They could wish for a fine house, but he would be stuck with a sausage on his nose for the rest of time. Should they wish for a carriage, but have children run from him shrieking? How quickly the hope of fortune had come and gone. There was only one thing to do.

"I wish that that sausage was not on your face," the wife said bravely. And it was gone. And so were the wishes. But the woodsman and his wife were ever thoughtful about what they wished for, and the woodsman was always careful to look out for tree sprites in the forest.

SOURCE

Wisdom Tales from Around the World, retold by Heather Forest (Little Rock: August House, 1996).

PICTURE BOOK

The Three Wishes, retold by Paul Galdone (New York: Whittlesey House, 1961).

This is a simple, humorous, and poignant tale with a valuable lesson. You can choose how angry you want the wife to be, or how much time is spent fantasizing what they could have with their wishes. Have fun pantomiming the wife trying to pull the sausage off her husband's nose.

- **Dramatic retelling:** Let the students retell the story by acting it out. Younger children: Have the students identify the characters in the story and volunteer for parts. Then narrate the story as they act out the parts. Older children: Have the students identify the characters in the story and volunteer for parts, including narrator. Then let them retell the story dramatically.

- **Questions, discussion and story sharing:** What lessons did your students find in the story? Would they have wished the sausage off the husband's face if they were the wife? This is a tale told in many lands, probably told to help people to think about making wise and careful choices with their wishes and words. I suggest emphasizing the negative banter that people often get into, of calling each other names, or saying things like: "I wish you would blah, blah, blah…" "Well I wish you would…" Has this ever happened to them? What can happen if you make statements like this to others?

- **Creative adaptation:** Let your students personalize this story. Where would it take place? What would they be likely to wish for without thinking? What would they wish for if they really thought about it carefully? How would they avoid making foolish wishes without careful thinking?

- **Brainstorming:** See if the class can agree upon three wishes collectively. One wish would be to make the world, their town, or their classroom a better place. The wife uses the last wish to free her husband from disfigurement. In what ways would they use a wish to help others?

- **Visual representations:** Let the students draw pictures of three wise wishes that they would make. Invite your students to make a book (construction paper stapled is the simplest) of their story in which they are given three wishes and they use them wisely. Share the books around.

Follow-up activities

Tip for story retention

Making a personal connection

Creative exploration

Turning the story ideas into action

How the Turtle Got Its Cracked Shell

India and Native American sources

Grades K-4

THEMES: Self-control, self-respect, responsibility, friendship

Once upon a time long ago, deep in the forest there was a beautiful pond. The pond was home to many animals. Among the animals was a large turtle. This turtle was a very sociable sort. He loved nothing better than to sit upon his favorite rock or log and to chat much of the day away to the various birds and water creatures living there. The turtle didn't like to be alone. Talking to himself wasn't much fun, and he liked to have appreciative audiences for his stories.

One spring no rain fell. The summer became even drier. The pond, once so full, began to shrink in size, forcing the water creatures to share a smaller and smaller space. Food was scarce. Many creatures left in search of a better place to live. One day, two swans, the turtle's best friends, came to him and told him that they couldn't stay and listen to his stories any more. They had decided to leave that day to find another pond. The turtle was crushed.

"You can't leave without me!" he cried. "Who will I talk to? I'll be all alone." The thought was unbearable. "Please, there has to be a way that I can come with you."

"But you can't fly, Turtle," they reminded him.

"I know," he said, "but please think of something. You can't leave me here alone."

So the swans thought and at last came up with a difficult plan. "Turtle," they told him, "we will try to fly you with us to our new home. We will carry a stick in our talons. If you can hold onto the stick with your mouth, we will be able to fly you there. But you can't talk. You can't open your mouth or you will drop. Do you think you can do it?"

The turtle was so delighted with the idea that he said, "Of course I can do such a simple thing!"

And off they flew. The turtle held on to the stick with his mouth and the two swans held either end in their talons. As they flew higher and higher, the turtle wanted so much to comment on how wonderful it was to be up in the air. He almost opened his mouth a dozen times to point out some spectacular site, but he would always remember at the last second to be quiet.

Then they flew over a town. The stick was heavy with turtle on it so the birds could not fly as high as usual. They flew over a place where students were playing. The students saw the strange sight and began to point and laugh.

"Look at the flying turtle!"

"That is the funniest thing I've ever seen!"

"That turtle looks ridiculous!"

That was more than the turtle could stand. How dare they make fun of him? If they only knew his story, they would understand.

"Don't you lauggggghhhhh—" Down he fell! He turned over and over in the air until his shell hit the ground. It cracked into the thirteen pieces.

Some of the students felt sorry for turtle and gently turned him over. He was in pain and he was baking in the sun. The students carried him to the edge of a small pond where the mud was deep. He slowly dug himself down into the mud. It felt nice and cool in the painful cracks of his shell. There he stayed all winter, quietly dreaming his stories to himself. From that day to this, the turtle has a cracked shell, and it sleeps deep in the mud all winter.

SOURCES

Jataka Tales Fables from the Buddha, edited by Nancy DeRoin (New York: Dell Publishing, 1975).

The Jataka Tales of India, retold by Ellen C. Babbitt (Upper Saddle River, N.J.: Prentice-Hall, 1940).

Storyteller Dovie Tomason tells a version of this called "Turtle Learns to Fly" on her CD, "Tales of the Animal People." (Somerville, Mass.: Yellow Moon Press, 1996). www.yellowmoon.com. Dovie learned the story from her Lakota-Dakota tribe.

PICTURE BOOK

How Turtle's Back Was Cracked: A Cherokee Tale, by Gayle Ross, is out of print.

Tips for the telling

This is a pourquoi story that explains how the turtle got his cracked shell, so it would be helpful to show the students a turtle's shell, or at least a picture of one. You should decide if you want to portray the turtle as overly talkative, or simply curious and friendly. Some teachers like to address the problem of overly chatty students through this story. This can work if it is done strictly through humor and doesn't single students out. The humor in the tale is with the turtle's difficulty in not speaking while he is holding the stick with his mouth. You should feel free to improvise more scenes that they fly over and more things that he wants to say. You could also animate the swans.

Follow-up activities
Tip for retention

- **Dioramas for simple retelling:** Give the students each a lump of clay and have them shape a turtle and two swans. Give them a piece of paper on which they can draw the two ponds. Have them manipulate the clay characters to show and tell what happened in the story to a partner or small group.

Making a personal connection

- **Questions and discussion:** What did the students identify with in this story? Did they have a favorite scene? Let them draw or talk about this.

- **Personal story sharing:** Help the students to talk about times when someone laughed at them or made them mad. What choices did they make and what happened as a result? This helps them to see that they need to be responsible for the way in which they respond to stress. Have they ever said or done something to someone that they later regretted because they were angry?

Creative exploration

- **Create a new ending:** Have your students create a new ending to the story starting in the air when turtle is being laughed at. Have them come up with different strategies for helping him to keep his mouth clamped around the stick. Let them share these with one another. It is good to see what they come up with first, but here are some strategies to teach and practice with them:

  Count to ten in their heads before taking an action.
  Plan to talk to someone about it later.
  Ignore the bully, by keeping your mind on what you are trying to do.
  Imagine that the bully has donkey ears and is braying.
  Talk about each anger management skill, and practice them together.

Turning the story ideas into action

- **Visual representations:** Let the students make posters that show the flying turtle with a balloon quote over its head counting to ten or focusing on something else. Maybe he is saying, "Wait till I get to my new pond. I'll have the best story to tell!" Help the children to remember the coping skills when they feel angry, by referring to the story or the posters.

- **Anger management training:** In some school settings, more intensive anger management training may be helpful. See the Resource section.

The Samurai and the Monk

A Zen Tale from Japan

Grades 6-8

THEMES: Self-control,
self-respect,
anger management

There once lived a powerful Samurai. As a youth, he had excelled at swordsmanship and had risen quickly through the ranks. While still a young man, he had become a member of the Emperor's personal guard. Despite his stature, the Samurai was not content with his life. He worried often about what would happen as he grew old, and if someone more talented than he came along. He had no peace of mind. One of his friends, seeing his trouble, suggested the Samurai go to visit the wise old Master Hakuin and seek his advice.

When the Samurai was finally standing before the Master Hakuin, he asked him, "Master, tell me, is there really such a thing as heaven or hell?"

The Master was quiet for quite some time while gazing at the man. "Who are you?" he asked at last.

"I am a Samurai swordsman and a member of the Emperor's personal guard."

"You are a Samurai?" Hakuin said doubtfully. "You look more like a beggar!"

"What?" the Samurai stammered, growing red in the face and reaching for his sword.

"Oho!" said Hakuin. "So you have a sword, do you? I'll bet it's much too dull to cut off my little finger!"

The Samurai's anger grew and he began to shake. "How dare you insult me!" he shouted as he drew his sword.

"Think you are tough, do you?" the old man queried. "I bet you couldn't hit me from two feet away!"

The Samurai could no longer contain his rage. He lifted his sword to strike the Master.

Hakuin responded quickly, "That is hell!"

The Samurai stopped just in time, understanding the truth in the master's words and seeing the risk he had taken to teach him. He sheathed his sword and bowed.

"Now," said the master. "That is heaven."

SOURCES

"Heaven and Hell," in *Doorways to the Soul: 52 Wisdom Tales from Around the World*, edited by Elisa Pearmain (Cleveland: Pilgrim Press, 1998).

"The Difference between Heaven and Hell," retold by John Porcino in *Spinning Tales, Weaving Hope: Stories, Storytelling, and Activities for Peace, Justice and the Environment*, edited by Ed Brody et al. (Philadelphia: New Society Publishers, 1992).

"The Gates of Paradise," in *Zen Flesh Zen Bones: A Collection of Zen and pre-Zen Writings*, by Paul Reps (Rutland, Vt.: Charles Tuttle Co., 1957).

Tips for the telling

Explain that a Samurai was a highly trained warrior retained by a Japanese emperor in medieval times. This story is especially effective if told standing up and letting yourself embody both characters. Take some time to feel what it would be like to be a Samurai swordsman. How would you stand? Where would you hold your sword? Feel what it would be like to be the old master? How does he hold himself? What does it feel like when the Samurai is insulted? Let the insults build naturally so that it is believable when the Samurai readies to strike.

My hope with this story is that the listener will grasp the idea that one's actions and identity can be ruled by one's ego, or that one could rise above ego and find peace. Some seventh and eighth graders "get" the story right away, while others need to rehash it to find meaning. I usually have those who think they "get it" explain how they see it for those who do not. The first-person retellings will also help.

Follow-up activities

Tip for retention

- **First-person retelling:** Put students into pairs and have them retell the story to one another in turns, as if one were the swordsman and one the master. Then ask them to switch partners and switch parts so that each gets a chance to be each character telling the story from each perspective.

Making a personal connection

- **Discussion and story sharing:** After students have a chance to retell the story from both perspectives, help them to reflect on what they learned. How did it feel to be the swordsman and to be insulted? Have you ever felt insulted that way and wanted to strike out at the insulter? What did you do and how did it feel? Why did the master do what he did to the swordsman? What did he mean that the Samurai's actions were like hell or heaven? Encourage your students to think metaphorically about this one, and to talk about the role of ego and pride in our lives and identity. Remind them also that whereas some religions believe that there are actual places called "Heaven" and "Hell," other religions, including Buddhism, use the terms to imply the states of mind that one can experience while alive.

Creative exploration

- **Creative adaptation:** Have your students modernize this story, imagining another character besides a Samurai who might have an enlarged ego, and who would seek help from the Master. Examples might be famous singers, movie stars, or political figures.

Turning the story ideas into action

- **Journaling:** Suggest that your students keep a log for a few days of situations in which they find their egos being threatened, or in which they otherwise find themselves feeling angry, or feeling like they are in heaven or hell. Have them make note of what brought on those feelings, and what they did about them. Let them share in class, as they are comfortable.

- **Explore anger-management strategies:** Have your class brainstorm situations that cause them to feel angry or threatened. Brainstorm strategies for responding instead of reacting in those situations. What can they do to avoid a fight in situations where they feel hurt or their pride is bruised? How can they help themselves to remember that they are more than their egos? Keep a list of those anger-management skills on the wall of the classroom. These can include: counting to ten, walking away, taking three deep breaths, deciding to look at the situation from another angle, asking a question, telling the person they are mad at that they want to discuss the situation after a short time out, and using "I" statements to express their feelings. See *The Kids' Guide to Working Out Conflicts*, by Naomi Drew (Minneapolis: Free Spirit Publishing, 2004) for more detailed exercises.

The Oak and the Reeds

Aesop

Grades 6-8

THEMES: Pride, ego, compromise, yielding, flexibility vs. rigid thinking and behavior

Once a giant oak tree stood near a riverbank. Close by lived some slender reeds. When the winds blew, which they often did, the great oak stood straight and tall, and only its highest branches swayed to and fro. But down by the riverbank, the reeds bowed low to the wind, and the wind seemed to moan sadly as it passed through them.

One day the great oak spoke to the reeds. "It is shameful how you must bow before the slightest breeze. Wouldn't you rather be like me and stand straight and tall, even in a high wind?"

But the reeds laughed and replied, "We do not mind bending in the wind. We thinking of it as bowing, and we know that that way we will not break. You, on the other hand, cannot bow if you want to."

"And why should I wish to bow to another?" asked the proud tree.

The answer came soon. One day a hurricane wind began to blow. The reeds bent their backs and let it run over them. The great oak stood straight and tall and fought as the wind tore through the air with all its fury. Finally, the great oak could no longer stand against the wind. Its great trunk toppled over, and its roots were pulled up out of the ground. It lay dying among the reeds.

"Ah," moaned the reeds sadly. "If only you had not been so proud, you would have learned that sometimes it is better to yield and live, than to resist and be destroyed."

See page 44 for information on Aesop.

This simple story is fun to act out and to observe in nature. It can be seen in most places: A sturdy tree and a thin, bending reed or grass. It is a metaphor story and may need to be identified or introduced as such.

Tips for the telling

- **Retelling with props:** This simple story will be easily remembered and grasped by older students. Younger ones would benefit from working with twigs and pieces of grass to reenact it, or by going outside to observe it.

Follow-up activities
Tip for retention

- **Questions, discussion and story sharing:** Here is a place to introduce the idea of being a flexible thinker. What does it mean to be a flexible person? Are we able to change our ideas about something? When do we yield or compromise, and when do we stand up and fight for something that we believe in? We might think that we are always right, but we will soon learn that we are not. We may think that the best way to be "strong" is to be rigid or tough, but we will be better served if we can sometimes bend. Share some examples of how you as a teacher have changed your ideas or learned to accept something that was difficult and how it benefited you. Ask the children to share examples from their own lives. These may include not being accepted onto the basketball team or chosen for a particular award, or having a friend move away. What did you learn about accepting these changes?

Making a personal connection

- **Looking for other metaphors in nature:** What other plants or animals in nature are flexible or adaptable to allow for changes in weather? Make a poem with your lists. How are you flexible and adaptable to changes in weather, plans, etc.?

Creative exploration

- **Visual representations:** Have the students make posters of things that represent flexibility to remind them to keep open minds and to be accepting of change and things not going their way.

- **Journaling:** Older students can keep journals and note times when they butt up against situations that are hard to accept, or when they find that they need to change their minds, and how it feels to try to be more accepting.

Turning the story ideas into action

The Three Dolls

Mongolia and India

Grades 6-8

THEMES: Wisdom, thoughtfulness, cleverness, listening skills, loyalty, qualities of friendship

Once upon a time, a Maharaja wanted to test the wisdom of his King. The Maharaja sent him a gift of three beautiful dolls. The dolls were exactly alike in appearance. They weighed the same and were all made of pure gold. The Maharaja's messenger told the Great Khan that his master wished to know which of the dolls was of the greatest worth, and which the least.

The Great Khan was intrigued for he loved a riddle, and he set about studying the dolls himself, but he could see no differences. He called in his advisors. These wise men examined the dolls, but also could see nothing to set them apart. Then he called on the men of his court, who also found nothing of note.

Rumors of the challenge spread around the kingdom until everyone was wishing for a chance to answer the riddle. The Great Khan decided to offer a reward to the person who correctly answered the Maharaja's question. People came from far and wide and stood in lines all day to have their few moments to gaze at the mysterious dolls.

A farmer's son who also loved riddles received permission from his father to journey to the city. While they worked hard all day, his family had a long tradition of solving riddle stories around the fire in the evenings. Finally, the farmer's son was given a chance to sit before the three dolls. He noticed right away, as others had, that each doll had an identical hole in its right and left ear. He asked a servant to bring him a thin and flexible piece of straw. This the servant did. Being intrigued by this request, the Great Khan came to watch.

The farmer's son quickly passed the thin piece of straw into the hole of the first doll's head. To the Great Khan's surprise it came out, not the other side of its head, but out of the doll's mouth. The young man then picked up the second doll and passed the piece of straw into the hole in its head. This time the piece of straw came out of the other side of its head. The Great Khan's brow became furrowed. A third time the young man passed a piece of straw into the hole of the third doll's head. This time the straw went further and further into the doll until it disappeared into the doll's stomach.

"There," said the young man. "I think we have an answer to the question. The first doll is like the man who takes whatever is told to him and immediately tells it to anyone who would listen, whether friend or foe. The second doll is like the man who listens to what you say, and then immediately forgets, or gives it no thought. It goes, like the straw, in one ear and out the other. The third doll, however, is like the man who listens carefully and wisely and digests every word. He would think carefully before speaking what he has heard, but he would remember it well."

"Ah," said the Great Khan, "you have indeed made the differences clear. The third doll is of the greatest value as a friend or counselor. The second doll listens but does not hear, so he is not of much use as a friend or counselor, but the first listens and then tells all, so he may be dangerous. I would say that this doll is of the least worth. Thank you for your keen observation."

The young man was rewarded and his family lived well after that. They still worked the land, but always had time to spend their evenings sharing riddle stories and wisdom with each other, and with any else who was wise enough to really listen.

SOURCES

Eurasian Folk and Fairy Tales, by I.F. Bulatkin (New York: Criterion Publishers).

"The Three Dolls," retold by David Novak in *Ready-To-Tell-Stories*, edited by D. Holt and B. Mooney (Little Rock: August House Publishers, 1994).

Tips for the telling

Why not leave off the ending of the story and let the students make the final decisions. You can do this in two ways. The first is to tell the story up until the point where the young man explains the meaning of the way the straw moves through each doll. Then let the students tell you which doll has the greatest and least value, and why. Alternatively, you can end the story sooner, after the young man has passed the straw through each doll, but has not yet explained the meaning. In this case, the students will be asked to do more metaphorical thinking about what each means. This can best be done in small groups. Have each group explain their ideas to the class. You might phrase the question this way: Imagine that each doll was a friend. The straw represents what they do with the things you tell them. Which kind of friend would you most want to have?

Follow-up activities

Tip for retention

- **Dramatizing:** Your students will enjoy watching classmates reenact this in front of the class. Get three pieces of straw for the props and let students be the dolls.

Making a personal connection

- **Questions and discussion:** In which situations would it be best to keep information to yourself? In which would you tell everyone? In which would you forget that you heard it or would not listen? Discuss these and make up scenarios.

- **Personal story sharing:** Discuss times when you have acted like each of the three dolls and times when an anonymous friend has acted like one of the dolls.

- **Telling at home:** Have your students take the story home and retell it to their family members. Let them decide which is the best doll or best kind of friend.

Creative exploration

- **Story making:** Let small groups create original stories based on this one, in which a person has three friends who respond as the three dolls would in this story. How does that person learn to value the friend who can keep information to himself?

Turning the story ideas into action

- **Gossiping:** This story can be used to teach about gossiping. Discuss the students' options for when they hear someone else talking about someone in a negative way. Which of the three dolls would they best emulate then?

- **Visual representation:** Have the class draw representations of the three dolls with the straw coming out different ways, and keep it in the classroom to remind people to listen well and to think carefully about what they do with what they hear.

The King and the Falcon

One day long ago, a King went hunting. On his forearm perched his favorite trained hunting falcon. His bird would fly high in the air, spot a rabbit or some other prey, and swoop down upon it, stunning or killing for his master.

It had been a long day, and the King had left his hunting party and continued alone far from home. By the end of the day, the King was very thirsty and began to look for a place to drink.

At last, he saw some water trickling over the edge of a high rock. He got down from his horse and unpacked his cup. As the King held his cup under the trickling drops, his pet falcon left his arm and flew overhead looking for prey. When the cup was nearly full, the King put it to his lips and was about the drink. All of sudden his falcon swooped down and knocked the cup from his hands, spilling the water.

Annoyed, the King waved the bird away and began to fill his cup again. When it was half full he could wait no longer, and again put it to his lips. Again, the bird swooped down and knocked the cup before he could drink.

"You imbecile!" he swore as the bird alighted on a rock. A third time the King filled his cup and a third time the bird knocked it away.

His anger was growing into rage; the King declared that if the bird dared to knock the cup a fourth time, he would pay dearly. So saying, he got out his sword.

He filled his cup but a third of the way, and then put it to his lips. Again, the falcon swooped down, but this time the King was ready. He sliced the bird as it passed, but not before the bird knocked the cup from his hand. The cup rolled past the dying bird and into an unreachable crevice.

Determined to quench his thirst, the King climbed up the steep rocky bank until, out of breath, he at last reached the spring. There it was, a pool of water—a pool of water in which a dead and very poisonous snake floated.

The King looked down at his dead bird, the bird that had saved his life. He climbed down and sadly put his loyal friend into his hunting bag. He rode slowly home that day, vowing never to act out of anger again.

Variants from Asia and Europe

Grades 4-8

THEMES: Anger management, awareness, greed, violence, living with consequences of our actions

SOURCES AND VARIANTS

Doorways to the Soul: 52 Wisdom Tales from Around the World, edited by Elisa Pearmain (Cleveland: Pilgrim Press, 1998).

"The Loyal Mongoose," in *The Panchatantra*, translated by Arthur W. Ryder (Chicago: University of Chicago Press, 1956).

Fables and Fairy Tales, by Leo Tolstoy (New York: Simon and Schuster, 1993).

PICTURE BOOK

The Mightiest Heart, by Lynne Cullen (New York: Dial Books for Young Readers, 1998). She states that this is a true story, at least by degrees, from Wales.

Follow-up activities

Tip for retention

- **Gossip retelling:** Put students into pairs and have them retell as if they were members of the king's court passing on what they had heard about his experience.

Making a personal connection

- **Questions, discussion and story sharing:** This is a great story to help us think about anger management. Try introducing the idea of "triggers" for anger. Help each student to write or share some of the situations that trigger them to be angry or upset. Many of us have had experiences in which either we tried to help someone and they got angry with us, or we got angry with someone who was trying to help us. We have also all acted in anger and later regretted what we did or said. Share these tales with one another.

Creative exploration

- **Exploring cultural variants:** Give small groups of students several cultural variants of this tale as listed above, and have them present these to the class.

- **Creative adaptation:** Once they have explored more variants on this theme, they will be ready to write their own version that might relate more to present-day events. Let them share these with the class.

Turning the story ideas into action

- **Brainstorm anger-management strategies** with the class. What would have helped the king, or other characters you read about, to avoid having killed his bird? Make a list of things that your students do to keep themselves from acting out of anger when they are triggered. (See suggestions under the story "The Samurai and the Monk" on page 345.) Have the class make posters or a poster of these strategies so that they can refer to them in the future. Suggest that they tell this story at home and discuss anger-management strategies with their families so that they can all practice them together.

The Lost Horse of China

Once upon a time in China, a farmer and his son lived in peace. They had a fine white stallion that the son trained and rode every day. One day the horse ran off and they could not find it. Soon all of the neighbors had gathered to offer their condolences. "What terrible luck," they cried.

"Well," said the farmer, "it could be bad, or it could be good. I will withhold judgment." The neighbors shook their heads and walked away.

A few days later, the farmer's horse returned with a beautiful black stallion at its side. Now the farmer and his son had two horses. Soon all of the neighbors had gathered to offer their congratulations. "What wonderful luck!" they cried.

"Well," said the farmer, "it could be good, or it could be bad. I will withhold judgment." The neighbors shook their heads laughing and walked away.

The son began to tame the black stallion. After many weeks, he was able to ride it. One day, however, the son fell off and he broke both of his legs. Soon the neighbors had gathered to offer their condolences. "What terrible luck," they cried. "Surely you must now admit it!"

"Well," said the farmer, "it could be bad, or it could be good. I will withhold judgment." The neighbors shook their heads in disbelief and walked away.

Not long after, when the son was just beginning to walk with the aid of crutches, the Emperor's soldiers marched into the village demanding that every young man come away with them to a war being waged on their borders. The farmer and his son watched as the young men marched from the village, leaving behind many a grieving family. Soon the neighbors were again at their door.

"What wonderful luck that your son had two broken legs, or he too would have gone," they cried.

"Well," said the farmer, "it could be good, or it could be bad. I will withhold judgment." And no matter what came their way, the farmer and his son lived in peace.

China

Grades 5-8

THEMES: Acceptance, peace of mind, non-judgment, mindfulness, faith, positive philosophy

SOURCES

"When the Horse Runs Off," in *Kindness: A Treasury of Buddhist Wisdom for Children and Parents,* adapted by Sarah Conover (Spokane: Eastern Washington University Press, 2001).

"The Lost Horse," in *Favorite Folktales from Around the World,* edited by Jane Yolen (New York: Pantheon Books, 1986).

"The Farmer's Horse Ran Off," in *Wisdom Tales from Around the World,* by Heather Forest (Little Rock: August House, 1996).

PICTURE BOOK

The Lost Horse: A Chinese Folktale, retold by Ed Young (New York: Harcourt Brace Co., 1998).

Tips for the telling	Make use of the simple repetition in the story. Have fun with the responses of the villagers to the farmers' steadfast philosophy and inner calm.

Follow-up activities *Tip for retention*	• **Gossips:** Put the students into small groups and have them retell as if they were villagers who had witnessed the whole thing.
Making a personal connection	• **Questions, discussion and story sharing:** Encourage students to share stories about experiences that happened that at first they thought were "bad," but later saw that something good came from them, or was learned from them.
Creative exploration	• **Creative adaptation:** Let students make up their own modern-day versions of this story in which things keep happening to them that could be considered "good" or "bad." Include the responses from the villagers.
Turning the story ideas into action	• **Adopting the philosophy for a day:** Encourage your students to adopt the positive philosophy in this story for a day. Every time they have the inclination to judge as a situation or feeling as "good" or "bad," have them say to themselves instead, "I will withhold judgment." Have them journal about their experiences and share in class the next day.

Favorite picture books	*The Carrot Seed*, by Ruth Krauss Pre-K-1 (New York: Harper & Row, 1989). In this short story, a little boy keeps the faith that his carrot seed will grow despite the negative predictions of his family members. This is a great story to act out with the youngest of storytellers. I add in a little song that the boy sings to urge his carrot to grow which the students can repeat over and over: "Grow little carrot, grow, dudududududu." Repeat. *The Three Questions*, adapted and illustrated by Jon J. Muth (New York: Scholastic Press Inc., 2001). The author states that this story is based on a story by Leo Tolstoy called "The Three Questions," published in 1903. I wonder if Tolstoy adapted it from a Buddhist tale. In this children's version, a boy asks three questions about the most important time, the most important people to be with, and the most important things to do. He learns through experience that the answer always lies in doing your best in the present moment. *Gluskabe and the Four Wishes*, retold by Joseph Bruchac (New York: Cobblehill Books, 1995). In this traditional story of the Wabanaki peoples of New England, Gluskabe grants four wishes to four men. Only one man wishes for something that will help others, and only one has the self-control to wait and discover how his wish may be granted, and to learn from his animal teachers. *The Lady Who Saw the Good Side of Everything*, by Pat Decker Tapio (New York: Clarion Books, 1975). One catastrophe after another takes the old lady and her cat from a picnic in the park to the middle of the ocean on a log, to a nice little house in China. As the title implies, no matter what happened, this old lady found a positive way of looking at it.

Bullying Prevention

NO MATTER WHAT KIND OF SCHOOL YOU WORK IN—public, private, urban, suburban, or rural—you will have some children who bully others. In some places this is a small issue; in others it's the biggest disciplinary issue for the school.

Bullying behaviors take many forms, and all of them have a victim or victims. Some are mild, such as public teasing, and some that involve physical injury may be quite severe, even illegal. They are aggressive behaviors, rather than assertive means of self-defense. They are behaviors in which one person or a group attempt to exert power over another person or persons. The difference between bullying and friendly poking fun is the intent with which it is done and/or the way if feels to the one who is being bullied.

The first step in reducing the frequency of bullying in your school community is having a clear awareness and consensus among all members of the school community about what constitutes an act of bullying. Coming to this definition collectively must be a part of the process. Studies by leading researchers on bullying show that conducting student and staff surveys about how and where bullying occurs in the school community is a necessary first step in addressing the problem.

Facts About Bullying

- Bullying is the most common form of violence in our society.
- The aggressive behavior of children who bully starts in the preschool years.
- In the United States, 4% of children in grades K-3 are targets of bullying.
- Nearly 30% of students in grades 6-10 are involved in bullying behavior or are being bullied by others.
- 160,000 students a day skip school for fear of being picked on and bullied.
- Throughout the world, one in ten young people are frequently bullied at school.
- From 1994-1999 there were 253 violent deaths in school.
- Bullying is most often a factor in school deaths.
- Many children who are bullied suffer long-term psychological effects as adults including depression and lower self-esteem.
- More than 60% of people who bullied in grades 6-9 have least one criminal conviction by age 24.
- Membership in either bully or victim groups is associated with school drop out, poor psychosocial adjustment, criminal activity and other negative long-term consequences.

Bullying behaviors include:

- teasing
- making jokes at the expense of someone
- gossiping in person, through notes or over the internet
- ostracizing
- exclusion

- picking on
- name calling
- hurtful graffiti (often racially prejudicial in nature)
- threats of harm to persons or property
- stealing

- destruction of person's property
- inappropriate touching
- neglect
- sexual harassment
- physical and sexual abuse
- homicide

You might make note of which behaviors fall within the threshold of "acceptable" behaviors in your school, and which ones are unacceptable but present. In the process of leading your students through lessons on bullying, they will be able to identify bullying behaviors more clearly and can perhaps add to this list.

Who bullies?

We all have probably bullied someone else to some degree in our lives, even if it was just a younger sibling. Many of the bullying acts mentioned above are socially sanctioned, or at least seen as within the normal range of children's behaviors. Sometimes adults bully children, particularly in dysfunctional homes where families are blended. People bully because they want to feel more powerful than someone else. Bullying happens across all socioeconomic levels and in many cultural groups, and sometimes bullying is called abuse. The line between bullying and abuse is thin and spreads across a broad spectrum, from largely accepted behaviors to those that are illegal. Bullying is not something that only children do. Adults are bullied at home, in the workplace, and in various social settings, including bars, nursing homes, and recreational sports.

Studies show that boys bully three times more often than girls, but those statistics are changing in some demographics. The type of bullying they do is also different, with boys resorting more frequently to physical bullying and girls to relational bullying, such as exclusion, gossip, and stealing. However, more girls are resorting to violence.

Studies also show that those who bully most often come from homes where there is little or no warmth or empathy expressed. These children get little positive attention in their families. Discipline is inconsistent and physical. Often the bullies have themselves been bullied, but this is no excuse for their

Who are the most frequent victims of bullying among young people?

- Children with low self-esteem.
- Children who are shy, anxious or nonassertive.
- Children who have difficulty reading social signals. (This includes children with various disorders such as learning disorders, autism spectrum disorders, and ADHD.)
- Children who react emotionally or cry easily.
- Children who are smaller or different in some way, including those who wear glasses, who dress differently than their peers, and who have a disability.
- Bullying can happen to anyone. Erika Arnold, a recent Miss America, was bullied repeatedly in ninth grade.

behavior. Young bullies tend to be arrogant and controlling. It may look as though they have high self-esteem, but they do not—it is false bravado.

In addition to my stories and follow-up activities, I suggest that you read these two excellent books for self-check lists and other suggestions for helping students to acknowledge and stop bullying behaviors.

- *Stopping Bullying at School: A Curriculum for Grades 5-8*, by Carol Wintle (Self-published, 1997, 2002).
- *The Kids' Guide to Working Out Conflicts*, by Naomi Drew (Minneapolis: Free Spirit Publishing, 2004).

How can you help the victim?

Victims of bullying need support from teachers, parents, and peers. Being bullied can be traumatizing. Having parents, teachers, and friends ignore, downplay, or dismiss the reality of bullying can be worse. Victims of bullying need to know that they are not alone. Frequently people who are bullied do not tell anyone because they feel shame, or they think that people will say that they brought it on themselves or are exaggerating for attention. They need to know that it is better to speak out than to keep the problem to themselves. This is one reason why school-wide education on bullying prevention is essential. Victims of bullying need to know that there is a safe person to tell, preferably someone whose job it is to know about incidents of bullying. Victims of bullying also need practical advice and training on assertiveness, and how not to react emotionally to bullying. Training in use of confident eye contact, posture, and speech when dealing with bullies can be helpful. Victims also need help in knowing when to ignore bullies, and when to get away.

Where does bullying occur?

School bullying occurs most often in less supervised school-related settings, such as at recess, in the cafeteria, hallways, and restrooms, and on school buses and at bus stops. Children are also bullied after school on the telephone, internet, on the street, and in their neighborhoods.

What about the bystander?

Probably everyone has been a witness to bullying at least once, and likely many times over the course of their lives. Those who do not do anything to help the victim often suffer from guilt afterwards. There can also be trauma associated with witnessing bullying, depending on the individual and the situation.

Children need to know that there is a safe way to report bullying. The clearer they are as to what constitutes bullying, and what the school policy is, the more comfortable they will feel with reporting or speaking out.

Children need to know that by laughing at a bully's actions they are participating in bullying. They need to know that the bully gets a reward for his or her behavior when the bystander responds positively. They need to know that the bully is encouraged when no one speaks up to stop his or her actions. The bully also becomes encouraged or gets an emotional reward when the victim is allowed to suffer alone.

What you can do about bullying

Here are some essential steps toward decreasing bullying and increasing safety in your school and classroom:

- Identify with your students and faculty the many forms that bullying takes. Research has shown that this is best done by letting students and staff fill out anonymous surveys at least yearly.

- From the surveys and group discussions, generate a list of behaviors that are considered bullying and thus unacceptable.

- Acknowledge that bullying does go on in every school, and identify the places and times where bullying happens most often in your school.

- Acknowledge that bullying happens outside of school, and identify those places and scenarios. This is important for many reasons, among them the fact that sometimes bullies at school are victims at home. I find that children readily identify having been bullied by a sibling, relative, or neighborhood child.

No-Tolerance Policies

If your school decides to have a no-tolerance policy, everyone must know what this means. It is actually a detriment to students if you espouse "no tolerance," but actually tolerate many milder forms of bullying. Studies have shown that up to two-thirds of students believe that schools respond poorly to bullying. Respondents believe that adult help is infrequent and ineffective. Studies have also shown that up to 25% of teachers see nothing wrong with bullying or put-downs and consequently intervene in only 4% of bullying incidents.

- Sensitize all students to the effects of bullying. Because so many aspects of bullying are socially sanctioned, the hurtful effects are often minimized by those who bully or those who observe bullying.

- Help students to acknowledge and think about times in which they might have been involved with bullying as a bully. (Make a checklist from the behaviors they have identified.)

- Help students to acknowledge and think about times in which they might have been involved with bullying as a bystander. Point out that every person who witnesses bullying and laughs or plays along is involved in bullying.

- Help students to acknowledge and think about times in which they might have been involved with bullying as a victim.

- Discuss the challenges that students and teachers face in knowing how to speak up when bullying is happening.

- Empower students and faculty with the communication tools and confidence to speak out against bullying, and help to stop it when it is happening. Research has shown that it is effective to have a Bullying Officer to report to who is separate from the chief disciplinarian (usually the assistant principal). The students will have greater sense that their efforts will be heard and less fear that the result will be punitive.

- Have clear and enforceable consequences for bullying behaviors.

- Support victims of bullying and their families in finding healthy ways to cope with and to respond to bullying. Blaming the victim, or focusing on the victim's behaviors as a cause of bullying (except in how to respond and protect themselves), is rarely helpful, and usually harmful.

- Work supportively with bullies and their families to address underlying causes of this behavior. Often it is necessary to involve a professionally trained counselor, as there are usually problems in the family system and parents can be very defensive.

- Educate every parent in the school community about the bullying policy. Some parents still tell their children to "ignore it," or even to "hit back" when they are bullied. You can help them to be more supportive in productive ways.

- Focus on ways to strengthen the sense of community identity within the school. This helps students to feel safe, as well as connected to and responsible for one another.

- Teach students how to recognize the difference between assertive and aggressive styles of communication. Help them to learn the tools of assertiveness through practicing assertive means of asking for what they need and expressing their feelings. Many students who are bullied end up responding with aggressive means for lack of better training or skills.

- Teach anger-management techniques. This involves becoming more sensitive to feelings of anger, and recognizing them before they are too strong. It also includes learning safe ways to express anger, needs, and feelings.

- With younger students it is important to teach the difference between "tattling" and telling. When we tattle, we are trying to get someone into trouble. When we tell, we are trying to prevent trouble. Create scenarios to discuss this and bring it up every time there is a question. Tattling can be a form of subtle bullying in young children.

- Teach the difference between teasing and bullying. It has to do with the intent of the behavior. Is it meant to intimidate or hurt another, or is it merely an affectionate way of being silly? Does it hurt the person it is directed towards? Is it a way to have power and control over another? Is it meant to point out one person's differences in a way that would ostracize them?

How Can Stories Help?

As I have identified, there are a number of factors that serve to foster or discourage bullying behavior. Stories help to:

Create a shared vocabulary about bullying—what, who, where, when, how.

Allow us to look at bullying from multiple perspectives.

Approach a difficult subject with open hearts and minds.

Provide a vicarious experience of being bullied to increase empathy.

Help us to make a personal connection to the reality of bullying.

Offer examples of ways to intervene in bullying situations.

Help people to identify and develop the character traits needed to stand up to bullies.

Foster respect for differences, and to encourage tolerance and inclusion.

Create springboards into dialogue and introspection on the issues.

Foster a sense of responsibility for our actions and those of our peers.

Serve as reminders for the rewards of positive behaviors.

Allow us to integrate bullying-prevention work into the language arts curriculum.

- Talk about joking and when jokes are funny and when they are mean. Black humor is always done at someone else's expense. It is a put down. White humor is just meant to be funny without hurting anyone. Help students to be more sensitive to when and why they laugh. Often we respond to something that makes us uncomfortable with nervous laughter.

- Train everyone in the school community about bullying, including bus drivers, cafeteria and recess monitors, and substitute teachers.

- Create opportunities for students to get to know those outside of their immediate peer group beyond superficial stereotypes.
- Reward teachers for getting bullying-prevention training. It does make a difference.
- Reward victims for speaking up about their abuse.
- Reward bystanders for speaking up on the behalf of victims.
- Reward bullies for learning and practicing new behaviors at school.

What you can do about bullying

- Use the stories in this book, as well as biographical and autobiographical stories to show examples of bullying.
- Have students make up scenarios to address each of the possible forms of bullying.
- Share stories from your own experience. Have the students gather stories from other students and faculty to identify examples of bullying, bystanding, and bullying prevention. Share and discuss them.
- Let the students write and/or tell personal stories of times when they felt bullied. They will think of quite a few examples once they get started. If you have any children who have emotional problems, you may want to advise the school counselor in advance what you are doing. Generally, it is a positive experience for students to hear each other's stories, but some stories may be traumatizing for students to tell, or for other students to hear. Most of the time storytelling provides a vehicle for self-expression that is helpful to all.
- Have students voluntarily play "hot seat," in which they pretend to be characters in the stories, while their peers ask them questions in character to experience in an non-traumatizing way how it feels to be bullied. (See details is the Pre-Story and Follow-up Activities sections.)
- Allow students to grapple with situations in which they have been witnesses to bullying behavior, or have even been the bully. They can do this in writing if it gives them greater comfort. Were they able to stand up to bullying of others? How did this feel?
- Create class dramatic reenactments in which a student is bullied and others participate by laughing or doing nothing. Then have a class discussion about the responsibility of the observers. Here again, roles should be voluntary so that students who are frequent victims do not end up playing victims.
- Once you have established a list of rules around bullying behaviors, have students make up stories or tell stories from the ones listed in this book to demonstrate behaviors and consequences. If these are shared school-wide, the sense of community understanding and adherence will be much stronger. This needs to be repeated to some degree each year.

"How Beetle Got Her Colors" (Respect)—Describes many ways of bullying, and bystander behavior. The story includes a helping character who intervenes and teaches the bully not to judge others by surface appearances.

"Sir Gawain and Lady Ragnell" (Diversity Appreciation)—A bully casts a spell on his sister, making her "ugly" when she won't act the way he wants. The "spell" can be a metaphor for ostracizing. The hero helps to break the spell by respecting the heroine and allowing her to choose how she will look and act in the world.

"The Leopard's Revenge" (Courage)—Describes the bullying behavior of picking on someone weaker than you, and bullying to seek revenge.

"The Sun and the Wind" (Cooperation)—Demonstrates assertive vs. aggressive styles, and the effects of using power-over vs. creative conflict resolution.

"The Stonecutter" (Respect)—Demonstrates the essential need of the bully to feel more powerful and to have power over others, and the realization that what is really needed is more self-acceptance and respect.

"The Tail of the Linani Beast" (Responsibility)—Stealing to impress someone, and getting others to do illegal things for you.

"Necklaces" (Empathy)—An example of how groups bully.

"Feathers" (Respect)—Shows the effects of gossiping and teasing.

"The Butterfly Friends" (Diversity Appreciation)—Demonstrates exclusion and sticking together.

"The Lion and Tree Sprites" (Diversity Appreciation)—Describes short-sighted judgment and exclusion of others.

"Sweet and Sour Berries" (Honesty)—Describes stealing and intimidation, and the transformation of a bully.

"The Secret Heart of the Tree" (Respect)—Describes bullying by threatening and stealing. It also models respect.

"The Answer Is in Your Hands"—(Responsibility) Peer pressure and choosing not to bully.

"The Children and the Frogs" (Responsibility)—Doing violence by disregarding others' feelings. The ending offers a choice for change.

"The King and His Falcon" (Self-Mastery)—Describes the dangers of lashing out in anger.

"The Man in the Moon" (Empathy)—Describes an example of doing violence to someone to make them give you something you want.

"King Solomon and the Hoopoe Bird" (Leadership)—Describes how one can take advantage of power over others to hurt them or to empathize with them.

Stories with examples of bullying behaviors

The stories

Just about any story in this book can be used to cultivate awareness of the qualities of character that will help students to stop engaging in or allowing bullying behaviors. I have chosen a few stories here that specifically address three areas: bullying behaviors, bystander responsibility, and cultivating empathy. The stories are listed here, but developed in the sections listed in parentheses. Follow-up activities are listed after each story, but some specific suggestions are listed here for a unit focused on bully prevention.

"Who Started It?" (Responsibility)—Describes how taking revenge creates its own cycle of violence.

"How Turtle Got Its Cracked Shell" (Self-Mastery)—Describes an example of making fun of others, and emotional reactions to teasing.

"The Dervish in the Ditch" (Empathy)—Describes as example of someone taking power over someone else, or disregarding their feelings. Also a creative way to respond.

Bystanding and standing up to bullies

The following stories can help to build your students' awareness about the role of the bystander in a bullying situation. They explore examples of characters standing up to bullies individually and collectively.

"A Drop of Honey" (Responsibility)—This story offers an opportunity to look at a bystander's role in preventing or allowing violence.

"How Guinea Hen Got Her Spots" (Friendship)—An example of bystanders taking action.

"How Beetle Got Her Colors" (Respect)—Describes bystander bullying behavior, and a helper who comes to the victim's aid.

"The Stork and The Cranes" (Friendship)—Demonstrates peer pressure and guilt by association.

"The Butterfly Friends" (Diversity Appreciation)—A bystanding flower offers to help when others have refused.

"The Children and the Frogs" (Responsibility)—Group pressure to stop bullying.

"Legend of the Panda" (Empathy)—The heroine finds the courage to take action to protect a victim of violence.

"Heads or Tails" (Cooperation)—Working together stops bullying.

"The Farmer, Son and the Donkey" (Self-Mastery)—A good story to help build awareness about how much we worry about what others are thinking about us, and how this affects our actions.

"Tipingee" (Cooperation)—A group acts in solidarity with one girl who is threatened.

Use the stories in the Leadership section to generate discussion about following or standing up to a bullying leader. Students also need inspiration to be leaders in the fight against bullying.

Building empathy for the victims of bullying

Don't take for granted that all of your students know how to empathize with others. If this is not modeled and valued in a family, a child may have a very limited capacity to offer it to others. These stories can help to start a dialogue and foster new awareness.

"Talk" (Empathy)—A bridge to discussing empathy for those whose feelings are not heard or considered.

"The Seal Hunter" (Empathy)—Building empathy in those who have bullied or been bystanders.

"Magic Listening Cap" (Empathy)—Helping others to see the effects of their actions.

"Necklaces" (Empathy)—Helping others because it is the right thing to do.

"The Children and the Frogs" (Responsibility)—Seeing the results of our actions.

"The Answer Is in Your Hands"—(Responsibility) Peer pressure and choosing not to bully.

"The Wise Teacher's Test" (Honesty)—Cultivating self-awareness so that we no longer let ourselves get away with cruelty towards others.

"The Dervish in the Ditch" (Self-Mastery)—Offers the victim of bullying a philosophy for not taking bullying personally by remembering that if the bully were a happy person, he would not be needing to hurt others.

Picture books

Mr. Lincoln's Way, by Patricia Polacco (New York: Philomel Books, 2001). Mr. Lincoln is an African-American principal in an elementary school. A white boy named Eugene bullies other students, calling them names about their ethnicity, as his father does at home. Mr. Lincoln finds a way to reach Eugene by noticing his interest in birds and enlisting his help in bringing birds of all kinds into the school atrium. He helps the boy to see that people of all kinds can get along just as birds do.

My Secret Bully, by Trudy Ludwig, (Ashland, Ore.: Riverwood Books, 2003). A girl who is bullied by her best friend gets some help from her mom in figuring out what to do. Includes discussion topics, tips, and resources.

Crow Boy, by Taro Yashima (New York: Penguin Books, 1987).

Say Something, by Peggy Moss, (Gardener, Me.: Tibury House, 2004). Addresses the bystander and imparts an important lesson in civic responsibility.

Sources

"Bullies, Victims, & Bystanders: Intervention Strategies," by Steve Berk, Ph.D. Given at a workshop by the same name at Community Program Innovations, Inc. Fall 2004. www.communityprograminnovations.com. This workshop is an excellent introduction to bullying prevention for teachers, counselors, and administrators.

Stopping Bullying at School: A Curriculum for Grades 5-8, by Carol Wintle (Self-published, 1997, 2002). This booklet offers much information, handouts, classroom exercises to explore many aspects of bullying, and lots of very short biographical stories describing aspects of bullying. E-mail: carol-wintle@earthlink.net.

The Students' Guide to Working Out Conflicts, by Naomi Drew (Minneapolis: Free Spirit Publishing Inc., 2004). This book has many practical chapters for teens, such as Be Smart about Bullying, Manage your Anger, and Gain Control, and others that help with aspects of conflict resolution.

Other bullying prevention resources

Odd Girl Out: The Hidden Culture of Aggression in Girls, by Rachel Simmons (New York: Harcourt, 2002) Exposes the nature of adolescent girl bullying behaviors through many girl's stories.

Schools Where Everyone Belongs: Practical Strategies for Reducing Bullying, by Stan Davis (Wayne, Me.: Stop Bullying Now, 2004)

The Bully Prevention Handbook: A Guide for Principals, Teachers, and Counselors, by J. H. Hoover and R. Oliver (Bloomington, Ind.: National Educational Service, 1996).

New Perspectives on Bullying, by Ken Rigby (London: Jessica Kingsley Publishing, 2002).

Stop Bullying: A Handbook for Schools, by Ken Rigby (London: Jessica Kingsley Publishing, 2003).

They Don't Like Me: Lessons on Bullying and Teasing from a Preschool Classroom, by Jane Tatch (Boston: Beacon Press, 2003). Great insights for teachers in why students bully, get bullied, and how to intervene.

Bullying at School: What We Know and What We Can Do by Dan Olweus (Oxford, UK: Blackwell Publishers, 1993).

How to Handle Bullies, Teasers and Other Meanies: A Book that Takes the Nuisance Out of Name Calling and Other Nonsense. By Kate Cohen-Posey (Highland City, Fla.: Rainbow Books, 1995)

Why is Everybody Always Picking On Me? by Terrance Webster Doyle (New York: Weatherhill, 2000). Stories, role plays and questions help students not to be bullies or victims.

Stick Up For Yourself! Every Kid's Guide to Personal Power and Positive Self-Esteem by Gershen Kaufman, et al. (Minneapolis: Free Spirit Publishing, 1999).

Websites

Anti-bullying Network—Dr. Ken Rigby's site. http://www.education.unisa.edu.au/bullying

Stop Bullying Now—Stan Davis's site. http://www.stopbullyingnow.com.

Bullying.org http://www.bullying.org. Includes pictures and stories about bullying from students around the world.

Hotline

For students who need to talk to someone anonymously about bullying, whether as the victim, the bystander or the bully.

Girls and Boys Town National Hotline: (800) 448-3000. A free 24-hour confidential hotline.

Resources

Character Development Group

Excellent source of books and videos on character education.
www.CharacterEducation.com (888) 262-0572

Character Education Partnership

The national umbrella organization for all character education organizations.
Resources, bulletin board, links. Look here to find a group in your region.
www.character.org (800) 988-8081

Character Counts

Identifying six character traits with resources, curriculum ideas, and articles.
www.charactercounts.org (310) 306-1868

Center for the Advancement of Ethics and Character

Boston University, 621 Commonwealth Ave., Boston, MA 02215
www.bu.edu/education/caec. (617) 353-3262
Includes sample lessons.

Character education organizations

Elisa Pearmain's website features stories with follow-up suggestions
www.wisdomtales.com or www.wisdomtales.com/character

The Healing Story website features stories and discussion, with links to local
organizations nationwide. Jonesborough, Tenn. www.healingstory.org

National Storytelling Network offers many links to storytelling sites:
www.storynet.org

Yellow Moon Press is a great source of storytelling books and tapes. PO Box
1316, Cambridge, MA 02238. www.yellowmoonpress.com (800) 497-4385

Storytelling websites and resources

The Barefoot Book of Heroic Children, by Rebecca Hazel (New York: Barefoot
Books, 2000). Short biographical stories told in first-person narrative of
young people who achieved greatness against tremendous odds.

Building Character in Schools, by Kevin Ryan and Karen Bohlin (San
Francisco: Jossey-Bass Publishers, 1999). A great argument for character education in the schools and descriptions of how to make it happen.

Books on character education

Character Education Through Story: Lessons to Build Character Development Through Multicultural Literature, edited by Joseph P. Hester (Chapel Hill, N.C.: Character Development Publishing, 2001). Over 200 stories from literature for grades K-6 that offer examples of various character traits. The stories are briefly described, with follow-up suggestions.

Characters with Character: Using Children's Literature in Character Education, by Diane Findlay (Fort Atkinson, Wis.: Alleyside Press, 2001). Focusing on 10 character traits, this book offers examples of children's literary stories that help students to explore the various traits. Brief descriptions of stories and follow-up exercises and games are practical for classroom use.

Educating for Character: How Our Schools Can Teach Respect and Responsibility, by Thomas Lickona (New York: Bantam Books, 1992). Also see *Character Matters*, 2004.

How to tell stories

A Beginner's Guide to Storytelling, by Katy Rydell (Jonesborough, Tenn.: National Storytelling Press, 2003).

Children Tell Stories: A Teaching Guide, by Martha Hamilton and Mitch Weiss (Katonah, N.Y.: Richard C. Owen Publishers, 1990). Includes 25 short tales for telling.

Creative Storytelling: Choosing, Inventing and Sharing Tales for Children, by Jack Maguire (Somerville, Mass: Yellow Moon Press, 1985).

Storytellers Sourcebook, by Margaret Read Macdonald (Farmington Hill, Mich.: ThomsonGale, 1982).

The Storyteller's Start-up Book, by Margaret Read Macdonald (Little Rock: August House Publishers, 1993).

Super Simple Storytelling, by Kendall Haven (Teacher Ideas Press, 2000).

Aesop's Fables

Aesop's Fables, illustrated by Jerry Pinkney (New York: Sea Star, 2000).

Aesop's Fables Retold and Illustrated, by Louis Untermeyer (New York: Golden Press, 1965).

The Aesop for Children (New York: Checkerboard Press, 1947).

Collections specific to character education or wisdom

The Book of Virtues: A Treasury of Great Moral Stories (New York: Simon & Schuster, 1993).

The Book of Virtues for Children, edited by William J. Bennett (New York: Simon & Schuster, 1995).

Bringing Out Their Best: Values Education and Character Development through Traditional Tales, by Norma Livo (Westport, Conn.: Libraries Unlimited, 2003).

Buddha Stories, by Demi (New York: Henry Holt and Co., Inc., 1997).

Dharma Family Treasures: Sharing Buddhism with Children, by Sandy Eastoak (Berkeley: North Atlantic Books, 1994).

Don't Think of a Monkey, by Swami Prakashananda (Fremont, Calif.: Sarasvati Publications, 1994).

Doorways to the Soul: 52 Wisdom Tales from Around the World, by Elisa Pearmain (Cleveland: Pilgrim Press, 1998).

I Once was a Monkey: Stories Buddha Told, edited by Jeanne M. Lee (New York: Farrar, Straus and Giroux, 1999).

Kindness: A Treasury of Buddhist Wisdom for Children and Parents, by Sarah Conover (Spokane, Wash.: Eastern Washington University Press, 2001).

Lessons from the Rocking Chair: Timeless Stories for Teaching Character, by Deb Austin Brown (Chapel Hill, N.C.: Character Development Group, 1997).

The Moon in the Well: Wisdom Tales to Transform Your Life, Family and Community, by Erica Helm Meade (Peru, Ill.: Open Court Publishing, 2001).

The Moral of the Story, by Bobby and Sherry Norfolk (Little Rock: August House Publishers, 1999).

Ordinary Splendors: Tales of Virtue and Wisdoms, by Toni Knapp (Los Angeles: The Scott Newman Center, 1993).

Peace Tales, by Margaret Read Macdonald (Hamden, Conn.: Linnet Books, 1992).

Spinning Tales, Weaving Hope: Stories of Peace, Justice and the Environment, by E. Brody, et al. (Philadelphia, Pa.: New Society Publishers, 1992).

The Wisdom of the Crows and other Buddhist Tales, by S. Chodzin and A. Kohn (Berkeley: Tricycle Press, 1997).

Wisdom Tales from Around the World, by Heather Forest (Little Rock: August House, 1997).

Best Loved Folktales of the World, by Joanne Cole (Garden City, N.Y.: Doubleday, 1983).

The Emerald Lizard: Fifteen Latin American Tales to Tell, by Pleasant De Spain (Little Rock: August House Publishing, 1999).

Favorite Folktales from Around the World, by Jane Yolen (New York: Random House, 1986).

Jewish Stories One Generation Tells Another, by Peninah Schram (Northvale, N.J.: Jason Aronson Inc., 1987).

General collections containing many great wisdom tales

Ready to Tell Tales from Around the World, by D. Holt and B. Monney (Little Rock: August House, 1998) Also More Ready to Tell Tales (2000).

Tales of the Hodja, by Charles Downing (New York: Henry Z. Walck, 1965).

Thirty-Three Multicultural Tales to Tell, by Pleasant De Spain (Little Rock: August House, 1993).

Diversity awareness through story	*The Need for Story: Cultural Diversity in Classroom and Community*, by A. Dyson and C. Genishi (Urbana, Ill.: National Council of Teachers of English, 1994).
Respect for the Earth	*Earth Care: World Folktales to Talk About*, by Margaret Read Macdonald (North Haven, Conn.: Linnet Books, 1999). *Earth Tales from Around the World*, by Michael Caduto (Golden, Colo.: Fulcrum Press, 1997). *Keepers of the Earth: Native American Stories and Environmental Activities for Children*, by Joseph Bruchac and Michael Caduto (Golden, Colo.: Fulcrum Inc., 1988).
Cooperative games for building trust, cooperation and other character traits	*Quicksilver: Adventure Games, Initiative Problems, Trust Activities*, by Steve Butler and Steve Rohnke (Dubuque, Iowa: Kendall Hunt Publishing, 1995). *The Second Cooperative Sports and Games Book*, by Terry Orlick (New York: Pantheon Books, 1982). *Silver Bullets: A Guide to Initiative Problems, Adventure Games and Trust Activities*, by Karl Rohnke (Dubuque, Iowa: Kendall Hunt Publishing, 1984).

Index of Stories by Title

Index of Stories by Theme

About the Author

Elisa Davy Pearmain is a professional storyteller, licensed therapist, and the award-winning author of *Doorways to the Soul: 52 Wisdom Tales from Around the World*. She began her career as a storyteller in 1987 with a position as Storyteller in Residence in the Boston Public Schools. In doing research for her storytelling, she learned to love stories from many cultures, and to appreciate how different cultures teach shared values such as honesty and kindness. Since then she has performed for thousands of students across New England in grades pre-K–8, and has come to believe that every child and every teacher can be a storyteller. The students' delight in hearing and telling stories keeps her eager to teach storytelling as a means to help young children grow in character, wisdom and respect for all living beings. Elisa has worked for fifteen years training teachers from across the United States to integrate storytelling across the curriculum through the Lesley University Creative Arts Masters Program in Cambridge, Massachusetts.

Elisa lives with her husband and daughter in Massachusetts. You can learn more about Elisa's programs and resources at www.wisdomtales.com, or reach her directly at elisa@wisdomtales.com.